Arab American Drama,
Film and Performance

ALSO BY MICHAEL MALEK NAJJAR

Four Arab American Plays: Works by Leila Buck, Jamil Khoury, Yussef El Guindi, and Lameece Issaq & Jacob Kader (McFarland, 2014)

Arab American Drama, Film and Performance

A Critical Study, 1908 to the Present

MICHAEL MALEK NAJJAR

McFarland & Company, Inc., Publishers
Jefferson, North Carolina

LIBRARY OF CONGRESS CATALOGUING-IN-PUBLICATION DATA

Najjar, Michael Malek, 1972–
    Arab American drama, film and performance : a critical study, 1908 to the present / Michael Malek Najjar.
       p.   cm.
    Includes bibliographical references and index.

    ISBN 978-0-7864-9516-0 (softcover : acid free paper) ∞
    ISBN 978-1-4766-1865-4 (ebook)

    1. American drama—Arab American authors—History and criticism. 2. American drama—20th century—History and criticism. 3. Arab Americans in literature. 4. Arab Americans in motion pictures. I. Title.

PS153.A73N35 2015
812'.5098927—dc23   2014040018

BRITISH LIBRARY CATALOGUING DATA ARE AVAILABLE

© 2015 Michael Malek Najjar. All rights reserved

No part of this book may be reproduced or transmitted in any form or by any means, electronic or mechanical, including photocopying or recording, or by any information storage and retrieval system, without permission in writing from the publisher.

On the cover: Amal (Chelsee Carter) in the University of Oregon production of Heather Raffo's *9 Parts of Desire*, directed by Michael Malek Najjar, produced by the University of Oregon (photograph by Ariel Ogden)

Printed in the United States of America

McFarland & Company, Inc., Publishers
  Box 611, Jefferson, North Carolina 28640
    www.mcfarlandpub.com

Table of Contents

Acknowledgments — vii
Preface — 1
Introduction: Defining a Genre — 15

1. "Unresolved sorrow and uncomprehending anger": Contemporary Arab American Identity Formation — 31
2. "We are not of the East or West": Origins of Arab American Drama in the Works of Rihani, Gibran and Naimy — 70
3. "There's nothing funny about your people": Arab American Comedy and Stand-Up Performance — 98
4. "It's not profiling, it's deduction": Post–9/11 Arab American Drama — 125
5. Suffering for Palestine: Palestinian American Playwrights — 156
6. Arabs Filming Arabs: Contemporary Arab American Films — 186
7. "A psychic civil war onstage": Arab American Solo Performance — 204

Conclusion — 231
Appendix: Abridged Chronology of Arab American Drama, Film and Performance, 1896–2015 — 243
Chapter Notes — 247
Works Referenced — 261
Index — 269

Acknowledgments

Creating a manuscript takes a great deal of time and support. I wish to thank the talented writers, filmmakers, and performers included here who have devoted their careers to dramatizing the experiences of Arab Americans in their plays, films, and performances. Your works are truly inspiring, and I hope this volume helps to make those unfamiliar with this genre aware of your talents.

I also thank my mentors—professors Sue-Ellen Case, S.I. Salamensky, Carol Fisher Sorgenfrei, Nouri Gana, and Susan Slyomovics—for their guidance during my studies at UCLA. Thanks to the Eugene V. Cota-Robles Committee for allowing me the opportunity to study within the University of California System. I especially wish to thank Jamil Khoury and Malik Gillani for supporting my artistic endeavors by allowing me to direct both *Precious Stones* and my own play *Talib* at Silk Road Rising. Of course, I wish to thank all of my colleagues at the University of Oregon for their continued support and guidance. I have found both an artistic and academic home at the University of Oregon, and I'm grateful for the opportunity to work at such a supportive and collegial institution. I wish to especially thank May-Britt Ostersen for her assistance in securing the permissions for the photographs included within this book. I could not have done this without your help. Also, I wish to thank the Oregon Humanities Center and the University of Oregon College of Arts and Sciences for providing me subvention funds for this publication.

I also thank everyone who aided me with my research in the United States and abroad. There have been many who assisted me, including Mona Arslan, Cherien Dabis, Christine Fish, Joseph Fakhri, Guita Hourani, Hisham Naimy, Nadeem Naimy, Ameen Albert Rihani, Nefertiti Takla, and Christopher Tayback. Special thanks to those who allowed me permission to utilize photographs, including Andrea Assaf, Holland Baird/The Alliance Theatre,

Sayed Badreya, Sarah Bazzi/AJYAL Theatrical Group, Cherien Dabis, Malik Gillani, Bill Huntington, Jennifer Jajeh, Jamil Khoury, Nadeem Naimy, Rana Halabi Najjar, Noor Theatre, Ariel Ogden, Ameen Albert Rihani, Heather Raffo, Christopher Tayback, Leon Milad Tuma, Wesleyan University, and Winnie Hershewe.

Lastly, I must thank my family, especially my cousin, Dr. Nada Najjar, and my uncle Dr. Abdallah Najjar, for instilling in me the inspiration to learn more about my rich heritage and culture. To my mother, Samia, and my sister Dina: your love, patience, and support have made this entire venture possible, and I could not have achieved my life goals without you. Thanks to my cousin Dr. Linda Najjar and my dear friends Roger Jameson, Jason Riggs, Khaled Hamadeh and Gary M. Bowne. Thanks too, to my extended family: Abbas, Julie, and Deanna Halabi and to my mother-in-law, Salwa Kantar. Thank you for welcoming me to your beautiful family and helping me achieve my goals.

To those actors, choreographers, stage managers, assistant directors, and designers with whom I've collaborated, I thank you for helping me bring my own productions to fruition. Also, thanks to my students who teach me so much every day.

Finally, I dedicate this volume to my beautiful wife, Rana, and my precious daughter, Malak. You're my heart, my soul, and my inspiration. I love you always and forever.

Preface

The idea for writing a book about Arab American drama, film, and performance came to me years ago when I spoke to another theatre colleague about an Arab American play I was reading. This colleague, who was well versed in many forms of intercultural and international theatre, asked me, "Is there such a thing as Arab American drama?" I realized then that there were few, if any, in the theatre who knew of the many playwrights, filmmakers, and performers who are, and have been, inadvertently creating a genre for over a century. The omission of these works from the theatrical canon is worth questioning. As a former theatre student with three advanced degrees who has studied in the United States and abroad, I can tell you that I was never assigned a novel, play, or book of poetry by an Arab American. Why was that, I wondered? Was it a matter of ignorant omission or outright exclusion?

My desire to meld my passion for the theatre and my interest in my Arab culture has led me to examine the history and literature of those writers who have traditionally been excluded from the theatrical canon. I have come to realize that this exclusion has occurred for many reasons: the inability (or aversion) of scholars to translate these plays from Arabic to English, the lack of access to many unpublished works, the exclusion/omission of these plays and productions by professional and semi-professional theatres, and the lack of books and anthologies about the subject that attempt to define and study this literature. Because of the paucity of information on the topic, I decided to focus my energies on directing, writing, and writing about Arab American drama.

My first strategy was to direct plays by these playwrights. I have directed Jamil Khoury's *Precious Stones*, Heather Raffo's *9 Parts of Desire*, Denmo Ibrahim's *Ecstasy: A Water Fable*, and my own play *Talib*. Second, I edited and published an anthology of Arab American plays titled *Four Arab American*

Plays: Works by Leila Buck, Jamil Khoury, Yussef El Guindi, and Lameece Issaq & Jacob Kader* (also published by McFarland). Now a historical analysis of the genre seems in order, which is the book you see before you.

My interest in this field of study is twofold: I am a theatre practitioner and scholar, and I am a second-generation Arab American of Lebanese Druze heritage. My parents, who immigrated to the United States in the 1940s and '50s, brought with them many important traditions and values from their upbringing in the villages of Lebanon. In fact, I might have been a third-generation Arab American had it not been for my grandfather's unexpected return, with his two young children, to Lebanon from the United States after the tragic death of his wife. My grandfather remarried in Lebanon and died there, leaving my father a naturalized American citizen. My father emigrated from Lebanon at the age of 17, worked in the coal mines of West Virginia, served in the U.S. Army during the Korean War, and spent the rest of his life as a self-employed businessman. My mother, a registered nurse who treated patients as far back as the 1958 crisis in Lebanon, immigrated to the United States in the 1960s and worked as a registered nurse her entire life. I was born and raised in the United States and, as with many of my contemporaries, I feel neither fully Arab nor fully American. Instead, I am a hybrid of two vibrant and profound cultures, and I am a self-proclaimed Arab American. Indeed, I didn't even know my birth name was Malek until well into my teen years. As with most Arab Americans, I was given a "safe" name (Michael) that my parents believed would deflect any anti–Arab prejudice that they thought I was sure to encounter in school. Little did they know that it takes more than a name to hide one's Arabness.

I am not proposing that my "descent relation" to this Arabness makes me any more or less qualified to write about Arab American literature. I do not claim an authenticity as an essentialist, or a "biological insider" as Werner Sollors suggests.[1] Instead, I come to this work as one who is deeply interested in his Arab and American roots and sees these plays as a scholar and theatre practitioner first, and as an Arab American second. However, despite this caveat I will say that growing up in an Arab American household and having the Arabic language and culture as part of my life provides insights into these works that one who has not interacted with this culture might not have. The cultural traditions that include language, music, dance, and (perhaps most importantly) food are all ones I have experienced first-hand and have spent a lifetime integrating into my own life. Furthermore, I study this genre because I believe it speaks to me and others like me, specifically as Arab Americans. These plays introduce American audiences to a culture that is known most often only for its negative aspects, broadcast on news reports whenever a calamity occurs in the Middle East. Conversely, these plays provide a look into the Arab American culture that displays Arab Americans for who they are—multi-dimensional individuals who are sometimes good, sometimes bad, but mostly compelling. Also, as a lifelong theatre director, playwright, and scholar, I find these plays and performances interesting as works of dramatic art. Since I have directed several of the works studied here and have met and befriended several of these writers and performers, my hope is that this has not placed me at a critical disadvantage since I have compressed my critical distance from my so-called "subjects." It is my sincere wish that any critiques I do level are read as a desire to elevate the genre, not to diminish it. Following the advice of the great director and critic Harold Clurman, I am attempting to be aware of my prejudices and blind spots and to "err on the side of generosity rather than an opposite zeal."[2]

One need not look far for examples of Arab Americans' literary work being omitted or overlooked. Kahlil Gibran's[3] book *The Prophet*, which has sold more than nine million copies in its American edition alone, is not regularly taught in American literature classes and is not shelved in the "literature" section in bookstores. Instead, it is often found under the category of "spirituality" or "new age."[4] The first Arab American novel, Ameen Fares Rihani's *The Book of Khalid*, has only recently been republished and is virtually unknown by many literary scholars, let alone taught in any college literature classes. As for Arab American drama, it is only within the past decade that any of these dramas were published at all. Until the anthology *Shattering the Stereotypes: Muslim Women Speak Out*, published in 2004, there were no Arab American playwrights who were anthologized. Even the anthologies that followed, such as *Salaam, Peace: An Anthology of Middle Eastern-American Drama*, which includes no less than five Arab American playwrights, still categorizes these plays under the larger rubric of "Middle Eastern-American Drama." Although there is no doubt that these works are, indeed, the works of Middle Eastern Americans, not specifying them as "Arab American" elides the difference between these writers and other Middle Eastern American writers such as Iranian Americans or Armenian Americans.[5] The issues facing Arab Americans are different in many ways from their Middle Eastern American counterparts, mainly due to the fact that some Arab Americans are Muslims and the complicated political situation that exists between the United States and most Arab nations is often fraught with tension, if not outright war. Furthermore, in the post–9/11 context, these geopolitical tensions have led to specific governmental persecutions that are not always shared by Armenian Americans, Israeli Americans, and others. This is not to say that Arab Americans are special—only that living in the United States and having ties to the Arab world in the twentieth and twenty-first centuries is fraught with difficulties.

Some, like Silk Road Rising Artistic Director Jamil Khoury, argue that this is a "both/and" and not an "either/or" proposition.[6] Although I agree with him, I also believe it is critical that, as theatre scholars and practitioners, we strive to educate our audiences about the multifarious nature of these people and their works. It is clear to me that we should not be satisfied with lumping all Middle Easterners, or their dramatic works, into this category. There is no reason we cannot have larger categorizations, but it is also necessary for us to understand the nuances and various subject positions of the writers and performers we study. This knowledge might dispel stereotypes, educate audiences, and lead to greater understanding of different Middle Eastern and Arab groups. There are other excellent anthologies that work in this mode, including Velina Hasu Houston's *But Still, Like Air, I'll Rise: New Asian American Plays*, Nishan Parlakian's *Contemporary Armenian American Drama: An Anthology of Ancestral Voices*, and Ellen Schiff's *Awake and Singing: 7 Classic Plays from the American Jewish Repertoire*.

Luckily, there have been great strides in the past few decades in fields of ethnic studies, postcolonial theory, queer theory, feminist studies, and Arab American studies. In addition, the early Arab American scholars, activists, and poets have created a large body of literature since the late 1960s. Instead of applying an overarching critical stance for this study, I will rely on the various theories and methodologies that I believe best convey, in a theoretical mode, what I believe these playwrights and performers are attempting to transmit in their performance modes. This polyvocal approach is necessary to address the complicated concepts, ideas, and expressions these artists are dramatizing. In addition, since these artists come from so many varying backgrounds, utilizing various dramatic and performative techniques, it is vital that the theories applied match the styles of the works. In other words, my desire is not to create a new theoretical framework but rather to elucidate these works by utilizing productive theoretical perspectives that have not yet been applied to dramatic interpretation or the study of these particular plays, films, and performances.

Theories explored are those of ethnicization, cultural exclusion, deassimilation, and pan-identities in regard to Arab American identity formation and Arab American performance. These plays serve what Barbara Harlow defines as "resistance literature," providing agency for these writers and performers who have traditionally been excluded (both by internal and external forces) from the mainstream American theatre and film industries. Harlow describes resistance literature as that which wages a struggle for political and cultural liberation.⁷ Although Harlow's study focuses mainly on the post-colonial aspect of resistance literature, it is my contention that contemporary Arab American plays and performances are focused on the neo-colonial conflicts relating to Arabs and Arab Americans in the twentieth and twenty-first centuries.

I deploy the term "restaging" in relation to Homi K. Bhabha's use of it in his book *The Location of Culture*, where he writes that the purpose of "restaging the past" is that "it introduces other, incommensurable cultural temporalities into the invention of tradition."⁸ For Bhabha, postmodernism is marked by existence in the "beyond," which is a moment where difference and identity exist within the in-between spaces that provide "a terrain for elaborating strategies of selfhood—singular or communal—that initiate new signs of identity, and innovative sites of collaboration, and contestation, in the act of defining the idea of society itself."⁹ These Arab American writers' and performers' works signify from the periphery of an authorized hegemonic power, which does not depend on the persistence of a previous Arab or American tradition. Instead, these artists estrange the access to their originary identity and received traditions by creating works that complicate notions of ethnicity, culture, hybridity, and homogeneity. By doing so, they speak from the margins of society, from the margins of accepted minority discourse, and from a multicultural/intracultural position that does not currently exist for them in the American theatrical landscape. However, this position is one that has both strengthened and weakened their voices. They have the creative license with which to speak about the issues that interest them, yet their marginalization can render them obscure to the larger discourses that surround them. Because of this, their works are not fully embraced by either the American theatre mainstream or by Arabs living in America.

The tropes of restaging and recasting are deployed for several reasons. As this is a study of theatre and performance, it is only fitting that theatrical and performance-based metaphors are utilized. More important, it is clear from both the works studied, and interviews with the artists themselves, that the hallmark of this wave of Arab American theatre and performance is the desire to re-imagine Arab Americans in theatre and film more humanistically and dimensionally, thereby replacing malicious stereotyping from popular media and the arts with more positive representations. In essence, these artists are attempting to seize the power of representation that has been denied them for so long. Their works answer the call of media scholar Jack G. Shaheen, who believes "to quash the Arab stereotype we must first identify it as unacceptable and commit to its eradication by speaking out."¹⁰ As the poet Khaled

Mattawa writes, "However slow and painful the recovery, Arab-American destiny will continue to come under Arab-American control so long as the image of the Arab-American comes increasingly under the control of Arab-American writers."[11] Holly Arida writes, "Arab Americans are constantly made to define and defend who we are. Otherwise, our image will be defined for us, either by those who commit violence in our name or by those who assert that Arabs and Muslims are somehow monolithic or deserve collective blame for 9/11."[12] I argue that these artists have, both successfully and unsuccessfully, made it their artistic mission to speak out against negative stereotyping through their writings and performances.

It is also my belief that, despite their attempts to abolish negative stereotypes, some of these writers and performers sometimes reify them by restaging several of the negative tropes they so ardently refute. For instance, the tropes of the hijacker, the hostage taker, and the oppressed Arab woman are sometimes recreated in their works. Despite the elevated visibility these writers and performers have achieved, it is clear that their work has not always served their stated purposes. As Peggy Phelan astutely observes, "gaining visibility for the politically under-represented without scrutinizing the power of who is required to display what to whom is an impoverished political agenda."[13] At times, these artists have confused their heightened visibility with their ability to create the positive representations they desire. In their attempts to enter the mainstream of the entertainment industry they have often been typecast in Orientalized, terrorist, or oppressed Arab female roles. Some of these artists have considered this a necessary compromise in order to "break in" to the entertainment industry, while others have shunned the industry altogether and have created works that remain outside the mainstream. This book examines how Arab American performing artists employ visibility and how it is sometimes unexamined by the artists themselves.

I also contend that the works of contemporary Arab American playwrights, filmmakers, and performers are a direct reflection of the Arab American civil rights movement that was born in the aftermath of the 1967 Six-Day War between Israel and several Arab nations. The work of Arab American scholars who created some of the seminal advocacy groups also led to publications of essays, poetry, and academic papers that would inform the very notion of what it meant to be Arab American. Therefore, a study of these groups and their founders is necessary. Of course, the work of one of these scholars, the late Edward W. Said, is foundational to a study such as this mainly because he was able to speak to both the modern and contemporary Arab American condition. Regarding the modern period, his seminal book

Orientalism provides the historical framework for the creation of the orientalist discourse by which the people of the Middle East have been framed by their colonialist and neo-colonialist "masters" for centuries. For contemporary Arab American studies, I will rely primarily on Said's seminal 1967 essay "The Arab Portrayed." In it, Said cogently dissects the pernicious stereotypes of Arabs that he perceived were in circulation following the events of the Six-Day War. I believe that it was this essay that was the spark for the entire contemporary Arab American civil rights movement and also informed the valuable work regarding anti–Arab stereotyping found in the media and in Hollywood films by scholars like Shaheen. Therefore, I will rely on Said's texts as frames through which I will view the Arab American dramas of the twentieth and early twenty-first centuries.

I have chosen the included plays and playwrights for several reasons: their importance to Arab American drama as deemed by other scholars, artists, and critics; the availability of texts and reviews about these performances; my own familiarity with these texts through personal research or performance; and my own belief in their inherent theatricality and dramaturgical value. Also, if a playwright has written multiple plays and if some of these plays have previously been studied, I have opted to choose plays that currently have no corresponding academic articles available. I have included many plays and films I believe are representative of the genre, but by no means included a study of all of the works in this genre.

This study is not meant to be a history of Arab American theatre and performance simply because there is so much more to research about this field. I have made it one of my goals to rescue many unpublished and unstudied works from obscurity, to contextualize them within their periods, and to understand what they have to say to both Arabs and Americans. As I noted, very few Arab American plays have either been translated from Arabic to English or have been performed on stage. Some of these plays have languished in archives (personal archives and libraries) or have remained untranslated for over a century. Imagine if the works of Chekhov, Pirandello, or Genet had never been translated to English; what would we have lost in our understanding and study of modern Russian, Italian, or French drama? How would contemporary English-language plays and dramaturgy have been different had we not had access to these works? A similar situation has occurred regarding Arab and Arab American dramas. Only now have certain works (such as Rihani's *Wajdah*) been published, and only due to recent efforts have works by Gibran and Naimy been translated. Furthermore, other works such as S. K. Hershewe's *An Oasis in Manhattan* might never have been known had they not been retrieved from obscurity. I have continually worked to "unearth" these scripts and performances, but there is much more to do—especially for the period between the demise of The Pen Group in 1931 and the first staging of Hershewe's *An Oasis in Manhattan* in 1965.

Instead of a linear, chronological history of this form, I will attempt instead a thematic approach that focuses on several important aspects: the early playwrights, comedy, solo female performance, post–9/11 dramas, films and performances, and works that focus primarily on the Arab-Israeli conflict. My hope is to continue this research and scholarship through the publication of books, articles, anthologies, and by my own directing of these works. A book like this one is meant to bring greater perspective to the growing number of studies of different American dramatic forms, to introduce theatre practitioners and scholars to works that they most likely have never encountered, and to establish Arab American drama as a distinct genre that has its own original voice.

This book departs from earlier studies by positioning Arab American theatre, film, and performance as a distinct genre and by identifying what makes these writers, plays, and performances unique and separate from other forms of diasporic literature. One of the main issues that separates Arab Americans is that some, though not all, Arabs are Muslim and that Arabophobia and Islamophobia have been a constant throughout the colonialist and neo-imperialist eras in Western Europe and North America. Also, unlike Armenians, Assyrians, and Israelis, the primary conflicts that have arisen from the Middle Eastern region involve Arab nations; this is especially true of the Palestinians in their conflict with Israel, the various issues regarding oil from Arab nations, and wars and conflicts with Arab leaders and political groups. These conflicts, more than any others abroad, have directly impacted American views of Arabs. I agree that there is no question that Arab American drama is a subcategory of Middle Eastern American Drama. However, in order to understand the genre in greater depth, a more specific and nuanced definition is necessary. To group Arab American drama with Middle Eastern American drama both amalgamates these ethnicities and gives the impression that all Middle Eastern groups are somehow the same. Instead, I advocate that these diversities be defined not for the purposes of division and segregation, but rather that we attempt to educate and enlighten readers by helping them understand the plethora of voices that exist within the context of the Middle East. As Steven Salaita makes clear, even the term "Arab American" elides the many different religions, sects, nationalities, and ethnicities that make up those of Arab descent, but at least the term underscores the commonalities Arabs share culturally that are wholly distinct from others from the Middle East.

I draw upon playscripts, films, live performances, recorded performances, interviews, and my own experience directing these works. A great deal of time and money has gone into the acquisition, translation, and analysis of these works. Some of more recent works are available as published playscripts, widely distributed films, and online videos. Other plays have been found in library archives, personal archives, and in museums in the United States and in the Middle East. Some playwrights have been very generous with their works, sending me their plays that have not been published. Other works were acquired by the survivors and relatives of playwrights who passed away. In other instances I have, through the University of Oregon, commissioned translations of some of these works specifically for the purpose of this study.

Although this genre is technically over one hundred years old, there has been surprisingly little written about it. The first Arab American play in English was written in 1908. Eighty years later, scholar Ala Fa'ik wrote of how there had been no attempt to record, study, or analyze the Arab American theatre movement.[14] Over the last decade, several scholars have adopted the term Arab American when referring to these performances. These scholars include Dina Amin,[15] Dalia Basiouny,[16] Marvin Carlson,[17] Anneka Esch-Van Kan,[18] Ala Fa'ik,[19] Erith Jaffe-Berg,[20] Somaya Sami Sabry,[21] and Jack G. Shaheen.[22]

Chapter 1, "'Unresolved sorrow and uncomprehending anger': Contemporary Arab American Identity Formation," examines the beginning of Arab American identity formation following the 1967 Arab-Israeli War. Prior to 1967, Arabs living in America were not referred to as "Arab Americans." Not until the 1967 War and the subsequent backlash against Arabs in America did Arabs living in America come together to form activist groups whose aims included informing Americans about Palestinian issues, U.S. foreign policy toward Arab countries, educating youth about the people of the Middle East, and combatting negative stereotypes of Arabs in the media. This movement also coincided with the third wave of Arab immigration to the United States that brought more diverse and educated Arabs. As part of the burgeoning civil rights movement of the 1960s, the Arab American identity movement was one that brought together many prominent Arab intellectuals who attempted to change the discourse regarding Arabs in the United States. Several advocacy groups formed, including the Association of Arab American University Graduates (AAUG), the Arab Anti Discrimination Committee (ADC), and the Arab American Institute (AAI). These groups, and their advocacy, became the philosophical foundation for the Arab American artistic movement that followed. By studying this history and understanding the missions of these groups it becomes clear that the Arab American plays written from the late

1980s to early twenty-first century are the theatrical equivalents of the academic advocacy that these early Arab American scholars were creating.

Chapter 2, "'We are not of the East or West': Origins of Arab American Drama in the Works of Rihani, Gibran and Naimy," investigates the first Arab American dramatists who were known primarily for their work as novelists and poets. Ameen Rihani's *Wajdah* (1908–09) is considered the first Arab American drama written in English. Rihani's work as a Shakespearean actor, and his fascination with the art of the theatre, led him to write dramas based on medieval Arab history, sometimes containing many fanciful Orientalist elements. His contemporary, Kahlil Gibran, wrote several plays during his lifetime, though he is best known for his longer poetic works such as *The Prophet*. Mikhail Naimy's *Fathers and Sons*, which contains the same title (but not the same subject matter) as Turgenev's novel, is an example of how Russian drama (as experienced by Naimy while living in Ukraine), is seen through the eyes of an Arab intellectual. Like Rihani, Naimy was also influenced by the theatre and was entranced by its power. However, unlike Rihani, who looked back into Arab history, Naimy decided to dramatize the lives of his contemporary Lebanese living in Lebanon and dealing with the moral and societal strictures found in his Christian village of Baskinta. The plays studied, Rihani's *Wajdah*, Gibran's *The Chameleons*, and Naimy's *Fathers and Sons*, were the first Arab American dramas, providing fascinating insights into what the first Arab immigrants were creating in the early decades of the twentieth century. These three writers provide an artistic foundation for the works of Arab American playwrights who followed.

Chapter 3, "'There's nothing funny about your people': Arab American Comedy and Stand-Up Performance," examines the long tradition of Arab comedy and how it has been adopted by Arab Americans. Beginning with Danny Thomas's nightclub act "Ode to a Wailing Syrian," the chapter explores how Arab Americans have always referenced their own culture in comedy and how, in some instances, they have reified the very stereotypes they may have meant to dispel. The chapter then examines S. K. Hershewe's play *An Oasis in Manhattan*, the first known Arab American theatrical comedy. The focus then turns to the AJYAL Theatrical Group, a Dearborn, Michigan–based, semi-professional Arab American theatre company that performs primarily in Arabic and is wildly popular with Arab American audiences. Following the events of 9/11, many Arab American stand-up comedians took on the mantle of Arab American identity and incorporated that identity into their comedy routines. Contemporary Arab American stand-up comedians Dean Obeidallah, Ahmed Ahmed, and Maysoon Zayid have found ways to play up their heritage while playing down the irrational fear many Americans have about Arabs and Muslims. The question remains as to whether this comedy actually changes the perceptions many have about Arab Americans or if it only reinforces those misperceptions through repetition.

Chapter 4, "'It's not profiling, it's deduction': Post–9/11 Arab American Drama" examines the works of artists who self-identify as Arab American after the real and perceived threat of persecution following the 9/11 attacks. These playwrights, who found themselves living with a palpable sense of fear in the aftermath of the terrorist attacks, wrote plays that reflected that state of being. The first group to form was Nibras, an Arab American collective that created a work titled *Sajjil* as a documentary theatre piece that explored American attitudes toward Arabs after 9/11. Egyptian American Yussef El Guindi, arguably the most prolific Arab American dramatist, has written several works that dramatize the pervasive sense of fear that racial profiling exerts on Arab Americans. El Guindi's works *Back of the Throat* and *Language Rooms* both explore what Judith Butler calls "the derealization of the 'Other'"[23] that is experienced by Arab Muslims in the post–9/11 era. These playwrights and performers provided the first forms of resistance literature in Arab American drama.

Chapter 5, "Suffering for Palestine: Palestinian American Playwrights," focuses on the work of several prominent Arab American playwrights of Palestinian descent including Ismail Khalidi, Betty Shamieh, Lameece Issaq, Jennifer Jajeh, Jacob Kader, and Najla Said. By examining the notions of trauma and postmemory as described by Marianne Hirsch[24] and Dominick LaCapra,[25] and also by examining the works of Edward W. Said, these plays are seen as reflections of second-generation American-born playwrights who attempt to recreate two Palestines: one that pre-dates the founding of Israel and another that exists under Israeli occupation. Given that some of these playwrights, such as Najla Said and Ismail Khalidi, are the descendants of post–1967 intellectuals (Edward W. Said and Rashid Khalidi, respectively) who were engaged in the academic activism that advocated for Palestinian rights, these plays are the dramatic equivalents of the scholarly work attempted by previous generations. The chapter explores how postmemory and trauma operate within this genre of theatre and how these playwrights advocate through their dramaturgy for a heretofore unrecognized Palestinian state and Palestinian people.

Chapter 6, "Arabs Filming Arabs: Contemporary Arab American Films," focuses on the small, but growing number of Arab American filmmakers. The three films *American East* (written by Hesham Issawi and Sayed Badreya and directed by Hesham Issawi), *Amreeka* (written and directed by Cherien Dabis), and *Detroit Unleaded* (written and directed by Rola Nashef) are all examples of Arab American films that attempt to recast and restage the Arab image in American cinema. Despite limited releases and modest production budgets, these filmmakers have decided to tell their own stories about their experiences as Arab Americans in a time when the Arab American image on film has primarily been dominated by what Shaheen calls "reel Arabs," or the stereotypical Arab characters who are comprised of either rich sheikhs and belly dancers or dangerous veiled and militaristic terrorists. By creating self-portraits, these artists are also attempting to reclaim damaging stereotypical images of Arabs that have been created in Hollywood cinema for over a century.

Chapter 7, "'A psychic civil war onstage': Arab American Solo Performance," explores the solo performances of several Arab American artists including Andrea Assaf, Leila Buck, Jennifer Jajeh, Laila Farah, and Heather Raffo. These solo performances, primarily by women, explore the tensions and complications of living as an Arab American woman in a time of persecution and tension that dictates women's conformity to the standards of what Nadine Naber calls "good Arab families, good Arab girls, and compulsory heterosexuality."[26] These women are also fighting against other Orientalist stereotypes of what Amira Jarmakani calls the "veil, harem, and belly dancer."[27] By not only writing, but also performing, their own works these women have created a space for themselves in a theatrical landscape that has both omitted, and/or erased the Arab woman entirely.

Arab American writers, performers, and filmmakers are all attempting, in their own way, to bring their personal stories to the stage and screen. This means telling stories based on their history and culture, writing fully dimensional characters, and creating works that humanize Arabs and Arab Americans in their full complexity. These writers are the first to state that it is not their goal to glorify Arab Americans in their works, but rather to offer portraits of human characters surviving human struggles whether about growing up Arab in America, being persecuted by the government as a suspected terrorist threat, dealing with the horrifying repercussions of wars, or trying to negotiate two very different cultures when it comes to dating, marriage, or childrearing. What makes these plays, films, and performances unique is that they are offering a perspective that is not often heard in mainstream media, theatre, or film. These artists are sharing their dual perspectives, American and Arab, telling us something about places we only read about in sensational newspaper articles or have seen imagined in Hollywood films. They are portraying the hopes, fears, and dreams of Arabs and Arab Americans living in this country during a time when tensions between the United States and Arab nations are at their worst. It might behoove all of us to listen.

Notes on Transliteration and Nomenclature

Arab American dramas often contain Arabic words transliterated into English. Although there are official Arabic Romanization systems (such as the International Phonetic Alphabet, Hans Wehr Transliteration, or the Qalam Transliteration Convention), Arab American authors often rely on their personal transliterations within their scripts. Rather than standardize these transliterations, or provide a glossary for each play, I have decided to keep the plays in their original forms, since the playwrights wrote them to be read as printed.

Also, some writers include a hyphen between the words "Arab" and "American" while others do not. I have chosen not to include the hyphen since I believe that the connection between these two words is more of a gulf than a bridge. Arab Americans live in this space between these two identities in a state of constant negotiation. It is from that interstitial space that I believe these writers and performers create their works.

Introduction: Defining a Genre

In October 2002, as the rubble of the World Trade Center was being cleared, a strange rectangular stone engraved with a cross and Latin text was found. It read "Saint Joseph's Roman Catholic Maronite Church." The church, originally located at 127 Washington Street in Lower Manhattan, was bulldozed for the construction of the original World Trade Center.[1] Recognizing that the first Arab American community was located over one hundred years before in the exact area where the "ground zero" of Arabophobia[2] is found today, demonstrates the complicated and contentious relationship America has with its Arab/Arab American population. What is overlooked, however, is that Washington Street was home to thousands of shopkeepers and priests, peddlers and journalists, parents and children, factory workers and writers. Different nationalities also mingled: Syrians, Greeks, Poles, Lithuanians, Czechs, Armenians, Turks, Hungarians, Ukrainians, and Slovaks. What came to be known as the "Syrian Quarter" or "Little Syria" was the first place immigrants of Arab descent visited to meet lost relatives, eat familiar foods, and to find work. More importantly, Little Syria was also home for the first Arab American writers, many of whom were poets, novelists, and playwrights. In fact, the first Arab American novel by Ameen Fares Rihani, *The Book of Khalid*, was inspired by life as an immigrant in New York City. The first professional Arab American writing group, The Pen League, which included playwrights Ameen Rihani, Kahlil Gibran, and Mikhail Naimy, was also founded on that long forgotten street.

¤ ¤ ¤

I begin with the Saint Joseph's cornerstone because it is a symbol of how the idea of "Arab American" began, a measure of how far it has come, and testament to how damaged the history and reputation of this group has become

Cornerstone of St. Joseph Maronite Church from Little Syria, found in 2002 beneath the ruins of the World Trade Center. St. Joseph's was the first Maronite Church in Manhattan (photograph by David Dunlap/*The New York Times*/Redux).

from the mid–twentieth century to the present. Three buildings from that earliest period remain to this day on Washington Street, although they are under threat of destruction. No signs, statues or memorials exist to commemorate the history of the early Arab American settlement there. Now housed in Our Lady of Lebanon Maronite Catholic Cathedral in Brooklyn, the cornerstone of Saint Joseph's Church is a perfect metaphor for this book because it reminds us of how Arab American history can be unearthed, reclaimed, and reevaluated in the twenty-first century.

Modern and Contemporary Arab American Drama

I define modern Arab American theatre as the genre that spans 1908 to 1967; from the publication of Ameen Fares Rihani's four-act English language drama *Wajdah* to S.K. Hershewe's comedy *An Oasis in Manhattan*. By contrast, I define contemporary Arab American theatre, film, and performance as the genre that spans 1967 to the present. Contemporary Arab American refers to the plays, films, and performances of self-identified first and second-generation Arab Americans whose works are a direct response to the backlash against Arab Americans following the 1967 Six-Day War through the post–9/11 era. I create these distinctions because there are major differences between the concerns of the pre–1967 playwrights and the post–1967 playwrights, filmmakers, and performers.

The differences between these two groups include the following:

Modern Arab American Drama (1908–1967)	Contemporary Arab American Drama (1967–Present)
Writers hailed primarily from Greater Syria and were primarily Maronite Christians.	Writers are descendants of Arabs from many different Arab countries and represent many religious faiths and/or sects.
Writers were known by various hyphenated identities.	Writers adopted the "Arab American" identity.
Writers were concerned with issues such as the poet/prophet ideal; East-West interactions; stories that revolved around disagreements with the church versus the individual; plays about Arab history.	Writers are concerned with issues such as identity politics; racial profiling; governmental persecution; assimilation; the Palestine-Israel conflict; women's rights; homophobia.
Plays written in English and Arabic.	Plays written primarily in English.
Playwrights were not theatre professionals and few of their plays were produced.	Playwrights are primarily theatre professionals and the plays are widely produced.
Plays were primarily written to be read.	Plays are primarily written to be staged.
Primarily wrote dramas.	Write plays, monodramas, screenplays.

Modern Arab American Drama (1908–1967)

Modern Arab American playwrights like Ameen Fares Rihani, Kahlil Gibran, and Mikhail Naimy were interested primarily in writing poetry, novels, and biographies. Their playwriting output, in comparison with the other genres in which they worked, was relatively small. These writers each wrote a handful of plays, primarily for publication and readings rather than full theatrical productions. Furthermore, many of these plays were not published or translated until decades after the authors' deaths. Some of these plays were read in front of audiences, and very few were staged. Also, none of the writers, except Rihani, had any formal theatrical training. Therefore, they were writing in a genre without knowing the intricacies that a professional playwright might have known such as staging a play, the uses of theatrical design elements, and working with actors. Instead, it is clear they attended and read many plays, and viewed playwriting as yet another outlet for their literary output. Their plays allowed them to level scathing critiques against the Maronite Church, their Syrian/Lebanese society, and their compatriots both in the United States and back in their homelands. Without having any productions or reviews, it is impossible to know how these works were received by readers or audiences.

Gibran, Rihani, and Naimy's works were written primarily in Arabic, though both Rihani and Gibran wrote plays in English as well. Most of Gibran's plays were written in his "poet-prophet" style, reminiscent of his works *The Prophet* and *Jesus, Son of Man*. According to his cousin, and namesake, Kahlil Gibran, "These were 'test' plays, symbolic short trials which synthesized his personal philosophy."[3] One play studied here, Gibran's *The Chameleons*, is a modern drama that focuses on the hypocrisy and jealousy Gibran encountered within New York's Arab immigrant population. Other plays by Gibran were Symbolist in nature. Rihani's plays were more interested in dramatizing Arab history. According to Nijmeh Hajjar, "Rihani was also the first Arabic playwright to experiment with political drama in an original way. At least one of his plays with a clear political message was staged in Beirut shortly after the overthrow of Sultan 'Abd al-Hamid in 1909."[4] Naimy focused his play *Fathers and Sons* on current issues from the villages of his native Lebanon. Naimy wrote the fewest plays from this triad, but his work, unlike the work of Gibran and Naimy, was heavily influenced by his years of study in Ukraine and his deep knowledge of Russian literature and drama. Also, unlike Gibran or Rihani, Naimy left several essays that elucidated his views on Arab theatre.

These three playwrights were all Maronite Christians, and their work contained deep ambivalence, if not outright anger toward the church and its officials. They also operated under their understanding of Phoenicianism, a belief held by Maronite Christians that they are descendants of the Phoenicians, and not Arabs. This hostility toward the Eastern Church and the distance these writers felt from Arabs and Arabism informs the style, tone, and political nature of their works. Since Maronite Christians from Greater Syria (now Lebanon) were the majority of the immigrants and the writers of this time, it was their religious beliefs and the "poet-prophet" ideal that informed their writing. This factor also separates their work from later Arab Americans who are from a variety of religious and sectarian backgrounds. By viewing their plays through these lenses, the contrast between the early Arab American writers and those who succeeded them becomes much clearer.

According to Nada Najjar, these writers' works contained an ambivalence that was historically, politically, and culturally tied to Western interventions within the Arab world in the late nineteenth and early twentieth centuries. She also writes that these artists existed in what she calls "the space in-between" their homelands and their newly adopted United States, which included the dichotomies between the East and the West, Christian and Islamic social systems, and the tension between their identities of consent versus descent.[5] According to Najjar, these writers isolated themselves from both the struggles of their homelands (by leaving those places and immigrating to the United States) and from the American experience (by never fully integrating into the culture and by literally isolating themselves from other Americans). Furthermore, these writers were deeply influenced by what Sarah M.A. Gualtieri calls "Phoenicianism," the ideological tool they used to construct a Lebanese nationality.[6] Phoenicianism was taught in the pro–French schools where these writers were first educated and distanced the Maronite community from notions of Arabism. Therefore, these writers viewed themselves less as Arabs and more as descendants from Phoenicians who were part of a long Christian tradition. In their later years some embraced their Arabness (Rihani) while others continued to view themselves as Christian mystics (Gibran and Naimy). This self-definition informed their writing and affected their political views.

One trait that was prevalent in the modern period was the anti–Ottoman sentiment that these writers professed. Gibran, Rihani, and Naimy all protested Ottoman rule of Greater Syria and even worked to raise funds to assist those suffering under the yoke of occupation. Rihani's house in Freike, Lebanon, became a gathering place for Arab intellectuals active against Ottoman rule.[7] For his part, Gibran formed the Syrian-Mount Lebanon Relief Committee. Serving as its secretary, Gibran wrote of his disdain for his fellow countrymen and their apathy regarding the war effort. Gibran wrote poems about the decimation of his country by the Ottomans, and about his guilt at not being able to be of more service to his homeland in works like "Dead Are My People." In the poem he wrote,

> Gone are my people, but I exist yet,
> Lamenting them in my solitude...
> What can an exiled son do for his
> Starving people, and of what value
> Unto them is the lamentation of an
> Absent poet?[8]

Following World War II, Rihani and Naimy's political attentions turned toward an anti-colonialist European Zionism regarding the settlement of Palestine. These writers were, in their own ways, cognizant of the colonial machinations of Britain and France during their lifetimes, and they could foresee the dangers inherent in the British partition of Palestine. In Rihani's 1932 essay, "Palestine and the Proposed Arab Federation," he wrote:

> Prior to the Mandate and the Balfour Declaration, the Arab-Jewish problem in Palestine did not exist. No one can deny that. Nor will any deny that in those days the Arabs and the Jews were peaceful, neighborly, and friendly towards each other. We want that happy era—the era of brotherhood and peace—to return; and any document that impedes its return, that raises barriers, that sows the seeds of hatred and strife, that produces riots and bloodshed, that creates an everlasting enmity between people, is a criminal document and should be abolished.[9]

For his part, Naimy also protested against the Balfour Declaration. In his autobiography *Seventy*, he wrote:

> The Balfour Declaration decreed that a stranger enter a house occupied by its people and that he enter it forcibly and with the armed support of the British sovereign. Then he tells the habitants: "Do not worry. The house will remain yours, but it will be my 'national home,' nothing more." That is a promise which even the demons of our lord Salomo cannot give—let alone fulfill.[10]

After 1967, this criticism of the British involvement in the partitioning of Palestine later transformed into a salient critique of the occupation of the Palestinian territories by the Israeli government. According to scholar Yossi Shain, the Arab-Israeli conflict provided the foundation for pan–Arab ethnic identity in America.[11] The late Arab American scholar Edward W. Said even went so far as to say that the Arab American identity was primarily based on the Israeli Palestinian conflict. Although Shain's analysis speaks specifically to the post–1967 Arab American condition, the examples above demonstrate that there was first a tension related to the European Zionist colonization of historic Palestine. The greatest difference between modern and contemporary Arab American writers is that the former seldom included political themes in their dramatic works, whereas many of the contemporary Arab American writers incorporate political themes in their dramas, films, and performances.

Contemporary Arab American Theatre, Film and Performance (1967–Present)

Contemporary Arab American[12] theatre, film, and performance in the United States refers to the plays, films, and performances of *self-identified* Arab

Americans after the 1967 Arab-Israeli War. The writers, directors, and performers of this period came of age during several major events that shaped Arab American consciousness in the United States: the Immigration Bill of 1965, which created sweeping changes to U.S. immigration policy; the reaction in opposition to Arabs and Arab Americans following the Arab-Israel Six-Day War in 1967; and the backlash against Arabs and Arab Americans following the events of September 11, 2001. It is my contention that Arab American theatre, film, and performance are neither mainstream cultural forces nor minority art forms. Instead, the works included in this genre serve as a form of resistance literature, providing agency for the writers and performers who have traditionally been excluded (through internal and external forces) from mainstream American academia and the theatre and film industries. In addition, contemporary Arab American plays, films, and performances are concentrated on neo-colonial conflicts relating to Arabs and Arab Americans in the twenty-first century.

Origins of the Arab American Identity

The term Arab American is a construction that, by most accounts, did not exist prior to the late 1960s. Prior to the 1967 Arab-Israel War, and the ensuing backlash against Arab American groups by the U.S. government, the terms "Arab," "Arabs in America," "Americans of Arab Descent," or being named by one's national or sectarian affiliation was more prevalent. An examination of the origin, construction, and deployment of Arab American identification is necessary to understand how this identity was created in the United States through juridical rulings, governmental acts, and group advocacy. Activist groups such as the American Arab University Graduates (AAUG), the American-Arab Anti-Discrimination Committee (ADC), and the Arab American Institute (AAI) shaped and defined contemporary Arab American identity formation. Post–9/11 surveillance of Arab Americans also is an extension of U.S. government persecution that can be traced back to the early 1970s. Furthermore, it is clear that the term Arab American is both embraced and refuted by the very community it seeks to represent. Therefore, as with most ethno-racial constructions, it is a complex and on-going identity formation that is neither stable nor definitive.

Arabs, first, are Semitic people who speak the Arabic language. Their "race" is not different from other Semitic people from the Middle Eastern region. Second, not all Arab Americans come from dual Arab parentage, making their racial or ethnic identification a less crucial factor. Third, what complicates this identity formation is that Arab American is not an officially recognized group by the United States government, yet the government employs this racial categorization for its own purposes of racial profiling, surveillance, and prosecution. For their part, not all of those of Arab descent living in the United States accept the term as an adequate description. Some of those who identify as Arab American find themselves interacting and affiliating with those most similar to themselves either tribally, religiously, or nationally, rather than with an imaginary pan–Arab community. To further complicate matters, some artists deny the moniker "Arab American" altogether, despite employing Arab American themes in their works. Therefore, it is clear that the Arab American identity is a political, not an ethnic or racial, identification that aims to reclaim agency for Arab Americans in all aspects of their lives. However, scholars like Gary C. David have pointed out that those who do not conform to the political, cultural, and linguistic expectations of the Arab American ideal are sometimes marginalized and rendered invisible by the very people who are meant to provide them agency.[13]

Defining a Genre

Defining this genre is somewhat difficult since I do not subscribe to the theory of essentialism or the belief that one is born into a race. Instead, I prefer Omi and Winant's theory of "cultural nationalism" that proposes cultural elements provide for collective identity, community, and a sense of belonging. Part of this categorization is the idea of "cultures of resistance" that resist hegemonic domination and promote a sense of collective identity.[14] Using this theory as a backdrop, I define Arab American theatre, film and performance as the following:

Works specifically created by self-identified Arab Americans as a response to the post–1967 and post–9/11 persecution and misrepresentation of Arab Americans. Because race has been proven an unstable and unessentialist category, I focus on self-identified Arab Americans. In a sense, these Arab Americans all lay claim to what is sometimes labeled "Arabness."[15] Since there are no racial markers that define an Arab, and because some Arab Americans are born of two parents of Arab descent while others are born of parents of differing ethnicities, I rely on whether or not Arab American artists identify themselves as such. This approach is fraught with its own difficulties, however, since some of the artists whose work I believe is exemplary of this genre actually refute the "Arab American" appellation. Instead of omitting these authors if I believe their works are exemplars in the field, I include them but I also note that they have refused to be categorized as such. My approach is not without precedent; Arab American history is rife with those who have litigated through the U.S. federal courts to be categorized as "white."[16] During the early decades of the twentieth century, this was done for a variety of reasons including their desire to vote, purchase property, and travel without difficulty. Some second and third generation Arab Americans have actually reversed this trend and have reclaimed their Arab heritage and their desire to be known as Arab Americans. This reclamation is part of many of the identities of Arab American artists, as I demonstrate in the following chapters. Although the term Arab American was not used until the 1960s, I utilize the term to include artists from the first decades of the twentieth century to the present time. This is done as a shorthand method since there were many terms for these writers prior to 1967, including: Americans of Arab Descent, Arabs in America, Syrians, Turks, Arabian, Semites of the Caucasian race, Ottomans, and Asiatic. Given the racist and exclusionary laws of the time, it is not unreasonable that Arabs would wish to legally petition for "whiteness" and to distance themselves from any connection with these groups. Many contemporary Arab American artists discuss the fact that they began self-identifying as such because of the political events that led to anti–Arab and anti–Muslim surveillance and persecution in the post–9/11 era. Therefore, this is clearly a political, rather than an ethnic or racial, category.

Works written in dramatic form either primarily in English or Arabic, or a mixture of both languages. Some of the works included here were originally written in Arabic, others in English, and still others in a mixture of the two which is often jokingly referred to as "*Arabeezi*," or a mixture of Arabic and the Arabic term for English—*Engleezi*. Because so many of the early Arab writers in America wrote their plays in Arabic, none of those works were performed or translated into English in their lifetimes.[17] Writers like Naimy wrestled with the linguistic use of *fusha*, or "high Arabic," versus *aamiyah*, or "low Arabic," in their plays. Contemporary playwright and director Najee Mondalek, of the Dearborn-based company *AJYAL* (Generations) Theatrical Group, writes his plays primarily in Arabic, but with English phrases and scenes added for comedic effect. Still other writers like Yussef El Guindi, Betty Shamieh, and Heather Raffo write their plays primarily in English with Arabic phrases and words embedded in the dialogue for a sense of cultural/linguistic authenticity. This book examines all of these combinations since they all have one element in common—a relationship with Arabic language and culture.

Works that utilize American dramatic forms such as two- or three-act realism, monodrama, and stand-up comedy. Arab American dramas mostly utilize what might be called "Western" or "American" Realism as their form. This form stands in contrast to traditionally Arab theatrical forms such as *hakawati* (storytelling), *zajal* (improvisational poetry), *khayal al-dhul* (puppet theatre), or *raqs al-Sharqi* (traditional Eastern dance). Almost all of these writers were students, or practitioners, of Euro-American comedy and drama. Their plays follow traditional forms such as one-, two-, and three-act dramas; solo drama or monodrama; stand-up comedy; or the "choreopoem" format. Arab American films are also written in the traditional three-act screenplay structure, much like the majority of mainstream American or European films. While this makes these works somewhat traditional in structure, they are unique in their perspectives into Arab and Arab American lives. In this sense, they join the canon of what is often called "multicultural," "intracultural," or "ethnic" theatre in the United States, much as is found in Asian American, African American, or Latino plays and films. In contrast, Arab dramatic/theatrical forms that predate the European influences of the eighteenth through twenty-first centuries are traditional forms specific to the regions where they were practiced by Arab storytellers, puppeteers, dancers, and poets.

Works that are interested in issues such as assimilation and acculturation within U.S. society, and the complications that arise from that identity negotiation. Many Arab American writers focus their works on the complicated relationships and conflicts they endure living between American and Arab cultures. For the early immigrant writers, the tension between leaving home and establishing themselves in "the West" was often fraught with difficulties that included longing for their homelands, struggling to assimilate into American society, and facing critiques and conflicts with other Arab immigrants. For second generation writers, the conflicts are similar. These writers also struggle with issues such as the inability to speak or understand the Arabic language, feeling a disassociation from Arabs and Americans, conflicts regarding endogamy versus exogamy, struggling with their religious heritage, dealing with governmental profiling, and their complicated relationship with American foreign policy and its effects on their Arab relatives living abroad.

Works that focus on more political, rather than cultural, themes. Many of these plays embody the adage "the personal is political." Because these writers are bi-cultural, they share both American and Arab heritages. This dual perspective lends itself to a critical stance regarding issues such as foreign policy regarding U.S. relations with foreign governments, internal U.S. policies that profile and persecute Arabs and Arab Americans, protests against Israeli governmental policies, and virulent critiques of Arab customs and traditions that are perceived unjust and antiquated. The plays simultaneously reflect the lives of Arabs who live in the Arab world and Americans who have ties to that world. Because these writers are born of immigrant parents and often travel and work in the Middle East, they chronicle life both in America and in their ethnic homelands. Often, the long, complicated, and violent history between the United States and Arab countries is dramatized in these works.

Works that discuss issues that are not often dramatized in traditional Arab theatrical forms, including identity politics and women's and queer subjectivity. Over the past five decades, Arab theatre in the Middle East has become more transgressive. However, due to censorship in most Arab states, experimental or avant-garde theatre in the Arab world remains poorly attended, underfunded, and somewhat scarce in comparison to the more popular art forms.[18] By comparison, Arab American theatre freely dramatizes contentious issues in Arab society including rape, women's rights, racism, and homosexuality.

Plays that focus on issues such as Arabophobia, Islamophobia, and the complicated relationship between mainstream American society and Muslim American culture. An uneasy relationship has historically existed between the Judeo-Christian values that many Americans hold and the Muslim religion that some Arabs practice. Islamophobia[19] is also tied to Arabophobia, and these issues manifest in many different ways—through discriminatory social acts, negative stereotyping/portrayals of Arabs and Muslims in American media and film, opposition to the building of mosques and Arab/Muslim cultural centers, and hostility against those who dress in a traditional Arab/Muslim fashion. Some Arab American playwrights and performers focus their attention on dispelling stereotypes of Arabs and Muslims and seek to create more multi-dimensional portrayals.

Of course, even categorizing these plays as "Arab American" is a large umbrella category that elides the multifarious composition of the group. Arab Americans, as Salaita reminds us, are not a single, unified entity.

> Arab Americans are Muslims (Shia and Sunni and Alawi and Isma'ili), Christian (Catholic and Orthodox, Anglican and Evangelical, and Mainline Protestant), Jewish (Orthodox and Conservative and Haredi and Reform), Druze, Bahai, dual citizens of Israel and twenty-two Arab nations, multi- and monolingual, progressives and conservatives, assimilationists and nationalists, cosmopolitanists and pluralists, immigrants and fifth-generation Americans, wealthy and working-class, rural and urban, modern and traditional, religious and secular, White and Black, Latin American and Canadian.... Sometimes Arab Americans are non–Arabs such

as Circassians, Armenians, Berbers, Kurds, and Iranians ... likely to inhabit any American industry and are represented across the social and political spectrums of the United States.[20]

However, Arab Americans have become an entity of their own that is related to, but distinct from, other Middle Easterners. Although they share a great deal in common with Armenian Americans, Iranian/Persian Americans, and Israeli/Jewish Americans, Arab Americans are distinct because they all share a common Arab heritage and Arabic is their common language. The greatest difficulty in defining a genre like this is that smaller and smaller subgenres (i.e., Lebanese American drama, Maronite Lebanese drama, etc.) are always possible. However, the category "Arab American" is large enough to encompass this entire group. By utilizing Arab American, I hope to provide a framework that includes the commonalities among these artists while working to clarify their specific identifications.

The Political Impulse in Arab American Writing

Long before there were any studies of Arab American drama or performance, Arab American poets were anthologizing their poetry and writing about the particularities of their positions as artists in America. Several anthologies of Arab American poetry have been published in the past few decades that argue for the specificity of the Arab American label attached to these works. Gregory Orfalea and Sharif Elmusa define Arab American poetry as poetry stands firmly against injustice and is "tempered by a kind of bitterness that America has not lived up to its ideals."[21] This critique is one that is shared by many Arab Americans who believe in the foundational principles and promise of America, but are frustrated by the foreign policies in the Arab world that often contradict those values. Orfalea and Elmusa write that, by taking an oppositional stance to U.S. policies, the Arab American poet is placed outside the mainstream dialogue and finds herself powerless, both politically and literarily. For his part, Hayan Charara writes that the term Arab American is relatively new and remains contentious within the community as a marker of identity. He writes that "literally, from poem to poem, and from poet to poet, 'Arab American' is accepted, rejected, maintained, and altered."[22] Charara also finds that engagement with politics, especially regarding U.S. foreign policy in the Middle East, seems to bring Arab Americans together more than other experiences can. In addition, themes regarding diaspora, 9/11, and the desire to dismantle "misguided and imbalanced" representations are all hallmarks of

Arab American writing. Nabil Alawi writes that teaching and studying Arab American literature suffers from two difficulties: lack of criticism on the subject and the constant focus on political issues in Arab American writing. These political issues make the study of such literature difficult because it requires an understanding of Middle East politics. Like others, Alawi finds the political aspects of these writings inseparable from the poets themselves:

> The political impulse in the poetry of Arab American writers is part of their consciousness; it is not much of their choice, but as ethnic writers their nostalgic feelings take them home where memories of childhood are being burned and the flames of endless wars and consequent hatred resulting from successive colonial periods leaves little room for optimism. But as all Arabs, Arab American writers long for freedom and they have a humble ambition—a home of their own unoccupied and without siege.[23]

It is evident that those who study Arab American poetry have created the bulk of critical thought regarding contemporary Arab American writing. The creation of specifically Arab American anthologies of poetry has led to a wider acceptance of the genre, as have newer critical writings that have elevated the discourse regarding Arab American literature. Although Arab American theatre has a long history, it has not had much in the way of publications, productions, and critical interventions. As Darcy Zabel writes in the introduction to her book *Arabs in the Americas: Interdisciplinary Essays on the Arab Diaspora*, the trend to justify or celebrate Arab Americans in early writings has given way to scholarship about specific aspects and representations which, in her opinion, is the only way to advance the field of Arab American Studies.[24] Therefore, if the genre of Arab American theatre, film, and performance is to advance, more critical engagement is necessary.

Since 1967, Arab Americans have found themselves on the defensive, adopting a sense of internal colonialism. In addition to an external locus of control, this internal colonialism has a negative effect upon those within the Arab American community. Arab American scholars Nadine Naber and Hatem Bazian describe this condition as "internment of the psyche" and "virtual internment" (respectively). Naber defines internment of the psyche as "the ways that the culture of fear produced a sense of internal incarceration that was emotive and manifested in terms of the sense that, at any moment, one may be picked, up, locked up, or disappeared."[25] Similarly, Bazian describes virtual internment as "a quasi-visible but repressive, intimidating, and confining structure employed by the U.S. administration and its allies on a global scale against individuals, communities, and organizations deemed unsupportive, and possibly hostile, in the worldview toward American and 'global' interests."[26] Because many Arab Americans retain dual citizenship and even dual allegiances with their homelands, conflicts between the United States and Arab countries exacerbate this sense of psychic and virtual internment.

Carol Fadda-Conrey writes that the transnational connections to Arab homelands create a space for Arab Americans to reformulate their understandings of citizenship and belonging within the United States. It is her view that Arab American writers simultaneously assert themselves within legal and cultural citizenship while maintaining their transnational connections and, by doing so, they challenge the notion that assimilation is a necessary goal for Arab Americans.

> Arab-American writers, by focusing in their work on complex and transnational engagements with the self-same constructs that Otherize them in the eyes of a U.S. public, revise hegemonic and binary configurations of racial, ethnic, religious, national, political, and gendered identities. In doing so, they challenge and push against the limits of purportedly inclusive structures of U.S. citizenship and belonging as conceived of and imagined by neoliberal U.S. multiculturalism.[27]

It is this transnational perspective, which is born of the fact that many Arab Americans are either legally or culturally tied to their ancestral homelands, that creates the political impetus to produce cultural works that engage with the critical political and social issues that concern them. Therefore, these writers, filmmakers, and performers find themselves creating from this transnational, interstitial space which often requires confronting a society that accepts them only when they conform to normative national frameworks. Their works, which challenge patriotic notions of what it means to be "American," often place them squarely outside the acceptable mainstream culture.

Arab American identity formation was, and remains, a reaction to the post–1967 and post–9/11 derealization of Arab Americans. Derealization is a term deployed by Judith Butler to describe the condition that renders the "Other" as neither alive nor dead, but "interminably spectral."[28] For Butler, this derealization constitutes an infinite paranoia that imagines the war on terror as a war without end against a spectral enemy. Through dehumanization, physical violence, and omission, the derealization of the Arab/Muslim Other has served to create a Foucaldian carceral system whereby this group has been systematically surveilled and persecuted. Plays like Yussef El Guindi's *Back of the Throat* and Ismail Khalidi's *Truth Serum Blues* dramatize these perceptions of internal carceration and derealization. Although this condition serves as interesting material for artists, it is also a state that leads to what Gualtieri charges is constrained scholarship for scholars and what Nouri Gana calls coerced imagination for artists. Gualtieri and Gana rightly fear that, by being so preoccupied by the ongoing stereotyping of Arab Americans and the fears of governmental surveillance and persecution, Arab American scholars and artists are limiting both their imagination and their potential. This fascinating dichotomy will be explored in depth in the following chapters.

Chapter 1 specifically explores Arab American identity formation in both the modern and contemporary periods. In the modern period, Arab American writers like Gibran, Rihani, and Naimy were more interested in the issues regarding their homeland of Greater Syria/Lebanon, than those that were taking place in their new homeland of the United States. As the United States became imbricated with the political affairs of the Middle East, and as the children of Arab immigrants were born and raised in America, that preoccupation shifted. Although contemporary Arab Americans remained deeply interested in the social and political issues that concerned the Arab world, they also included the American perspective on those issues. As the next chapter demonstrates, the values and principles that were first established by contemporary immigrant scholars were fundamental in the social and political aesthetics that would come to define the artistic works of the Arab American playwrights, performers, and filmmakers who followed.

1
"Unresolved sorrow and uncomprehending anger": Contemporary Arab American Identity Formation

By 1966, Professor Edward W. Said was content teaching classes in English literature and comparative literature at Columbia University. A Palestinian born in Jerusalem and displaced in exile to Cairo with his parents after 1948, Said was a model student in the British colonial school system. In many ways he, along with his affluent school colleagues, was being primed to become the Egyptian ruling class: educated Arabs who would eventually take control of Egypt after Britain's occupation. His classmates included such notables as King Hussein of Jordan and a young Michel Shalhoub, who would later go to Hollywood to transform into a star named Omar Sharif. Said and his parents immigrated to the United States in 1951. They made sure young Edward would attend the prestigious Mount Hermon School in eastern Massachusetts. After achieving a bachelor's degree at Princeton and a master's and Ph.D. at Harvard University, garnering a tenured faculty position at Columbia University in 1963 must have seemed the culmination of Said's ambition. The devastating 1967 Arab-Israeli War, which led to the Israeli occupation of the Sinai Peninsula, the Golan Heights, the West Bank, the Gaza Strip, and East Jerusalem, dealt a crushing blow to exiled Palestinians who believed that one day they might be able to return to their homeland. To make matters worse, American journalists and filmmakers, who were once content dramatizing Arabs as exotic sheiks and sexualized belly dancers, now perverted those stereotypes, transforming them into the violent Arab terrorist and the burqua-clad female suicide bomber. Suddenly, Said's entire life had been upended. His focus shifted from topics like postmodernism, deconstruction, and poststructuralism, to how the Arab image was being, and had been for centuries, manipulated and distorted for Western consumption. In his memoir *Out of Place*, he wrote:

> Until 1967 I succeeded in mentally dividing U.S. support for Israel from the fact of my being an American pursuing a career there and having Jewish friends and colleagues. The remoteness of the Palestine I grew up in, my family's silence over its role, and then its long disappearance from our lives, my mother's open discomfort with the subject and later aggressive dislike of both Palestine and politics, my lack of contact with Palestinians during the 11 years of my American education: all this allowed me to live my life at a great distance from the Palestine of remote memory, unresolved sorrow, and uncomprehending anger.[1]

Portrait of Edward Said, Palestinian American literary theorist, cultural critic and political activist (photograph by Francis Tsang/Cover/Getty Images).

Other Arab American intellectuals like Said also had a radical shift in consciousness after 1967. It was their political awakening that defined Arab American identity politics, community activism, and resistance to traditional media representation for generations that followed.

¤ ¤ ¤

The plays, films, and performances discussed in this book are representative of three major periods that correspond to the three major waves of Arab immigration to the United States: the first wave included the early Arab community (1880–1945); the second wave comprised the post–World War II immigration (1945–1965); and the third wave spans the period of 1967 through the present time. For my study I have combined the first and second waves into what I call the "modern" Arab American period, and the third wave I call the "contemporary" Arab American period. By dividing these periods in this way, I hope to elucidate the shift that occurred both in the political orientation of Arab Americans, but also in their artistic motivations.

The works of the early Arab community, best exemplified by the three seminal first-generation writers Kahlil Gibran, Mikhail Naimy, and Ameen Rihani, were interested in several major tropes: the poet-prophet model, a

Phoenicianist perspective on Arab history, and their contemporary views of life in their homeland and in their newly adopted country, America. By contrast, during the post–1945 second-wave immigration, plays were primarily amateur productions written in Arabic for different social and church groups in order to maintain cultural unity and group identity. The contemporary plays, films, and performances from 1967 onward are much more political in nature. These works are interested in issues such as the Arab-Israeli conflict, societal and governmental persecution of Arabs and Arab Americans, and the perspectives of those embroiled in the numerous conflicts between the United States and Arab nations. It was only after the 1960s civil rights movements that included the work of Arab American scholars that the term "Arab American" was finally coined, utilized, and embraced.

Setting the Stage for Arab American Identity

Most Arab American scholars concur that there were three major "waves" of Arab immigration to North America: the early immigrants (1880–1945); the post–World War II immigrants (1945–1965); and the contemporary wave of immigrants (1967 to the present day).[2] These three waves of immigration roughly correspond to Omi and Winant's "ethnicity paradigm" that is also broken into three periods roughly corresponding to the waves of Arab immigration: the ethnicity based paradigm (pre–1930s); the assimilationism/cultural pluralism phase (1930s–1965); and the group rights phase (post–1965). By comparing these three phases from Arab American studies and the discipline of sociology, it is clear that these movements dictated the sense of citizenship and belonging Arabs felt throughout the twentieth and into the twenty-first century, but also how these movements shaped the theatrical and literary landscape of Arab America.

The first wave of Arab immigration (1878–1924) was composed mainly of Christian Syrians (named so because they emigrated from what was then Greater Syria). Some of these immigrants were fleeing the persecution they endured under Ottoman rule where they were the religious minority, while others fled the crippling economic conditions that befell the country due to the decline of the silk trade. These immigrants were primarily isolationists who came to the United States to earn enough money by working as peddlars, coal miners, and factory workers for an eventual return to their homelands. Omi and Winant describe the pre–1930s ethnic paradigm as containing both a biologistic and "insurgent approach." It was during this time that whites were considered the superior race, and race was equated with distinct hereditary and biological characteristics. This later gave way to the ideas of cultural pluralism and assimilationism that suggested race was a social category. Also, ethnicity was based on culture and descent. Although this mode of thinking was preferable to the biologistic one, it still gave preference to the notion of assimilation as the best model for immigrants in America.[3] Following World War I, these immigrants were barred from returning home due to the fighting overseas and took on an assimilationist mode of acculturation.[4]

The ethnicity based paradigm directly affected the early Arab immigrants since they existed outside the normative American status because they were neither considered "white," nor were they considered "native." Instead, the Immigration and Naturalization Act of 1906, created by the Bureau of Immigration and Naturalization in the Department of Commerce and Labor, limited naturalization of "free white persons" and aliens of African nativity or descent. Syrians were considered threatening because, "they possessed cultures and habits that were fundamentally at odds with southern traditions and values and that immigrants would not abide by the 'white man's code.'"[5] Arabs found themselves in the position of litigating for their "white" status. This litigation led to further distinctions between Christians and Muslims, lighter skinned Arabs and darker skinned Arabs, and the geographic origins of the immigrants. Also, when Arabs first arrived in the United States, they were not classified by nationality, but were deemed as coming from what was then called "Turkey in Asia" due to Ottoman rule of the nations from which they hailed. In order to litigate for their whiteness, Syrians attempted to claim that they were of the Caucasian race, that they were Semitic or members of Semitic nations, and that the historical connections with Jewish and Christian peoples could not possibly exclude them from this category.[6] In addition, intelligence, attitude, and even sexuality were considered racial characteristics.[7] Socially, Arabs were often attacked with the same racial slurs leveled at other minority groups. Words like "nigger" or "dago" were used by some Americans to describe these early immigrants. Other immigrants were subject to physical abuse, personal humiliation, summary arrests and deportations, and anti-alien antipathy.[8]

The so-called second wave of Arab immigrants (1947–1966) was motivated by the exodus of Arabs following the creation of the State of Israel and a migration of the intelligentsia from Arab regions such as Egypt, Syria, Iraq, Jordan, and North Africa. During this phase of immigration, two major themes were prevalent—assimilationism and cultural pluralism. Again, the period was defined by the presence of a majority Anglo culture. Despite absorbing immigrants and granting them some rights, considerable nativist hostility still existed toward these groups. Assimilation is defined as the point when "the group considers cultural or ethnic maintenance to be less important than acceptance by the host society. The group is prepared to abandon its cultural identity as a price to be paid for belonging to the host society."[9] When the United States effectively stopped emigration from Arab regions, those Arabs living in the United States who felt isolation and separation created several clubs and federations. In addition, many of these immigrants participated in American political parties, in voting, and public service.[10] Because their children were growing up in the United States, many of these first-generation immigrants began speaking English much more frequently than speaking their native Arabic and began assimilating into the culture. This Arab group's political activism included issues related to Palestine, the deteriorating conditions in the newly formed state of Lebanon, and participation in the U.S. armed forces.

The changes to U.S. immigration laws in the 1950s and 1960s, and the 1967 Arab-Israeli War, shaped what is often called the third wave of Arab immigration to the United States. The Immigration and Naturalization Act of 1952 ended Asian exclusion and race-based citizenship, and the change in quotas increased the number of immigrants allowed to emigrate from each country, setting aside 50 percent of the quota for immigrants with skills that were desirable to the United States. The law, which increased the number of immigrants from professional classes, was more of a "retooling of the national-origins system that favored white immigrants."[11] The law also excluded those deemed "immoral" or "subversive" in order to target or exclude subjects considered communists. The subsequent Immigration Act of 1965 dismantled the previous system, allowing "six percent of the annual quota ... set aside for refugees, namely persons deemed to be fleeing persecution from communism, those rendered homeless by wars in the Middle East, and victims of natural disasters."[12] The 1965 Immigration Act allowed more diversity—persons engaged in commerce, skilled workers, professional classes, and college students. These immigration changes impacted the religious and the intellectual demographics of Arab immigrants to the United States.

Unlike the previous waves of Arab immigrants, the third wave (1967–2005) accelerated due to the 1967 Arab-Israeli Six-Day War, and continued on because of wars in Lebanon, Kuwait, and Iraq, and political turmoil in Arab countries. The third-wave immigrants were mainly educated professionals and technical workers, and many were Palestinian. Half of these immigrants were Ph.D. graduates in science and engineering.[13] These immigrants were also in a better financial position than their predecessors, and they were more highly educated. Many immigrated specifically because they were seeking a better education in the United States. According to Gualtieri, these students formed the foundation of an activist and self-consciously Arab population in the United States. Therefore, the new immigration laws brought Arabs who were more educated and inspired by notions of Arab nationalism, issues relating to Palestine, and civil rights for those of Arab heritage. More importantly, many of these new immigrants were Muslims who often felt alienated from the Judeo-Christian values that dominated American life. They sometimes opposed U.S. foreign policy, leading to a cultural shift away from the Anglo-American core and into a de-assimilationist mode of existence. This increase in Muslim migration would transform the Arab American community and the religious composition of the United States for decades to come.

Contemporary Arab American Cultural Production

Arab American playwrights, filmmakers, and performers utilize their cultural production to rearticulate, recast, and restage their experiences in defiance of plays, films, and performances that traditionally staged and cast them negatively.[14] Omi and Winant's book *Racial Formation in the United States from the 1960s to the 1990s* states that social movements offer their adherents "a different view of themselves and their world; different, that is, from the worldview and self-concepts offered by the established order." Groups do this through what is called "rearticulation" that produces a new subjectivity by utilizing information and knowledge already present in the subject while taking elements and themes of the subject's culture and tradition and infusing them with new meaning.[15] Similarly, Bhabha writes of the need to think beyond the narratives of originary and initial subjectivities, with a consequent focus on the moments that are produced when cultural differences are articulated.[16] Bhabha views what he calls "in-between spaces" as the fertile terrain for establishing "strategies of selfhood" that can initiate new identities and sites for collaboration, contestation, or definition. He also writes that the "terms of cultural engagement, whether antagonistic or affiliative, are produced performatively." Therefore, the minority social articulation of difference is an ongoing negotiation that authorizes cultural hybridities in moments of historical transformation. "Restaging the past" introduces incommensurable cultural temporalities into the invention of traditions, thereby estranging the immediate access to an original identity or received tradition.[17]

I argue that the space between "Arab" and "American" is one such "in-between space." In that space scholars and artists have created their own contestatory sites from which they engage culturally and produce work performatively. I utilize the term "recasting" to mean that those who are in the periphery of the dominant culture, and whose narrative has been inscribed and reinscribed by that culture, have the agency to rewrite those narratives by recasting themselves in the roles that were previously written for others. In essence, they have recast themselves in the "Arab" roles that were often played by non–Arabs, and they have restaged scenarios that have been written for them by others, often in negative and stereotypical fashions. Their agency is subversive since it seeks to remove the power others hold over the production of narratives, reinscribing new narratives in their place. Therefore, Arab American writers and performers are in a constant process of rearticulating, recasting, and restaging the Arab American experience through their dramas, comedy performances, and films. This ethno-political activism becomes a productive space where subjects who identify as Arab American take their various encounters with filial conflicts, discrimination, profiling, and violence perpetrated against family or religious/cultural group and transform them into works of art. The interstitial space between Arab and American then becomes a positive, rather than a negative, space for identity formation and expression through various artistic mediums.

In the modern period, these Arab writers were working to establish themselves at a time when Arabic was their primary language and their works were often viewed through an Orientalist lens. By portraying themselves as bridges between the East and the West, casting themselves as poet-prophets, and clearly distinguishing themselves as descendants from the Phoenician-Maronite Christian tradition, these writers were able to establish themselves within the American literary scene. They understood that they had differing audiences—those in the Arab-speaking communities both in the United States and abroad, and those who read their works only in English. Sometimes, these writers actually highlighted their "Oriental" nature. In contrast, as the post–1967 generations came of age, and as more playwrights and filmmakers became professional artists, the desire to rearticulate their space within the professional world of theatre and film caused them to eschew stereotypical performances of Arabs and Arab Americans and to rearticulate their self-image as both Arab and American. Therefore, they are reclaiming agency through these restagings and recastings in an attempt to change the theatre and film industries in which they work.

I contend that contemporary Arab American theatre, film, and performance share many of the same principles and ideals that the early Arab American scholars and activists espoused beginning in the late 1960s. It was the activism of these scholars that established the foundational principles that both defined what it meant to be Arab American and how that identity would later be expressed in performance. It is fundamental, therefore, to examine these early activist groups, their individual missions, and their trajectories in order to understand how these foundational thinkers and ideologies later influenced contemporary Arab American playwrights, filmmakers, and performers.

Arab American Identity as a Culture of Resistance

The term Arab American is one that is generally used to describe Arabs in America and Americans of Arab descent. Sometimes the term is ascribed to Canadians of Arab descent, however the terms Arab Canadian, Canadian Arab, or Canado-Arabe are utilized in Canada. According to Michael Suleiman, "the term 'Arab Americans' refers to the immigrants to North America from the Arabic-speaking countries of the Middle East and their descendants."[18] These terms were created by Arabs in North America during the civil rights movement in the 1960s in order to create a pan–Arab solidarity for Americans of Arab descent "that cut across religious and country-of-origin identities and essentially introduced the concept of 'Arab American' into the consciousness both of Americans at large and the various sub-group identities (Lebanese, Syrian, Palestinian, Egyptian, etc.)."[19] For some, this term is one of empowerment, and for others it bears negative connotations. According to Naseer H. Aruri, during the late 1960s, most Arabs born abroad did not identify themselves as Arab Americans because to do so would be a concession to those who advocated assimilation. Aruri goes so far as to say that it was "almost sacrilegious" to include the American label, even as a hyphenated identity, because it produced feelings of disloyalty to Arabism, Arab causes, and to the issue of Palestine in particular.[20] For those who immigrated after 1965, identifying Arab American was a choice that pitted Arab Americans in a battle between ethnic isolationists and ethnic integrationists. Ethnic isolationism is defined as a group's desire to "maintain its ethnic identity and cultural traditions but voluntarily or involuntarily does not participate in the life of the host society. When isolationism occurs by choice, the result is separation; when it is imposed by the host society, the acculturating group experiences segregation."[21] Ethnic isolationists believe that immigrants and Arab Americans are "driven in part by a desire to preserve and transmit their cultural identity to the next generation, usually through the maintenance of ethnic institutions and endogamous marriage patterns. The isolationists' marginal status can only augment their cultural identity and ethnic endogamy." Ethnic integrationists, on the other hand, are mainly assimilated second- and third-generation Americans of Arab Descent who desire to win acceptance of their cultural background by mainstream American cultural and political institutions, and to counter what some believe is "the pro–Israeli bias in U.S. foreign policy."[22]

Economist Ibrahim Hayani describes this tension in another way—as one between assimilation and integration. Both of these processes are forms of acculturation, which Hayani describes as the changes that occur when groups of individuals of different cultures come into continuous first-hand contact, with subsequent changes in original cultural patterns in either or both groups.[23] After the events of September 11, 2001, the governmental backlash against Arabs and Muslims in particular led to a neo–Muslim movement whereby Muslims feel that it is both a duty and obligation to reconnect with their Muslim heritage. Many young Muslims are reclaiming this identity by dressing more traditionally, studying the Koran, learning the languages of their ethnic ancestry, and speaking out against measures intended to assimilate them, such as the banning of Islamic dress and practice.

The desire to identify as a contemporary Arab American is an identification that can be made consciously by most, as Arab Americans have "passed" as whites in the United States since their arrival in the late nineteenth century.[24] Those Arab Americans who are either darker skinned, or whose traditions mark them as an Arab "Other," find they have the most difficult task if they wish to identify as "white." The political decision to identify as Arab American includes many factors such as the desire to maintain ties with one's Arab heritage while simultaneously retaining one's identification with life in the United States, a desire to fight for a more equitable and less prejudicial portrayal of Arabs and Arab Americans in the media, and a political desire to reject and change the more problematic aspects of U.S. foreign policies. Perhaps no other feature of Arab American identity is more prevalent than this desire to speak out and criticize U.S. foreign policies, especially in regard to Arab countries.

Not all agree that Arab American identity runs counter to mainstream American thought or that it is always a positive identificatory marker. According to Abraham and Shryock, the identity of Arab American "gives meaning to individual lives even as it circumscribes them with yet another potentially reductive label."[25] They argue that Arab American identity is one that is learned and that much of this learning takes place in colleges and universities at the hands of academics and activists. They also argue that this is a solidly middle class identification that is identified with mainstream institutions, political action groups, human services agencies, and for the most assimilated and least Arabic-speaking of the population. "Being Arab American," they argue, "is a way of surviving in these special contexts; in short, it is a way of entering the American mainstream."[26] I would argue that Abraham and Shryock's analysis negates the political and social activism that actually alienates Arab Americans from the American mainstream. Indeed, by being politically outspoken against many American policies (both international and domestic), Arab Americans are often targets of governmental and social actions that seek to silence their oppositional voices. Abraham and Shryock further argue that "Arab American identity is an abstraction, a convenience, a substitute for history, or a political sensibility" that most Arabs do not understand.[27] If this identity is an abstraction, it is because it has been adopted by those who embrace it as a political identification that stands apart from those Arabs living in America who prefer to assimilate in order to avoid prejudice. If Arab American identity is learned in colleges and universities, it is because analysis of Arab American identification has a history that has been developed and chronicled mainly by academics in an attempt to further understand the group.

Race Theory and Arab American Identity

In order to understand the formation of Arab American identity, it is necessary to explore both sociology and race theory. In their concept of racial formation, sociologists and race theorists Omi and Winant locate race at the center of American political history. Their definition of racial formation emphasizes the social nature of race, the absence of essential racial characteristics, the historical flexibility of racial meanings and categories, the conflictual nature of race, and the "irreducible political aspect of racial dynamics."[28] Previous models focused on ethnicity theory that views race as a variety of ethnicity that is applied to racially defined groups with certain standards and values whose exemplars were European immigrants. Class and nation based theory rejected this European immigrant analogy and suggested that racial minorities could be incorporated into American life in the same ways as white ethnic groups. The problem with such models is that they neglect the institutional and ideological nature of race in America and the systemic presence of racial dynamics in the social spheres of education, art, social policy, law, religion, and science.[29] The model that best describes the Arab American group may be one that Omi and Winant title "cultural nationalism," which focuses on cultural elements that give rise to collective identity, community, and a sense of "peoplehood."[30] In addition, this identity formation underscores the centrality of cultural domination, racial oppression, and cultural resistance with the desire to unify and promote collective identity.[31] Cultural nationalists prefer building countercultural institutions and what they call elite-led negotiations with the hegemonic power structure. The major accomplishments of cultural nationalists groups such as black nationalists or the Chicano movement were consciousness-raising and the creation of "cultures of resistance" that promoted collective identity among the oppressed.[32] Charara also points to the fact that more people tend to identify less with what he calls "limited social constructions of nationalism" and more with postmodern/postcolonial identities.[33]

Philosopher and political theorist Falguni A. Sheth argues that race is a technology and an existential mode of sovereign power that simultaneously threatens and coheres. This violent power, both regulatory and disciplinary, is hidden behind moral discourses of inferiority, criminality, and evil, and "encourages the deployment of racial divisions by different populations in attempts to become less vulnerable to the law."[34] Sheth divides racial discourse into biological race (BR) and political othering (PO). Biological race utilizes or challenges biology, genetics, phenotype, and genealogy for its argumentative grounding. Political othering refers to political structures such as Orientalism, colonialism, and imperialist methods by which populations have been construed as "foreign" or "Other" on the basis of culture, political structure, status, and territory.[35] Sheth suggests Arabs and Muslims are racialized as "evil" and "less rational" because they are considered a threat to "reasonable" and "law abiding" members of the American polity.[36] Sheth refers to groups that have been deemed in this way as "the unruly" because they are not heterogeneous, they are unable to live "neatly" within the community, and they hold vacillating allegiances with multiple cultures, conventions, nations, and territories. This racialization of Islam has led to legitimizing the withholding of human rights and constitutional law.[37] In addition, Sheth argues that it is the "strangeness" or "foreignness" of Arabs and Muslims that makes them outcast, which includes the wearing of the *hijab* for women, the growing of long beards for men, reading and reciting the Koran, open religious worship, and political speech that expresses dissent through Islamic tenets. Therefore, the public perceptions of Arabs and Muslims are ones of threat and a possible insurgence to the American order that therefore should be suppressed.

Arab American identity formation relies on this culture of resistance, especially in terms of resistance to U.S. foreign and domestic policy that has historically targeted this group since the late 1960s. In his essay "Edward Said's Out of Place: Criticism, Polemic, and Arab American Identity," Hosam Aboul-Ela writes that a dissident relationship to U.S. foreign policy in the Middle East is foundational to the Arab American experience. This dissent from American foreign policy has played the same role in cultural formation as codified legal discrimination has played for African Americans, Mexican Americans, Chinese Americans, and Native Americans. According to Aboul-Ela, "part of being Arab American ... is to think in a more sustained and in a different way about American foreign policy in the Middle East. For better or worse, this is a major source of Arab American identity for many."[38] Arab American feminist scholar Evelyn Shakir wrote in her book *Bint Arab: Arab and Arab American Women in the United States*,

> Another major conflict is grounded in ambivalence toward the United States, a country that may offer immigrant women new opportunities for self-direction and achievement, yet often seems dangerously hostile to the Arab world. For daughters and granddaughters, the conflict is similar, a tug of war between attachment to the land of their birth (the United States) and anger or frustration at American policies in the Middle East. Though men also face these conflicts, they take on special meaning for women; female and Arab, they may feel doubly victimized.[39]

As these examples illustrate, there is a great dissatisfaction among those who identify as Arab Americans with the political tenets that define U.S. foreign policy including the tacit approval of Israeli settlement expansion in Palestinian territories, U.S. financial support for dictatorial Arab regimes that oppress their own populations, the extrajudicial killing of American citizens abroad, and the deliberate targeting and profiling of Arabs living in America.

No single event crystallized this identity formation more clearly than the 1967 Arab-Israeli War. The Arab defeat and the ensuing Israeli occupation of Palestinian territories were the catalysts that precipitated Arab American identity formation, activism, and much of the art that followed. According to Michael W. Suleiman, after the 1967 War and its ensuing backlash, some Americans of Arab Descent resented the partisanship America showed toward Israel, and opposed the hostility that was directed toward Arabs in America. The consequence of this was a desire to organize to fight against negative stereotyping of Arabs and to work to create a more balanced American policy toward the Middle East. Because of this, many de-assimilated, openly identified as Arab, and joined political groups that advocated for Arab American causes.[40] Anti-Arab bias in the entertainment industry and the media and the opposition to U.S. governmental policies in the Middle East were galvanizing issues for Arab Americans. It was the confluence of U.S. foreign policy in the Middle East, and the negative stereotyping of Arabs in film and television, that prompted Arab Americans to advocate for change.

The Aftermath of 1967

It is difficult to express the magnitude of the impact of the 1967 Six-Day War on Arab consciousness worldwide. The defeat of the armies of Syria, Egypt, and Jordan was tremendous, but the ensuing occupation of the West Bank, Gaza Strip, the Golan Heights, and East Jerusalem was a devastating blow with repercussions that resonate to this day. Many Arab and Arab American writers chronicled their feelings about the war. Journalist Samir Kassir wrote of "the Arab malaise" and how it manifests itself in perceptions and feelings with the notion that "Arabs have no future, no way of improving their condition."[41] This malaise is bound up with "the gaze of the Western Other— a gaze that prevents everything, even escape.... It ridicules your powerlessness, foredooms all your hopes, and stops you in your tracks time and again at one or other of the world's border crossings."[42] According to Kassir, this condition is so debilitating that "Arab history has been entirely hollowed out. What remains is a state of permanent powerlessness that renders any chance of a revival unthinkable."[43] In his novel about the 1967 War titled *Days of Dust*, novelist Halim Barakat echoes Kassir's sentiment:

> On the seventh day the Arab did not rest. And he did not know how long this seventh day would last. He sensed that there were to be many days of dust and cries of children from beneath tents in the desert. His seventh day would be months, perhaps years.... All the Arab had created in the first six days was dust, and now the tempests were revealing the true nature of his creations. There was nothing but the future left for him now, but he still reached back for the past.[44]

Another Arab American activist, Jamil Jreisat, wrote, "The Israeli invasion of 1967, and the occupation of Arab lands in Palestine, Syria, and Egypt, was one of the most far-reaching events in the past century of Arab history. The invasion shocked the Arab people, sidelined their governments' public policies, and left an indelible impact on Arab psyche and culture."[45] The late Palestinian-American scholar, Ibrahim Abu-Lughod expressed his feelings about the aftermath of 1967 in this way:

> '67 was a watershed, I think, for all of us in America. What I saw in '67 was totally unexpected; shocking for two reasons: one is obviously the complete dashing of the Arab states and the hope that we had pinned that there would be a battle and

we would be liberated and we would be able to go home, and the way the Arab states were shattered—the armies I mean—was unbelievable. I never realized how racist American society was at that moment in terms of the Arabs. How pleased of the media [*sic*] showing the pictures of the Egyptian soldiers in the desert and so forth, and how happy they were with this victory of the Israeli army. I realized there were no voices in America for our point of view.[46]

Many Arab Americans were immigrants from the defeated countries, and many still had family and homes there. In her book *A Country Called Amreeka*, Alia Malek writes, "Arabs in America and Americans of Arab descent had [also] been bewildered by the incredible defeat; the occupation by Israel of East Jerusalem, the West Bank, the Gaza Strip, and the Golan Heights directly affected them, their families, their property rights, and their homelands."[47] Palestinian Americans were the ones most directly impacted by this war, since the occupation of Palestinian territories was the greatest and most pressing factor for their community. However, many Arab Americans still believe that the occupation is both illegal and unjust.

The Media War

The media war waged against Arabs in the late 1960s was the most difficult issue Arab Americans faced. Referring to the 1967 War, Edward Said wrote, "this was a war fought as much in the media as on the battlefields; the struggle was felt to be *immediately historical* because it was fought simultaneously in the scenes created by actuality and those created by television, radio, newspapers."[48] Just as the Vietnam War was lost in the American consciousness by the terrible images witnessed each evening on television, the 1967 War was won in the minds of the American public through the media's coverage of the event. According to Robert Ruby, senior editor of the *Pew Research Forum on Religion & Public Life*, a Gallup poll conducted during the three days before the outbreak of the 1967 War and extending through the first three days of fighting, found that 45 percent of Americans sympathized more with Israel than with the Arab states, 4 percent sympathized more with Arab states, and 26 percent with neither.[49] According to Baha Abu-Laban, "in the wake of the 1967 War, there was an enormous increase of attention given towards Arabs in American mass media, and much of it was stereotyped, negative and racist."[50] AAUG member Rashid Bashshur believed the U.S. media was gloating about the Israeli defeat of Arab armies and that the information provided to the American public was inaccurate and one-sided.[51] Similarly, Elaine C.

Hagopian believed that the media was promoting anti–Arab racism in their reporting of the events,[52] and Michael W. Suleiman stated, "American coverage of the 1967 war was clearly among the worst, if not *the* worst, and most biased reporting of any period since World War II. Indeed, the American media practically celebrated the war as if the United States was involved in the fighting and won a decisive victory against the Arabs. Hardly any attempt was made at objective reporting."[53] This perceived imbalance in American media reports regarding the war led many Americans of Arab Descent to shift their views and become Arab American activists. In the months following the 1967 War, left-leaning Arab Americans would join forces in the name of this cause, putting aside their religious, tribal, and national differences in favor of a pan–Arab American identity. The first group to organize, the Association of Arab American University Graduates (AAUG), represents the first major step in Arab American identity formation, and the work they accomplished would inspire Arab American activism for generations to come. Over time, the fractious issues that followed such as the Iranian Revolution in 1979, the first and second Gulf Wars, the Lebanese Civil War, and the Palestinian intifadas would all strain and split the coalition built by the AAUG, leading to its eventual demise.

AAUG and the Beginnings of the Arab American Intellectual Movement

During the fall 1967, the World Congress of Orientalists[54] met in Ann Arbor, Michigan. Several prominent Arab American intellectuals, who were in established positions at several major academic institutions, discussed the issues facing the Arab community in the United States. These intellectuals included Bashshur, Adnan Aswad, Fawzi Najjar, and Abdeen Jabara. These scholars were admittedly frustrated over the aftermath of the 1967 War and were asking themselves how they could instigate change. One of the main issues discussed was how to counter biased and prejudicial information about Arabs and Americans of Arab Descent that they believed were saturating U.S. news, media, academia, and popular entertainment.

Bashshur proposed that academics and professionals should be the "source of reason and accurate information" in order to build a bridge between their countries of origin and their country of adoption. The group would be open to Arab American university graduates and its responsibility would be "to present factual, accurate and reliable information about our history, geography, culture as well as our objective assessment of the Arab-Israeli conflict, its causes and its resolution."[55] Other objectives included disseminating information about Arab culture and contributions to areas such as science and technology, educating Americans about Arab history, and to advocate for, most specifically, the Palestinian perspective following the 1967 War. Their ultimate goal was to "contribute to a better understanding between the Arab and American people that would ultimately lead to a more balanced U.S. policy toward our region."[56] These intellectuals clearly understood that Arab nations and regimes had been some of the worst advocates for their own causes, hampered by corrupt leadership and aggregious violations of human rights. According to Bashshur, the AAUG was established more as a social movement than as a political platform. Their goals included creating educational materials that could be incorporated into school curricula, publishing a professional journal that would include scholarly work and scientific study, and producing reports and white papers with issues of relevance to the American public and scholars. The members would be volunteers, and members of the group agreed not to affiliate with any political group in either the U.S. or in their countries of origin.

One of the first efforts undertaken by the AAUG was a public relations effort that took the form of a full-page advertisement in *New York Times* titled "Needed, a Nixon Declaration for Five Million Jewish, Christian, and Moslem Palestinians"[57] that appeared on November 2, 1969. The letter, addressed to "peacemaker" Nixon who could bring peace to "the tormented land of Palestine," included a statement that the Balfour Declaration of 1917 favored the "dismemberment of Palestine, its mutilation from a land sacred to and inhabited by Moslem, Christian and Jew, to a land which is the exclusive domain of a few." The group called upon Nixon to issue a "Nixon Declaration" that would "commit the Government of the United States to the cause of a lasting peace in Palestine." The advertisement, funded by donations, received a great deal of praise from supporters and equal scorn from detractors. Critics wrote angry letters that accused Arab states of amassing arms from the Soviets, asserted they were communist nations, and accused the members of the AAUG of being "not students but paid propagandists."[58] Although many believed that the members of the AAUG were paid advocates of dictatorial Arab regimes, the members stated they had no ties to Arab governments.[59]

The ensuing years led to annual conventions that began in 1968, seminars, public speakers, networking with like-minded Arab American organizations, and the 1979 founding of the journal *Arab Studies Quarterly* (*ASQ*). The journal was started by Abu-Lughod, Edward W. Said, and Fouad Moughrabi. Said and Moughrabi co-edited the journal for eight years.[60] The journal was created with an all volunteer staff, and their work with AAUG would later lead to important contributions to Arab American studies, including Edward Said's 1970 essay "The Arab Portrayed" and his 1975 essay "Orientalism and the October War: The Shattered Myths," both of which led to his seminal text *Orientalism*.[61] The *ASQ* featured scholarship about the Arab world and Arab American issues, and critiques of U.S. foreign policy regarding Middle Eastern matters. According to Abbas Alnasrawi, "its intent was to help its members break from isolation, to create and maintain bridges to the Arab world while at the same time providing forums within the United States to express an Arab American position on the issues of the day."[62] According to Hani A. Faris, "within a relatively short period, ASQ established itself as a leading periodical in the field of Middle East studies. By 1986, ASQ was ranked among the top three U.S.–based academic journals on the Middle East, and one of the top twenty most read academic journals in the U.S. ... in addition, the Journal attracted renowned intellectuals from many nations and disciplines."[63] Years later, in a reflection on the AAUG and the *ASQ*, Suleiman wrote that the organization's work to combat negative stereotyping through scholarly studies and activism was ultimately fruitless. After his experiences he wrote, "a substantial increase in the number of scholarly studies detailing American media bias concerning Arabs, especially in relation to Arab-Israeli issues, had hardly any impact on the media and their representation of Arabs and Arab Americans. It was exasperating and extremely disappointing."[64] Suleiman was not the only one to lament the demise of the AAUG and its inability to change the course of American political thought.

This desire to target and change the unfair and stereotypical portrayals in popular media was one of the main issues that concerned the AAUG and remains a central issue to Arab Americans to this day. However, despite the decades of work that has been dedicated to this effort, many of the same issues remain. Not all members of the AAUG believed media representations should be the sole focus. Khalil Nakleh wrote,

> The task and challenge for our Arab-American institutions are much more radical than the mere rebuttal of negative images and stereotypes; it is much more radical than shallow international campaigns whose goal is to equate and balance American imperial interests with those of the Arabs. Official American logic aggresses upon our legitimacy and historical continuity as a people and as a nation.[65]

For members like Nakleh, change meant redefining accepted notions such as "turning a 'terrorist' into a freedom-fighter, a 'fanatic' into a defender of indigenous culture against foreign penetration, a 'rejectionist' into the energy of steadfastness and struggle."[66] Nakleh's view represents the depth of frustration many AAUG members felt about their alienation and rejection by the American mainstream. It is apparent that, when the members of the AAUG believed they were struggling for justice, the nation to which they belonged regarded them as rejectionists and propagandists. This fundamental disconnect between striving for justice and being perceived negatively is central to the Arab American condition.

Over the decades, AAUG membership dwindled, funds were scarce, volunteers were harder to recruit, and fewer youth became involved. Other factors that contributed to the organization's demise included ongoing crises in the Middle East that led to polarization among AAUG members, lack of success in its efforts to lobby Washington on behalf of changing U.S. foreign policy in the Middle East, and the difficulty its members found in both criticizing Arab regimes while attempting to lobby the U.S. government for more favorable policies toward the region.[67] Other foreign issues also fragmented the AAUG, including Egyptian President Anwar Sadat's peace initiatives with the United States and Israel, American policies regarding Lebanon and Iraq in the 1980s and 1990, and various intra–Arab conflicts. Looking back, the enduring legacy of this group was the *Arab Studies Quarterly* journal, the breadth of scholarship created, and the inspiration it provided other Arab American activist groups that followed.

Forty Years of Institutionalized Surveillance

Contrary to conventional thought, U.S. surveillance and monitoring of Arab Americans did not begin after September 11, 2001. As far back as 1968, several days after Richard Nixon's election, New York police arrested three Yemeni men for plotting to kill the president-elect. The case was later thrown out of court.[68] By 1972, the Nixon Administration instituted Operation Boulder that authorized the FBI to monitor the activities of Arab students and politically active Arab Americans following the massacre of 11 Israeli athletes during the Munich Olympics. According to *New York Times* article "U.S. Checks Arabs to Block Terror," the Nixon Administration began a major effort to "identify Arabs residing in this country who are suspected of planning terrorism and to screen travelers from Arab nations more carefully."[69] According to Nadine Naber, "Nixon's Operation Boulder marked the beginning in a series of FBI policies that entailed the harassment of individuals of Arab descent in general and Arab students in particular, who were targeted by the state and denied their constitutional rights, specifically those related to free speech."[70]

Individuals of Arabic speaking descent were interrogated, photographed, and fingerprinted by FBI and immigration officials. Their friends, employers, neighbors, and family members were also interviewed by FBI agents. The suspects were profiled, surveilled, and their visa applications were subject to a mandatory waiting period while they were checked through U.S., European, and Israeli sources.[71] Naber writes, "'Operation Boulder' was initiated as a result of pressure from Zionist groups both within the U.S. and from Israel to silence Arab Americans from voicing opposition to U.S. and Israeli policies in the Middle East."[72] Whether or not Naber's analysis is correct, Operation Boulder set the standard for nearly every other U.S. administration in their handling of Arabs living in the United States.

The 1978 Operation ABSCAM (the code name for the FBI investigation that combined the name Abdul Enterprises Ltd. and the word "scam") was another FBI operation created to catch corrupt members of Congress and members of organized crime with the impression that Arabs were a threat to the American political system.[73] FBI agents posed as Arab oil sheiks and were taped manipulating several members of Congress on video. In the process, six congressmen and one senator were convicted of bribery in 1981. This performance of Arabness by FBI agents underlies the menacing prejudice against Arabs, especially during the 1973 OAPEC (Organization of Arab Petroleum Exporting Countries) oil embargo that also turned American sentiment against Arabs in the United States. Alia Malek writes:

> No Arab or Arab American had ever been accused of bribing an American politician. For Arab Americans, ABSCAM's unquestioned use of the "Arab sheikh" indicated that the stereotype of the slimy, wealthy, and corrupt foreigner lived not only in the media and pop culture, but at the highest levels of U.S. power as well. They saw these omni-present portrayals as creating the perception in the United States that anything Arab was almost inherently bad or anti–American; therefore Arabs, Arab Americans, their speech, or their perspectives were easily dismissible and politically risky.[74]

The first Arab American to be elected to the U.S. Senate, James Abourezk, voluntarily quit the Senate in 1978 during the ABSCAM affair and went on to found the Arab American Anti-Discrimination Committee (ADC).

In 1987, seven Palestinians and a Kenyan were arrested, with the intent to deport them under the provisions of the McCarran-Walter Act of 1952. The McCarran-Walter Act was originally meant to target suspected communists. The group, later named the LA 8, was charged with allegedly raising money for the PFLP or Popular Front for the Liberation of Palestine, labeled a terrorist organization by the United States. The case was a 26-year attempt to deport two Palestinian Americans, Khader Hamide and Michel Shehadeh, and the six others. Ultimately, the defendants were not deported because a federal appeals court declared the anti-communist law unconstitutional. In 2007, an immigration judge called the case "an embarrassment to the rule of law" and ruled the case violated the defendants' constitutional rights.[75]

Following the Oklahoma City Bombing, the Clinton Administration passed both the Anti-Terrorism and Effective Death Penalty Act (AEDPA) and the Illegal Immigration Reform and Immigrant Responsibility Act (IIRIRA). These acts utilized a combination of secret evidence deportations and denial of bond, and were "used almost exclusively against persons of Arab ethnicity and/or Muslim religious affiliation to detain them for long periods in jail without charge or the ability to mount any form of effective defense."[76] The acts called for the federal government to deport noncitizens based on governmental evidence unknown to the public. These acts were passed despite the fact that neither of the two suspects charged with the bombing were of Arab descent.

Following 9/11 the persecution of Arabs and Arab Americans increased with Bush Administration acts such as the USA PATRIOT (The Uniting and Strengthening America by Providing Appropriate Tools Required to Intercept and Obstruct Terrorism) Act and Special Registration, and Operation TIPS (Terrorism Information and Prevention System). Mass arrests, secret and indefinite detentions, detention of material witnesses, closed hearings, use of secret evidence, illegal wiretapping, removal of aliens with visa violations, and mandatory special registration became the new order. Up to 1,200 (some report up to 2,000) Muslim and Arab noncitizens were arrested and detained, however none were found to have any links with terrorism. Up to 5,000 individuals were summoned for what were called "voluntary interviews," yet, "the interviews yielded no information relating to the terrorist attacks."[77] The Patriot Act reinforced Clinton's 1996 Anti-Terrorism Act, with indefinite detentions, searches, seizures, wiretapping, and guilt by association. Many were given secret hearings, summarily deported with no due process, and "on one occasion, 132 men were shipped off by plane to Pakistan and told not to come back."[78] The Special Registration program, meant to promote national security, "has resulted in the exact opposite ... special registration has violated the civil rights of an important immigrant population that the United States relies upon for crucial terrorist related information."[79] Likewise, Operation TIPS was voluntary and intended to be a means of reporting suspicious terrorist activity. Gana wrote, "the goal of Operation TIPS boiled down to inciting everyday citizens to spy on one another and report whatever they deemed suspicious by calling a special hotline."[80] The subsequent Homeland Security Act of 2002, the National

Security Entry-Exit Registration System (NSEERS), U.S.-VISIT (United States Visitor and Immigrant Status Indicator Technology), and other decisions by the U.S. government to single out travelers from more than a dozen, mostly Middle Eastern countries, for increased security caused many in the Arab/Muslim-American community to feel that they are being singled out, racialized, and collectively punished. Despite the demise of the AAUG, several other Arab American activist groups filled the void. The Anti-Arab Discrimination Committee (ADC) and the Arab American Institute (AAI) were founded in response to the many governmental actions leveled against Arab Americans, and many of their members had been AAUG activists. Issues for these groups are the same—proving that the issues that plagued the community over 40 years ago continue to inspire resistance and activism.

The Anti-Arab Discrimination Committee

One group inspired by the activities of the AAUG was the Anti-Arab Discrimination Committee (ADC). Formed in 1980 by Abourezk, the ADC mission includes empowering Arab Americans, defending the civil rights of all people of Arab heritage in the United States, promoting civic participation, encouraging a balanced U.S. foreign policy in the Middle East, and supporting freedom and development in the Arab World.[81] According to the organization, one of the major missions of the ADC is "combating defamation and negative stereotyping of Arab Americans in the media and wherever else it is practiced ... by promoting cultural events and participating in community activities, ADC has made great strides in correcting anti–Arab stereotypes and humanizing the image of the Arab people."[82] Like the AAUG before it, the desire to combat negative stereotypes remains central to the purpose of the ADC. In addition, the ADC has its own communications department that combats defamation, stereotyping, and bias in films, television and news reporting, and serves as a media watchdog. Following the 1982 Israeli invasion of Lebanon and the Sabra/Shatila massacre, the ADC organized demonstrations, marches, press conferences, and other events aimed at protesting the invasion and educating Americans about what was occurring in Lebanon. Following Israel's partial withdrawal from Lebanon in 1983, the ADC also became active in monitoring the anti–Arab stereotyping and the exclusion of Arab Americans from academia and politics. According to Malek, university academics have been silenced or harassed by labels such as "pro–Arab" or "anti–Israel" for focusing on issues regarding the Arab world or for receiving funding from

Arab sources. In addition, these charges have been leveled against scholars offering narratives of the Arab-Israeli conflict that is either critical of Israel or sympathetic to the Palestinian point of view.[83]

Arab Americans have been refused and attacked within the American political arena as well. The 1985 murder of ADC West Coast regional director Alex Odeh in his Santa Ana, California, office again led to ADC action. Following an FBI investigation that named the Jewish Defense League (JDL) as the "possible responsible group," the Subcommittee on Criminal Justice of the House Committee on the Judiciary held a hearing titled "Hearing on Ethnically Motivated Violence against Arab-Americans" in 1986. The hearings found that violence against Arab Americans had become "a national tragedy" and that Arab Americans were in "a zone of danger."[84] Since then, the ADC has continued its mission of political activism, which became especially important following 9/11. In addition, the ADC has created several scholarships for Arab Americans in the fields of medicine, journalism, and communications.

The Arab American Institute

The Arab American Institute (AAI) was founded in 1985 in order to "nurture and encourage the direct participation of Arab Americans in political and civic life in the United States."[85] In addition, the AAI mission states that it strives to promote Arab American participation in the U.S. electoral system, focusing on campaigns, elections, policy formation, and research. In addition, the AAI conducts media research. Through their publications *Congressional Scorecard* and *Election Report*, as well as their cable program *Viewpoint*, the AAI spends a great deal of its time and energy on combating negative and pernicious stereotyping. The AAI has become the strongest of the remaining Arab American activist organizations, and, their president, James Zogby, has become a leading voice of the Arab American movement since 9/11.

Formations of Negative Arab Stereotyping

Edward Said's salient critique of Orientalism speaks specifically to the representation of other cultures, the relationship between power and knowledge, the role of the intellectual, and questions regarding methodology between different texts and histories. Said's later book, *Covering Islam: How the Media and the Experts Determine How We See the Rest of the World*, is pertinent to any study of Arab and Arab American media bias because it examines contemporary issues, especially pertaining to Muslims who as a group are most targeted by negative stereotyping. Said writes that his subject is "Western and specifically American responses to an Islamic world perceived, since the early seventies, as being immensely relevant and yet antipathetically troubled, and problematic."[86] This anti–Muslim antipathy has grown since 9/11, and there have been several controversies since that time that involve anti–Mosque protests and organized Koran burnings.

Said's critique focuses on how the term "Islam" has been created as a monolithic entity, while in reality it is "part fiction, part ideological label, part minimal designation of a religion called Islam."[87] Said returns to the central critique stated by many other Arab American scholars before him—namely that "Islam" has been mislabeled, subject to ethnocentric and racial hatred, and inaccurately portrayed in what is meant to be a balanced or responsible coverage of the subject, primarily by the media. Said labels this media coverage as both covering and covering up Islam with easy and instant generalizations. The media portrays Islam as underdeveloped, fanatical, and a menace to Western civilization. Said views the term "Islam" as a scapegoat for everything not liked about the world's political, social, and economic patterns. For the political right, Islam represents barbarism; for the left it represents medieval theocracy. For the center, it is "a kind of distasteful exoticism." Overall, he argues that "even though little enough is known about the Islamic world there is not much to be approved of there."[88] While Said concedes that some Islamic societies are repressive, abrogate personal freedoms, contain unrepresentative and minority regimes, he also notes that Islam is "doctrinally as blameless in this regard as any other great universal religion."[89]

The confluence of the academy, corporations, media, and the government have all grossly simplified Islam "so that numerous manipulative aims can be realized, from the stirring up of a new cold war, to the instigation of racial antipathy, to mobilization for a possible invasion, to the continued denigration of Muslims and Arabs."[90] For Said, Orientalism and anti–Semitism have common roots based on "reductive formulae and the abstract but potent kind of thought that leads the mind away from concrete human history and experience and into the realms of ideological fiction, metaphysical confrontation, and collective passion."[91] In addition, Said criticizes the mass media for focusing ahistorically and sensationally on war and on the demonization of an unknown enemy "for whom the label 'terrorist' serves the general purpose of keeping people stirred up and angry, media images command too much attention and can be exploited at times of crisis and insecurity of the kind that the post–9/11 period has produced."[92] Said's work on Arab American issues has completely changed the way intellectuals approach Arab American identity, pedagogy, and activism. From the time Said changed his focus from strictly literary issues to political ones that deal directly with the Arab world, his works provide a standard by which most Arab American scholars, artists, and activists have conducted their own research.

Jack G. Shaheen has continued Said's work regarding the media representation of Arabs. Shaheen labels anti–Arab racism as "the New Anti-Semitism," reminding readers that Arabs are Semites and are being subjected to the same kind of anti–Semitism Jews were subjected to through Nazi propaganda. Shaheen's wider point is that the corrosiveness of these negative stereotypes affects both non–Arabs and Arabs alike. Shaheen is also concerned about Arab American youth and their exposure to such images: "Our young people are learning from the cinema's negative and repetitive stereotypes. Subliminally, the onslaught of the reel Arab conditions how young Arabs and Arab Americans perceive themselves and how others perceive them, as well."[93] Shaheen does not propose that Arabs never be portrayed as villains; instead he asks that not all Hollywood depictions of Arabs be bad ones.[94] Shaheen's pioneering work in the field of anti–Arab stereotyping in the media, popular film, and even cartoons has provided a wealth of knowledge to those in media studies focusing on Arab and Arab American issues.

Palestinian American media and political analyst Ray Hanania writes in his book *I'm Glad I Look Like a Terrorist: Growing Up Arab in America*: "Arab Americans who tried to advocate their 'cause' never had a chance in this country. First of all, we did not and still do not understand the concept of 'perception.'"[95] It is Hanania's contention that most Arab Americans view the media, television, or Hollywood as a threat rather than as an instrument of salvation. As with other Arab-American critics, Hanania writes that the tension between Arabs and Jews is caused primarily by the Palestinian situation, bigotry, and American policies that discriminate against Arabs.[96] Through the mediums of journalism, stand-up comedy, blogs, and his writings, Hanania has attempted to find solutions to contentious issues like the Israeli-Palestinian conflict. Hanania believes that, through communications, Arab Americans can help Americans understand the complexities of the issues facing the Arab world and Arab Americans.

Constrained Scholarship and Coerced Imaginations

As contemporary Arab American history has shown, scholarship in this area has been fraught with the contentious and difficult issues regarding the multiple wars in the Middle East, the backlash against Arab Americans, and the difficulties faced by Arab Americans combating negative stereotyping and racism. As Gualtieri states, "the preoccupation with defending a culture under siege in the United States ... has constrained Arab American scholars and consumed their time, impeding more thorough explications of Arab culture here and abroad."[97] I agree with Gualtieri that Arab American scholars have spent an inordinate amount of time writing about their resistance to these issues. One can only speculate on how many other interesting and productive topics could have been explored in the past 40 years by those scholars had they not been continually compelled to defend their communities under siege. In his essay "Writing While Muslim, Writing While Arab," Gana addresses the unfortunate fact that Arab/Muslim American cultural production post–9/11 is colored and distorted by the backlash, fanaticisms, and exigencies of the nation's work of mourning. "Small wonder, then, that Muslim- and Arab-American literary and cultural productions have been remarkably counternarrative, reactionary, and corrective in their overall propensity—in short, products of the coerced imagination."[98] This sense of coercion is one that some Arab American artists have, for better or worse, made central in their work.

If there is a major critique to be leveled against Arab American performance, it may be that it too closely emulates the tone and voice of the post–1967 intellectuals. Instead of these works being free to explore aesthetic and imaginative concepts, writers and performers are often constrained artistically by the need to create works that defend their community. Arab American plays and performances in the post–9/11 era are not always as formally adventurous as other American plays because they are consistently inspired to write in a manner that expresses their polemical and political views in a linear storytelling format. Many post–9/11 works revolve around the same issues: stereotyping, racism, profiling, exclusion from the mainstream, and Othering.

Arab American scholar Hatem Bazian labels this condition "virtual internment." Bazian defines this concept as "a quasi-visible but repressive, intimidating, and confining structure employed by the U.S. administration and its allies on a global scale against individuals, communities, and organizations deemed unsupportive, and possibly hostile, in their worldview toward American and 'global' interests."[99] Bazian writes that the war on terrorism is really a collective criminalization of Arabs and Muslims, a "guilt by association" that targets the entire community as a way of "possibly, finding the 'terrorist' hiding among them."[100] These strategies, employed across governmental and security agencies and modes of public discourse, operate on a mentally induced state of control.

As a result, communities are being transformed into virtual prison states without leaving their homes, jobs, and friends.... The individual sitting at home, watching television, listening to the radio, or reading the newspaper must be induced to feel guilty for belonging to a now criminal class—Arabs, Muslims, and Asians—and the only way to prove otherwise is to cooperate with the authorities against one's own community. Failing to do so becomes a sure sign of harboring sympathies toward the criminal terrorists.[101]

Given the events that have occurred since the late 1960s, it is little wonder that this state of mental siege exists in the Arab American community. An atmosphere of fear, surveillance, and suspicion has been created whereby Arab American activism can lead to all sorts of harassment by governmental officials. For instance, a December 2009 *New York Times* article, "Muslims Say F.B.I. Tactics Sow Anger and Fear," chronicles how, eight years after 9/11, the FBI continually infiltrates mosques and uses its agents as "provocateurs to trap unsuspecting Muslim youth."[102] According to the article, Muslims have been told to spy on relatives overseas in order to secure green cards and have canceled trips abroad to avoid suspicion. In addition, Muslim charities are finding it difficult to recruit volunteers willing to work with them for fear of suspicion. According to the American Civil Liberties Union (ACLU), Muslims have a pervasive fear of arrest, prosecution, and targeting for law enforcement interviews. In 2010 the FBI's hiring of convicted criminals to secretly spy on mosques throughout Orange and neighboring counties in Southern California was discovered. A *Washington Post* article, "Tension Grows Between California Muslims, FBI After Informant Infiltrates Mosque," reported that an FBI informant utilized high tech devices such as a key ring microphone and lapel cameras to infiltrate mosques and entrap worshipers.[103] As these cases demonstrate, the post–9/11 governmental hysteria that was created by the Bush Administration continued during the Obama Administration despite public rhetoric to the contrary.

Arab American Cultural Production and Resistance Literature

Studying the cultural production of Arab Americans reveals many productions and performances in the past four decades. Few of these productions, however, have achieved any notoriety. The reasons for this are both internal and external. The internal reasons include the fact that Arab Americans typically gravitate toward fields such as medicine, engineering, and law and not toward educational or artistic fields. Therefore, prior to 2001, there has not been a major influx of Arab American artists. When Gregory Orfalea asked Edward W. Said about his views on Arab American arts and artists, Said replied:

> Sociologically there aren't enough—or there isn't a tradition yet of Arab Americans who write, who are involved in the arts. Second, it's not perceived as particularly important. You know, maybe there are other issues that are more important, like surviving, maintaining your identity, and so on.... But the question is, can you make an impression in the face of the dominant culture? ... You know, there's a lot of very important work in its own terms. Not only in its own terms, but in absolute terms, very good cultural discourse in essays or fiction and so on. And in that, the Arab American simply plays a very tiny, marginal, unimportant role.[104]

This statement by one of the foremost Arab American literary critics demonstrates that, even among the Arab American community, there has been little or no knowledge of Arab American artists, even among the intellecuals of the community. As late as 2007 Suleiman wrote that there was a paucity of research on Arab Americans; what did exist was mainly to be found in the form of theses and dissertations. In his opinion, the lack of publication has to do with a scarcity of courses or programs that focus on Arab American studies on U.S. campuses, a lack of interest in the subject by publishers, and lack of Arab Americans in positions of influence.[105]

While it is true that the majority of the plays written by Arab Americans prior to the 1990s were cultural productions that had more to do with upholding Arabic traditional arts such as music and dance, the post–9/11 writers and performers have attempted to shift their focus onto more political issues. Since the 1980s, Arab American involvement in theatre has grown dramatically in cities such as Detroit, New York, Los Angeles, and Chicago.[106] The most political plays written by Arab Americans can be categorized as works of virtual internment, being overwhelmingly preoccupied by the fear and paranoia of being Arab in America. Furthermore, the kinds of plays that Arab Americans write are critical of U.S. domestic and foreign policies, and therefore are not the kind of entertainment that could be considered popular by mainstream standards. According to playwright Betty Shamieh, most regional American theatres only produce one play per season by artists of color, and trying to get an Arab American play produced in the current politicized and racialized market is very difficult.[107] In addition, where most minorities have the ability to receive specialized grants from U.S. governmental organizations such as the National Endowment for the Arts, Arab Americans are excluded from these categories.

Resistance Literature

In her dissertation, *The Space In-Between: The Ambivalence of Early Arab-American Writers*, Arab American scholar Nada Najjar posits that the works of Arab American writers and performers are a form of resistance literature, as defined by Barbara Harlow in her book *Resistance Literature*. Harlow writes of postcolonial resistance literature and its place within the Western canon. Although Harlow primarily discusses works by so-called "third world" writers, her paradigm is useful in discussing works of diasporic writers as well. Harlow parallels resistance literature with national liberation movements. This literature demands recognition of its independent status and its existence as literary production. In addition, resistance literature presents a challenge to the canon of theory and literature as it has developed in the West.[108] For Harlow, the struggle of authors of resistance literature is one of liberation "on many levels and in many arenas" and is part of their political and cultural agenda.[109] Harlow further identifies this form of literature as access to a history for those who have been historically denied an active role in world politics. She also explores the social/political transformation from a genealogy of filiation to one based on affiliation.[110]

If Arab Americans do indeed form a culture of resistance, it only follows that the scholarship and literature produced by the group would mirror such a culture. I argue that contemporary Arab American theatre, film, and performance are also forms of resistance literature. First, Arab Americans have historically been denied their active role in the politics of the United States, because they have been grouped under the category of "white" in the American cultural imaginary without being able to reap all the positive benefits of whiteness. Second, the question of contested political terrain exists not in the United States itself, but in the Arab countries from which many of these writers' parents emigrated. The experience of vicarious victimhood via grandparents and parents becomes a topic of great importance. Many of these writers retain connections with their lands of ancestry through dual citizenships and family ties. Last, the Arab American experience is one not only of filiation (through kinship, ethnicity, and race) but also through affiliation, since these artists were born in the United States, were educated and raised in the American system, and hold dual allegiances to their lands of ancestry and their land of birth. What has occurred since 1967, and especially after 9/11, is that their land of birth has sometimes treated its citizens as aliens through governmental persecution, surveillance, and racism (even against religion such as Islam). Therefore, after 9/11, these writers resisted their own society's persecution, believing that they have been deemed third world citizens within their own country.

Analyzing the plays, performances, and films by Arab Americans after 9/11, their preoccupation with the attacks, both literal and figurative, on Arabs and Arab Americans is clear. Playwright Yussef El Guindi's dramas and comedies often revolve around themes of governmental coercion, media stereotyping, and intra–Arab violence. Betty Shamieh's dramas speak to the displacement and persecution of Palestinians both in the Middle East and in America. Heather Raffo's work focuses on the cruel difficulties of surviving as an Iraqi exile. Ismail Khalidi's plays explore how Palestinians live in a state of flux—labeled and treated as "terrorists" both in Palestine and in the United States, regardless of their guilt or innocence. Because of the extraordinary backlash against Arab Americans of all faiths, the state of siege that developed in the years following 9/11 created works of coerced imaginations. Ironically, this has also further defined these Arab American artists and allowed them to utilize their talents in order to defend their community through their performances.

If these works are works of constrained scholarship and coerced imaginations, it is because the society itself has constrained and coerced its own citizens. As the following chapters demonstrate, these artists were compelled to create these works because their culture was under siege by those who usurped power and turned it against its citizens. Rather than silently accepting their victimization, these writers and performers made the decision to out themselves from the "white" status they had often consciously or unconsciously assumed in order to speak out against this oppression. Various ramifications have resulted. In some circles, such as stand-up comedy, there has been a measure of acceptance and even fame. In other genres, such as theatre and film, the response has been tepid at best, and post–9/11 works are rarely produced outside of theatres that have a mission that focuses on writers from the Middle East and its diaspora.

Hybridity and Arab American Identity

Bhabha's idea of cultural hybridity has been rejected by some Arab American scholars like Salaita, who believes that focusing on ethnic identity comes at the expense of more pressing concerns. Salaita believes that focusing on issues of ethnicity constrains and contains Arab American scholarly engagement. In Salaita's view, "to reduce discussion of this community to subject identities (an approach that relies inevitably on amorphous, and thus ineffectual, criteria) is tantamount to forestalling productive scholarly engagement."[111] Gana expresses a similar concern in his essay "Everyday Arabness" where he discusses the Arab Canadian predicament that is not unlike the Arab American experience. "The fact remains ... that Arab Canadian artistic productions—however long-established, rich, or profuse they might be—did not help Arabs to override their minority status in Canada but became themselves variably hostage to such a minority status, paradoxically mirroring and warranting their ultimately mutual marginalization."[112]

The suspicion of many Arab American scholars regarding notions of hybridity and visibility are therefore problematized, especially in light of the events of 9/11. Ironically, however, the events of 9/11 have simultaneously increased visibility of Arab American artists while forcing them to focus their works primarily on their status as outsiders and ethnic "Others." Instead of moving away from notions of hybridity and ethnicity, scholars and writers have instead become particularly interested in these notions. If anything, the post–9/11 environment hostility toward Arab Americans left many artists feeling that addressing these issues rather than avoiding them was the only way to speak out against governmental actions such as racial profiling, interrogations, internment, and renditions. Charara writes that Arab Americans have taken on the notion of hybridity by both expressing and embodying it. Arab American artists in particular choose complexity over positive or apologetic images of their culture and challenge the stereotypes and discourses that Orientalize them.[113]

What characterizes contemporary Arab American theatre, film, and performance is the fact that these works spend less time dealing with issues of ethnic identity and more time dealing with the political implications of what it means to be Arab American, especially in the post–9/11 context. Unlike previous American writers of Arab Descent (such as Kahlil Gibran, Mikhail Naimy, or Ameen Fares Rihani), these new writers explore the condition of being a first- or second-generation Arab American whose parents came from Arab countries, but who themselves do not necessarily have an affiliation or desire to return to those places. However, some of these writers hold dual citizenships and have family members in Arab countries. Therefore, the events that are occurring in those countries have a direct impact upon their lives. Where previous generations of writers spent their time on the subject of yearning and longing for their homelands, contemporary Arab American writers frequently travel back and forth between their ancestral homelands and their land of birth. These writers, filmmakers, and performers create works that grapple with what it means to be Arab in America today. Their work is not nostalgic; rather, it is dynamically seeking some means to understand how they can negotiate their American identity (their Americanness) simultaneously with Arab identity (their Arabness).

The "New" Abjects

Despite their desire for acceptance, Arab Americans have become yet another abject group in a predominantly "white" society. In this regard, many Arab American scholars have likened the current state of Arab American affairs to those of Asian Americans in the middle of the twentieth century. In her book *National Objection: The Asian American Body Onstage*, Karen Shimakawa discusses Asian American as "a category both produced through and in reaction to abjection within and by dominant U.S. culture—a discursive formation that both describes a demographic category and calls that category into being."[114] Like Arab Americans, Asian Americans are a "panethnic, self-identified political and social coalition/identity ... a late–twentieth-century creation, an antiracist coalitional strategy."[115] Shimakawa suggests that Asian Americanness functions as abject in relation to Americanness, but does not result in the formation of an Asian American subject or even an Asian American object. Asian Americanness is characterized by its shifting relationship to Americanness, its movement between visibility and invisibility, foreignness and domestication/assimilation. "It is that *movement between* enacted by and on Asian Americans ... that marks the boundaries of Asian American cultural (and sometimes legal) citizenship."[116] Shimakawa warns that scholars of the politics of representation, particularly of performance, "must grapple with the connections linking the body, the image, and the polis, in other words, connections between affect and effect."[117] Shimakawa also writes that Asian Americans have, at times during American history, been embraced while at other times were excluded or segregated. She notes that these contradictions are understood as a product of the continually collapsing project of abjection as a fundamental element of national identity formation.

While some hyphenated groups have had periods of acceptance by the dominant culture, it can be said that Arab Americans who have not assimilated (especially those who are Muslim or who dress in traditional Arab/Muslim dress) have never really been accepted by the majority of American society. This is primarily due to the fact that many Arabs in America are Muslim, and those who are not are often mistakenly thought to be Muslim. In addition, some Muslim Arabs often do not assimilate into American culture, preferring an isolationist stance. Yazbeck Haddad and Idleman Smith write that American

Muslims find themselves forced to choose between their conformity to Islam and honoring the pluralism of the United States.[118] Because of these facts, Moustafa Bayoumi writes that Arabs and Muslims "now hold the dubious distinction of being the first new communities of suspicion after the hard-won victories of the civil-rights era."[119] Since 9/11, Americans' mounting suspicions about Arabs and Muslims in their midst finally came to fruition, as if to reinforce their preexisting fears. Bayoumi writes of how terms such as "radical," "sleeper cells," "alienated Muslims," "homegrown terrorists," and "radicalization" are spoken of so frequently that they have become devoid of all meaning. What is missing is the human dimension of how Arabs and Muslims live their lives, experience their religion, and deal with the prejudices they face on a daily basis.[120] This desire for more understanding of Arab lives is shared by Shakir, who writes in her book *Bint Arab*, "the more I answered to Arab, the more I puzzled over the discrepancy between what most people believed about Arabs and what I knew of Arab Americans."[121]

The stereotypes Shakir experienced in popular culture did not match the pedestrian lives Arab Americans lived every day. Furthermore, the Arab women she knew could not be confused with notions of harem girls or domestic slaves that are often associated with Arab culture. However, whenever Shakir identified as Arab American, the stereotypes would return, most unexpectedly, even from American feminists. "Instead, they [feminists] have sometimes seemed to have a vested interest in broadcasting stories of savage Arab men and perpetuating the stereotype of the passive, pathetic Arab woman, needing to be roused from her moral, intellectual, and political stupor."[122] It is Shakir's view that, if the real stories of Arab American women were to be told, Arab American women have to be the ones to tell them. For her part, Amira Jarmakani believes that Orientalist images of Arab womanhood limit the human potential of the women they represent, opting for caricatures rather than thoughtfully reflected images. The "veils, harems, and belly dancers" she experienced in American culture were directly linked to patriarchal domination, erotic fantasy, and rationalizations of militarism.[123] Also included in the post–1967 and post–9/11 contexts is the cultural mythology of the dangerous, *burqa*-clad Arab/Muslim female terrorist/suicide bomber who has been added to Jarmakani's list of negative representations of Arab womanhood.

Searching for Identity

There is a crucial distinction, however, between those Arab Americans who have consciously self-identified as such and those who have not. Americans of Arab Descent who have assimilated and who have successfully passed as white have found that their post–9/11 experience is vastly different from those Arab Americans or Arabs in America who have chosen integration, assimilation, or isolation. Those who have chosen assimilation have changed their appearance by dressing more "Western," anglicizing their names, changing their physical appearance (dyeing their hair, having plastic surgery), reducing or eliminating their accents, and changing their religion. By contrast, those who have chosen either an isolationist or acculturative path have found themselves less accepted and more scrutinized by mainstream society. Some who wear traditional Muslim garb (such as women who wear *hijab*), who speak Arabic in public, and who retain their Arab/Muslim names, have found themselves on the margins of society. Often, it is this group who is excluded from the opportunities and fiscal rewards of being assimilationists.[124] Living on the margins of society, however, presents its own opportunities. Bhabha writes:

> Increasingly, "national" cultures are being produced from the perspective of disenfranchised minorities. The most significant effect of this process is not the proliferation of "alternative histories of the excluded" producing, as some would have it, a pluralist anarchy.[125]

This pluralist anarchy challenges the hegemony by introducing traditions and lifestyles that are often counter to the dominant culture. Although this causes tremendous disruptures, such as the debates in the United States and some European countries regarding issues of multiculturalism,[126] it also creates opportunities to hear voices that are often not considered in mainstream American discourse. Arab American writers, especially after 9/11, have embraced this alternative history of the excluded in their works.

In her article "A Quest for Identity: Racism and Acculturation Among Immigrant Families," Sandra Mattar studies the mental health consequences of the acculturation process. Mattar asks, "As the United States becomes increasingly more multicultural or culturally diverse, does this increase risk for psychological conflicts due to acculturation processes and forces?"[127] For immigrants, defining ethnic and racial identity are part of a developmental process that is connected to acculturation. The process of defining ethnic identity becomes an active negotiation with the environment and is mediated by many forces. According to Mattar, many immigrant children learn that society has different rules for them because of their foreign background, forcing them to struggle to integrate different lifestyles into their lives in order to understand themselves.[128] Mattar finds that families of color and their children must deal with several unique tasks, including living with racism, the development of coping mechanisms, and living with rage and internalized oppression. Questions arise about choice of language, stereotypes, self-identity, self-esteem, and internalized racism.

> How can you teach your children to be proud of their ethnicity when the message in the community around you is "you either assimilate or else you don't belong." There is no possibility of embracing one's culture unless mainstream society confronts its own fears around difference and is willing to embrace "the other" as he/she is.[129]

Mattar concludes that children of immigrants try to maintain cultural allegiances for their parents' sake, while being pushed by their mainstream peers to accept mainstream discourses and to deny their backgrounds. She adds, "I will feel at home when I am no longer forced to be the 'other,' or what the rest of the group wants me to be in order to diminish its own anxieties. Home means peace, and peace means exactly what the Pledge of Allegiance prescribes: 'liberty and justice for all.'"[130] Most disappointing about the post–9/11 situation for many Arab Americans was the government's singling out people—citizens—of Arab descent by placing them on watch lists, surveilling places of worship, and creating a culture of fear regarding Arab/Muslim Americans.

Realizing Abjection

In the writings and performances of these authors, the realization of their abjection occurs quite suddenly and at different points in their lives. In Najla Said's drama, *Palestine*, her othering as an Arab American occurs as she watches the events of 9/11 unfold:

> Thus I was crowned and outed as an "Arab-American." I'd never been a hyphenate before—it was kind of nice to be an "officially franchised minority" but then it was horrifying. This part is sort of hard to explain. I don't feel entirely American, never have, but it's not because I don't want to or because I don't seem it—I do, I am. I don't feel entirely Arab though either, for the same reasons. But I certainly don't feel like any *combination of the two* either.[131]

This dichotomy, where one is deemed a minority, is a disconcerting realization because it creates an identity that must either be denied or embraced. If it is denied, the subject faces isolation from their heritage group; if it is embraced, the subject faces isolation from their adopted society. For graphic artist and writer Toufic El Rassi, this self-realization occurs later in life. In his graphic novel, *Arab in America*, the main character named Toufic realizes his abjection when he looks back at a video of himself acting in a school production of *The Wizard of Oz:*

> I think that most non-white people who grew up in a mostly white environment have a story about the first time they realized that they were not white. I vividly remember the first time I discovered my brown skin when I was in the 8th grade. Growing up, I naturally assumed equality or (thanks to my doting mother) even superiority to my peers ... imagine my shock upon discovering that, in sharp contrast to the angelic white faces arrayed in the chorus, the dark splotch on the grainy tape was me! That was a very jarring thing to come to grips with as a boy, and it was at that moment I realized that I was different from other kids. I felt panic, I didn't know what to do, I just wanted to leave the room.[132]

Likewise, for Hanania, growing up Arab in America was an uneasy experience. "I worked at being an American, but I was treated like a foreigner, an alien, a stranger in my own country."[133] The at-school experience was one where Hanania felt the most alienation, as there were no Arab authors or topics covered in his studies. Hanania writes about how "Arab role models were not among our curriculum. Few Arabs were presented to us in school as real heroes or role models. There wasn't one that I was encouraged to admire. Still, I was inspired as an American, with a gaping hole in my ethnic heart."[134] Only when Sirhan Sirhan shot Robert Kennedy was Hanania taught about Arabs in school and on television (though Sirhan is not Arab), and it was in a negative context. No matter how hard Hanania tried to be American, there was always something that alienated him from the experience:

> We pushed our ethnicity down because we wanted dearly to be a part of this country. We changed our names, gave ourselves nicknames, to make it easier for Americans to accept us. Kaffirs, or sub-humans.[135] Discriminated against. Victims of bias and stereotyping. Defenseless against the fears and frustrations of society. These words have meaning to us. No one can really understand the truth of their own ethnicity until they have experienced the pains and joys of another's. In the American melting pot, Arab Americans are a small bubble, an ingredient that still floats apart from the rest of society's brew. As Americans, we Arabs must accept part of the blame. As Americans, we all must stir that pot to bring us all together.[136]

As all of these examples illustrate, there is a common sense of frustration found within these works. The feeling of alienation and abjection is not one that is inherent to a child—it is thrust upon them through various negative social interactions. The selections by Said, El Rassi, and Hanania demonstrate the inability for Arab Americans to find their place in American society and how writers attempt to explain these realizations. After 9/11, the alienation became even greater. While some Arabs in America retreated further into their assimilation, those who identified as Arab American made the decision to confront the discrimination they experienced by writing and performing works that they hoped would humor and educate the society around them. These artists attempted to confront the concepts of surviving racism through developing coping mechanisms that deal with their internalized oppression.

Recasting and Restaging

In order to understand how Arab American artists restage and recast themselves within the American imaginary, it is helpful to understand how these ideas function within a performative context. In her introduction to the anthology *Performance and Cultural Politics*, performance scholar Elin Diamond defines the nature of performance as "always a doing and a thing done."[137] On the one hand, performance is an embodied act in a specific site witnessed by others, however performance is also a completed event, framed in time and space that is "remembered, misremembered, interpreted, and passionately revisited across a pre-existing discursive field."[138] Since performance embeds features of previous performances that include gender conventions, racial histories, and aesthetic traditions, each performance contains within it both "now-absent performances" and "other now-disappeared scenes."[139] According to Diamond, it is impossible to write about the pleasurable aspects of performance without engaging with the cultural stories, traditions, and political contestations that make up a sense of history. Diamond notes the terminology of "re" in performance, such as *reembody, reinscribe, reconfigure,* and *resignify*. The "re" acknowledges the pre-existing, the repetition, and the desire to repeat in performance, and by doing so it asserts the possibility of something that exceeds our knowledge and imagines "unsuspected modes of being."[140] Performance and power are inextricably linked to one another, as these reinscriptions are negotiations with the regimes of power, and viewing performances within the matrix of power "encourages a permeable understanding of history and change."[141]

Arab American writers and performers, especially in the years following 9/11, utilized their performances to challenge the matrix of power that had called for understanding and tolerance while simultaneously persecuting Arab and Muslim Americans under the guise of the so-called "war on terror." These artists decided to challenge the regime of power by writing about the incarcerations, interrogations, renditions, and tortures that had taken place all in the name of homeland security. Although these artists did not utilize any radically different art forms in order to do this, they did reinscribe existing art forms in order to make these political stances. By utilizing forms such as the one-act play structure, the graphic novel, stand-up comedy, and the three-act film, these artists recast themselves in roles in traditional American theatre and film in which they never would have been cast, as well as restaged their lives in ways that had not been seen by American popular culture audiences. Diamond believes that the critique of performance reminds us of the unstable improvisations within cultural performances, exposing the fissures and revisions that have settled into our reenactments. These performances attempt to explore the pernicious stereotypes that have been circulating within popular culture regarding Arabs and Arab Americans and, in so doing, they seek to change the reception of these stereotypes in the minds of the audience.

Identity and Difference

In their book *Middle Eastern Lives in America*, Amir Marvasti and Karyn D. McKinney explore how Middle Eastern Americans deal with daily acts of discrimination through what they call *resistance strategies*.[142] This repertoire of coping mechanisms is learned "both through personal experience and through collective memory."[143] They divide the repertoire into two types of responses: attitudinal coping mechanisms and action-oriented resistance strategies. The former entails being prepared for discrimination, avoiding internalization of the discrimination and feelings of anger and bitterness, knowledge of oneself, and using spirituality and mental withdrawal. The latter mechanism includes verbal confrontation, educating others, protesting through formal channels, use of humor, and using physical withdrawal. Marvasti and McKinney apply these resistance strategies to the lives of Middle Eastern Americans because "the issue of accountability has become an everyday reality for Middle Eastern people in light of official policies that systematically demand that they explain their every action."[144] The action-oriented resistance strategies are categorized as: *humorous accounting*, which entails making jokes about one's name to diffuse prejudice; *educational accounting*, where the subject attempts to educate the person they are speaking with about the origin/history of their name and culture; *confrontational accounting*, where the subject confronts the person with their anger and frustration at being prejudiced against; and *passing/avoiding accounts* where one puts off the question or gives no account at all of their ethnicity. According to Marvasti and McKinney, humorous accounting is a way of acknowledging the need to explain oneself while simultaneously subtly mocking the necessity of the encounter; this mode of accounting is the one most utilized by Arab American stand-up comics. Educational accounting "may be the most intelligible and productive accounting strategy for one's identity" and "it is also the most time-consuming and potentially misleading approach."[145] Confrontational accounting, on the other hand, "is a risky approach that could, on the one hand, rid them of a potentially humiliating process," but it can also generate additional requests and demands.[146]

Confrontational accounting, as seen in the plays of Yussef El Guindi and Ismail Khalidi, is often dramatized as a failing strategy since those who attempt to confront the hegemonic power structure are often crushed by it. Passing or avoiding, according to Marvasti and McKinney, is sometimes the best strategy because it results in not having to give an account at all. In their opinion, passing is a strategy that eliminates the need for accounting for one's identity altogether. Passing strategies include manipulating appearance, trading Middle Eastern identity for "a less controversial one," giving an ambiguous account in response to ethnic identity questions, and stating the name of a city as one's ancestral origin rather than one's country of birth.[147] The authors admit, however, that passing strategies are "not without complications," such as being accused of "selling out" and alienating other ethnic minorities who resent having outsiders confused with their group. I disagree with the authors that passing and avoiding are successful accounting strategies. Americans of Arab Descent have attempted passing and avoiding for decades through both personal and juridical means, yet this strategy failed terribly after 9/11 when they were once again called upon to account for themselves. Therefore, Arab Americans realized that this method was not viable given the precarious circumstances they faced in the post–9/11 decade and beyond.

Reassessing the Arab American Experience

This chapter sought to explain how Arab American identity formation has coalesced since the late 1960s through community activism, academic scholarship, and artistic production. When threatened by governmental and societal pressures, it is clear that Arabs in America found it necessary to group themselves together under the inclusive term "Arab American." While this strategy found some efficacy by Arab American immigrant scholars, the following generation gradually realized that it was necessary to carry this struggle forward through a variety of means. Two of the most valuable modes of communication they discovered were performance and filmmaking. Their work, which began in earnest in the 1990s, and continues to the present day, has reshaped how Arab Americans express themselves culturally. Despite their relative success, these artists owe a tremendous debt of gratitude to an earlier generation of writers who emigrated from Greater Syria to the United States in the early twentieth century and established the model for Arab American literati that is emulated to this day.

2
"We are not of the East or West": Origins of Arab American Drama in the Works of Rihani, Gibran and Naimy

In 1928, Lebanese novelist, poet, and playwright Mikhail Naimy isolated himself in a small cabin along a river near Walla Walla, Washington. Up to that point, life had been both eventful and difficult for the writer. For his education, he traveled from his native Lebanon to Palestine, then to Ukraine where he became bilingual in Arabic and Russian. Naimy then immigrated to the United States where he studied law at the University of Washington, adding English to his linguistic repertoire. After graduating, he journeyed to New York where his Arabic poetry was published in several prominent Arabic newspapers. He volunteered to fight for the United States in the World War I not because he was obligated to do so, but because he felt it was his lawful and moral duty. After witnessing the horrors of that war, he studied in France and returned to New York to found, along with Gibran and Rihani, *al-Rabitah al Qalamiyah*, or The Pen League. This influential group of writers established Arab American writing in the early decades of the twentieth century. After a disillusioning sojourn back to New York, he returned to Washington state where he lived simply, in a little hut, much as his idol Henry David Thoreau once did almost a century before him. During that time he wrote, "Here I feel as if I am a different person—not the same person who was in New York. This little hut seems to me like a palace in the paradise which the lost, the tortured, and the displaced dream of." This feeling of loss, of torture, of displacement was one shared by the early Arab American authors who simultaneously found their authorial voices in America, but also lost themselves in the process.

2. *"We are not of the East or West"* 71

◻ ◻ ◻

The origins of Arab American drama can be traced as far back as March 14, 1896, when the Syrian Youth Society performed a play titled *Andromak* in New York "which had a large audience of 'Syrians' and Americans" according to the Egyptian newspaper *Al-Mushir*.[1] The years that followed this performance led to the emergence of the Arab American literary movement that was led by Syrian/Lebanese writers Nasib Arida, Kahlil Gibran, Abd al-Masih Haddad, Mikhail Naimy, and Ameen Fares Rihani. Nada Najjar writes that the growth of Arab American literature from 1890 to the 1930s can be attributed to two historical events: the influx of Arab immigrants to the United States and the establishment of Arab American newspapers starting in 1892.[2] These newspapers, which included *Mir'at al-Gharb* (*Mirror to the West*) (1899–

A 1920 photograph of four of the members of The Pen League. From left: Nasib Arida, Kahlil Gibran, Abd al–Masih Haddad, and Mikhail Naimy (courtesy Nadeem Naimy).

1961), *as-Sayeh* (*The Ttraveler*) (1916–1931), *al-Funun* (*The Arts*) (1913, 1918), *al-Huda* (*Guidance*) (1902–1976), and *The Syrian World* (1926–1932), provided a platform for writers to publish their works (including plays), to educate immigrants about life in America, and to express the struggle between Americanization and the desire to retain ties to their respective homelands.[3] It was due to these newspapers that Arab American writers, who were also playwrights, were able to publish some of their early works.

Kahlil Gibran, Ameen Fares Rihani, and Mikhail Naimy, who were arguably the most famous and important of the early Arab American writers, are known now primarily as novelists and poets. Few, in their native Lebanon and abroad, have knowledge of their plays because the plays were often not produced or translated in their lifetimes and because these works comprised the smallest number of works in their literary oeuvres. These writers' plays, however, provide a fascinating view into how they viewed their world, their cultures, and their art. Like later Arab American playwrights, these writers were resistant to some aspects of their home cultures, to American life, and to the ways their compatriots conducted themselves as immigrants. Their plays, which include Rihani's Orientalist fantasy of pre-modern Iraq, Gibran's scathing critique of his fellow Syrians living in New York, and Naimy's critical view of Lebanese village life, are the foundational works that defined how Arab Americans would create dramatic literature after being influenced by life and study in Europe and the United States.

Ameen Rihani's Wajdah

Ameen Rihan's play *Wajdah* was written in 1908 and 1909 during Rihani's first return to Lebanon. Rihani was born in 1876 in the Metn village of Freike, Lebanon, to a family who owned a raw silk factory. He was educated in both Arabic and French in a private, secular school that was overseen by Na'um Mukarzil (1863–1932), who would later accompany Rihani to the United States and who would become editor of *al-Huda* (*Guidance*), the Arabic newspaper that would eventually print Rihani's early written works. Rihani immigrated to New York at the age of 12 in 1888 with his uncle Abduh and his teacher Mukarzil. He continued his schooling at a Catholic school in Newburgh but was forced to leave school to assist his father as a bookkeeper for their family export-import business. Rihani continued his study independently, reading works by Dante, Emerson, Hugo, Montaigne, Rousseau, Shakespeare, and Voltaire.[4] By 1895 Rihani left his family and joined the Henry Jewett Theatre company for six months before the company folded due to bankruptcy. There he was exposed to their productions of *Hamlet* and *Macbeth*, from which he would later draw sketches of the actors dressed in their Elizabethan garb.[5] Rihani, who was deeply influenced by Shakespeare, demonstrated his love of the theatre through his Shakespearean-influenced play *Wajdah*. In all, Rihani wrote five Arabic dramas: *The Prisoners, or Abdul Hameed in Asitana* (1908), *The Tragedy of the Rasheed Family* (1928),[6] *The Trilateral Treaty in the Animal Kingdom*, a play in six acts (1903, published 1972), *The Register of Repent* (1909, published 1951), *Faithful Time* (1934), and four English dramas: *Wajdah* (1909), *The Crescent Moon: A Fantasy in One Scene* (c. 1922), *The Travellers: A Vision of the Eternal Dual* (c. 1922), and *The Tragedy of Shammar*, a short play in four acts (1928). His play *The Prisoners, or Abdul Hameed in Asitana* was staged in Beirut's New Theatre in 1909 starring Petro Paouli, editor of *al-Watan (The Nation)*. Paouli and other pro-nationalists were later hanged by the Ottoman forces in Beirut's Martyrs Square on May 6, 1916. A statue commemorating their death, created by Italian sculptor Renato Marino Mazzacurati and inaugurated by late Lebanese President Fouad Chehab, has been a centerpiece of Beirut since its unveiling in 1960. Despite Rihani's best efforts, his play *Wajdah* was never produced in his lifetime.

Rihani achieved notoriety in New York City, publishing the first pieces about the Middle East by an Arab writer in *New York Times*, *Atlantic Monthly*, and *Harper's*. He also wrote the first Arab American novel in English, *The Book of Khalid* (1911), and the first Arab American play in English, *Wajdah* (1909). Rihani is widely cred-

Ameen Fares Rihani's statue in Deek al-Mehdi-Deir Tamish, sculpture by Nihat Biyar Karam (author's photograph).

ited with introducing what he called "prose poetry" or free verse into Arabic. Rihani visited Paris in 1910 and spent time with Kahlil Gibran, who was there studying painting. They also travelled to London together, where Rihani gave poetry readings and attempted (and failed) to get his play *Wajdah* staged.[7] Upon returning to New York he published several books, literary and political articles, and art critiques in English. After marrying in New York, Rihani travelled to Arabia, then Lebanon. He spent the years 1923 to 1940 travelling back and forth between the Middle East, Europe, and the Americas. Between 1915 and 1917, Rihani belonged to the first Pen League, even signing his Arabic articles "member of the Pen League."[8]

After 1920, Rihani broke with the second Pen League, mainly because he had disagreed with some of the other writers, claiming his interests did not reflect those of the group. According to scholar Nijmeh Hajjar, Rihani reproached Gibran and Naimy for their interest in literature over their attention to the strife in their native Syria/Lebanon. According to Ameen Albert Rihani, the reason Ameen Fares Rihani broke with the group was that he "had a different literary and political agenda with a focus on his English literary works like *The Path of Vision* (1921) and *A Chant of Mystics and Other Poems* (1921), and another focus on planning for his upcoming trip to Arabia."[9] By this time Rihani was publishing books in Arabic and English and was a member of several literary associations including the Poetry Society of America (1904), the National Art Theatre Society of New York (1904), the American Asiatic Society (1918), the Authors' Club (1921), the American Press Club (1922), and the American Oriental Society of Yale University (1930).[10] Rihani's travels to Arabia influenced him greatly and gained him the friendship and confidence of Arabian rulers. These affiliations led to Rihani playing a major role in the economic and political matters of the kingdom, including negotiating with British oil companies on behalf of Bahrain, Kuwait, and Najd, as well as on a mediation mission between Ibn Sa'ud and King 'Ali Ibn al-Husayn.[11] Rihani published several books about his travels in Arabia, and he was even gifted the personal sword of King Abdul-Aziz, the founder of Saudi Arabia; this was the first time such an honor was bestowed upon a Christian. Rihani was granted an honorary Ph.D. from the University of Illinois in 1937. By the time of his death in 1940, after a bicycle accident in his home village of Freike, Rihani penned 25 books in Arabic and 11 books in English.

Rihani's views of theatre were not collected into one treatise, however a reading of his essays, *Ar-Rihaniyyaat* (Volume 1, 1910; Volume 2, 1911, Volumes 3–4, 1924), provide some insight into his beliefs about the purpose of art. In his essay "From Brooklyn Bridge," he wrote:

> If you are a poet or a photographer or writer ... then I ask you to do the following: look at nature for Divine inspiration, and gather from it gorgeous colors, beautiful elegant sceneries and heavenly melodies. Then look towards Paris to learn the precision of industry and the elegance of style, the beauty of art and amazing creations. Finally come to New York to learn to be industrious and patient, and learn from its people independence in work and constancy after failure. Nature, art, and hard work—these are the bases of intellectual work, and the pillars of spiritual life.[12]

In Rihani's "The Great City," he writes that freedom is the food for the arts and sciences, where "its arts bear fruits and its literature is glorified," where writers and artists should stand apart from those with money, and where the literati live for truth, not gain. Rihani believed that prophets, writers, and poets of earlier ages were in pursuit of honor, loyalty, love, and glory and that his contemporaries were more interested in groveling to the powerful and flattering them for their personal gain. Rihani believed that his home nation of Syria (now Lebanon) did not appreciate its artists, despite the importance of their literature:

> Literature has an invisible yet strong spiritual power that is not revealed at once in the human society as do the factors of politics. This strength reveals itself slowly and in mysterious ways that are almost unnoticed. This is why we see men of letters, especially in a nation like ours always complaining of neglect and oversight, and that is why they often live alone, isolating themselves from people, denied of the fruits of life and the pleasures of living. But if we look closer the truth will reveal itself to us; then we have no right to complain or nag.[13]

Rihani, a writer in both Arabic and English, was steeped in the literature of both cultures. He was a poet, a novelist, an essayist, a philosopher, and a critic. He was so revered in his time that he was labeled "the philosopher of Freike." His wide-ranging intellect, coupled with his world travels and his multifarious experiences, made him a true intellectual.

Rihani's play *Wajdah*, which was written in English, presents a dilemma for Arab American critics and writers: how can one write a historical play about Arabs without simultaneously Orientalizing them? The play *Wajdah* is set in the seventh century ACE in Koufah (in present-day Iraq) and "the Desert." Wajdah, born a pagan Yemeni princess who was captured by Imam Ali's Muslim forces after the defeat of her father's empire, lives in Kufah with her husband Mustafa and his son Kice. Meanwhile, Imam Ali is facing pressure from the armorers who refuse to work until they get paid and from a rebellion led by Moawia, a Muslim leader who is threatening Ali from Damascus. Ali is suspected of murdering the previous Khalif, Othman. For her part, Wajdah is unsure whether Kice is her son, since she was separated from her child during the siege of Yemen. Another character, Ahmed, who is in love with Wajdah, is suspicious of Mustafa and Kice and openly accuses them of conspiring with Moawia against Ali, causing Wajdah to renounce God. Meanwhile, rumors circulate that Wajdah is secretly in love with her son, Kice. After the war between Ali and Moawia begins, a rumor that Kice has left Kufa to join Moawia's forces emerges, and that Wajdah's son can be identified by a tattoo of an amulet on his arm. Wajdah rides out to find Kice, but to no avail. Ahmed tells Wajdah that he would save Kice if she could only love him. After she rebuffs his offer, he vows revenge on her. Ali vows to protect Wajdah since she saved his life by extracting poisonous venom from his arm during the siege of Yemen. In prison, Wajdah discovers that Kice has been killed on Ahmed's orders. She discovers his body but finds no tattoo. She weeps over the loss of the man she loved and, when Ahmed discovers them, she kills Ahmed with her dagger only to discover that Ahmed bears the tattoo on his arm and is, therefore, her son. She contemplates suicide but, after hearing the call of the *muezzin*, she decides to devote her life to God once more.

The structure, language, characterizations, and dramatic conventions Rihani employs in his play are highly influenced by the works of Shakespeare. Rihani, who was intimately familiar with Shakespeare both as a reader and as a theatre practitioner, was clearly attempting to write his own Shakespearean style tragedy. Rihani employs blank verse, iambic pentameter, rhyming couplets, and includes Shakespearean staging devices in order to accomplish this goal. In his essay "The Spirit of the Language," which concerns writing in Arabic and English, Rihani writes,

> My style does not vary much in either language, except where it concerns the right focus of ideas, some literary figures of speech, and social positions that might permeate my writings. For, as I already mentioned, each language has a spirit that aspiring writers look to possessing. I, who direly needs the compassion of both Al Ma'arri and Shakespeare, am in possession of two distinct spirits that the conditions of birth and emigration have dictated. When I write in English, I express my thoughts English-style, so I desist from saying, "Night has 'camped' on the town," since English speakers do not live in camps. And I never write, "He shook his hand" when writing in Arabic since shaking hands for us does not imply greeting.[14]

Rihani outlines other differences between Arabic and English. Arabic is a language that allows one to express particular thoughts, tender emotions, and great imagination, yet falls short in expressing new or foreign ideas of modern life. Arabic is a sensory language, with little ability for abstract facts

> (2)
>
> WAJDAH
>
> ****
>
> ACT I
>
> PUBLIC SQUARE in KOUFAH: a crouching place for camels U. R. with two palm trees and a large earthen basin for water near them. Houses, flat-roofed and thatched, to left and right, with entrances 2R. E. and 2 L. E. An arch-way U. L. corner leading to the Mosque, whose minaret--practicable--rises in the rear. An open view R. C. showing part of City wall and palm groves on horizon. A well in the centre of the Square with an earthen jar tied to a rope. Well practicable.
>
> Time: Morning, flush of dawn.
>
> In the MINARET the MUAZZEN is calling the Faithful to the morning prayer.
>
> MUAZZEN Allahu akbar, Allahu akbar!
>
> La ilaha illallah, la ilaha illallah!
>
> CITIZENS pass U. L. on their way to the MOSQUE
>
> Enter U. R. HUMMAD, SHEIBAN and other ARMORERS in their working clothes.
>
> HUMMAD And this will also be
>
> A year of blood and steel.
>
> SHEIBAN And for the armorers prosperity.
>
> Allah's slaves the armorers must live.
>
> HUMMAD Thy neighbor's curse thy blessing then shall be.
>
> SHEIBAN Allah is all-seeing and all-wise--
>
> Allah be praised!
>
> HUMMAD But wait till thou art paid.
>
> Thy pious hope might yet bark at thy heels
>
> For bread. (Drums heard) Hear that. It is for thee, for me,
>
> For all of us.

Ameen Fares Rihani's original annotated manuscript for his play *Wajdah* (courtesy Ameen Albert Rihani).

in figures of speech. Rihani writes, "It is as through we can only comprehend ideas if they are illustrated for us in order for our senses to comprehend them before our mind does." English, on the other hand, is an intellectual language that is much more rational and practical. Rihani's use of English has been criticized, especially in his novel *The Book of Khalid*. Rihani's desire to combine Arabic and English literature through his somewhat convoluted style can be alienating for some English readers. According to scholar Waïl S. Hassan, *The Book of Khalid* "is both archaic and at times unintelligible to readers unfamiliar with Arabic and its cultural frame of reference because of its infusion with words, expressions, proverbs, and even rhetorical strategies characteristic of nineteenth-century Arabic literature, such as parallelisms and rhymed prose, in addition to verbal humor and ironic tone characteristic of the Arabic *maqama* genre."[15]

Unlike his novel, the play *Wajdah* is Rihani's attempt to introduce an ancient Arab/Muslim story into a Shakespearean *mise-en-scène*. By appropriating Shakespeareanesque language, structure, and characterizations, Rihani allows readers to enter seventh-century Iraq through a form, style, and structure they can understand. Clearly, Rihani did not have the poetic range or versatility of Shakespeare and his contemporaries, but viewed within a modernist perspective, the play is a viable attempt at restaging a Shakespeareanesque play in an Arab context. Hassan also notes that "Rihani's poetry and drama may have exhibited more literary ambition than talent, but they nevertheless stand as a testimony to his effort to 'expand' American consciousness of the Orient."[16] Because the play was never staged, it is difficult to ascertain whether or not this expansion of consciousness would have been accomplished in his time.

Is *Wajdah* an Orientalist fantasy, or a genuine attempt by an Arab writer to write a convincing Arab drama for Western audiences? In his seminal book *Orientalism*, Edward W. Said writes that the relationship between the Orientalist and the Orient was a hermeneutical one, with the Orientalist standing at a distance from the civilization or culture, translating, portraying it sympathetically, and reaching toward an unattainable object. "Yet the Orientalist remained outside the Orient, which, however much was made to appear intelligible, remained beyond the occident."[17] Regarding representation of Oriental subjects, the Orient is often transformed from a far, distant, and threatening "otherness" into something that is relatively familiar so that the representation becomes how the non–Oriental makes a symbol of the Orient. According to Said, the representational aspects that should be explored are style, figures of speech, setting, narrative devices, historical and social circumstances, and *not* the "correctness" of the representation or its fidelity to some great original. Given that there is not an original Wajdah story for comparison to Rihani's play, the other aspects of Said's analysis must be relied upon for scrutiny of the text. Regarding style, the play is written in a Shakespearean style, which means that it is already extracted from the performance styles of Arab culture including *hakawati* (storytelling), *zajal* (improvised poetry), or *Qasida* (poetry). Therefore, the play operates much like Shakespeare's own dramas that are set in foreign countries such as *Othello, Romeo and Juliet*, or *Hamlet*. To our knowledge, Shakespeare had no intimate knowledge of these cultures, only that he was creating a dramatic fantasy that occurred there based on his own Elizabethan experience and norms. Several characters and scenarios are also appropriated from Shakespeare including Rihani's Tabtaba, the wise fool character who speaks truth to power via his poetry; Wajdah's "Blow on, blow on" speech in Act III, Scene I, that is reminiscent of Lear's speech on the heath, and the tragic ending based on misunderstanding and revenge. As for figures of speech, those used in the play are a mixture of Shakespearean utterances and Arabic forms. For instance, the text is littered with sayings such as "Why look upon me thus?," "I pray thee," "Thou knowest well," "forsooth," and "What dost thou mean?" All of these phrases can be found in Elizabethan dramas, and it is obvious that Rihani reappropriated them for his own uses. However, he also infuses the text with Arabic words and phrases such as "*jehad*," "*koufiyeh*," "*Muazzin*," "*Allahu akbar*," and "*billah*." He also uses the word "*Allah*" instead of "God" despite the fact that the former is the Arabic translation of the latter. The setting is clearly stated as "KOUFAH and the DESERT" in "Seventh Century A.D." Rihani's scene descriptions are fairly unembellished:

> Public Square in Koufah: a crouching place for camels with two palm trees and a large earthen basin for water near them. Houses, flat-roofed and thatched, to left and right, with entrances. An arch-way corner leading to the Mosque, whose minaret—practicable[18]—rises in the rear. An open view showing part of City wall and palm groves on horizon. A well in the centre of the Square with an earthen jar tied to a rope. Well practicable.[19]

Rihani does not include fantastic or unusual characters or elements often found in Orientalist fantasies such as snake charmers, genies, magic lamps, or flying carpets.[20] For the most part, the character descriptions are similar to those of any dramatist who is attempting to create dynamic and colorful charac[ters. For instance, Wajdah is described as a forty-year-old woman with a magnificent physique who is "tall and commanding, dark-complexioned, more magnetic than beautiful." Likewise, Imam Ali is described as "dressed as an ascetic, wearing plain sandals, a cotton tunic, and his sword hung from his shoulder by a cord made of hemp." There is only one section of the play that treads upon Orientalist fantasy. In Act Two, Scene One, Wajdah's slave-girls dance a veil dance:

> Salwah claps her hands; four or five slave-girls enter and stand in a line up stage, while she, with a veil in her hand, and Mahmoud, with the reeds, dance around

the incense-bearing column in the centre; one of the slave-girls plays the rebab, and Zeid, with rhythmic accompaniment, pounds the coffee in the wooden mortar. After Salwah has executed the veil dance, she turns her step towards the slave-girls, who immediately take up the cue and dance down stage, and then around the column with her.[21]

This scene in particular plays upon many of the Orientalist notions that have been passed down for generations, including veils, dancing slave-girls, and burning incense. Jarmakani writes that the images of Arab women in U.S. popular culture are either the erotic, sexualized versions of belly dancers or harem girls, or they are portrayed as helpless, silent victims of patriarchy. In either regard, they are cultural mythologies that are constantly represented as innocent and natural forms.[22] Rihani, like the orientalists who preceded him, does not challenge this representation of the Arab female—instead, he opts to reintroduce the dancing harem girls without any critical stance toward their representation. Like the entertaining aspects found in Shakespeare's work, the characters are necessary for spectacle and entertainment, not for historical accuracy. In contrast, historical and social circumstances of Islamic figures are portrayed in a more historically accurate and realistic manner. The play takes place during the reign of Imam Ali in Kufa, Iraq, spanning the years ACE 656–661. Given the historical facts, Rihani did attempt to portray the events of the conflict between Imam Ali and Muawia in a fairly realistic manner. Since there is no historical personage known as Wajdah, the entire subplot of Wajdah, Kice, and Ahmed was pure invention.

It is notable that Rihani wrote such a strong and dominant leading female character at that time in theatre history. In an age of the *Ziegfeld Follies*, *The Merry Widow*, and *The Man Who Owned Broadway*, the character Wajdah was far ahead of her theatrical contemporaries. Her character is described as a hunter, expert javelin thrower, noted for her horsemanship and her prowess fighting in battle, and her bravery in saving one of the most important historical figures in Islam. More importantly, in her character description Rihani writes, "She is never veiled." This sets her apart from the other Muslims in the play for two reasons: first, she is a pagan convert to the religion, but also that she is strong enough to reside in an Ummayad Muslim society without conforming to its strictures. Although she sometimes reads more like Racine's Phadre than Shakespeare's Joan la Pucelle, she still commands a strong presence in the play and refuses to be subject to the will of any of the men, including her husband Mustafa or Imam Ali himself. If there is a defect in Wajdah's character it has to do with Rihani's use of Shakespearean tragic dramaturgy. The necessity for a mercurial character temperament, a climax that demands death or murder, and the notion of tragic reversal all ensure that Wajdah is destined to accidentally kill her son. Instead of creating a laudable female heroine, Rihani creates yet another flawed Shakespearean-esque character that becomes a stereotype rather than a dimensional and powerful female protagonist.

I contend that, despite Rihani's being born in Greater Syria, living and travelling abroad multiple times, and returning to Lebanon for the final years of his life, his play *Wajdah* is ultimately Orientalist in attitude, as defined by Edward W. Said. First, Rihani was of a Maronite Christian tradition that traced its roots not to Arab history, but to Phoenician history. Therefore, although Rihani was technically Arab, he was viewing Wajdah's story as a religious, if not cultural, outsider. In addition, because he relied so heavily on the Shakespearean/Elizabethan form for his storytelling in the play, his treatment of the subject is much more aligned with how Shakespeare viewed Othello or Shylock than how an Arab author might view a character if told through another indigenous art form such as *hakawati* storytelling. The inclusion of the slave-girl veil dance, the fanatical followers of Islam, and the setting in the Islamic past, all point to a modern artist interpreting Islam for a Western audience. Given the fact that Rihani lived in the United States and France, it is clear he was influenced by the theatrical forms of these cultures and sought to meld his view of the East with his view of the West. Whether or not he was entirely successful is unclear since the play was never staged. It would be a fascinating experiment to produce the play now with the intention of avoiding the very Orientalist tropes that are inherent in the script itself. Would the play speak to a "Western" audience the way Rihani had hoped? Any theatre practitioner knows that a play's true worth is not only in its writing, but in how it plays on the stage before an audience. Only there, based on the audience's reaction to the work, can the truth of the script be known.

Kahlil Gibran's The Chameleons

On April 20, 1916, Lebanese-American Gibran Kahlil Gibran's one-act play *The Colored Faces* was published in the New York publication *As-Sayeh* (*The Traveler*). The play, whose title was translated by Michael Suleiman as *Chameleon-Like Personalities* and by Nefertiti Takla as *The Chameleons*, dramatizes a bitter critique on the then–Syrian New York community for their duplicitous manner of criticizing Arab writers and intellectuals of their day. Gibran's defiant stance, published in a paper that reached many Arabs living in New York at the time, is a controversial play that calls for scholars' reconsideration of previous notions of Gibran as a writer of abstract, spiritual works with little political attitude.

According to the first major Arab American critic Mikhail Naimy, Gibran "praises to Heavens and damns to Hell."[23] Naimy was one of the first to objectively critique Gibran's work as an authentic voice that successfully wrote about the Arab experience. Naimy critiqued Gibran by calling his initial works both "incomplete and deformed" while heralding Gibran for ushering in a new dawn in Arab literature.[24] However, after joining the Pen League, it is clear Naimy's objectivity toward Gibran's work shifted toward a kind of uncritical praise. Gibran's relationship with the Syrian community was not a good one. According to Suheil Bushrui, "He told Mary [Haskell] that he was a Syrian and would always remain so; but although Rihani and the other Syrian immigrants understood one another, he did not understand them nor they him."[25] Gibran went so far as to say that he would find himself an alien even in his own homeland. Gibran, who served as secretary of the Syrian-Mount Lebanon Relief Committee, was angered as well by the apathy he felt the Syrian Americans had toward the worsening situation in Syria under Ottoman rule.

> As for the Syrians, they are even *stranger* than they used to be. The bosses are getting bossier, and the gossips more gossipy. All these things make me hate life ... and if it had not been for the cries of the starving which fill my heart, I would not have stayed in this office for one second ... and had I been given the choice of death in Lebanon or life among these creatures I would have chosen death.[26]

Given his anger about the Syrian situation, the attitudes of his countrymen living abroad in the United States, and Gibran's growing isolation, it is little wonder that Gibran felt a frustration so great that he wished to lash out vehemently against his compatriots. *The Chameleons* is a dramatic representation of his antipathy toward his fellow Syrians living in New York.

Gibran was known primarily for his poetry, his short stories, and his artworks. Few know that Gibran was also a dramatist, though, unlike Rihani, there is no evidence that he actively sought to have his dramas produced for the stage. Gibran's dramas written in Arabic include the works *The Beginning of the Revolution, Between Night and Morn, The Chameleons, The Invisible Man, The King and the Shepherd, The Blind* (written in Arabic and English), and his English plays *The Banshee, The Last Unction, The Hunchback or the Man Unseen,* and *Lazarus and His Beloved*. Gibran biographer Robin Waterfield writes that "Gibran was perennially interested in writing plays" and that the themes revolved around "the unfortunate Westernization of Lebanon, the true artist's contempt for wealth and isolation from the norms of society."[27] Indeed, he even planned to write a play for Lionel Barrymore.[28] The only record of any of Gibran's plays being presented in his lifetime was a public reading of *Lazarus and His Beloved*, which he read to a private audience. Gibran was forty-six years old when he read the play aloud at a private celebration of his birthday in New York on January 6, 1929. Ravaged by solitude, alcoholism, and a feeling of artistic impotency, Gibran suddenly faltered while reading and abruptly left the room. His good friend, Mexican painter José Orozco, rushed to his side and found Gibran sobbing, confessing that he felt he had lost his artistic power. "I know the truth and I face it," he told Orozco. "I can no longer write as I once did."[29] Gibran died two years later of cirrhosis of the liver and tuberculosis.

His two English plays *Lazarus and His Beloved* and *The Blind* were "the most developed of five short dramas Gibran wrote in his last years."[30] These final plays were what Kahlil and Jean Gibran called "test plays"; short plays of a symbolic nature that synthesized Gibran's personal philosophy of "Gibranism" that Gibran defined as "freedom in all things." Some other themes that are present in these works include predestined lifemates, twin/sister souls, preordained love, the idealized creator, and art as the ultimate salvation.[31] What differentiates Gibran's early Arabic play *The Chameleons* from Gibran's other plays like *Lazarus and His Beloved* is that it takes place in a Syrian-American setting, it is a Realist drama, and it has a definite and scathing tone that is not present in his more ethereal works. Also, unlike Gibran's other plays, there is little that is spiritual about the characters or the action. The play was published on April 20, 1916, in a special edition about Gibran in *As-Sayeh* (*The Traveler*), the Arabic newspaper owned and edited by Abdul Massih Haddad, who was also a member of the Pen League.

Kahlil Gibran sculpture by Rudy Rahme outside the Gibran Museum in Bsharri, Lebanon (photograph by Rana Halabi Najjar).

The Chameleons opens with "prominent Syrian merchants" sitting in a large room filled with "expensive yet gaudy" furniture "lacking in color coordination, indicating both the wealth and tastelessness of the master of the house."[32] From the start we understand the dramatist's view of the antagonist, Yusuf Efendi al-Gamal—he is wealthy but does not know how to spend his wealth tastefully. Furthermore, he has employed an older Syrian woman named Hanna al-Bashawati; a widow from Lebanon who goes by the name Umm Nofal. She must have been a person of some importance in her homeland, for she says "Who could have believed that the wife of Khalil al-Bashawati would become a servant in a foreign country?"[33] Making matters worse, al-Gamal's wife, Maryam, speaks about Umm Nofal with disdain: "She is a poor woman we took in as a servant two days ago. She is exactly what I thought she would be—unpleasant and unfit to be a servant, but we did it for the sake of charity."[34] Other antagonists are Farid Efendi Ghantous, a journalist; al-Khoury Na'mat Allah Bakhous, a priest; Dr. Suleiman Beitar; and a merchant and writer named Anis Efendi Farhat. Through his *mise-en-scène* and his description of these characters, it is clear that Gibran has posited them as antagonists in his drama.

The protagonists of the drama are Miss Warda al-'Azar, a Lebanese American writer who speaks "with a calm voice and an accent that reveals her strong command of the English language," and Salim al-Marjani, a Lebanese American writer.[35] Miss Warda enters carrying an English language newspaper and declares herself to be an unmarried woman. Despite her being among fellow Lebanese in this setting, she feels estranged from them. First, she does not share her compatriots' view of al-Marjani and, because she is an unmarried woman, she believes that her point of view is discarded based on her marital status. Miss Warda represents Gibran's ideal "young American of Syrian origin" as outlined in his essay "Gibran's Message to Young Americans of Syrian Origin," published in *The Syrian World* in July 1926. Although Gibran outlines many points that define such a young Syrian, Miss Warda best exemplifies his tenet: "to create the useful and the beautiful with your own hands, and to admire what others have created in love and with faith."[36] This principle is something that Miss Warda and Salim al-Marjani possess that others in their culture do not. Like Rihani, Gibran writes a strong female protagonist in his play at a time when other crowd pleasing plays like *A Kiss for Cinderella* and *Stop! Look! Listen!* were hits on Broadway.

As with some of his other writings, Gibran features himself in his own drama. According to the play, al-Marjani is a writer who lives in Boston (the city where Gibran and his family first settled), and who "is full of empty dreams and thinks that he can keep up with both Eastern and Western art and literature."[37] In addition, the antagonists chide al-Marjani for being a disbeliever who attacks the Church (something Gibran himself was accused of doing) and who grows his hair, wears western-style clothing, and carries a cane. Furthermore, al-Marjani speaks much like Gibran's character Al Mustafa from *The Prophet* when he incants lines like "We have all left our country, Umm Nofal, and this saddens our hearts. Yet sadness does not break the heart but rather makes it grow" and "All of us are servants, Umm Nofal. All of us are servants. He who doesn't serve doesn't deserve the light of day."[38] Lastly, al-Marjani is called "crazy about coffee and drinks it night and day,"[39] something Gibran himself was known to do.

The play's conflict lies between the assembled Syrians and their distaste for al-Marjani, coupled with Miss Warda's defense of him. Al-Marjani is hated for multiple reasons: he has attacked the Church, he has been praised by Americans for his genius, he dresses like a "Westerner," and he attempts to remain knowledgeable of both "Eastern" and "Western" art and literature. The Syrians in the room are suspicious of American newspapers, saying they are "full of lies, and in this respect they are worse than the Syrian newspapers."[40] One character, Dr. Beitar, a novice writer himself, levels this attack:

> There are so many crazy Syrians out there and so many people who devote themselves to things that neither benefit them nor anyone else. What's worse is that whenever a crazy person like this appears among us, our newspapers get riled up about him. As for the American newspapers, it is well-known that they are tabloids that like to blow up trivial issues.... It wasn't enough they called him a novelist and creative writer, but to add insult to injury they called him a Syrian genius.... What did this man al-Marjani do to be labeled a genius? ... The Syrians don't know what they are doing. There is no one among them that can distinguish gold dust from ashes. They call anyone who graduates from medical school a doctor and anyone who composes a poem a poet. If it weren't for this defect, there wouldn't be anyone among us calling Salim al-Marjani a genius or even mentioning his name. We have lost our way and since most of us are blind, how will we ever find it again?[41]

When Miss Warda, who has remained silent throughout the barrage of insults leveled against al-Marjani, is finally asked for her opinion, she breaks into a page-long monologue defending the absent writer. She praises an American philanthropist "Mrs. Hamilton" (surely a dramatic representation of Gibran's own patron Mary Haskell) for throwing a party for al-Marjani and makes it clear that the only reason she did so was a shared passion they both had for literature. Miss Warda also praises the Americans for their appreciation of others' talents:

> Why do you think the American people would treat a writer with so much respect? Is it because of the darkness of his eyes or the length of his hair or the foreignness of his accent? Do you think they respect him because he was born in the desolate valleys of Lebanon or because he is a descendent of the old prophets of Syria or because he represents the new Ottoman state? No, Americans do not care about such things. They have the insight to select those foreigners who have brilliant minds or produce outstanding work and to put them on a pedestal to honor and encourage them. For the American people are progressive and they are aware that each nation has its share of geniuses.... They give every distinguished individual what he deserves, which is something that you are all incapable of.[42]

Miss Warda's blistering attack on her Syrian compatriots continues when she asks them if envy is a characteristic of the Syrian people, if patriotism has died, if they do not know the value of their own people, how Syrians are inclined toward materialism, and how Turkish rule has destroyed the noble sentiments in their hearts. She tells them that she hopes that the awakening of the Western nations will lead to the awakening of their sons and grandsons.[43] Her deepest anger arises from her perspective as a woman in her society where she states, "I am a woman and the voice of a woman is never heard among the Syrians.... I am an unmarried woman and according to your longstanding tradition, an unmarried woman should remain as silent as a grave and as still as a corpse."[44] When al-Marjani suddenly arrives to give a letter with money transfer to Hanna al-Bashawati, everyone begins praising him, inviting him to dinner, and offering to publish his works in their newspapers. Once al-Marjani realizes he has been the object of their disdain for the evening, he excuses himself. After his departure, Miss Warda tells the men,

> This last hour has shown me how well a Syrian can lie and fabricate ridiculous stories.... We all have many faces. In the blue hour we put on our blue faces, in the yellow hour, we put on our yellow faces, in the red hour we put on our red faces, and so on until we have exhausted all the colors of the rainbow.[45]

Miss Warda's sudden departure, "like someone who is running away from hell," is the most telling stage direction of the play. The rest of the company is left alone "silent, staring at the ceiling as if they were looking at a dreadful demon carrying a journal in which he had recorded everything they had said about Salim al-Marjani shortly before the night brought him into their midst."[46]

For Gibran, at that time, spending time with the Syrian community in New York must have been a difficult experience. He was always critical of his Syrian/Lebanese countrymen, as witnessed in his poem "My Countrymen," where he wrote:

> I hate you, My Countrymen, because
> You have glory and greatness. I
> Despise you because you despise
> Yourselves. I am your enemy, for
> You refuse to realize that you are
> The enemies of the goddesses.⁴⁷

    This short play is so remarkable because it breaks from the form, content, and language that identifies the majority of Gibran's writing. Gibran has been heavily criticized for his romanticism, sentimentalism, moralizing, and his deliberate and affected tone. As Gregory Orfalea and Sharif Elmusa rightly note, perhaps Gibran's strength may lie in his social and political works. *The Chameleons*, like his poem "My Countrymen," lashes out at some of his fellow Syrians/Lebanese for their attitudes regarding social status, for jealousy of those who have achieved success in America, and for the prejudices against those who dare to call themselves writers without the proper pedigree. Al-Marjani bears a striking resemblance to Gibran, and it seems painfully clear that Gibran inserted himself in this play in order to criticize his community from within his own personage. The fact that Gibran printed the play in *As-Sayeh*, a paper circulated widely within his Syrian community in New York, was a bold and defiant move on his part. According to Gibran biographers Suheil Bushrui and Joe Jenkins, Gibran became more and more isolated from the Syrian community in New York during the Ottoman siege of his homeland. He wrote to his benefactor and then-fiancée Mary Haskell, "I'm continually tortured by people's talking; I can't stop listening to what they say. A stream of words, words, words—just the workings of an active mind and a bubbling heart said without realization in the saying, gives me actual pain."⁴⁸ Given Gibran's bitterness toward his fellow Syrians in New York, it is little wonder that he would write a play like *The Chameleons*. Given his grief over the horrors his countrymen were enduring, his frustrations toward the Syrians in New York and their apathy toward the suffering, and the defamation he heard from the community, Gibran lashed out in one of the only ways he knew—as a dramatist.

    Gibran's play is important because it is a modern drama written in the language of the time, directly aimed at its audience. Like *Wajdah* before it, the play was never staged in Gibran's lifetime. The play must have been read by many in the Syrian community at that time and Gibran surely understood the consequences of its publication. Given that Gibran had written works that led to his excommunication from the Lebanese Maronite Church, perhaps he felt he had little left to lose by virtually excommunicating himself from his own community in the United States as well.

Mikhail Naimy's Parents and Children

Mikhail Naimy (1889–1988) is considered by many to be one of the greatest Arab American poets, fiction writers, critics, and biographers. In addition to his work in these areas, Naimy also wrote the play *Fathers and Sons* (1916, revised 1953) (translated by Takla as *Parents and Children*), *The Last Leaf* (1958), and *Job* (1967). Naimy was born in 1889 in the small Lebanese (then Syrian) mountain village of Baskinta, thirty-three miles from Beirut. His father, a farmer, immigrated to the United States, but returned to his homeland after finding little financial success. Naimy was raised in a devoutly Maronite Christian household and had an attachment to his home village that would last throughout his lifetime. Naimy was educated first in an Orthodox Christian school staffed by graduates of the Russian Teachers' Institute at Nazareth, Palestine. Seeing his promise, the schoolmasters invited Naimy to study at the Institute in Nazareth in 1902 where he was taught Arabic and Russian. While in Palestine, Naimy visited all of the Biblical sites he could and stated, "I have never doubted the truth concerning the miracles ascribed to Christ."[49] In 1906 Naimy was sent to Poltava, Ukraine, in order to join the Theological Seminary (a secondary school devoted to theological and ecclesiastical studies). There he was exposed to the poetry, short stories, and plays of the prominent Russian writers, including Lermontov, Turgenev, and Tolstoy. He attended operas and ballets, where he was impressed with the beauty of a Russian culture that contrasted greatly with the plight suffered by those in his homeland. According to Professor Nadeem Naimy, it was during his time in Tzarist Russia from 1906–1911 that Mikhail Naimy read Russian dramatists, particularly the plays of Chekhov and frequented theatre productions whenever possible. By 1911, Naimy's studies in Russia had come to an end and his world view had drastically changed, especially regarding an anti-establishment view of the Church. His return to Baskinta left him with a desire for more knowledge and experience. Naimy left for the United States to work with his brothers Najib and Adib, who owned a furniture store in Walla Walla, Washington. There he concentrated on his English studies, learning the spoken language and reading American literature. Upon receiving the periodical *al-Funun* (*The Arts*), he was inspired by the works of fellow Syrian writers Kahlil Gibran, Ameen Rihani, and Nasib Arida. He submitted articles that *al-Funun* published and that were well received. Naimy studied at the University of Washington from 1912–1916 under the name Michael Joseph Naimy, receiving a Bachelor of Laws degree in 1916, the same year he wrote *Parents and Children*.[50] He moved to New York and joined The Pen League while working odd jobs. He joined the U.S. Army during World War I out of a sense of duty and a desire to abide by the law. His experiences in battles during the war troubled him greatly and only strengthened his resolve as a pacifist. After the war he was sent to Rennes University in France where he studied French history, literature, and art. He returned to the United States once more, again working odd jobs, including selling *Encyclopaedia Britannica*, and continuing his writing. It was during this time that he worked in establishing The Pen League in New York with Nasib Arida, Kahlil Gibran, Raschid Ayoub, Wadi Bahout, and William Catzeflis, where he served as vice president. After several years in New York, Naimy returned to Walla Walla, where he took refuge in his little cabin by the river.

Although the play *Parents and Children* is of literary value to Arab American drama, it is Naimy's preface to the first edition that is of great theatrical interest since it explores Naimy's view of where Arab American drama is situated within the drama of the Arab world and the drama of Arabs in America. Naimy, who was part of the original Pen League, agreed with his fellow members Gibran and Rihani that the work of Arab American writers should remain in the interstitial space between Arab literature and American literature. Naimy wrote that some Arabs blamed Western civilization for injecting immorality and blasphemy into Arab lives, while others worship the West and everything it creates. Naimy prefers to remain neutral. "We will leave them to settle their differences with knives and axes, if they so wish, provided that they allow us to boldly admit to the superiority of the West in

Mikhail Naimy sculpture at his gravesite in Shakhroub, Lebanon (photograph by Rana Halabi Najjar).

one thing—its literature."[51] Naimy writes that the Arab literary renaissance, or *nahda*, was the result of Arab writers being influenced by Western writers who inspired new ideas and modes. Naimy writes, "Thanks to the West, we are now aware that there is more to poetry than love and eroticism, praise and defamation, lamentation and representation, vainglory and heroism."[52] The greatest contribution, in Naimy's estimation, is the novel that allowed Arab writers to "describe life and touch people's hearts and minds through the written word."[53] However, by 1916, Naimy believed that the Arab literary renaissance was still underdeveloped, mainly due to the fact that Arab literature had overlooked the significant field of drama. Naimy wrote of his praise for theatrical art, which I will quote at length:

> Drama has always been closely associated with Western literature and it has become one of its cornerstones. Westerners have erected theaters for it, and thus it has become a part of their daily lives like school, home and church. For in the theater, his soul, famished and overburdened with work and worries, finds rest, comfort, and enjoyment. His spirit is lifted from the endless mire of his life where the days all blend together and is transported to a world where human emotions roam freely, ranging from beautiful to ugly, weak to strong, honorable to contemptible. On stage before his very eyes, he sees people like himself fully engaged in the struggle for survival, revealing to him the untold secrets of their hearts and minds. He finds a part of the being he calls "I" embedded within their secrets, and he uses them to better himself and adds them to his treasury of life experiences. The playwright and actor—the first through his thoughts and the second through his speech and gestures—join forces to penetrate the sanctity of his solitude. They enter into the crevices of his heart and strike its deepest chords, as they rummage through the folds of his subconscious and set his thoughts in motion. Altogether, they awaken him with all the forces of his being, and he feels alive. Many a word falls on his ears and is immediately nestled in his mind and ripened in his soul; many a gesture on the part of the actor makes his heart tremble; many a scene shakes his entire being the way a storm shakes a tree from its roots.[54]

For Naimy, the playwright and the actor must work in a collaborative, symbiotic manner if they are to affect the audience: If one or the other is weak, the story loses its force and splendor. Because of the power of the theatre, he believed the West elevated the role of the actor over the playwright, lavishing them with gifts, fame, and honor. Conversely, in the Arab world, Naimy wrote that the theatre was viewed as nothing more than a coffee house, and actors were treated as no better than stuntmen and whores. Arab playwrights had not depicted scenes from life that the audiences of his time would have found familiar. He blamed the writers, not the people, for this since the playwrights of his time were content to only offer a few plays translated from other European languages into Arabic. In order to address this dilemma, Naimy proposed that a national theatre be created where scenes from daily life could be performed. "This will first require that our writers turn their attention to the life that they see around them everyday—with all its faults, all its joys and sorrows, all its beauty and ugliness, all its good and evil—and use this as material for their writing. For they will find that it is rich with material if they know how to look for it."55 Another difficulty was the misconception that theatre corrupted morals, especially for women.

Yet another deficit was the lack of playwrights and national plays. A remedy for this would be that playwrights write their characters in vernacular Arabic, as opposed to the more classical Arabic that pervaded the translations during his lifetime. "For the writer who attempts to make an illiterate peasant speak like a poet or a linguist does a great injustice to his farmer, himself, his reader and his listener. He makes his characters appear comical when no comedy is intended, and he commits a crime against an art whose beauty lies in depicting people the way in which we perceive them in real life."56 Naimy's solution was somewhat Shakespearean in nature: The educated characters in his play would speak in classical Arabic while the illiterate characters would speak in the vernacular. For other characters who fit neither mode, the style would be dictated by the character's personality and background. Naimy admitted, however, that this is not a perfect solution and called upon the greatest linguists and writers to work together in something like a literary council or academy to solve the dilemma for the future.

In his preface to the second edition of the play, Naimy returns to this question of classical versus vernacular Arabic. In his revision, he attempted to re-write all of the characters in classical Arabic, however, "each time, I felt like a boy who was forced to swallow a foul medicine."57 Naimy takes the blame for this inconsistency once again, writing, "The problem lies not in the playwright's need to use the vernacular in some parts of the play, but rather in our inability to accurately transcribe it and refine it with the means of communication available to us."58 He rightfully notes that Arabic dialects differ from country to country, region to region, and that, "in spite of ourselves, everything we write is colored with regionalism and sectarianism because of the constraints of these dialects."59 He notes that, if theatre makers wish to perform the play outside of Lebanon, they should translate his writing of Lebanese vernacular into their own vernacular dialects.

The diglossic debate over the use of "High"/classical Arabic (*fusha*) and "Low"/vernacular Arabic (*aamiyya*) in Arab drama is one that had been confounding playwrights as far back as the mid-nineteenth century. Marun al-Naqqash's 1847 translation of Moliere's *The Miser* (translated as *al-Bakhil*) was written primarily in classical Arabic with colloquial sayings scattered throughout the text. The published version of the play, edited by his brother, apologized for the use of colloquial Arabic and urged readers to see his other play *The Envious One* (*al-Hasud*) as proof that al-Naqqash knew proper Arabic language and grammar. According to Arab theatre scholar Elsaid Badawi, "By the end of the nineteenth century, hundreds of translated, adapted or original plays—some in Fusha, some in colloquial Arabic and some in a mixture of both—were staged."[60] The debate continued on throughout the twentieth century. What makes Naimy's play relevant in this debate is that it was the first to incorporate both the classical Arabic and colloquial Arabic languages within a play that was both original and specific to Naimy's own time.

In many ways, Naimy's play is reminiscent of the dramatic works of Turgenev and Chekhov, whose plays he surely encountered during his studies in Ukraine. In his autobiography *Seventy*, Naimy writes:

> I wanted to write a play and perfect the art of drama after I visited the theatre for the first time in Poltava, and there I saw and heard how plays and actors function. What, then, can I say about the opera, the ballet, of the freedom of unhindered movement between two bodies, in the home, in the street, and in the country?[61]

The play takes place at the beginning of the twentieth century in a small town in Mount Lebanon and revolves around the life of the Samaha household. Umm Illyass, widow of Butrus Bek Samaha, rules her house with an iron fist. Her oldest son, Ilyaas, her youngest son Khalil, and her daughter Zeina are all powerless within the household and are subject to their mother's rules. Another character, Naseef Bek, a wastrel who is engaged to Zeina, is also under the dictates of his father Musa Bek 'Arkoosh. The only other characters who are relatively free from the patriarchal/matriarchal structure are Dawud Salama, a poor schoolteacher, and his single sister Shaheeda. Given the dramatic circumstances, the play is more properly titled *Parents and Children* than it is *Fathers and Sons*. The title *Fathers and Sons* is meant as an homage to Turgenev, whom Naimy considered a great thinker and master of literature. Although Naimy claimed that the title was merely a point of departure for his work, it is clear that he adopted the dramatic structure of the late nineteenth-century Russian playwrights as the work is reminiscent of Turgenev's *A Month in the Country* and Chekhov's *Uncle Vanya*. He wrote the drama in three weeks and was fully aware that he was utilizing the title already made famous by Turgenev. He also realized that the struggle between generations is presented in an entirely different manner than that written in Tugenev's novel.[62]

I see nothing wrong in this. After all, the title is not original: On the contrary, it is perhaps the first thought that comes into the mind of any writer who wants to examine the conflicts between two generations. This title is not unlike, say, "Poetry and Poets," "East and West," "Life and Death," and so on. In such situations, where the titles and ideas are similar, what is required is a different approach to the theme.[63]

The play deals directly with intergenerational conflicts between parents and children, religious conflicts between the Church and the individual, societal conflicts between tradition and individual free will, and moral conflicts between goodness and profligacy. These theoretical themes are dramatized and embodied by Naimy's characters. On the side of tradition and the church are Umm Ilyaas, Khalil, Musa Bek 'Arkoosh, and Naseef Bek. On the side of free will and goodness are Ilyaas, Zeina, Dawud, and Shaheeda. In the play Naimy works to create a moral universe where the dogged pursuit of tradition, of societal custom, and of marriage that exists only to improve one's social status is in direct conflict with one's individualism, freedom to marry for love over money and status, and the importance of righteousness over profligacy. Naimy also makes a strong moral statement against the ills of sectarianism in Syrian/Lebanese society. As a playwright, Naimy understands the power of opposites in the theatre and utilizes both stage setting and characterization in order to portray the diametrically opposed nature of his characters.

The setting of the play symbolizes much about the world of Butrus Bek Samaha, Umm Illyaas, and of old Lebanese traditions. The living room contains swords, rifles, daggers, and spears along with pictures of saints and angels. Ilyaas invites Dawud into the household, and Dawud exclaims, "House?! This is a museum of antiquities." Ilyaas tells Dawud he despises war and its trappings, though his mother relishes displaying the weapons that were used to massacre many Druze, Mutawallis, and Kurds. Ilyaas is frustrated with living under the control of his mother, who symbolizes matriarchy in the play:

> I am on the verge of suffocating, Dawud. I am suffocating in a world that is stuck in the past and is blind to the present and future. I have begun to hate the past, present, and future. I have begun to consider life a burden, and my existence in this world just continues to deteriorate.[64]

For Ilyaas, suicide is preferable to the miserable life he is living. He asks Dawud, "What is the point of a life in which hardship far outweighs happiness, a life that begins in the darkness of a womb and ends in the darkness of a tomb?"[65] Worse still, his sister Zeina is forced to live a cloistered life and has been engaged, against her will, to Naseef, an unemployed gambler and rhymester who is only attractive to Umm Ilyaas because his father, Musa Bek al-'Arkoosh, is a nobleman in the town. What Umm Ilyaas does not know is that both Musa Bek and Naseef are destitute and are marrying only to acquire Umm Ilyaas's wealth.

Where Ilyaas represents cynicism and despair, Dawud represents knowledge and hope. Dawud does not ascribe himself to any religion (though he does call himself a Christian), which instantly casts him as a heretic in the eyes of Umm Ilyaas. Dawud, who, like Gibran's al-Marjani, is an obvious reflection of the playwright himself, responds, "I believe that Jesus, Moses and Muhammad are all equals. There is only one God in this world; he is the God of mankind. There is no Christian nor Muslim nor Jew." For Dawuud, the blind allegiance to one's parents is anathema to evolution:

> I am surprised that after all these years of studying, you still don't realize how normal it is for parents and their children to differ in their beliefs and dispositions. Without that, we wouldn't have what we call progress.... The saying is "Honor your father and mother," not "Obey your father and mother even when they are wrong." Obedience to truth is a virtue, but the struggle against falsehood is an even greater virtue. And falsehood can come from your mother just as it can come from a stranger. In either case, you have to fight it with all your might.[66]

Dawud and Ilyaas's opening philosophical discussion is one that could very well be taking place in the contemporary Arab world. Ilyaas reminds Dawud that his mother's prejudices represent her entire generation and are deeply rooted in the souls of the people. He tells Dawud that if he pulls out one root, a thousand will grow in its place. Dawud refuses Ilyaas's pessimism. "Those who want to cause destruction can destroy whatever they like," he tells Ilyaas. "That will not stop me from building. Moreover, I love destroying as much as I love building. If you don't destroy, you cannot build."[67] Naimy proves here his unwillingness to give in to the destructive impulses that were tearing his homeland apart.

Khalil, Ilyaas's younger brother, along with Naseef, represent the new generation that is mired in the prejudices of their parents' generation and believe in a life of hedonism. By creating these characters, Naimy is creating yet another set of dramatic conflicts that shows an intra-generational division between those who are educated and moral and those who may be educated, but prefer a life of leisure. By use of dramatic setting, Naimy explains much about his character Dawud. On the eastern wall of his home hangs a painting of Tolstoy and on the western wall a painting of Christ. These polar opposites—Tolstoy and Christ—are a perfect metaphor for the divergent interests that preoccupied Naimy. He strived for the purity of Christ in religion and the transcendence in literature found in Tolstoy. Shaheeda, Dawud's sister, is also pure of heart. She, like the other women of her generation, understands that the societal and religious traditions of her culture oppress women: "This is the story of our life here in the East," she tells Dawud. "A girl's parents marry her off without asking her opinion as if her wishes mean absolutely nothing."[68] Dawud, the eternal optimist, tells her "yes, this is the story of our life here in the East. But it needs to change and hopefully it will. It has to change because this generation was born into a different world than the one our parents were born into."[69]

Naseef, who is obviously educated and considers himself a poet, believes that he lives in an age of enlightenment and civilization, yet he finds no other occupation than gambling, drinking, and composing improvisational poetry. He tells his father, "You have a son who is renowned and you don't even know his worth or social stature. We were born in different eras—so how could you expect me to follow in your footsteps?" Musa Bek replies,

> You, the sons of this generation, learn how to conjugate verbs in school and then grow up thinking that you are philosophers and that your fathers are like a cracked water jug, not good for anything but breaking.... Lord save us from this generation. In all our lives and our grandparents' lives, we never heard of a girl disobeying her parents. Today they're coming up with all sorts of new ideas. One day, they say that marriage without love means nothing. Another day, they want to get married without a priest. Another day, they want to get divorced for no reason. Enough already. We're lucky God hasn't sent the heavens crashing down on us.[70]

The transformation that occurs in the fourth act begins to stretch the plot's and characters' plausibility. Umm Ilyaas's transformation from the rude, vengeful woman of the first half of the play to the kinder and gentler person in the latter half is due to Zeina's near-death illness and Shaheeda's overwhelming kindness. She relents on her desire for Zeina to marry Naseef Bey and even provides consent for her marriage to Dawud. The only part of her sudden transformation that seems plausible is her fear that others will speak badly of her if something happens to her daughter, thereby keeping consistent with her previous characterization. In another moment of *deus ex machina*, Naseef Bek and his father are thrown in debtor's prison, Khalil becomes a happy-go-lucky drunk who befriends Dawud, and both Dawud and Zeina and Ilyaas and Shaheeda are destined to be married. The most that Umm Ilyaas can say at the wondrous turn of events is, "My God, what a crazy world we live in."[71] Here, it seems, Naimy shows life not as it was, but as he hoped it could be.

Scholar Muhammad Badawi criticizes Naimy's play for its plot, characterizations, and dialogue. The play, he writes, is really no more than a melodramatic story with an unsatisfactory plot, shallow and unconvincing characterization, excessive abstract discussions and a seriously flawed dialogue in which, instead of opting for either the colloquial or the classical, Nu'aymah resorts (albeit inconsistently) to the method advocated by Farah Antun, that of making the educated speak in the literary idiom while putting the colloquial in the mouths of the rest, with artificial and at times downright ridiculous results, as when two brothers engaged in a conversation are not made to speak the same language.[72]

Scholar Aida Imangulieva agrees that the characters are poorly defined and that the Dawud character is less of a fully dimensional character and more a mouthpiece for the playwright's positive ideas. Although, as a scholar and playwright myself, I agree with both Badawi and Imangulieva's critiques, as a theatre director and theatre historian, I tend to view the play within its historical and dramatic context. First, the play was one of the first dramas written in its time in the Arabic language that spoke against the societal and religious norms that were tearing apart Syrian/Lebanese society. By contrast, the Arabic plays that preceded *Parents and Children* were mainly adaptations of other Western dramas and comedies written primarily in classical Arabic. Second, the use of classical Arabic for educated and noble characters and the colloquial Arabic for uneducated or peasant characters, while not a new device in world drama, was one that was new within the Arab dramatic context. Naimy was struggling to capture the language of the land he inhabited, and he found a solution that worked within this particular context. As for the play's unsatisfactory plot and shallow characterizations, the play, when viewed as a comedy, is actually consistent with the comedic romances of Shakespeare, such as *As You Like It*. Thinking of the seemingly incomprehensible reversals that occur in comedies by Shakespeare or Moliere clearly places *Parents and Children* within the romantic/comedic mode where characters change drastically when confronted with overwhelming emotions such as love or death. When viewed with this perspective it is clear that Naimy was not writing a drama in the Chekhovian mold (though it should be noted that Chekhov himself viewed his own plays as comedies); rather, he was writing a pastoral comedy that dealt with serious issues, but was meant ultimately to entertain its audience.

Rihani, Gibran, and Naimy were writers committed to reenvisioning their places in their respective Syrian/Lebanese societies as well as their places in the literary pantheon of the Arab world. Although none had trained as dramatists, they contributed important works of drama to the canon of Arab dramatic literature by introducing new plots instead of relying on translations of existing ones, by experimenting with language in order to fully convey both the social class structure and the dialects of their characters, and by melding the Arab literary traditions and histories with those familiar to Western audiences by incorporating styles found in the works of Shakespeare and other contemporary American and Russian dramatists. By doing so, these writers were instrumental in shaping the foundations of both Arab and Arab American drama. Despite their shortcomings, these are important plays for their respective time periods. Since none of these plays was staged during the writers' lifetimes, it is impossible to fully understand whether they are successful dramas. By examining these works solely as literature, only half of their true nature can be comprehended. Perhaps, in the future, after these works are produced, staged, and reviewed, a fuller accounting of their worth as works of theatre will be possible.

3

"There's nothing funny about your people": Arab American Comedy and Stand-Up Performance

Egyptian-American stand-up comedian Ahmed Ahmed struggled in Hollywood. A trained actor, Ahmed repeatedly found himself cast as a cab driver or a terrorist (his role in the film *Executive Decision* was literally "Terrorist #4"). Finally, Ahmed decided to take control of the narrative. He began writing and performing stand-up comedy routines. Once, a Hollywood executive told him, "There's nothing funny about your people." Little did this executive know that Arabs have been producing comedies in theatre since 1850 and on film since the 1940s. Arab American comedians have been part of the comedy landscape too, starting with Danny Thomas's 1944 routine titled "Ode to a Wailing Syrian." In many ways Ahmed, and his contemporaries, are just part of a long lineage of Arab comedy that has vibrant roots in Arab theatrical and filmic history.

Arab American stand-up comedy has proven the most successful of all Arab American art forms. The comics in this genre began in relative obscurity but, over time, found their way into more mainstream success. For some, like Danny Thomas, the journey often entailed having to work in small nightclubs for decades before success was at hand. For others, like Ahmed Ahmed, the price for fame was playing stereotypical nefarious Arab characters in Hollywood films. Other Arab American comics like Dean Obeidallah found careers in other media as political commentators and internet content producers. In all cases, these comics relied on the humorous accounting coping mechanism in order to meld their personal experiences with their comedic impulses.

Humorous Accounting and Danny Thomas's "Ode to a Wailing Syrian"

Marvasti and McKinney explain that humorous accounting is utilized when one is faced with questions regarding one's ethnic identity and humor is utilized to diffuse tense situations. This form of active resistance strategy is one that has been utilized by many ethnic groups, primarily through the uniquely American form of stand-up comedy. In his book *Stand-up Comedy in Theory, or, Abjection in America*, John Limon notes that, around 1960, Jewish men were the group who produced most of America's stand-up comedians. Like Shimakawa, Limon also utilizes the concept of abjection to mean two things: the first being abasement, or groveling prostration; the second meaning the aspects of self that cannot be eliminated. Limon states that abjection is "self-typecasting" and that "what is stood up in stand-up comedy is abjection ... comedy is a way of avowing and disavowing abjection."[1] Therefore, comedians such as Lenny Bruce and, later, Richard Pryor, utilized abjection as their self-identification in an abjected race.[2] Thus, they are not the sufferers of abjection but, rather, they *are* the abjection itself:

> Stand-up has the structure of abjection insofar as comedians are not allowed to be either natural or artificial.... Reality keeps returning to stand-up performance, but the deepest desire of stand-ups is to be, with respect to their lives, unencumbered. All a stand-up's life feels abject to him or her, and stand-ups try to escape it by living it as an act.[3]

As with so many of the counter-cultural trends that arose in the United States, the stand-up comedy of the early twenty-first century came into existence during the late 1960s. Limon asserts that the contemporary stand-up tradition was made through the black body, the homosexual body, and the female body. Jewish and Protestant comedians took the human body and converted it into a gag, thereby abstracting its essence.[4] A theory of stand-up is a theory of what to do with your abjection at a moment of cultural history when abjection is startlingly pervasive. For Arab Americans, their particular moment of cultural history came after 9/11, and one of the major ways Arab Americans dealt with their abjection after 9/11 was through stand-up and sketch comedy. Long before that time the first Arab American stand-up comedian, Danny Thomas, created a fascinating comedic routine that combined Syrian history, the Arabic language, and his own experiences as a frustrated nightclub performer.

Danny Thomas and "Ode to a Wailing Syrian/Lebanese"

Danny Thomas's "Ode to a Wailing Syrian," also known as "Ode to a Wailing Lebanese," was his hallmark nightclub act that was reviewed by *LIFE Magazine* as early as 1944 and was performed live on television for *The All Star Revue* as late as 1951. In 1943, *LIFE Magazine* wrote that Thomas was "probably 1943's most promising new cabaret comic" and that "Ode to a Wailing Syrian" was "the funniest of his numbers."[5] Thomas, who was born to Lebanese parents, composed, enacted, and directed his first burlesque show in high school, which Thomas said was his true beginning.[6] Thomas began his professional career as a "would-be radio actor working in beer gardens."[7] Thomas recounts that he was desperate to be in show business, and he was repeatedly told he would never be successful. Thomas suffered so many setbacks that, at one point, he considered committing suicide. Then, upon meeting a friend whose wife was cured of cancer due to the intercession of St. Jude, Thomas made a vow that, if he succeeded in show business, he would build a shrine in St. Jude's honor. After moving to Chicago and working in nightclubs, one success followed another. He changed his birth name, Amos Jacobs, to Danny Thomas, an amalgam of his brothers' first names. Thomas later made good on his vow, creating St. Jude Children's Research Hospital in Memphis, Tennessee, which opened its doors in 1962. Today, St. Jude is internationally recognized for its work in the research and treatment of children who have cancer and other malefic diseases.

It was in his early years as a writer and performer that Thomas perfected his nightclub act that included "An Ode to a Wailing Syrian," which Thomas called "a brand-new idea, completely offbeat for a comedian."[8] What is most remarkable about Thomas's act is that it begins with a long lamentation spoken entirely in perfect Levantine colloquial Arabic. According to Thomas, the skit was created in a nightclub and was based on Tchaikovsky's "Arabian Fantasy of the Nutcracker Suite" and the clarinet cadenza from "Samson and Delilah."[9] In the act, Thomas equates the hanging death of a politically minded troubadour living under Ottoman occupation with his own struggles as a nightclub comedian struggling to make a career. The act combines deep pathos through the lamentable wail of the doomed Syrian singer with Thomas's own zany acting, singing, and dancing playing himself as a down-and-out comedian struggling against tyrannical nightclub owners. The only recorded version of the routine is the October 13, 1951, episode of NBC's *All Star Revue*, a show that Thomas also hosted.[10] During that taping Thomas opened the show with an altered version of the act. The show's announcer says in a large voice, "And tonight—Danny Thomas, the wailing Lebanese!" Smoke fills the screen and Orientalized music plays. Thomas appears from the smoke wearing a white sheet over his head, singing in a large voice, "As-salam aleykum, ahlan wa sahlan feekum ya ahl-Amrika!" which is an Arabic saying that translates to "Peace be upon you and welcome people of America!" He then begins introducing the guests.

Much later in the program, Thomas returns to the set wearing a tuxedo with a large orchestra in the pit and many seated guests sitting behind him as if in a large nightclub. Thomas launches into an introduction where he explains the piece. He first notes the influences of Tchaikovsky and Saint-Saens, then explains where the story originated:

> Lyrically, my friends, it is based upon an actual execution. And this is a true story. I beg you to believe it. The story is fast becoming legend amongst the Arabic and Hebraic speaking peoples of the world. It happened in the holy land. The year nineteen-hundred fourteen. When a compatriot of my father's, a Lebanese, was executed for singing propaganda against the government. The man was a street singer who roamed the streets singing for his daily bread. And every now and again he would extemporize a song against the government. They finally caught up with him and hanged him. And on the gallows, he extemporized this song. Incidentally, they say the song was recorded on the spot, the record later given to his widow. She, in turn, had over a million copies made and sold.[11]

Thomas then pauses, laughs, and says, "That's not really true but you were so quiet you scared me! But up until the part about the records, I swear this is a true story. I hope you find interest in it. This is the song he sang."[12] The audience joins him in his laughter, primarily because he is so serious in his delivery.

One might believe the entire story were not true, however, Thomas then places a sheet he has pulled from one of the cocktail tables over his head and begins a deeply moving and incantatory wail in colloquial Arabic that sounds as authentic as any Greek tragic ode. Thomas performs this with flawless Lebanese-Arabic dialect and with the seriousness one might expect from a classical tragedy. He then pauses, looks at another camera and says, "Oh, you poor English speaking people!"[13] The audience bursts out laughing. He then translates the Arabic incantation, explaining that these were the last words of a man to his wife as he stood on the scaffold before his execution. Thomas then asks, "Now what does all this have to do with my place as a saloon entertainer, you are probably wondering. Those of you who are seeing me for the first time I'm sure are saying to yourselves 'This kid has flipped his lid!'"[14] Again, the audience roars with laughter.

Thomas then goes on to explain how, eleven years prior, he was working in a small nightclub in Chicago for "a maniac who wouldn't give you one night off." He then recounts how he worked from the club circuit to the legitimate stage to Hollywood films and finally to television. "And yet, with all of these minor accomplishments, my friends, you find me where fate and destiny have decreed I belong—in a saloon! A television saloon yet!" He laments the fact that, as a nightclub performer he was never given a night off and, as a television performer, he still works endless hours. Breaking into a Russian accent, he decries the management, calling them "stinking bosses!" and vows that the peasants sitting in the back of the theatre will someday be allowed to sit in the front of the house "come the day of reckoning." He jokes with the nightclub "guests" onstage, sings nonsensical lyrics, dances in a silly manner, and recites limericks. He again returns to speaking and singing in Arabic:

> *Ya Habeebi*! That means, my lover. *Ya Habeebi*, ya habeebi, ya habeebi! That means, my lover, my lover, my lover. I didn't want you to be in the dark. *Ya salaam, salami*! Salaam, that means "peace." Salami, you know what that is. Put the two together comes out piece of salami. If you have been listening attentively thus far you have heard in an ancient tongue "my lover, my lover, my lover, give me a piece of salami!"[15]

Again, Thomas incorporates Arabic into his routine, oscillating between speaking and singing in Arabic and translating the lyrics for the audience while twisting and perverting the meaning of the translation. After another bit where he beats his microphone with a dinner roll, he begins to sing (with full voice) the final passage of the skit, "So you see, my friends, I have only, I have only to lament. So this is my lament! Yes this is a lament of a fool you see! Just a fool! That's me!"[16] The music crescendos and the audience laughs and applauds. The act must have been important at the time since the producers were willing to allow Thomas not only to perform a version of it on prime-time television but also to utilize it as the opening for the entire broadcast.

By most accounts, Thomas's act was a hit from its inception. Reading several reviews of the piece from 1944 to 1950, the skit was uniformly praised. *LIFE Magazine* wrote, "The almost childlike quality of his humor is fresh and exciting."[17] *Billboard* magazine wrote, "He's one of the few comics around who can take a standard gag and build it into a routine that just about kills 'em." Thomas was praised for his ability to switch from seriousness to subtleness. Regarding a 1946 version of the routine, a critic wrote:

> So far as his *Ode to a Wailing Syrian* is concerned, it's still a classic.... He works all kinds of bits into this routine, a couple of limericks, a talk on nightclub bookkeeping, a lecture on the downtrodden man. The tablecloth prop heightens the

effect of the worm that turned who subsequently got stepped on. The hands he got on his walk-off could be heard in the street. Boy has improved so much that there is no comparison between the Thomas caught here a few years ago and the Thomas of today. He's a comic today, a great comic.[18]

By 1950 *Billboard* wrote that Thomas was playing to packed houses, was called back for three encores, and "knocking them out every show."[19] By 1951, the television industry hired Thomas, making him a national star. Thomas wrote about how he came to create his "Ode" in a November 1955 issue of *The American Magazine*:

> Jerking a tablecloth from a table and draping it around my head like a shawl, I cried out against the burdens of the common man. And me, I was plenty common. Condensed into the wail was the story of my own hard times, from Cherry Street to now, but with only the funny aspects showing. The louder I moaned, the more hysterical was the audience's laughter. Why? Since all of us have our troubles and poking fun at misfortune makes it disappear, every man and woman in the 5100 Club was casting off his grievances by seeing the humor in them and I stood there denouncing my fate. We were brothers and sisters under that tablecloth.[20]

Thomas's "Ode to a Wailing Syrian" is fascinating because it mixes Arabic and English, pathos and comedy, and the past and the present. Given the current political situation, it is difficult to imagine that any comic performer could speak in Arabic for long stretches of time on a prime-time television program. Being a comedian, it is interesting that Thomas could be so serious in both his subject matter and his delivery. Furthermore, Thomas melds the story of a man who was of his father's generation, fighting for liberation from the Ottomans with his own trials as a nightclub performer. Viewing the performance now it is difficult to understand how or why the audience found it so hilarious given its serious content, or how an American audience in the 1940s and 1950s would be open to that much of a foreign language being sung and spoken to them as entertainment. In his autobiography, *Make Room for Danny*, Thomas recounts that his "Ode" skit was cut down to seven minutes by the producer of *The All Star Revue*, about which Thomas said, "it took me seven minutes to get into the nub of the routine—basically the absolutely necessary introduction, so the audience would know what I was talking about."[21] Given that assessment, the extant recording is really only a condensed version of the much longer routine that ran almost an hour in length. According to entertainment writer Marla Brooks, Thomas's act was "a dismal failure on TV" and led Thomas to criticize television as being suitable "only for idiots!" He vowed never to return to television. According to Brooks, "A detailed storyteller by nature, the mere seven minutes he was allowed to do any of his famous routines, like 'Ode to a Wailing Syrian' was barely enough time to set the story up, much less tell the whole tale, so he opted out and went back to his beloved saloons—as he called the nightclubs."[22] According to Thomas, in 1942 he was booked to perform at a benefit show at Madison Square Garden where he performed his "Ode." After being mistakenly introduced as Danny Kaye, he performed his "Ode to a Wailing Syrian." Thomas recollected, "I was out there almost an hour, the audience refusing to let me go, and the next day Ed Sullivan opened his Broadway column with, 'A new star is born.'"[23] Of course, after several years, Thomas did return with his *The Danny Thomas Show* (*aka Make Room for Daddy*) that ran from 1953 to 1971. It is a testament to Thomas's talent as a performer that he could integrate such varied material, could perform the material so expertly, and could find a way to transform such material into a performance that would garner national attention.

In many ways, Thomas was also performing a type of resistance by the incorporation of the peasant's lament in Arabic. The period from which Thomas drew his characterization, the Ottoman rule of Greater Syria, was one of great difficulty for the Syrian people, especially between 1914 and 1918 when the Ottomans conscripted hundreds of thousands of men to fight in World War I. Much like Gibran before him, Thomas recounts the Ottoman rule as one of the greatest tragedies in the history of what was then Greater Syria. Hundreds of thousands died of famine, which led to a revolt against the Ottoman army and later led to the summary executions Thomas refers to in his act.[24] As mentioned in the previous chapter, many prominent intellectuals were killed for their participation in this revolt, including the journalist Petro Paouli, who performed in Rihani's first play. If the street singer in Thomas's act was, in fact, a compatriot of his father's, Thomas is harkening back to the dark and painful history of the Syrian famine and revolt.[25] The most inaccurate aspect of Thomas's performance is that he wears the tablecloth over his head as a female might wear a *hijab*. If this story was about a man, as Thomas says it was, the male would not be wearing such a *hijab*. Thomas elides the difference between Arab men and womens' dress, thereby either confusing or misrepresenting the culture he was representing. Of course, the piece was meant for entertainment, but through this one costume/prop choice, Thomas may have inadvertently confused rather than enlightened his audiences regarding Arab customs and dress.

What is clear from the performance is that Thomas was an incredible performer, able to mix pathos and comedy, to sing with complete confidence and ability, and to capture an audience's attention for long periods of time. It may have been fortuitous for Thomas that he was rejected early on for this routine because that allowed him more time to hone his skills, which led to his later successes. Of course, his successful television work would force Thomas back into the proverbial closet since few of his later works had any traces of Arabness to them. Thomas's 1966 television special *The Road to Lebanon* (in which he costarred with Bing Crosby) was an outrageously Orientalized variety show with egregious Arab stereotypes, many performed by Thomas himself. Thomas's performance of "Ode to a Wailing Syrian/Lebanese," like many of the Arab American works that followed, demonstrates how these writers and performers were able to combine the political with the personal, Arabic with English, and pathos with comedy. However, these works also demonstrate how these performers were co-opted by television producers to reproduce atrocious Arab stereotypes in later films and television series.

Danny Thomas performs his "Ode to a Wailing Syrian." The image appeared in *LIFE Magazine*, January 10, 1944 (photograph by George Karger/Time & Life Images).

S. K. Hershewe's An Oasis in Manhattan

S. K. (Sober Khalil) Hershewe was the first professional Arab American theatrical playwright, and his play *An Oasis in Manhattan* was the first professionally produced play. Early in his career, people knew him by his nickname "Hershey." Hershewe, the son of Lebanese parents Oscar and Shafeeka, who emigrated in 1898 from Lebanon, was born in Ft. Dodge, Iowa. He was the youngest of six children, and served in the U.S. military in Africa and Italy during World War II. After returning from the war, he studied theatre at Southern Methodist University (SMU) where he met his wife Winnie. They married in the Episcopalian chapel at SMU and the reception was held at the Margo Jones Theatre in Dallas. He and his wife moved to New York where he worked as an actor. They moved to Los Angeles in 1961. They had three sons: Ron, Jamil, and Michael.

Hershewe began writing plays after the writer Ronald Alexander told him, "All you need is a yellow legal sheet and a bunch of number two pencils."

NBC offered Hershewe $10,000 for his teleplay *A Toy for Carmen*, but Hershewe refused the offer since he would have no control over the script after its sale. He was also head of the Playwrights Unit of the Actors Studio from 1972 to 1974 until Hershewe and fifty other playwrights had a falling out with Lee Strasberg after Strasberg cancelled The Playwrights Unit. "The emphasis at the studio is on the actors," Hershewe told the *Los Angeles Times* in 1974. "Which is fine, but then don't pretend to be anything else. We were constantly being reminded that the Actors Studio is for actors, not playwrights." For Strasberg, cancelling the Unit was best for the studio since he "did not feel the unit was sufficiently exciting and interesting to satisfy the standards of the studio." Hershewe moved the Unit to the Odyssey Theatre in West Los Angeles and renamed the group the National Playwrights Company.[26] Hershewe's biography claims that he had written for labor magazines, industrial films, television, movie scripts and stage plays.[27] He had open heart surgery in 1987, and recovered quickly, only to relapse due to a staph infection. After recovering, Hershewe never wrote again. He passed away from heart failure at his home in Carmel-by-the-Sea, California, on October 14, 2005.

In 1965 Hershewe produced his play *An Oasis in Manhattan* at the Stage Society Theater in Los Angeles starring Alan Reed, Magda Harout, and a young Vic Tayback. The play was directed by Mesrop Kesdekain. The preview for the play touted that "Hershewe based his play on incidents in his own early life as a member of a large and spirited Lebanese family."[28] The *Los Angeles Times* reviewer wrote, "There's a tendency to dismiss 'Oasis in Manhattan' as 'Abie's Lebanese Rose,' but the play won't let you. There's too much vitality and churning life and genuine humor in S. K. Hershewe's new comedy.... The thing you most object to is the moth-eaten premise of the daughter of a Lebanese family who chooses a Jewish boy for a mate with the resultant family explosion." The review praised Alan Reed's performance, but the play itself was criticized for an ending that was "a bit too pat and predictable, the passions dissolving into soapsuds."[29] For his part, Alan Reed, who was best known as a radio actor and as the voice of the cartoon character Fred Flintstone, said of the play, "Sure, you have a feeling you've seen his play before, but it has a warm, real quality. I think that's very much needed today."[30] Reed had hoped the play would be transferred to New York, but that never happened. According to Hershewe, the play was a success until the 1967 Arab-Israeli War had "dampened the interest" of audiences at the time.[31]

Hershewe and Richard Fulvio ran the Venture Theatre in Burbank that produced a variety of works. The play enjoyed a revival twenty-five years later when veteran Arab American actor Vic Tayback produced and starred in the play at the Venture Theater, directed by T. J. Castronovo. Tayback was best known for his role as Mel Sharples in the hit television series *Alice*, yet few know that Tayback also had a thirty-three-year career as a film, television, and stage actor. His films included *Bullitt, Papillon, The Gambler,* and *The Choirboys*. He also appeared in many television series including *Mission: Impossible, Star Trek, The Man from U.N.C.L.E., The Mary Tyler Moore Show, All in the Family, The Love Boat,* and *Fantasy Island*. His stage productions included *12 Angry Men, The Diary of Anne Frank,* and *Death of a Salesman*. Tayback, whose original name was Victor Tabbak, was born in 1930 to Syrian-immigrant parents. In 1959, Along with Richard Chamberlain, Leonard Nimoy, and Vic Morrow, Tayback co-founded the renowned Los Angeles theatre, Company of Angels.[32] Tayback's performance in *An Oasis in Manhattan* was widely praised by many newspapers that noted his masterful interpretation, his energetic performance, and his comic timing. *Los Angeles Times* reviewer T.H. McCulloh wrote that "Vic Tayback is a charmer as patriarch of a Lebanese family.... Tayback's performance holds it all together."[33] *Drama-Logue* wrote, "Taybeck [*sic*] is solidly splendid for the course of this two-hour-plus play. He has a few bad moments at the end of Act Two.... Other than this scenery-chewing, his is a masterful interpretation of a father too proud to bend to new winds and too loving not to make the ultimate compromise."[34] For Tayback, the play represented more than mere entertainment—it was a statement that he believed needed to be made given the ongoing Arab-Israeli conflict. "The play's message is that it's the kids who are going to take us away from prejudice between Arabs and Jews."[35] Tayback's interest in the Arab-Israeli conflict went far beyond the play *An Oasis in Manhattan*, prompting Tayback to work on his own comedic television script titled *St. Louie & Moh* in 1986. Tayback pitched the idea of his series this way:

> Arabs and Jews have been on opposite sides of many different issues and events for more centuries than either cares to remember. Throughout these centuries, there have been actual reports of Jews and Arabs who actually live in peace, with each other, who really laugh together at the same things, and some who even loved each other.[36]

Tayback's story for the TV pilot concerned an Arab and a Jew who operate a small deli/grocery store in St. Louis. This "odd couple" relationship is filled with arguments, yet there is love and respect between the characters. "Their areas of conflict are not related to the problems in the Mideast; instead, they contend as partners; two men, like Art Carney and Jackie Gleason, whose 'Honeymoon' is over."[37] In Tayback's personal notes on the project he wrote, "I think this type of show is over-due—I think it's needed—I think America

Youssef (Vic Tayback, left) is baffled by Richard (Bryan Kovacs) in the 1990 revival of S.K. Hershewe's *An Oasis in Manhattan*, directed by T.J. Castronovo, performed at the Venture Theatre in 1990 (courtesy Christopher Tayback).

is ready for it—I think it's a network's duty to show a *Positive* Arab-Jew Situation."[38] According to comments written by an unknown Hollywood executive found in Tayback's personal papers, the presentation was neither warmly received nor accepted. The script was never green-lighted for production.

As mentioned by the reviews, Hershewe's plot for *An Oasis in Manhattan* was hardly original. As noted by reviewers, many comparisons were made to Anne Nichols's 1922 play *Abie's Irish Rose*. The plot also resembles Kaufman and Hart's 1936 play *You Can't Take It with You*. The play opens in the New York City home of Youssef and Nijma Joseph, Lebanese immigrants who have two daughters, Olga and Miriam, both of whom were born in the United States. Olga, the older daughter, is dating a young Lebanese American named Freddie Beshare and Miriam is dating an Irish American boy named Richard Kelly. The play also features Youssef's sister Mary who is married to a Lebanese man named Benny Haddad. Unbeknownst to everyone, Olga is actually engaged to Freddie Schroeder, a Jewish boy with whom she is in love. Youssef is a mercurial man who has a bullish exterior and a kind heart; he's also determined to marry his daughters to good Lebanese boys. Upon learning that his daughter Miriam is dating Richard, he assaults the boy with Lebanese food and drink (including *kibbeh*, a raw meat delicacy) and drives him from the house. Olga successfully deceives her parents by pretending to be dating Freddie Beshare while secretly engaged to Freddie Schroeder. By the time Freddie arrives with his parents Seymour and Selma for the engagement party, Youssef becomes completely irate and irrational, and swears he will disown his daughter and never speak with her again. When Olga leaves the house Youssef believes he is dying, despite the fact that Doctor Kaplan assures everyone there is nothing wrong with the man. The final act is the reconciliation between Youssef, Freddie, and Olga with the final scene climaxing in an argument over whether a rabbi or a priest will officiate the wedding.

What makes this play important for its time is that it was a successful production written by an Arab American that provided a glimpse into the lives and culture of Arabs in America. Only one other play, Harry Chapman Ford's 1921 drama *Anna Ascends*, which premiered on Broadway and was later released as a silent film starring Rudolph Valentino, had given non–Arab audiences a glimpse into the lives of Arabs. In his article, "Why I Wrote a Syrian Play," Ford explains that he wrote the play based on a Syrian family he met in 1921 living in Washington, D.C. Ford wrote, "Their family life, their clean way of living impressed me and I decided that the Americanization of such a race was a big factor in making 'the melting pot' one of the greatest nations of history."[39] Ford also claims that the Syrians are a people who were reading and writing six-thousand years before Europeans and who have fewer people in prisons than any other in the world. He based his play on a young woman he met in a Syrian restaurant whom he befriended, taught English, and who went on to marry a wealthy Anglo-Saxon man and had four children.[40] That play, however, was written by a non–Arab about an Arab family. Hershewe's comedy is based, in part, on Hershewe's own experiences growing up in a Lebanese household. During the 1990 revival, Hershewe stated that "the time is right. In 1966 no one had ever heard of Lebanon. They sure have now. Besides that, all statistics point to intermarriage in the U.S., and 'Oasis' sets the scene."[41]

Hershewe's play is set in the Joseph household which contains many of the items one might find in a Lebanese home: dark brown cedar chairs inlaid with mother of pearl, *darbakee* drums, *Arkaley* water pipes, Oriental rugs, bottles of *arak*, and old scimitars. The characters also speak some Arabic, dance the *dabkee*, eat Lebanese food, and recite old stories from the homeland. Much like the play *Anna Ascends*, the main issue *An Oasis in Manhattan* presents is the tension between isolationism and assimilation. In her analysis of Ford's play, Gualtieri writes,

Anna is indeed a strong and likeable character, yet her story involves the *effacement* of her Syrian identity, not the retention of it. The film's message was antipluralist and assimilationist: Syrians could become Americans, but they would have to lose their language, history, and culture in order to do so. This was the "price of the ticket" for entry into the American mainstream.[42]

Likewise, Hershewe's play contrasts the old values of the parents' generation (adherence to cultural norms, retention of cultural values, and endogamy) against the new values of the younger generation (rejection of cultural norms, loss of the Arabic language, and exogamy). Given Hershewe's theme that love conquers all, either the Arab/Christian family loses their Arabness and their Christian faith, or the Jewish family loses their Jewishness and their Judaism, or both. The Lebanese American children have already given up on learning their parents' language, eating their mother's cooking, and dating other Lebanese.

Playwright S.K. Hershewe at work (courtesy Winnie Hershewe).

The play refers to the fact that there is prejudice against Arabs that prompts feelings of ambivalence within the characters. When Freddie Beshara tells Youssef that his father hates eating garlic, Youssef responds, "He's afraid the American people smell him and then they don't buy his life insurance. If you ask me, he become Americanized too damn fast."[43] When Miriam tells her father to forget the old country, he responds, "Forget Lebanon? (*He turns toward and points to the picture of his father and mother*) If your grandmother could hear you she would step down and give you a licking you'll never forget. Now you say you're sorry!" When Youssef believes Beshara has sent Olga flowers he complains that he has become too Americanized by spending his money on "damn foolishness." When the family believes that Youssef is about to die, one of the characters asks that his body be returned to the house for a traditional funeral so that the Americans would not laugh at the Lebanese funerary customs. Youssef is also prejudiced against non–Lebanese such as Greeks, Armenians, and Jews. In a 1990 interview, Tayback said,

> Those kinds of attitudes are a universal thing. People come over from another country and try to hold onto things from there. Youssef is definitely bigoted, but it's not against any particular race. He talks about Armenians, Greeks, Jews, Swedes, Italians, Irish and Turks—basically anybody who isn't Lebanese isn't OK. The play's message is that it's the kids who are going to take us away from that prejudice.[44]

Hershewe and Tayback, both second generation Arab Americans, viewed the assimilationist model as one that would remove Arabs in America from the prejudices of sectarianism that they brought with them when they immigrated. Where the first generations of Arab immigrants still retained cultural traditions, they also remained patriarchal, prejudiced, and inflexible. By contrast, their children who were born and raised in America would adopt American values that encourage liberalism, acceptance, and the notion of marrying for love.

Being a comedy, Hershewe's play begins with Youssef being completely intransigent in his views to his gradual transformation toward acceptance by the final curtain. In the final act it is revealed that Youssef "destroyed a village" for Nijma's love. By the end of the play Youssef's desire for the retention of his culture and beliefs is overcome by his desire for his daughter to be in love. As with Naimy's romantic ending to *Parents and Children*, Hershewe also undercuts Youssef's character and the dramatic tension that had been building throughout the play by a sudden reversal that seems implausible. As with *Anna Ascends*, the message of assimilation and unity prevails despite the protagonist's best intentions. In her book *Becoming American: the Early Arab Immigrant Experience*, pioneering Arab American scholar Alixa Naff writes about the changing values of first-generation immigrants:

> The persistent identification with the homeland continued to wane; loyalty to America began to take precedence. The pioneer generation registered its rush to assimilate in the saying "We came to America to become Americans and we exceeded." They will say it about themselves, often critically and sarcastically, when they reflect on how readily they adopted American ways without fully integrating them.[45]

Hershewe's play, written before the events of 1967, represents a lighthearted comedy designed to entertain American audiences and to give them a glimpse into the world of Lebanese/Arab culture. Tayback's 1990 revival of the play and his unproduced teleplay were also intended to entertain, but with a greater purpose of bridging the gap between Arabs and Jews that had been widening for decades prior. By promoting a comedic, assimilationist stance, these artists were working to overcome the caustic Arab-Jewish tensions they perceived around them in the entertainment industry and in the society in which they lived.

AJYAL Theatrical Group and Im Hussein

Dearborn-based theatre company *AJYAL (Generations)* Theatrical Group was founded by producer, director, actor, and writer Najee Mondalek in 1988. According to their website,

> Most of AJYAL Theatrical Group' [sic] shows poke fun at the everyday lives of Arab-Americans, who have recently become citizens and who are desperately trying to blend into the mainstream of American culture. The plays serve as a forum to help people laugh at their mistakes and mishaps but also to come to terms with social issues facing Arab-Americans, such as their difficulties adjusting to a new culture and lifestyle. These performances, like music, art and other entertainment media, are a very important piece of the fabric of Arab-American culture.[46]

Mondalek was born in Marjayoun, Lebanon, before the Lebanese Civil War. He immigrated to the United States in 1985 and received his Associates degree from Macomb Community College in 1988. He also holds a Bachelor's degree in Mass Communications, and a Master's degree in Virtual Reality, 3D Animation, and Visualization. While still a student at Macomb Community College, Mondalek began writing plays. In all, Mondalek has written, produced, and acted in twelve comedies over a twenty-five-year span: *What a Shame* (1989), *Students Nowadays* (1990), *Honest Thieves* (1991), *Smile You're in Dearborn* (1993), *We Became American* (1996), *Come See...Come Saw* (1998), *Happy Bairday* (1999–2000), *Me No Terrorist* (2001–2004), *Arabic & Broud* (2005–2006), and *Where Does It Hurt* (2012–2013). The plays tour throughout North America, and there have also been several international tours as well. The plays, and Mondalek's alter-ego Im Hussein, are well known throughout the Arab American community, and the shows usually sell-out wherever they play. Mondalek also records the productions and sells the DVDs on the www.ajyal.us website. The ensemble is made up of several other Arab American actors: Rima Amine, Nader Aoude, Hassan Haj, Rabih Jaber, Rodney Karromi, Christine Mondalek, Michael Modalek, Ayman, Safaoui, and Rita Srour.

Mondalek plays (in drag) a Lebanese matriarch named Im Hussein (mother of Hussein), a woman who mostly dresses in a floral-patterned, brightly colored *abaya*, a head scarf, and thick rimmed glasses with caked on makeup. The character is married to her hapless husband Abou Hussein (father of Hussein) who often dresses in cheap suits, an oversized knit hat, and sports a handlebar moustache. Im Hussein's best friends, Im Elias (mother of Elias) and Abou Elias (father of Elias), round out the main characters in the comedies. The rest of the cast are comprised of colorful characters who are both Arab and non–Arab. The Im Hussein character first appeared in a brief skit in Mondalek's play *Smile You're in Dearborn*. The character was so popular with audiences that Mondalek rewrote the character as a lead role in all of his future plays.

Mondalek's plays are primarily written in Arabic, but several combine English and Arabic into a hybrid language Mondalek calls *Arabeezi* (combining the Arabic words for the Arabic language and English languages he calls *Engleezi*). This is how Mondalek describes his newly minted language:

Najee Mondalek as the matriarch known as Im Hussein (photograph by AJYAL Theatrical Group, courtesy Sarah Bazzi).

When I started writing *Smile You're in America*, I was faced with a small problem: we all read, write, and speak and understand Arabic. However, in the new and growing generation born here, or those who came here when they were young, there are some who read Arabic, there are some who write Arabic, and there are some who understand Arabic but the majority neither read, write, and maybe even do not understand Arabic. So the difficulty arose as to which road we would choose in order to attract this new generation. I wondered, should I write the play in Arabic or in English? So I ultimately decided to write the play in the language of *Arabeezi*. *Arabeezi* is Arabic and English combined, and all of us have started speaking *Arabeezi*. A woman walks into a place and says "Do you speak *Arabee* (Arabic)?" This is *Arabeezi*. Or another woman who is crossing the street shouts out to her husband "*Ya Yussef, wayn paraked al-Sayaara, ya Yussef*?" ("Hey Yussef, where did you park the car, Yussef!") This is what we call *Arabeezi*.[47]

Mondalek uses this mixture of Arabic and English to reflect the bi-cultural language that many Arabs speak in their daily lives. Mondalek uses this hybrid language to great comic effect, especially when his lead character Im Hussein speaks with American characters who neither speak nor understand Arabic. In one exchange, after Im Hussein and her husband return from a trip to their Lebanese homeland, they are stopped at customs and asked to declare any items they are bringing to the country. Im Hussein struggles to be understood by the increasingly frustrated customs agent. Im Hussein and her husband argue back and forth in Arabic until the agent asks if they have any food in the luggage. Im Hussein rattles off a litany of Arabic foods she's brought back with her from her travels, but focuses on one particular item:

IM HUSSEIN: We have *peanus* in ze luggage.
AGENT: You have *what*!
IM HUSSEIN: We have *peanus*.
AGENT: You have what?
IM HUSSEIN: We have *peanus* in the luggage.
AGENT: Hold on. You have *penis* in your luggage?
IM HUSSEIN: Yes, we have *peanus* in the luggage.
AGENT: Ma'am, why do you have penis in your luggage?
IM HUSSEIN: It's a gift.
AGENT: A gift!
IM HUSSEIN: It is for my son.
AGENT: For your son?
IM HUSSEIN: Yeah, my son loves to eat *peanus*.
AGENT: Your son eats penis?
IM HUSSEIN: Yes, every night before he go to bed. He drink *arak* and he eats *peanus*.

The combined use of Arabic and English, the intermittent use of rhyming Arabic proverbs, the comical costumes and acting, and the use of malapropisms all contribute to creating situations that are both comical and outrageous. Mondalek's plays also include interludes that contain Arabic song and dance, also adding to their entertainment for primarily Arab-speaking audiences.

Mondalek's character Im Hussein follows in a long tradition of British and American male actors playing older matriarchs such as Barry Humphries' Dame Edna, Tyler Perry's Medea, Eddie Murphy's Mama Klump, and Martin Lawrence's Big Momma. These entertainers rely on the notion that a strong female character with agency must be large in stature, have a homely appearance, dress garishly, and have the underlying threat of male violence. As Judith Butler states, there is no original or primary gender identity, and therefore drag acts can, and sometimes do, reveal the imitative structure of gender. However, as Butler also notes, there are drag acts that offer no subversive critiques or queering of the original subject and simply repeat cultural hegemonic norms. Mondalek's use of drag in his plays does not destabilize culturally hegemonic ideas about gender or the role of women in Arab/Arab American society. Instead, his Im Hussein character, along with the other female characters (also played by males), serve to perpetuate the reiteration of gender relations and norms that privilege males. Instead of utilizing drag as a liberatory device, it is simply utilized for comedic entertainment. In fact, as a preface to one of his skits, Mondalek tells audiences, "ladies and gentlemen, I ask from you for the next two hours to forget your worries and problems ... and laugh, laugh from the bottom of your hearts. And remember the saying that goes, 'laugh, and the whole world laughs with you.'"[48] By offering this preface, Mondalek is urging audiences to sit back in their chairs and to passively enjoy the entertainment without critical thought regarding its contents.

As a character, Im Hussein has agency. She is the driving force in the comedy and the reason the major events occur. She is also the wittiest, the funniest, and the most forceful character. Whenever her husband talks back at her, she either outwits him with a clever Arabic saying, she de-masculinizes him, or even tacitly threatens physical force. In essence, she is the "funny man" and her husband is the "straight man" in this comedic duo (both literally and figuratively). There are other less-examined aspects of Mondalek's comedy. The black-facing of another male actor in order to make them look like a South Asian maid for his 2005 comedy *Arabic and Broud* also proves problematic because it is yet another drag role and because it treads so close to blackface techniques. There is no doubt that Mondalek's plays are loved by the Arab

American/Arab Canadian community based on their widespread popularity, their sold-out performances, and their reputation within the community at large. Indeed, it is one of the few live theatrical experiences Arabs in the United States and Canada can attend that includes the Arabic language, Arab dance and music, and an opportunity for Arabs to gather and understand the cultural milieu that surrounds the works. However, the venture is primarily male-centric and treads upon old-fashioned notions of Arab female matriarchs, impotent male patriarchs, and cultural misunderstandings that remain between Arab and American societies. Like the previous comedies mentioned here, it is clear that the desire to entertain overrules any need for verisimilitude or cultural critique.

Post–9/11 Arab American Stand-Up Comedy

During the past decade there has been a proliferation of Arab American comedy through the different venues of the New York Arab American Comedy Festival, the Arab American Comedy Tour, The Watch List, The Allah Made Me Funny Tour, and the Axis of Evil Comedy Tour. Current Arab American stand-up comedians include Ahmed Ahmed, Fahad Albutairi, Ali Al-Kalthami, Mohammed (Mo) Amer, Ray Hanania, Geoff Johns, Aron Kader, Baha Khalil, Ronnie Khalil, Helen Maalik, Eman Morgan, Remy Munasifi, Dean Obeidallah, Nick Youssef, Amer Zahr, and Maysoon Zayid. Three of these comics—Dean Obeidallah, Ahmed Ahmed, and Maysoon Zayid—rose to relative prominence during this time primarily through the use of humorous accounting and abject comedy. As Palestinian American comic Zayid puts it, "the Arab comedy thing is actually the ultimate American story because when you look at any immigrant group that tried to make it in America—that tried to integrate, that tried to rage against discrimination, they all started out using comedy."[49]

In the decade that followed 9/11, in an attempt to combat the rising fear and hatred that was targeting Arab Americans in general (and Muslims in particular) these comics came together in order to find some semblance of unity. Obeidallah and Zayid founded the New York Arab American Comedy Festival to showcase the talents of Arab American actors, comics, playwrights, filmmakers, and to "inspire our fellow Arab-Americans to create outstanding works of comedy."[50] Obeidallah, an American born comic of Palestinian-Sicilian descent, came to the realization that embracing his Arab identity after 9/11 was more important than rejecting it altogether:

I started taking Arabic lessons after 9/11—never did before. I joined Arab-American groups, talked about it in my act much more. It became such a big part of me and because all of us came together, like circling the wagons to protect ourselves, we were under siege and then from that we're like, "well, let's collectively try to do something to define who we are the right way."[51]

Maysoon Zayid, who describes herself as a "Palestinian Muslim virgin with cerebral palsy from New Jersey," says that comedy has enabled these artists to create an identity and a community by identifying first as American, then by their Arab heritage.[52] Egyptian-American Ahmed Ahmed, who has found perhaps the greatest success among all Arab American comics, has appeared as part of the Arab American Comedy Tour, the Axis of Evil Comedy Tour, and has directed his own film about his experiences performing comedy in the Middle East titled *Just Like Us*. Ahmed states, "I think the general perception of Islam is so serious that we have a hard time laughing at ourselves and with ourselves, and if we can't laugh at ourselves or with ourselves, the rest of the world won't."[53]

The first major Arab American comedy tour to reach national prominence was the Arab American Comedy Tour. The DVD version of the tour highlights the comedy of Obeidallah, Ahmed, and Zayid. Obeidallah and Ahmed perform their stand-up routines in a theatre in Dearborn, Michigan, to what appears to be a mainly Arab and Muslim American crowd. Obeidallah's delivery is the least confrontational of the three, since he is able to approach his humor through his Arab and his Sicilian heritage. By his own admission, he does not look Arab to most, and this allows him a greater amount of freedom when it comes to his comedy.

> When the terror alert is raised we think of that, how is that going to affect us that night onstage? Can I tell this joke tonight, you know? Should I mention I'm Arab? Maybe tonight, you know, I can be a tourist; I'm different. Ahmed Ahmed can't be a tourist, you know. Some of those guys cannot be tourists. I can choose to introduce myself into the conflict or not.[54]

By his own admission, Obeidallah could "pass" as white, but decides to self-identify as Arab American.[55] Obeidallah's comedy is not obscene or outwardly political in nature, yet he jokes about issues that are of concern to Arab Americans. For instance, one of his recurring jokes is about the terror alert system. He says, "I'm jealous. We don't get a month that celebrates our heritage like Black History Month or Asian Awareness Month. You know what Arabs get? Orange Alert!" In another joke about his life after 9/11, Obeidallah says:

> Pre 9/11, honestly I was just a white guy living a white guy life. All my friends had names like Monica and Chandler and Joey and Ross. Then 9/11 happened and I,

Stand-up comedian Ahmed Ahmed performs with a young audience member in his 2010 film *Just Like Us* (photograph by Abdullah Nidal Mohiuddin/Cross Cultural Productions).

for the first time in my life, became an Arab and I'm happy about it. I've gotten to travel and perform in the Middle East.... It was fun. I was a hostage, but it was fun.[56]

Obeidallah, like the others, has poked fun at the experience of what he calls F.W.A., or "Flying While Arab." Obeidallah tells the audience, "I think, honestly, if you asked most Americans, more Americans would rather fly with snakes on a plane than with Middle Eastern people."[57] Obeidallah clearly finds that the genial approach is one that works best for his form of comedy. However, Obeidallah relies on images of terrorists, hostage takers, and dangerous Arabs on planes as material for his humor.

Ahmed Ahmed says he is the only "practicing Muslim" among his Arab American stand-up comedy peers in both the Axis of Evil Comedy Tour and the Arab American Comedy Tour. Ahmed's comedy revolves mainly around topics regarding Arabs in Hollywood, difficulty navigating the post–9/11 world (especially regarding travel), and growing up within an Egyptian Muslim family. He tells the audience that initially his father did not want him to pursue the arts because "Allah does not live in Hollywood."[58] Ahmed spent years in Hollywood as an actor first, even appearing in the Hollywood film *Executive*

Decision as an Arab terrorist who hijacks a plane. He later found that comedy would be a more viable and a more positive means to remain in the spotlight and have a lucrative career. Ahmed is under no illusions that his comedy stems primarily from his ethnicity. "When I go up onstage the first joke that comes out of my mouth, if it doesn't have anything to do with my name or my heritage or my religion, people aren't as interested."[59] Consequently, much of his humor revolves around terrorism, his Egyptian American heritage, Arab-Jewish relations, and Islamophobia:

> Both Jews and Muslims have more in common than any other religion ever. Both Jews and Muslims don't eat pork. We don't celebrate Christmas. We both use *[cchhhhh]* in our pronunciation. We're both hairy creatures of God. We both circumcise. We both yell on the phone when there's no emergency. Really, the only difference, if you think about it, between Muslims and Jews is that Jews never like to spend any money and Muslims never have any money to spend.[60]

Ahmed also makes fun of being Muslim and flying on planes after 9/11. "The only reason I fly Southwest [Airlines] is because they don't check Middle Eastern people. Try it. Every time I fly Southwest—'Mr. Ahmed, you're Arab and you're Muslim? Oh, go ahead. We'll probably crash before you do anything.'"[61] In another joke about flying while Muslim, Ahmed quips, "Whenever I get on a plane, I always know who the air marshal is. It's the guy holding the *People Magazine* upside down looking right at me."[62]

He also jokes about casting in Hollywood and how, even when he auditions with the most outrageously stereotypical Arab performance, he is still cast in films. One of his jokes revolves around his agent calling him to inform him he has been cast in the role of a terrorist. He replies that taking the role would be like "feeding the beast, it's like putting fuel on the flame. No way." When his agent responds that he will be paid $30,000 for a week of work, Ahmed puts his head in his hands, sighs, and then responds with the sound of gunfire, grenade blasts, and ululating.[63] As with Obeidallah, Ahmed's comedy relies on generating images of Arabs as terrorists and hijackers. Although Ahmed does tell audiences he is trying to break down negative stereotypes of Arabs, his use of these same stereotypes simultaneously revives and reiterates them.

Maysoon Zayid focuses her comedy on her Arabness in relation to her virginity, her cerebral palsy, and her Palestinian heritage. She jokes that being thirty and single is normal in New York, but that "thirty in Arab years is sixty-seven."[64] She also tells audiences about her volunteer work with refugees in Palestinian refugee camps where she admits that "the only reason I go to the refugee camps every year is because I feel it's the best place to catch a husband.

Because I have something they really want—an American passport!"⁶⁵ In another routine, she jokes about being Arab at an airport. "When I enter an airport, security sees an Arab. And you might ask yourself.... 'How do they know you're an Arab?' And it's because I have the kind of facial hair that no waxing in the world can deal with." She also remarks that "I'm terrified of flying ... because I know that if, God forbid, the plane I'm on crashes, they're gonna blame *me*. And all of my neighbors are gonna get on the news and say, 'Yeah, we always knew there was something really wrong about her—I think she was trying to become one of those virgins in heaven.'"⁶⁶ Like Obeidallah and Ahmed, Zayid reiterates tropes of terrorism, Muslim virgins in heaven, and even her father's likeness to Saddam Hussein.

Each of these comics believes their performance is a form of activism. Marvasti and McKinney write that Middle Eastern Americans use humorous accounting as a means of explaining themselves while subtly mocking the encounter. The use of stand-up comedy mocks the encounter, but hardly in a subtle manner. Their mocking of the post–9/11 hysteria against Arabs has been surprisingly successful. These comics have been booked nationwide, have had international tours, released DVDs of their works, and some have found work in Hollywood films. These performers have broken into an industry that historically has only had only a handful of Arab American performers. Therefore, by Hollywood standards, they have achieved a great deal of success.

The overriding question that begs to be asked of these performances of culture is whether they defy or reify stereotypes. These artists both implicitly, explicitly, and tacitly disavow negative stereotyping, and it is clear that their stated intention is to defy these stereotypes. However, in the constant focus and retreading upon the very stereotypes that have been used to portray Arabs and Arab Americans, some of these portrayals utilize the stereotypes and reify them. For instance, regarding the trope of the "Arab terrorist," Ahmed Ahmed often plays upon this idea and points it up for humor:

> I don't like flying any more than you. And I'm from the Middle East and I'm Muslim so I got everything going against me. When I get on a plane and I see another Arab or a Muslim sitting down, *I* get scared. I'll be looking for my seat, "let's see it says 16C ... (*he sees someone*).... Oh my God.... Excuse me.... Are you the guy? 'Cause I'm not the guy so you must be the guy. You're not the guy? (*skeptically*) Uh-huh. Okay. Well, I'm watching you *habibi*."⁶⁷

As this short excerpt demonstrates, Ahmed seems to be on both sides of the argument that Arabs are inherently terroristic. On the one hand, he joins the audience in their post–9/11 hysteria and fear of flying. He then acknowledges he is Middle Eastern and Muslim. However, it is his line "when I get on a plane and see another Arab or a Muslim sitting down, *I* get scared" that is most problematic. By assuming this position, Ahmed seems to be endorsing the former view that Arabs and Muslims are inherently dangerous passengers on planes. His next question, "Are you the guy?" also confirms the fact that, on each plane carrying an Arab or Muslim, there must be at least one person who is going to do something dangerous. Ahmed concludes with the line, "I'm watching you, *habibi*," as if to say that he is ultimately on the end of the spectrum that is on the lookout for dangerous Arabs and Muslims. The fact that even *he* would think that another Arab/Muslim would be dangerous makes it clear that the image of "the terrorist Arab/Muslim" is one fixed in his imagination and in the imaginations of the other passengers. Of course, during his routine, Ahmed often plays the account giver rather than the account taker. The very use of the stereotype, although humorous, can reify the fact that these comedians must rely on the stereotype itself for the comedy, and sometimes they must give in to the stereotype in order to "land" the jokes.

Zayid and Obeidallah also employ these stereotypes, but in a more self-effacing manner. Zayid plays upon the image of the virginal Arab woman who lives with her parents and desires sexual encounters, yet is hindered by her circumstances. This, by itself, would be humorous, yet Zayid ties this notion to the misconception that all Muslims are awaiting virgins in heaven. Furthermore, her deployment of images of Arab tyrants and hirsute women reinforces stereotypical notions of Arab womanhood. As Jarmakani notes, these mythologies of Arab and Muslim women function both as representations of backward, primitive others and as emblems of a traditional past.[68] Obeidallah's humor is the least stereotypical of the three comics. Instead of abjecting himself, his stand-up comedy deals with the way Arab Americans are abjected by others. For instance, when he jokes about the only holiday for Arab Americans being "Orange Alert" or the fact that most Americans would rather fly with snakes on a plane than with Arabs, he simultaneously mocks the encounter with prejudice while not subscribing himself to the stereotypical notions that abject him personally. In this regard, he subtly criticizes the society's abjection of others, while entertaining the audience. However, even he cannot resist playing upon negative representations when he cites the fact that he toured the Middle East as a "hostage."

What is most fascinating about Ahmed Ahmed's 2010 documentary film *Just Like Us*, which he directed and narrated, is the subtle difference in his stand-up material when he performs in Arab countries. As Ahmed Al Omran notes, when Arab American comics perform in the Middle East, they "prefer to stay away from politics and focus on Arab culture and everyday life—things like being late, talking at the movies, or fighting over who pays the check after they have a meal in a restaurant." The other difference between performing in the United States and the Middle East is that, when in the United States, these comics also have a mission to change negative perceptions of Arabs.[69] The film opens with interviews with different people who discuss their views about the differences between Arabs and Muslims. He includes images of U.S. food chains that are in the Arab world, clips of Obama speaking about Muslims, clips of Arabs and Muslims living in the Middle East, scenes from Ahmed's family both in the U.S. and in Egypt, and selections from Hollywood films that stereotype Arabs. He also interviews the same people about their views about comedy. Ahmed promises, "you're going to see the Middle East like you've never seen it before." Ahmed also provides educational accounting by explaining about the cities and countries he's visiting by telling the viewer what makes each place unique. Ahmed tells an interviewer in the film, "people, they want to laugh. It's a time for laughter, it's a time for a coming together. Comedy provides a cross-cultural dialogue for social change."[70]

At the outset, Ahmed tells his fellow comedians to treat their show "like a Tonight Show set." He also tells his comedians to avoid vulgar language and jokes about the royalty, politics, or religion. According to Ahmed, he told a joke in the past that banned him for a year in Dubai. Unlike his terrorist-centered jokes in The Axis of Evil Comedy Tour, Ahmed's jokes in his film *Just Like Us* are about his own Muslim culture:

> Listen, Muslims, we're responsible for a lot of inventions people use around the world, like ... we invented the mechanical clock. Which is ironic because we're always late for everything. (*looking at his watch*) Muslims are like, I'll get there when I get there. I invented time.... We invented the toothbrush, soap, and deodorant. What happened there?[71]

After a few non–Muslim comics perform, he says, "welcome to *haram* [forbidden] comedy." His other jokes revolve around dating, social customs, and censorship. Ahmed even brings children onstage for comic bits. He explains that, except for in Lebanon, there is censorship in Arab countries. Ahmed tells his fellow comedians, "you can say whatever you want in Beirut." The journey to the Kingdom of Saudi Arabia has the comedians performing under "consultant" visas since they cannot be listed as comedians. Ahmed talks about the religious police, the *mattawa*, which monitors entertainment and potentially could shut down the show. He also featured a female Saudi comic who performed, but the performance was not allowed to be filmed and the comic could only perform to a mixed male/female crowd.

Ahmed's journey back to Helwan, Egypt, his parents' village, is the emotional center of the film. The scenes from Helwan, and the narration about his parents' lives, provides a deeper aspect to the film—one that shows the Egyptians as normal people struggling to live their lives under difficult conditions. Ahmed narrates,

> Every time I visit the Middle East it gives me a great opportunity to see my family in Helwan, just outside of Cairo. It's from here that my parents sacrificed leaving their homeland in search of a better life.... I really enjoy seeing the happiness of my family and the people in Helwan. It makes me truly appreciate my roots and the values that have been passed on to me.... I'm really proud to be Arab and American. If it weren't for American stand-up comedy, our experiences would not have been possible. We want to show you have Arab culture and comedy being celebrated here in the United States.[72]

In this way, the film goes beyond simply documenting the journey of these American and Canadian comics to the Middle East. Instead, the film serves to humanize the people of the Arab world, to challenge the stereotypes that remain regarding Arabs, and to show Arabs as normal people engaging in different cultural activities. Of course, Ahmed focuses primarily on the positive aspects in these countries, not mentioning the difficult issues of the patriarchal hegemony in Gulf Arab states, the simmering sectarian conflicts that constantly plague Lebanon, and the political and religious conflicts that beset Egypt since the Tahrir Square protests were violently suppressed in 2011. Ironically it is the visit to Helwan, and not the stand-up comedy, that is the most compelling part of this documentary. In many ways, seeing Ahmed's family living simple, decent lives is more humanizing and impactful than any stand-up comedy routine.

Ahmed goes to great lengths to state how everything he and his fellow comics are doing are the first—the first stand-up comics in the Middle East, the first female comic in the Middle East, and how the comedians are helping the people gain a sense of humor. They also talk about the comedians being ambassadors, and how they are performing the first comedy shows "ever." The claims made in the film are somewhat exaggerated given that comedy has been a part of Arab entertainment since the mid-nineteenth century. Like theatre, comedy in the Arab world did not take on the exact forms that it did in the West. The form existed in Arabic translations of European plays, in oral improvised poetry, and in storytelling. If stand-up comedy did not appear until recently in the Arab world, it is only because the stand-up form is something that has gradually infiltrated world entertainment and was sure to reach Arab nations eventually.

Actually, There Is Something Funny About Your People

As this chapter demonstrated, Arab American comedy has come a long way from the early performances by Danny Thomas to the release of Ahmed's film in 2010. Arab comedy has its roots in the nineteenth century, and much of that sense of humor was transplanted with the immigrants from Arab nations. Despite the tumultuous political upheavals, the civil and international wars, and the violent inter-sectarian violence that remains in the Middle East, most Arab Americans can agree that there is humor in the Arab American experience that is based on cultural mistranslation, the interplay between the Arabic and English languages, and the attempt to find humor during a time of persecution. What is also evident is that the humor Arabs share with one another is different from what is shared with non–Arabs.

With the internationalization of entertainment and the proliferation of satellite television, there is increased coproduction and cooperation between North American and European producers who are working more closely with Arab artists and producers. This globalization of entertainment has meant that many U.S. productions have been replicated worldwide, including shows such as *Arab Idol*, *Dancing with the Stars*, *The Voice*, and *Who Wants to Be a Millionaire?* As Ahmed Ahmed's film demonstrates, acts of cultural translation have also led to more American comics traveling and performing in the Middle East and nurturing comedians in Arab countries. Arab Americans continue to find opportunities in mainstream entertainment. Dean Obeidallah is a CNN contributor and has co-directed a 2013 film titled *The Muslims Are Coming!* with Iranian American comic Negin Farsad which is meant to show that Arabs and Muslims can laugh and have a sense of humor. Maysoon Zayid has taken her "Laughing Without Teeth Tour" to Palestine. In 2013, The New York Arab American Comedy Festival celebrated their tenth anniversary and AJYAL Theatrical Group celebrated their twenty-fifth anniversary with a U.S./Canada tour. There are other Arab American comics touring with stand-up acts including Mohammed "Mo" Amer, Ray Hanania, Aron Kader, Ronnie Khalil, Remy Munasifi, and Amer Zahr. Although many of these artists have not broken into the mainstream of comedy, they have managed to create their own space within the greater American comedy scene. By doing so they have created a place where they can express their creativity, speak to Arab and non–Arab audiences, and work to change perceptions.

4
"It's not profiling, it's deduction": Post–9/11 Arab American Drama

On September 11, 2001, Najla Said's life changed forever. The daughter of Edward Said and an aspiring writer/actress from a Christian Palestinian family, she found herself in a strange position. As a native New Yorker, she saw her hometown under attack and felt the brunt of anti–Palestinian anger, despite the fact that the perpetrators of the attacks were not Palestinians. She had experienced the fear of warfare before, having been in Lebanon as a child during the civil war there, and she knew about the situation in Palestine having visited the West Bank and Gaza Strip with her father years before. She faced a choice: either hide behind the mask of whiteness and deny her Arab heritage or embrace her Arab American identity. She remembered her father's words: "there are two alternatives: either you go in and just obliterate your past, which some people have tried to do, or you cultivate your identity with a group of yourself." When she received a message on an ArabDrama listserv urging her to join an Arab American theatre company, she knew what she had to do.

¤ ¤ ¤

This chapter focuses on the concepts of derealization and infinite spectrality as proposed by Judith Butler and internment of the psyche as described by Nadine Naber, in relation to the plays *Sajjil* by the Nibras Theatre Collective, and *Back of the Throat* and *Language Rooms* by Arab American playwright Yussef El Guindi. The derealization of Arab Americans created the conditions whereby, after the attacks of 9/11, the American public was willing to allow, and sometimes become complicit in, their government's detention, extradition, and torture of Arabs and Muslims in black sites, or war prisons, around the world. Because to these factors, Arab/Muslim Americans are currently faced with an either-or dichotomy that pressures them to choose between their

Arab/Muslim heritage/religion and their Americanness. El Guindi's plays provide both a historical depiction of the post–9/11 paranoia and fear that engulfed the United States, as well as a reminder that, without fundamental changes in perception and attitudes, such persecution may occur again with even deadlier consequences.

Arab/Muslim Derealization: A Brief History

Previous chapters demonstrated the shift in attitude toward Arabs and Muslims after the 1967 Arab-Israeli War. As difficult as those governmental actions were during the 1970s, 1980s, and 1990s, nothing could compare to the post–9/11 anti–Arab/Muslim governmental actions that led to mass detentions, deportations, renditions to black sites, and torture. The PATRIOT Act (2001), Special Registration (2002), and Operation TIPS (2002) were enacted, creating a carceral system of fear and persecution among the Arab/Muslim population in the United States. Up to two thousand Arab and Muslim noncitizens were arrested and detained and five thousand were summoned for voluntary interviews. Indefinite detentions, searches, seizures, wiretapping, and deportations became commonplace. Most troubling, however, was the United States' establishment of international black sites, or war prisons. According to *New Yorker* reporter Jane Mayer, "enhanced interrogation techniques" that were tantamount to torture were used at these sites, including waterboarding, reducing detainees to a state of "learned helplessness," sensory deprivation, and other forms of physical abuse. One expert told Mayer, "it's one of the most sophisticated refined programs of torture ever.... People were utterly dehumanized. People fell apart. It was the intentional and systematic infliction of great suffering masquerading as a legal process. It was just chilling."[1] The post–9/11 creation of torture centers and black sites is not surprising given the fact that the U.S. government established The School of the Americas (SOA) (which is now renamed the Western Hemisphere Institute for Security Cooperation [WHINSEC]) in 1946. Since the end of World War II, the SOA/WHINSEC has trained soldiers allied with the United States in counterinsurgency techniques, psychological warfare, and enhanced interrogation techniques. The fact that these techniques have been developed and disseminated for decades demonstrates that the post–9/11 use of such techniques is hardly a new attitude by the U.S. government.

According to the Human Rights Watch Report, "We Are Not the Enemy," in the aftermath of 9/11, Arabs and Muslims—and those perceived to be Arabs and Muslims—became victims of a severe backlash of violence.[2] According to

FBI reports, "the number of anti–Muslim hate crimes rose from twenty-eight in 2000 to 481 in 2001, a seventeen-fold increase." The ADC reported over 600 September 11-related hate crimes committed against Arabs, Muslims, and those perceived to be Arab or Muslim, such as Sikhs and South Asians.³ These included verbal threats, beatings, shootings, murders, arsons, and attacks on mosques. Arab/Muslim communities were also targeted by the government. With increased detentions and deportations, these communities became fearful that reporting hate crimes would draw attention to those non-citizens who violated terms of their visas.⁴ These tactics, conducted in the name of homeland security, created a sense of anger and fear among Arabs and Muslims despite individual efforts to cooperate with governmental agencies.⁵

Arab/Muslim Derealization in Film and Media

Despite the common belief that Arab/Muslim derealization in the U.S. is a relatively new phenomenon, it should be noted that Edward W. Said studied and analyzed anti–Arab portrayals in the media as early as 1968. Although his book *Orientalism* is hailed as his most important work, it was his seminal essay "The Arab Portrayed" that was Said's original attempt to analyze how Arabs were misrepresented by the media in the contemporary era. Said argues that, whereas the European consciousness was at least shaped somewhat by Orientalist authors who acknowledged the Arab, the American psyche provides little space for their very existence. Said writes, "If the Arab occupies space in the mind at all, it is of negative value."⁶ For Said, the most negative change in perceptions regarding Arabs occurred during the June 1967 Arab-Israeli War, after which Arabs were represented as "mobs of hysterical, anonymous men" akin to savages bent on destruction. Said writes:

> The Arab, if thought of singly, is a creature without dimension. His history is obscure, for it is written neither in terms of institutions the American can recognize nor in a language he can read.... What is most telling about Western consciousness of the Arab is how few ordinary categories of human existence seem applicable to him. Suffering and injustice, it seems, can never be his lot.⁷

Said's greatest criticism is with how the media, including films, often dramatize Arabs as "over-sexed degenerates who were capable" of cleverly devious intrigues, but essentially sadistic, treacherous, and low."⁸ Arabs became caricatures depicted as primitive, subservient terrorists.

Other scholars corroborate Said's view of negative media and film portrayals of Arabs and Arab Americans. In their study of American film, Benshoff and Griffin separate Middle Eastern Arabs from Arab Americans. In their view, Arab Americans are rarely depicted in American film, whereas Middle Eastern Arabs are constantly depicted as villainous invaders, sexualized figures, belly dancers, harem girls, and Muslim terrorists.[9] In contrast, Arab Americans are viewed in American film as a group who cannot assimilate into Western society because they have pledged their allegiances solely to other countries. Furthermore, even when filmmakers attempt to individualize Arab American characters, they "still fall back into stereotypes," and Arab and Arab American actors in Hollywood still have difficulty finding challenging or complex characters to play.[10]

Film scholar Tim Jon Semmerling describes the depiction of "evil" Arabs in American popular film as "narrative tools used for self-presentation and self-identity to enhance our own stature, our own meaning, and our own self-esteem in times of our own diffidence."[11] He claims that the creation of "evil" Arab characters in these films is actually an oblique depiction of an insecure America projecting its insecurity on these stereotypical characters at their expense. By allowing these "evil" Arab characters to remain on the fringes of collective fear, these films provide no clear defeat of the Arabs or clear victory for the Americans; instead, they "keep the 'evil' Arabs as recurring characters and continual objects of the prejudicial act. The absence of a decisive resolution most likely produces a shared fear in an American audience, and thereby supports the prejudicial perceptions of the 'evil' Arabs with an impression of universality."[12]

The creation of this impression reacts with our ideologies and myths, which distorts the Arab image with our own concerns and self-interests. This anti–Muslim sentiment, as portrayed in popular entertainment and the media, has created a rehearsal for the violence that was committed against Arab/Muslim Americans after 9/11. Former UN Secretary-General Kofi Annan describes Islamophobia as a xenophobic phenomenon that dates back centuries, leaving Muslims today feeling aggrieved, misunderstood, and fearing for their safety. Annan encourages education, interfaith dialogue, and resolution of longstanding conflicts involving Muslims. According to Annan, "there is a need to unlearn the stereotypes that have become so entrenched in so many minds and so much of the media."[13] This entrenchment of stereotypes is rooted in concepts of derealization, spectrality, and internment of the psyche.

"Derealization," "Spectrality" and "Internment of the Psyche"

The discourse of derealization invokes the work of Judith Butler in her book *Precarious Life: the Powers of Mourning and Violence*. Butler's essay begins with three provocative questions: "Who counts as human? Whose lives count as lives? And, finally, *What makes for a grievable life*?"[14] Butler explores the concepts of the "social vulnerability of our bodies" and the idea of what she calls "fundamental dependency and ethical responsibility."[15] Bodies imply mortality, vulnerability, agency, and a physical dependence on one another as human beings. Butler defines violence as an exploitation of the tie that binds humans. She believes that the United States perpetrates violence and, having suffered violence itself after 9/11, plans infinite violence in the name of the war on terrorism.[16] In addition, Butler examines the conditions by which certain lives are considered more vulnerable and grievable than others. This concept of derealization of the Other makes the Other neither alive nor dead, but rather "interminably spectral."[17] In other words, the war on terrorism becomes a war without end, justifying itself in relation to a spectral enemy that may or may not exist in reality. In turn, this gives way to physical violence that delivers the message of dehumanization that is already working within culture.

Like Said before her, Butler specifically discusses the condition of Arabs and Muslims during this period, asking "to what extent have Arab peoples, predominantly practitioners of Islam, fallen outside the 'human' as it has been naturalized in its 'Western' mold by the contemporary workings of humanism?"[18] Because of this practice of dehumanization, entire groups have historically become suspect in times of national vulnerability. She describes post-9/11 hysteria as one of anxiety, rage, and a desire to secure U.S. borders from anyone perceived as alien—"a heightened surveillance of Arab peoples and anyone who looks vaguely Arab in the dominant racial imaginary."[19] The difficulty with this racial schematic, she argues, is that many other groups, such as Sephardic Jews, Sikhs, Hindus, and American-born Arabs, have all become targets as well. Perhaps there is no greater example of this derealization than the creation of black sites throughout the world where detainees were taken and held indefinitely without trial. Butler writes, "Indefinite detention ... extends lawless power indefinitely. Indeed, the indefinite detention of the untried prisoner—or the prisoner tried by military tribunal and detained regardless of the outcome of the trial—is a practice that presupposes the indefinite extension of the war on terrorism."[20] Prisoners in these war prisons are labeled detainees because they have no legal rights under the U.S. Constitution and protection of the law is indefinitely postponed. According to Butler, these prisoners are deemed dangerous and, therefore, there is no actual need to determine whether or not criminal acts occurred.

> The license to brand and categorize and detain on the basis of suspicion alone, expressed in this operation of "deeming," is potentially enormous. We have already

seen it at work in racial profiling, in the detention of thousands of Arab residents or Arab-American citizens, sometimes on the basis of last names alone; the harassment of any number of U.S. and non–U.S. citizens at the immigration borders because some official "perceives" a potential difficulty; the attacks on individuals of Middle Eastern descent on U.S. streets, and the targeting of Arab-American professors on campuses.[21]

This process of deeming is, according to Butler, a potential license for prejudice and a virtual mandate for a racialized manner of looking at, and judging, entire groups in the name of national security. Arabs and Muslims have been watched, monitored, and contained by those who believe themselves to be the foot soldiers in this war. Those deemed dangerous are indefinitely contained and can be taken outside the jurisdiction of the law, depriving them of their legal protections and transforming them into "humans who are not humans."[22]

In her essay "The Rules of Forced Engagement," Nadine Naber analyzes how the post–9/11 persecution of Arab/Muslim Americans led to what she calls an "internment of the psyche." Naber situates her analysis within the context of U.S. histories of racial exclusion and argues that the post–9/11 backlash represents "a recurring process of the construction of the Other within liberal polities in which long-term trends of racial exclusion become intensified within moments of crisis within the body politic."[23] According to Naber, the racialization of the "Arab-Middle Eastern-Muslim" Other is constituted by the dual process of cultural racism and racialization of national origin. The anti–Arab/anti–Muslim racism that has pervaded the national discourse in the United States for decades became more pronounced after 9/11 and rendered this group as embodying a culture/religion that is inherently different and inferior to American culture/religion.

> In this sense, the racial category "Arab-Middle Eastern-Muslim" has come to signify not only a moral, cultural, and civilizational threat to the "American" nation, but also a security threat. This racial project has been critical in generating support for U.S. nationalist arguments that claim that going to war "over there" and enacting racism and immigrant exclusion "over here" are essential components to the project of protecting national security.[24]

Naber also concludes that what has occurred since 9/11 is a sense of fear, apprehension, and intimidation that has encompassed the Arab/Muslim community for decades and has produced an "internment of the psyche."[25] This emotive form of internment engenders forms of power and control in the realm of the psyche that produces a culture of fear and internal incarceration leaving subjects feeling that they may, at any moment, be apprehended, incarcerated, or disappeared.[26] Being Arab/Muslim during this period, "one must 'drag' conformity and normativity and must become habitually concerned about hegemonic misrepresentations and mistranslations."[27] This state of fear inspired several Arab American playwrights to examine this condition through dramatic representations of persecution.

Truth Serum Blues

Ismail Khalidi's *Truth Serum Blues* is a monodrama that dramatizes issues of governmental persecution, inter-generational trauma, and the incarceration of prisoners at Guantanamo Bay. The play is set sometime between 2002 and 2007. Khalidi's dramaturgy employs multimedia, a chorus, and can be staged either as a one-person play or with multiple actors. The protagonist, Kareem, calls the prison in which he is incarcerated "Dubya's Gitmo," a reference to the Bush Administration's establishment of the Guantanamo Bay Naval Base (GTMO/GITMO). Kareem jokes about the difference between the Cuba of his imagination—replete with cigars, rum, and the *Buena Vista Social Club*—versus the totalitarian atmosphere he finds at the prison. He calls it, "more or less a mix of Attica and Alcatraz ... with a militaristic Caribbean vibe—a collection of Chicken and razor sharp barbed wire."[28] The most resonant statement he makes, especially in lieu of subsequent administration's promises to close down the prison, is *"this* place will always be around! Even if they shut the motherfucker down."[29] The ominous implication is, even without GITMO as a physical prison, the atmosphere of suspicion directed toward Arabs and Muslims will continue indefinitely.

Kareem's dilemma unfolds within a series of scenes of graphic torture intercut by flashbacks to a past with his Palestinian cousin, Waleed. Ismail Khalidi is the son of the respected Middle East scholar Rashid Khalidi, who is often branded a "terrorist" by hard-right-wing groups in the United States. Khalidi makes references to his own father through Kareem.

> Do you remember how my father used to give us lectures on Arab history? About Salah al-Din freeing Palestine and the invading crusading barbarians? And I listened as he talked between innings. Always between innings. See, Pops taught us about baseball and Holy Wars, but never taught us kids to be religious ... just history, politics and baseball, stats and dates, the recitations and repetitions of invasions and uprisings: '48, '67, '82, '87, '91, '96, 2000, 2002, 2003.... What's next? WHAT'S NEXT?!?[30]

Through exposition, the audience discovers Kareem is incarcerated because of his relationship with Waleed, a doctor whom the antagonist in the play, named only "Interrogator," insists is cooperating with Hamas. While he's being abused, Kareem tells Interrogator, "Look, man, I don't know what they teach you at West Point or the School of the Americas or wherever you got them brass knuckles, but Palestinians, we lost everything in '48, and '67, ... brothas are hopeless, just need money, need bread, want life, sick of death."[31] The recurrent traumas endured by the Palestinian people are recounted here in a series of dates marking the loss and mourning of what used to be Palestine.

Khalidi then adds characters who are named "Intellectual Factors"—conservative pundits who appear and discuss the Israeli-Palestine conflict in terms of "the Arab mentality," "pathological anti–Semitism," and "life and culture of hatred." These talking heads, dramatic representations of neo-conservative television and radio talk show hosts, add another layer to the script, giving a larger polemical context to the political imbalance of the situation. Kareem's flashbacks with Waleed (also called Abu Ali in the play) add moments of levity to the pervasive seriousness of the drama, but these interludes are brief. At one point, Kareem and Waleed discuss the schism they feel about their identities.

> KAREEM: You should have stayed in the states.
> ABU ALI: It was time for me to leave. The American in me started hating the Arab in me. So I smuggled that part of me back home. For safekeeping.
> KAREEM: What about me, huh? I have nowhere to go Waleed. Where's home for me? The diner? The taxi? I can't go live in Ramallah like you. That's not my home either.[32]

As with many Arab Americans, having divided loyalties between one's land of birth and one's ancestral homeland causes feelings of displacement, disattachment, and guilt. Added to these psychological factors, the contemporary paranoia regarding perceptions of terrorism pervades all of the play's dialogues.

> KAREEM: Waleed.... Someone said you were in Hamas...
> ABU ALI: Of course they did! We're all in some fucking group or another if you ask them. It's our nature habibi. And Aspirin factories are really explosive plants and our schools are actually training camps. I mean, honestly, talk about a "collective obsessional delusion."
> KAREEM: I'm just saying.... You didn't go funda-mental on a brotha did you???
> ABU ALI: Listen man, Iftah ar radio... (*Kareem switches on the radio*)
> RADIO: (*Voice Over or Chorus*): News Flash: Khan-Younis: peaceful demonstration turns deadly—4 shot, as missiles hit a building said to be used by weapons smugglers.
> ABU ALI: There's your answer...Get it?[33]

4. "It's not profiling, it's deduction"

Kareem describes the torture he endures in the detention camp, including extreme temperatures, sleep deprivation, verbal abuse, physical exertion, and broken bones. These physical abuses are also echoed by radio transmissions broadcasting Amnesty International reports of inhuman and degrading treatment of "aliens." By combining physical traumas with actual reports of abuses that have taken place in black sites, Khalidi merges fact and fiction in order to heighten the effect of the drama.

Through one dialogue, the audience learns that Waleed/Abu Ali is a doctor and a refugee from Palestine who was attacked and beaten while living in America. "I could never tell you," he tells Kareem. "Hard to talk about, getting my ass beat like that.... And for what, for being Arab, White, other? Who the fuck knows." Suddenly, The Chorus begins screaming epithets at Waleed: "You goddam camelfucker rag head motherfucker, you want some more.... I'll fuck your mother you terrorist motherfucker!!!"[34] Khalidi demonstrates that any feelings of resentment or anger Kareem harbors were the direct result of the prejudice and trauma he endured being an Arab in America.

Khalidi's playwriting style alternates between realistic dialogue, hip-hop lyrics and poetry. In one monologue/rap, Kareem speaks out "frantic, lost, crazy, preaching,"

> Look what they did to the panthers,
> Huey an Fred Hampton, the Chicano movement, man y'all, they are always
> *ready* ... aim ... SNCC! MLK! Malcolm! FIRE!!!! And the list goes on and on
>   and it 'aint
> just about Hoover or Nixon, or even the Bush boys ... it's all of them, democrats an republicans...
> 'cause this country was founded on the backs of slaves, the bloody tracks
>   of genocidal
> plagues
> of extermination,
> seeds that germinated into trade and expansion, open markets and mansions...
> But it's just divide and conquer in fashion, on runways, bombs dropped from
>   30,000 feet,
> the same show on repeat ... cause they can kill us fast.
> Or they can kill us slow.
> And the rest of us, the *rest* of us can be bought and sold ... it's that simple.
> One by one they get us out of the picture so we can't interfere with plans
>   hatched from
> the yoke of British rule,
> and fried on pans greased with cotton and sugar, tobacco then skewered
> with greed and gold,
> cocaine and soil

> and finally, that crude black oil...
> Now, let that shit simmer...
> Add corporate sponsors,
> use freedom as the moniker...
> divide and conquer.[35]

The title *Truth Serum Blues* refers to the barbiturates that Interrogator injects into Kareem throughout the interrogation process. The main antagonist, a character named Colonel Sangerson, justifies the use of these drugs by saying, "the real issue is what risks you all are willing to take to protect yer loved ones from these Izlamic [*sic*] zealots! Is it worth getting one of these rag-heads a lil tipsy to make him talk, to save lives in a fine hardworking American city? Well to take a line right out ole Rummy the defense secretary's book of gems, I would say: 'heavens yes!!!'" Later, the Colonel quotes from a fictional book titled *The Way Arabs Think* and says, "'Arabs only understand FORCE ... and the biggest weakness of the Arabs is shame and humiliation ... especially sexual variations since they are a severely repressed a backwards society ... good stuff!'"[36] As Edward W. Said demonstrated clearly in his *Orientalism*, books by scholars that seek to explain the thoughts and motivations of entire groups of individuals contain a bankrupt moral agenda. As contemporary books like *While Europe Slept: How Radical Islam Is Destroying the West from Within*, *America Alone: The End of the World as We Know It*, and *Londonistan* prove, the so-called "Islamophobia industry" is both lucrative and pervasive.

The tragedy that ends *Truth Serum Blues* is one that affects both Kareem and Waleed. After Waleed's clinic is obliterated by a missile strike, Kareem's guilt overwhelms him. In the play, cable news networks report that the clinic was a terrorist hideout, but Kareem refuses that indictment.

> there was no burden of proof, no room for me to question their version because the verdict had been passed, the punishment swift, just blood and broken glass.... No names, no faces, no ages, just the parroted statements of colonels and majors, analysts and haters justifying death of the other ... but this time it was the death of me, the death of my brother in struggle, in the hustle and I cried for our mothers who would rather die a thousand deaths before burying a son or a daughter ... any mother any mother, anywhere from Buchenwald to Bosnia and back and I cried habibi ... cried, cause any way you cut it I was guilty.... I was guilty any way you cut it! Any way you cut it I am part of it, complicit in this terroristic existence ... no matter what I know or believe, or believe I know, it is *my* tax dollars that helped send that missile.... And that's terror, man ... sheer fucking terror!!![37]

By play's end, Khalidi explains how Kareem ended up in GITMO. In order to keep from acting out irrationally after his cousin's extra-legal assassination, Kareem turned himself over to Homeland Security. The character realizes that, whether he is outside or inside the walls of GITMO, he is still a complicit actor in a situation that is directly afflicting his family. Instead of lashing out with violence, he submits to removing himself from the cycle of violence forever. This bleak ending to the play provides little room for hope for a peaceful resolution to the so-called "war on terror."

Nibras and Sajjil

Nibras, a former New York–based Arab American theatre ensemble, described themselves in this way:

> Nibras is an Arab/American theatre ensemble that is built upon a shared passion for theatre and is united by a common heritage. It is our belief that by fostering an understanding of the Arab experience in America, we will help to engender a greater understanding for all communities who feel left outside the equation of American society. Through our productions, we hope to aid in the process of inclusion, thereby enriching the colorful tapestry of American culture. Nibras also seeks to create a strong and viable support group for other Arab theater artists. We will work to build a network of young and old, acolytes and adepts, who can all benefit from one another's talent, experience and passion.[38]

The group's members—James Asher, Leila Buck, Maha Chehlaoui, Omar Koury, Omar Metwally, Najla Said, and Afaf Shawwa—began exploring their Arab American identities in the years following the September 11 attacks. According to *VOA News*, the group began the play *Sajjil* prior to 9/11, but "its aftermath underscored their efforts to challenge misconceptions and present the diversity of the Arab-American experience."[39] The production, which debuted as the International Fringe Festival in New York City in 2002, won a FringeNYC Overall Excellence Award for Ensemble Performance that year. Nibras members (the Arabic word for lantern), wrote *Sajjil* (the Arabic word for record [n.] or to record [v.]). The members of Nibras met online via an ArabDrama listserv. According to Said, the eventual members of Nibras became friends online long before they ever met in person. "For most of us, newly crowned 'Arab-Americans' by the agents and casting directors we had been getting to now, it was an opportunity to dip our foot in the waters of being Arab-American without diving all the way in."[40] For Leila Buck, the Arab American identification was one that provided artistic insight. "I cannot judge why people choose to identify with or write about their Arab-American heritage. For me, it is the reason I write—not an obligation but an inspiration."⁴¹ Regardless of their motivations, the members of Nibras found both a cultural and artistic home at a time when being identified as an Arab American performer was hardly desirable.

Nibras described the play as a "theatrical testimonial." The members of the group spent a year recording interviews with many different Americans "trying to get at the core of what it is to be Arab in America."⁴² With tape recorders in hand, they interviewed family, friends, teachers, and strangers. Antonio Sacre of NYTHEATRE.com wrote, "the result is an educational and entertaining show about the incredible variety, beauty, and struggle of what it is to be Arab and Arab American."⁴³ He went on to write that the performers were "committed, charismatic, and talented, expertly conveying more than thirty characters with passion, dignity, and much humor," though he believed that the ensemble could have benefited with some older actors.⁴⁴

> But the subject matter is crucially current: we are an ignorant people. Until 9/11, much of America knew nothing at all about Islam or what it means to be Arab in America. Many theatergoers want to be enlightened, want to be educated, want to know what we can do to make things better not just for ourselves, but for others as well. The questions are raised by Nibras, but never answered. Near the end of the show, they ask, "What should I do?" That's a question well worth exploring.⁴⁵

Said wrote that the 9/11 event made creating a piece like *Sajjil* urgent because "we were just trying to carve a place for ourselves in American cultural history, because it seemed not to be there. And then 9/11 happened, and it sort of lit the fire underneath us. We need to do this project now."⁴⁶ Omar Metwally wanted to confront misconceptions about Arab Americans, "to challenge those representations, and provide alternatives, and show a richer more complex picture ... and, hopefully, allow people to think about Arabs and Arab Americans in a different way than maybe they thought of them before."⁴⁷ Najla Said, told *New York Times*, "the point we were trying to make was that Arab culture is linked to Islamic culture, but not all Arabs are Muslim, and not all Muslims are Arab; and not all people from the Middle East are Arab; that we're a varied culture."⁴⁸ Following the 9/11 attacks, the rehearsals became a forum for the cast members to discuss how they were feeling about the political situation at the time.⁴⁹

Though in the mode of a documentary drama like *The Laramie Project*, the playscript itself is not as structured and does not have the same kind of dramaturgy as Kaufmann's play. For the members of Nibras, the central question of the piece is "What comes to mind when you hear the word 'Arab'?" According to Said, Arabs who were asked this question responded with words like "love," "food," "home," and "family." Non-Arabs used words like "desert,"

4. "It's not profiling, it's deduction"　　　　　　　137

The ensemble cast of Nibras (from left Leila Buck, Najla Said, Omar Metwally, Afaf Shawwa, James Asher and Omar Koury) performs in *Sajjil* (© Dixie Sheridan 2002).

"camel," "terror," "angry," and "Muslim."[50] James Asher said, "it was by no means finished and the significance of it is best appreciated by the performances which were based on mimicry of the actual people interviewed a la Anna Deavere Smith ... the play is really more of a transcript of a docudrama than a traditionally structured text."[51] The dialogue in the play attempts to capture, in a photorealistic manner, the speech patterns of those interviewed. The text, therefore, reads as if it is rife with misspellings, but that is due to the fact that it was meant for performance rather than reading. Despite the fact that there have been other Arab American theatre ensembles in the past (such as the Baghdad Theater, Firqat al-Youm, AJYAL Theatrical Ensemble, and The Arab Theatrical Arts Guild), Nibras was the first post–9/11 theatre ensemble whose mission was to confront the misrepresentation of Arab Americans. Therefore, a play like *Sajjil* is quite literally a "record" of a very dangerous and contentious period of time in American history for Arab Americans, and it speaks to the experiences of the Arab American community and to the experiences of those who have their own misconceptions of that community.

The theme of American-ness, and how one achieves it, is a prevalent one in the play. Claire and Jaquie, both of Syrian/Lebanese descent, tell James, they have difficulty knowing who they are.

CLAIRE: Do YOU tell everybody that you're Arabic?
JAMES: Um. Yeah.
CLAIRE: Why do they ask?
JAMES: Cause they think I look strange—(*Jacquie laughs*) er different, you know "ethnic."
JAQUIE: Ethnic. But you don't say you're American Arabic or—
JAMES: Arab-American? Sure.[52]

Claire then makes the observation, "if you want to know the truth, Arabics—Arabic people were not discriminated against until just the last sixty years. [...] The last—last ten years is when I became frightened."[53] This view coincides with the aforementioned political tensions that increased from the 1970s to the present day.

Another character, Ayman, is the described as an acting director of a Muslim center. His character says that his mission is to "teach our youth how to play their role in building the American society.... Because we consider ourself as a part of the American, American society at the large."[54] Ayman relates how he was profiled after 9/11, being pulled off of a plane for handing a book to his friend "in a suspicious way." When Ayman tells the officers that his friend, a man named Mohammed who is a physician, had tended to the victims of the World Trade Center, he was finally allowed to return to his seat. For Ayman, Arabs and Muslims took "more burden than the average American person" following the 9/11 attacks. "I mean like it's as if everybody suffers one time and you suffers two times." Ayman's conclusion is that isolation would be the worst possible reaction to the event.

> But I think what the Muslim community had realized after September eleventh, that we as a Muslims, we cannot afford to be isolated. From this society. Because as if you basically if you are isolated, you givin' the chance for people, to build up their own image about you. So you better take the initiative, you better come close to people, and let them know you.[55]

Edward W. Said is also a named character in the play. As would be expected, the most penetrating insights into the post–9/11 Arab American situation come from his character, named simply "Edward." Edward provides repeated instances of discrimination, both subtle and overt, that he has faced in his lifetime. For instance, when Edward was asked by his publisher for a list of books for translation, he said he provided a list that included the great Egyptian novelist Naguib Mahfouz. The publisher decided not to publish Mahfouz's work because "Arabic is a controversial language." In another instance, Edward recounts how he has seen discrimination aboard airplanes.

And I've seen it happen, and it happened to me, that somebody will be sitting on a plane, and the case is uh—simply to be reading an Arabic book or newspaper, and somebody will come and say, "could you put that away, it's disturbing."[56]

In another exchange, Said meets an Egyptian American who also rebuffs him when he speaks in Arabic.

So I started to speak to him in Arabic, I said um my name is Edward Said and I was told to look you up by, and I mentioned the name of the friend, and he said, "oh yeah, how is Freddy?" I said "he's fine," and uhhhha I spoke to him in Arabic. And he just cut me off. He said "no no." He called me brother. He said "no brother. I don't speak Arabic anymore. This is America, and I'm an American. That's it."[57]

According to Said, the difficulty with being Arab in America is a political one. The global politics and conflict between North America and Europe and the Arab nations is one that directly affects the situation of Arab Americans themselves. "Don't forget," he tells one interviewer, "the Arabs are on the other side. The other side of America. The wrong side." According to Edward, this has mainly to do with America's support of Israel. James questions Edward:

JAMES: How much do you think the issue of Israel has to do with—
EDWARD: Oh, 99.9 percent.
JAMES: —the identity of Arab-Americans, really?
EDWARD: Oh, absolutely. Absolutely. Of course. Of course.[58]

For Edward, the constant state of war between Israel and Arab nations has been the direct reason for the negative attitudes displayed by Americans toward Arabs. "That's why I'm telling you Israel is so important," he says. "Tell me, show me somebody, some other race where that is—no such thing. Never happen." Then, in a prescient moment, Edward says, "You know, Iraq is considered a danger to the United States because it's an enemy of Israel."[59] In his review of the production for www.offoffoff.com, Joshua Tanzer criticizes Edward's viewpoint in the play:

For the West, there is an equally difficult question to face: What is the history that fueled anti–Western opinion in the Middle East? The play touches on this question once, when an actor playing the scholar Edward Said argues that "99.9 percent" of the problem is rooted in the conflict over Israel, and yet there's much more to it. Britain, France, and the United States have a long history of influence or outright colonial domination in troubled countries from Algeria to Indonesia, and the uprising of Islamic fundamentalists against Western influence—of which the Israeli-Palestinian conflict is just one example—is obviously connected to Western colonialism that changed the shape of Middle Eastern societies.[60]

Tanzer's analysis is correct, however, it's clear that Said was speaking primarily to the post–1967 condition that focused its energies on the Israeli-Palestinian conflict. Edward Said's analysis, though based specifically on his own experience, does speak to his generation's view of Arab American identity formation; the members of Nibras, however, were much more preoccupied by their own post–9/11 condition.

The play also looks at non–Arab perceptions of Arabs. In one interview, James discusses these perceptions with two men (who only give their names as John Doe, or JD1 and JD2):

> JD: Y'all got different religions then we got. But we don't have one of them that keeps bombing places and going to heaven.... I just don't believe in terrorists. I don't care how—you got probably good people over there that's not tire-ists. We're not after every A-rab we're after the terrorists.... I'm not, don't think the United States is interested in defeating the A- the A-rabs we're after the terrorists ... y'all come over here and bombed us we didn't come over der and bob y'all. How would you feel if you lived over here?"
>
> JAMES: Ya ... well I live in New York.
>
> JD2: ...they just a bunch of crazy motherfuckers. Every time they catch one of them son a bitches they oughtta bring him over to let me shoot the son a bitch right there.... I'll kill the son a bitch right there. I-it wouldn't cost the state, the tax payers, the man whos working for a living it wouldn't cost him a damn thing—cause I'd kill the son a bitch.[61]

Another character, Kevin, says he thinks of Arabs as "evil."

> Evil comes to mind. Dark, shady. Um, uh, sneaky, dishonest ... the mass murders, the killing people, blowing up themselves, dropping bombs, running into pizzerias and blowing up uh, uh, kids and their moms, and turning jetliners into missiles and, you know, slamming em into the side of financial trade centers...[62]

An African American character named Vince, who loves eating Arabic food, also has misgivings about Arabs after 9/11. He says his perceptions have changed slightly, and "I do have a tendency to look—at a person and wonder what's going on in that person's mind" when flying with an Arab. Yet Vince, who has been racially profiled himself in the South, can understand the corrosive effects of the practice. "I felt like a second class citizen again. I felt like my ancestors—the fight for slavery was ... nil." He also recounts how the racist attitudes toward Arabs sound terribly familiar.

> You know, I hear people talking. Especially in the south you would hear. I don't know how much you hear about it in New York but in the south I would hear guys talk about, [...] You know, "Let's get all the A-rabs and get 'em all together

and just git 'em all outta here. Ship 'em back home." Well, you know, that's the same as telling me. You know, cuz when they're saying that they don't know it but they're talking to me about sending me back to Africa ... in a sense. And I don't like that. I don't like that at all.[63]

The character who perhaps most exemplifies what Arab Americans experienced in the post–9/11 New York context is Adil Al Montaser, a New York City police officer. Adil's parents, who were raised Muslim, emigrated from Yemen while teenagers, and he and his siblings were born in the United States. For Adil, the 9/11 period was especially difficult.

> I'm a police officer...—when you dial 911 fa help I'm here for your call to save you or you know ta assist you and—and you know ta catch the bad guy now I'm sworn—I'm a sworn police officer—now I'm a terrorist too? Cause I'm Arab and I'm Muslim?...—cause like myself my kids are born and raised here and dey wake up in the morning and they wanna eat Fruit-Loops and watch ... you know, Scooby-Doo, w-what makes 'em any different besides their name? Me? What makes me any different besides my name? Are you better than me? More patriotic than me? I don't gotta prove myself to anyone...[64]

Adil lost eight fellow police officers in the World Trade Center attacks. He was one of the first responders at Ground Zero.

> I remember working 12–14 hour shifts doing all types of investigative work and then going off duty and diggin for the next six hours you know, while the ground was still hot and steel beams hovering over your head you know y-you're just not thinking of your safety ... and ah, at the same time it's pinching you in the back thinking "is my father gunna have problem when he goes to work tomorrow?" "Is my wife gunna have a problem picking up the kids from school?"[65]

Adil's belief in law enforcement and due process is directly in conflict with his feeling for those who committed the heinous acts on 9/11. "I believe in law enforcement but it has to be fair, impartial and it has to be done perfect."

Sajjil ends with a passage regarding heritage and how Arab Americans can find the balance between their American selves and their Arab culture. For Edward Said, the choice is clear. "And so there are two alternatives: either you go in and just obliterate your past, which some people have tried to do, or you cultivate your identity with a group of yourself."[66] Adil finds that one can find a balance in their lives.

> Of course you should always try to hold on to your heritage. I mean I'm not saying to walk around hey all with like a ... ah you know turbin and, you know and play a flute ... but it's just like you know it's yer culture it's yer heritage I mean you should always hold on to something you shouldn't totally forget about it—[67]

Another character, Antonio, says "it becomes very muddy, you know; in effect America's greatest weapon is re-telling y'know, your history to you. In their terms." Yet another character, Hala, uses a metaphor that is often evoked by Arab Americans while discussing their place in North America.

> HALA: And I think ... that you're more than the sum of your parts. Cause you're more than just this or this and this and this. You're ... you're sort of a connector. And in a way you can never really fully belong to any of the parts. And that's hard!! But I think this is ... what makes you in a way, a bridge.[68]

In another exchange, an Indian character named Aroon speaks about how Americans perceive Middle Easterners:

> AROON: y'know they have shakes and uh, there's harems, and I guess you have people (mumbling) who like saying things like y'know what do they call 'em "camel jockeys" and "sand niggers." I've heard that term before I think once in Texas I don't know if it was somebody who called my sister a "sand-nigger" as a kid, I think so and she's like "what are you stupid we're Indian we're—we're not Arabic"...[69]

The term "sand nigger" is one that turns up frequently in Arab American writings, most famously in Lawrence Joseph's poem by the same name:

> "Sand nigger," I'm called,
> and the name fits: I am
> the light-skinned nigger
> with black eyes and the looks
> difficult to figure—[70]

Steven Salaita also discusses use of this pejorative. He writes that "*Sand nigger* is not only an epithet increasingly common among American purveyors of anti–Arab racism, but also a signifier of the alienation of minorities wrought by the majoritarian notion of American exceptionalism."[71] Salaita postulates that the term traps Arab Americans into a particular meta-narrative invented by settler-invented racism that would ensure that racism would be perpetuated by future generations. "Arab Americans, then, acquired an epithet because we or our forebears migrated to a nation in which some modernized variation of 'niggerdom' is a prerequisite for cultural naturalization."[72] One Arab American character, Ayman, speaks about his experiences of prejudice in the post 9/11 world:

> I think part of it, part of it, actually the Arab the Arab, or Muslims, I think they took uh more burden than the average American person. For somebody like me who lives in New York, and when September 11 took place, you as a human, as a

citizen, as a person who lives in this country, and you saw that ... horrible thing, and you see people dying, or you see people who are—eh families, family members who lost people or are suffering. That's something affect you as a human. At the same time, you have been accused as a Muslim or as an Arab, that you had something to do with that. So you have, I mean like it's as if everybody suffers one time and you suffer two times. For somebody like me, uh I understand, I mean I could tolerate. But so fo—for an average person, sometimes it does hurt them: you have some families, they decide just to leave, jus, they felt that they should leave.[73]

In the aftermath of the attacks, what many Americans failed to understand was that Arabs have called Manhattan home for over a century. The 9/11 attacks were as deeply personal and painful for Arab Americans as for any other group. Unlike others who were allowed to mourn openly, Arab Americans found themselves feeling defensive and afraid.

After the performances of *Sajjil* were concluded, there was a feeling of great accomplishment, but not a desire to continue on with Nibras. According to Said, "we were exhausted. Proud, elated, excited, overwhelmed, and exhausted. We were ready to take over the world with our company, we felt like we'd found our own voices, our way into our culture."[74] For Buck, understanding the complexity of her background was important to her as a writer and performer. "What I have come to realize is that it is only by acknowledging and confronting the negative aspects of Arab culture that we can truly begin a dialogue about the positive ones. At the same time I feel strongly that it is important to keep telling simpler, personal stories because that is what is missing in American culture—positive, human portrayals of Arabs."[75] Nibras never produced another play, but they were involved in several projects including *Aswat: Voices of Palestine* that was sponsored by New York Theatre Workshop in 2007. The group disbanded because of many factors. The artists involved were primarily focused on creating theatre and not administration, marketing, or fundraising. Although there were some "frustrations and frictions along the way," according to Maha Chehlaoui, the major reason for ending the artistic relationship had more to do with the tensions of trying to be an institution, especially after 9/11. "To build anything from the ground up is a challenge," Chehlaoui says. "But to do so in upheaval, while grieving, and feeling threatened on multiple fronts is especially so."[76]

Derealization in Back of the Throat *and* Language Rooms

Unlike the collective playwriting of Nibras, Egyptian American Yussef El Guindi is a playwright in the traditional sense of the word—creating plays in isolation and having his works produced at major theatres nationwide. In his plays *Back of the Throat* and *Language Rooms*, the sense of Arab/Muslim derealization is dramatized by utilizing several dramatic devices: situating the protagonists at the mercy of the hegemonic power structure around them, subjecting the protagonists to latent anti–Arab/Muslim prejudice and hysteria, and forcing the protagonists into situations that dehumanize them. El Guindi mirrors Naber's internment of the psyche by creating a dramatic environment rife with fear, suspicion, and surveillance. El Guindi's protagonists gradually realize that there is a governmental panopticon monitoring their movements, their habits, and their predilections.[77] El Guindi creates dramatic situations where post–9/11 persecution becomes both legitimate and acceptable because of the hysteria surrounding the past and the fear of future terrorist attacks. The so-called "enhanced interrogation techniques" proposed by the Bush Administration in the aftermath of 9/11 became standard practice. Much like a Foucaldian prison, which is rooted in strategies of power, any attempts toward the abolition of such a military state become futile. This new carceral network is meant to normalize and punish the Arab/Muslim into becoming more American, which aligns with removing allegiance to Arab/Muslim political/religious doctrine. El Guindi's dramas examine this new world order in harrowing detail.

Back of the Throat's protagonist, an Arab/Muslim American named Khaled, is a writer who is surprised by government agents who suddenly arrive and search his apartment after the 9/11 attacks. The agents, Bartlett and Carl, question Khaled about his reading habits, employment history, and social relations. Gradually, the line of questioning becomes more intense and menacing. The agents accuse Khaled of collaborating with a suspected terrorist named Gamal Asfoor. During a series of flashbacks, it is revealed that Khaled's female acquaintances, one of whom was a former girlfriend, have implicated him as someone aiding Asfoor. After the agents violently interrogate and physically abuse Khaled, they leave him with a threat to return the next day to complete their interrogation.

Language Rooms resumes where *Back of the Throat* ends. In this scenario, the Arab/Muslim agents, Ahmed and Nasser, are working for a U.S. foreign black site as Arabic translators and interrogators.[78] After their superior, Kevin, suspects Ahmed's interrogations have not provided the requisite information to convict the detainees of terrorism, Ahmed is suspected of disloyalty. The situation also divides Ahmed and Nasser, the only two Arab Muslims on the compound, by raising their fear and suspicion of one another. Ahmed is then put to the ultimate test—the interrogation of his own father, an immigrant from Egypt, about his dealings with a yet another suspected terrorist named Sheikh Al-Rawi. When Ahmed cannot garner the required information from his father Samir, he is forced into an isolation suit/tank where he is left to ponder "Was there something genuinely good in those initial impulses to make yourself a new home in America? And if so: What happened to them?"[79] Like *Back of the Throat*, the play *Language Rooms* ends with the protagonist alone and isolated in fear of further persecution.

When each play begins the respective protagonists, Khaled and Ahmed, are subjected to the power and control of the governmental structures surrounding them. The agents interrogate Khaled within his own apartment, rummage through his belongings, accuse him of conspiring with terrorists, plant evidence in his clothing, and verbally and physically abuse him. Likewise, Ahmed is questioned by both Nasser and his superior Kevin about his skills, his work ethic, and his lack of sociability. Whatever agency the protagonists possess in El Guindi's plays is subject to their ability to placate the hegemonic power structure around them. Although the agents tell Khaled he has not been accused of anything, his guilt is nevertheless implied:

> Here're your choices, Khaled, that you can think about. Either you're innocent. In which case proving that might be difficult. Or you're guilty, in which case telling us now would score you points because we'll find out soon enough. Or: you're innocent of being guilty. You didn't know what you were getting into. Stumbled into it. Through deception. Other people's. Your own stupidity. And that would be okay too. We can work with that. We can work with you to make that seem plausible.[80]

Khaled may be a U.S. citizen and may believe that he has all of the same rights as his fellow citizens, yet he is a guilty subject in the eyes of those in power because he is outside the normative. In *Language Rooms*, Nasser tells Ahmed he is guilty simply for being himself—an Arab and a Muslim. Ahmed is also dehumanized because the information he has gleaned from his interrogations did not provide the requisite intelligence the power structure demands despite his protestations to the contrary. Ahmed can only be trusted when he provides the kind of information that will definitively convict the detainees of terrorism; otherwise he is not useful to the system.

If derealization is the overriding political motif of both of these plays, internment of the psyche is the dominant psychological underpinning that works on and within the protagonists. Both plays revolve around the concept of loyalty to country and how Arabs/Muslims are not considered loyal subjects by the dominant hegemony in America. Like the characters Khaled and Ahmed, El Guindi is an Egyptian-born immigrant. El Guindi describes *Back of the*

Throat as "a paranoid thought game" written after 9/11 where "as an Arab/Muslim-American one wasn't quite sure where one stood."[81] El Guindi wrote the play in those mistrustful days after 9/11 when he himself was concerned about getting a surprise knock on the door in the middle of the night, about flying as a Muslim on an airplane, and about what someone would think of his own personal reading collection. As the war on terror ensued, El Guindi became more interested in the global/political, rather than the personal, nature of the conflict. He said, regarding his later play *Language Rooms*,

> At some point, the notion of these "black sites" crystallized into a perfect metaphor to talk about the current situation in America, and how I personally felt. It wasn't their function as places for suspected terrorists that interested me, it was their status as these non-acknowledged sites, a place of shadows, a no man's land where intense questioning took place, that tickled my interior and allowed me to talk about how I felt as an Arab/Muslim American in this current climate. These black sites became the perfect "objective correlative," if you will, by which I could laugh and rage at the alienation I was feeling as an American citizen in this hyper vigilant period.[82]

For Naber, this internment of the psyche explores the "connection between state policies, everyday acts of violence on the streets and the realm of the psyche or the emotive."[83] Both Khaled and Ahmed are infected with this paranoia of the psyche, believing they are being specifically targeted. Khaled tells the agents he is a citizen and that he meant to call them after the attacks so he could address their concerns. As the agents rummage through his apartment Khaled explains:

> I imagine you're getting a lot of calls. People with scores to settle. Or skittish neighbors. Was it George? He seems a little too curious about where I'm from. He doesn't seem to understand my connections with my country of birth are long gone. Was it—Beth? We had a falling out. It's very strange not being able to address whatever accusations have been made against me. It's like battling ghosts.[84]

The Bush Administration policies known as Special Registration and Operation TIPS were meant to promote national security. The Special Registration program required non-resident males in the U.S. from North Korea and twenty-four Muslim majority countries to be fingerprinted, photographed, and interviewed. According to Naber, "special registration resulted in the deportation of more than thirteen-thousand individuals. Not one terrorist suspect was found in the process."[85] As Gana notes, the entire goal of Operation TIPS was to incite Muslim Americans to spy on one another and to report suspicious persons by calling a special hotline.[86] Given this environment of surveillance and fear, it is little wonder that Arab/Muslim Americans experienced a sense of internal incarceration.

As a playwright, El Guindi creates this sense of fear and internment through secondary characters who look upon their protagonists retrospectively with suspicion. The non–Arab, non–Muslim characters in his plays are consumed with Islamophobia. In *Back of the Throat*, the FBI agents interview three people who had suspected associations with Khaled: a librarian named Shelly, his ex-girlfriend Beth, and a stripper named Jean. Both Khaled and Asfoor frequented the same library, leading the agents to suspect Khaled of consorting with a suspected terrorist. Khaled tells them, "This is like twenty degrees of separation. Then everyone in that library is a suspect. I use books, for chrissakes, I'm a writer."[87] Shelley, who had an encounter with Asfoor, describes him as dirty and evil; even going so far as to accuse Asfoor of trying to molest her. In the next interview with Khaled's ex-girlfriend Beth, the word "betrayal" is used, again raising suspicion against Khaled. Beth tells the agents that Khaled's life seems a lie and that Khaled "never seemed to come clean about anything." Beth also recounts that Khaled seemed secretive and even goes so far as to tell them Khaled gloated about the terrorist attacks. In a flashback it is clear that Khaled was actually attempting to convince Beth to reconsider U.S. foreign policies.

> KHALED: Why aren't you hearing what I'm saying?
>
> BETH: It was a rape, Khaled. It was a rape multiplied by a thousand. You don't go up to the woman who just got raped and say, you know what, I think you probably deserved that because you go around flaunting your ass so what do you expect. And if you want to make sure it doesn't happen again, then maybe you should go around in a fucking burqa.
>
> KHALED: (*Disbelief, then*) The United States of America is not a woman who just got raped. The United States of America is the biggest, strongest eight hundred pound gorilla on the block.... You can't rape an eight hundred pound gorilla, even if you wanted to.[88]

Khaled's desire to have Beth think more critically and dimensionally about the scourge of terrorism is rejected as a form of disloyalty to country, thus causing her to suspect his motives. Beth's Islamophobia is clear when she recites the stereotypical idea of the "fucking burqa," recounting the stereotype that all Muslim women are forced to wear the garment. Lastly, a stripper named Jean accuses Khaled of meeting with Asfoor at her strip club. Like Shelley, Jean cannot definitively identify Khaled and, like Beth, she carries deep-seated anti–Muslim prejudices herself:

JEAN: I'd say touch me, Kaled, so the bouncers can come in and smash your stupid face in. Coming here to get off on me while all the time wanting to do shit to us. Wrapping your women in black and then sneaking in here and getting your rocks off.[89]

Shelly, Jean, and Beth parrot the ugly and pernicious stereotypes that all Arab and Muslim men are lecherous female oppressors and all Arab and Muslim women are *burqa*-clad and docile. In each instance, the evidence against Khaled is circumstantial, yet the character is still targeted and threatened by the agents. Khaled is guilty by association; not association with the suspected terrorist alone, but also by the association of being Arab/Muslim himself. The agents, armed with their own prejudice and insubstantial evidence, come to the conclusion that Khaled must be a part of Asfoor's terrorist plot when, throughout El Guindi's play, it is clear that Asfoor is an immigrant who wishes to learn English and wants Khaled's assistance in doing so. Asfoor's guilt is never concretely established in the text of the play.

Likewise, in the play *Language Rooms*, Ahmed's motives become suspect. Ahmed notices that twenty-five new surveillance cameras have been placed within the compound to monitor his activities. The intelligence Ahmed has gathered has been deemed by his supervisor, Kevin, as suspect by the "higher-ups" in the organization. Ahmed's sympathies and loyalties are in question due to his Arabic translations, his not fitting in with his co-workers, and his lack of participation in group events. Along with the cameras, Ahmed recognizes the other means by which he is being surveilled. For instance, during their conversation in the locker room, Ahmed and Nasser discover Kevin has been listening in on their argument the entire time. In one exchange, Ahmed confronts Nasser about their place as Muslims within the compound:

I'm just saying. It's as if they can only like one Muslim at a time, and you're it. The designated Muslim. And I get to be the piñata. I think that's the psychology. I really do. I think you know that and play off it.[90]

This "playing off" one another is a theme that adds to the alienation between the men and to their general feelings of mutual mistrust. Kevin, their African American supervisor, understands their predicament well, himself being ordered to create divisions among African American groups during the civil rights era.

It saddens me to see the only two Muslims on this compound ready to tear each other's throats out. You're like a two-man version of the black militant groups I had to infiltrate back in the day. It tore me up to see them bring each other down. Yes, it was my job to plant that misinformation that led to their collapse. But to see how easily it could be done.[91]

4. "It's not profiling, it's deduction"

Bartlett (Tom Hickey, left) and Carl (Sean Sinitski) interrogate Khaled (Kareem Bandealy) in the 2006 production of Yussef El Guindi's *Back of the Throat*, directed by Stuart Carden, produced by Silk Road Rising (photograph by Johnny Knight, courtesy Silk Road Rising).

In another speech linking the Arab American and African American condition, Kevin tells Nasser and Ahmed, "You know what they say, sometimes the last person a black man wants to be arrested by is by a black cop, because that officer probably has something to prove."[92] With El Guindi's inclusion of Kevin, an African African American character, he invokes a trope that Arab American scholars have found to be a useful comparison—the Arab/Muslim and African American experiences in the United States. Arab American scholar Moustafa Bayoumi cites W. E. B. Du Bois' *The Souls of Black Folks* and his concept of African Americans "being a problem" within the racial matrix of the United States, in relation to Arab Americans.[93] Bayoumi calls Arab/Muslim Americans the "new 'problem' of American society," following the long line of other racial and religious groups such as Native Americans, Catholics, Irish Americans, Italian Americans, German Americans, Jewish Americans, Japanese Americans, and Hispanic Americans. Bayoumi writes that Arabs and Muslims "now hold the dubious distinction of being the first new communities of suspicion after the hard-won victories of the civil-rights era."[94] El Guindi references this notion of American exceptionalism when Bartlett tells Khaled:

> One more thing: at no time should you think this is an ethnic thing. Your ethnicity has nothing to do with it other than the fact that your background happens to be the place where most of this crap is coming from. So naturally the focus is going to be on you. It's not profiling, it's deduction. You're a Muslim and an Arab. Those are the bad asses currently making life a living hell so we'll gravitate toward you and your ilk until other bad asses from other races make a nuisance of themselves. Right? Yesterday the Irish and the Poles, today it's you. Tomorrow it might be the Dutch.[95]

This concept of the ethnic line of persecution, whereby each minority must be given its moment of scrutiny, becomes a dominant theme in El Guindi's works. El Guindi's protagonists have a naiveté regarding their views of American citizenship, and of the concept that all men are created equal; something debunked by the non–Arab/Muslim characters in his plays. Ahmed cannot seem to accept the fact that his allegiance is being questioned even though he believes he has embraced his nation by becoming a citizen, translator, and interrogator.

> I know with Europe, and other places, you might be born in the country and still not be considered French or English or Thai or whatever, but in my country, that *is* the point. It's *supposed* to be instant conversion. Anyone who becomes a citizen inherits everything. Which means never having to say I'm sorry for being foreign-born.[96]

The crux of the argument in both plays recalls notions of consent and descent as explained by Werner Sollors in his book *Beyond Ethnicity*. Sollors quotes John Quincy Adams who stated unequivocally that immigrants would be "disappointed in every expectation of happiness as Americans" unless they cast off their ancestral ties and "cling to the prejudices of this country."[97] Sollors explains that "descent relations" are those that emphasize hereditary qualities, liabilities, and entitlements; whereas "consent relations" are those that stress the subject's abilities as "mature free agents and 'architects of our fates' to choose our spouses, our destinies, and our political systems."[98] The characters in El Guindi's plays are in a constant struggle between their Arab/Muslim descent and their American consent as citizens. Their internal schism is exacerbated when their faith/ethnicity collides with their adopted homeland and they are forced to choose between the two. In the play *Back of the Throat*, Khaled's allegiance is questioned at every turn. When Khaled protests to the agents that they cannot violate his civil rights because he's a citizen, Bartlett quickly disabuses him of his notion of Americanness.

> "It's my country." This is your fucking country. Right here, right now, in this room with us. You left the U.S. when you crossed the line, you piece of shit.... It's galling.—Sticks in my craw. To hear these people who got here two hours ago quote back to me Thomas Jefferson and the founding fathers. They're not his fucking fathers.[99]

El Guindi's line "these people who got here two hours ago" underlines the prejudice and the fact that first-generation immigrants, especially from certain cultures, cannot possibly claim their Americanness no matter how long they have been citizens. Having been in America for at least a generation, and eschewing any former cultural/religious roots seems to be the underlying prerequisite for true citizenship. In another section, after physically abusing Khaled, the character Carl says:

> God: I know your type, so well. The smiling little Semite who gives you one face while trying to stab you with the other. You're pathetic, you know that. If you hate us, then just hate us. But you don't have the balls to do even that. You bitch and you moan and complain how overrun you are by us and all the time you can't wait to get here. You'd kill for a visa. That pisses me off. That's hypocrisy. Why not just come clean and own up that you hate everything this country stands for.[100]

Once the veneer of civility is removed from El Guindi's characters, the true nature of prejudice is exposed. As Benshoff and Griffin write, it is rare that Arabs are portrayed in American film as becoming part of the fabric of European or American societies. Instead, Arabs are portrayed as those who are inherently unable to assimilate.[101] Similarly, El Guindi represents the same image, but in his case, it is an attempt to reverse the image and to prove how prejudicial the image really is. The antagonists in El Guindi's plays consider those of Arab/Muslim heritage and beliefs to be anathema to the American system. Ahmed's boss Kevin explains it in this way:

> In America, son: you leave family—to find family. That's how it works. We're not tribal. We don't do blood feuds. We've evolved. You want to do family, join the Mafia. You're part of something bigger here.[102]

That "something bigger" is American hegemony in all of its forms. Both Ahmed and Khaled *must* make a choice. If they do not choose their American consent identity, they will be outside of the norm and subject to the uncertain future that isolation entails. Most importantly, El Guindi does not allow the protagonists to view this as a false choice; rather he creates it as a dilemma from which his characters cannot escape. This is the crux of El Guindi's dramaturgy and creates the dramatic tension within these works: if his protagonists retain their ties to their Arab/Muslim ideals, they are outside the normative Judeo-Christian framework that defines the American religious ethic; if they retain their Arab allegiances, they find themselves against the political ethic that is being carried out against Arabs both domestically and internationally. As President George W. Bush warned in his post–9/11 address to the U.S. Congress, "you are either with us or with the terrorists." This false binary utilizes the word "terrorists" not only to mean those who utilize violence and threats in order to achieve political ends, but also to mean anyone who disagrees with, or protests, U.S. hegemony in any manner. This false choice becomes real once backed by the full force of governmental actions. As much as El Guindi's plays may be works of fiction, they reflect the time period in which they were written, recreating the same sense of fear and paranoia that existed in the years following the attacks.

The final aspect that defines El Guindi's two works can be viewed through the lens of what Butler calls "interminable spectrality." Butler writes, "The derealization of the 'Other' means that it is neither alive nor dead, but interminably spectral."[103] Interminable spectrality is a state where subjects are forced into a liminal position where they are not allowed to live freely and instead become victims of an infinite paranoia. The detainees in black sites who have been incarcerated have not been tried in courts of law. Instead, they are left in a state where they cannot be freed until the so-called "war on terror" is realized. However, this is the kind of war that has neither a definitive enemy nor an achievable goal. The war, based not on a fixed enemy, but rather on a tactic, is one that could conceivably last for generations. By defining the war in this

4. "It's not profiling, it's deduction" 153

Ahmed (James Asher, left) pleads with his boss Kevin (Mujahid Abdul-Rashid) in Yussef El Guindi's *Language Rooms*, directed by Evren Odcikin, produced by Golden Thread Productions (David Allen Photography, courtesy Golden Thread Productions).

manner, the Bush Administration created an infinitely spectral situation, leaving the prisoners of this war with no means of legal recourse.

After Ahmed interrogates his father, Samir, and realizes that he is not, in fact, a terrorist, Kevin informs Ahmed that the real concern was not with the father at all, but rather with Ahmed's allegiance to the war on terror. Kevin sees Ahmed's hatred toward his father as more than a filial matter. After Kevin explains this, he commands Ahmed to wear an isolation suit and enter an isolation chamber. El Guindi creates this stage device in order to represent this interminable spectrality onstage.

> KEVIN: Look: we've figured out what that scuba looking suit is for. Turns out it's an isolation suit. A kind of time out for people to reflect. And that's what you need to do. Because I still believe there is room for you here. But you've got to get clear on some things. And focus. Can I ask you to do that for me? Get in that suit and reflect? And while you're in there, ask yourself: Do I know what I mean when I say:—"I belong."... When we've all now gathered to be a part of something new. And now that I've arrived, why does that set off such a war, in here? (*touching his chest*)[104]

Because Ahmed cannot claim his allegiance to the war's mission without any doubt, he is literally forced into a state of isolation and suspension indefinitely, much like the prisoners being held in the black sites themselves. There he can reflect on why he has dual allegiances, reflect on why he cannot give himself over completely to the war on terror, and reflect on why he still feels the pull of his heritage over the pull of patriotism. Similarly, by the end of *Back of the Throat*, Bartlett tells Khaled, "We're going to leave you to think about it. Come back later, tomorrow." In a darkly comic turn, the agents leave Khaled with evaluation forms to rate their interrogation performance.

> Think about it. And about those evaluation forms: they're no joke. It's your chance to respond. That's what this is all about. At the end of the day, we're fighting to safeguard that right. It sounds counter-intuitive. But that's the struggle for freedom for you. It's never as straight-forward as you'd like it to be.[105]

Again, El Guindi leaves his protagonist and his audience in a state of limbo—infinitely spectral beings, neither dead nor alive, in the war on terror. As Carol Fadda-Conrey puts it, Khaled is branded as a terrorist by his interrogators to the point that "he comes to embody that role, regardless of his innocence or guilt."[106] The implication is that, by placing Arabs and Muslim in this liminal state, we may create a false sense of security for our society, but we are simultaneously damaging the very principles that guide our nation. In El Guindi's plays the climate of fear that accompanies the war on terror perverts the foundational notions of American democracy.

Ongoing Anti-Muslim Prejudice

In the decade following 9/11, anti–Arab and anti–Muslim prejudice and governmental persecution have not abated. Arab American playwrights have continued to create works that address prejudicial attitudes regarding the building of mosques, the wearing of headscarves, and ongoing Arabophobia and Islamophobia. According to a July 29, 2014, Arab American Institute poll, there has been a continual erosion in favorable ratings given to Arab Americans and Muslim Americans. From 2010 to 2014, favorable attitudes towards Arab Americans had fallen from 43 percent in 2010 to 32 percent in 2014. For Muslims the favorable attitudes declined from 36 percent in 2010 to 27 percent in 2014. During that same period there had been a rise in support for profiling by law enforcement against Arab and Muslim Americans. The same poll found that 57 percent of Americans say they do not know enough about Arab history and people, and 52 percent say they do not know enough about Islam and

Muslims. The report concludes that "Education about and greater exposure to Arab Americans and American Muslims are the keys both to greater understanding of these growing communities of American citizens and to insuring that their rights are secured."[107]

Jamil Khoury's online playwriting development project, *Mosque Alert*, addresses the controversies over the building of mosques in communities that oppose them. Ayad Akhtar, a Pakistani American playwright who identifies as Muslim, won the 2012 Pulitzer Prize for Drama for his play *Disgraced*. These plays serve as cultural barometers for the time periods in which they were written as well as necessary reminders of how, when governments overstep their bounds and societies become infected with fear of the Other, it is necessary to *re*-realize the humanity of members of all communities.

5

Suffering for Palestine: Palestinian American Playwrights

When Betty Shamieh was approached by a group of American playwrights to travel to Palestine, her first reaction was "Hell, no!" That reaction was not due to her lack of desire to visit her parents' homeland, but rather because she "did not want to confront what my life could have been like if my parents had not immigrated to America in the 1960s." Shamieh, born in San Francisco and not Ramallah, did not know life under military occupation. Instead of Harvard and Yale, she might have attended Bir Zeit University and endured the many shutdowns that university often faces. She might have had to live under military curfew. "I know myself, and I am not a brave person," she writes candidly. Ultimately, she decided going to Palestine was the right choice. "The cost of ignoring what is happening there—and ignoring how those happenings affect the stability of the entire world—is unbearable."[1]

¤ ¤ ¤

If the persecution of Arab Americans in the post–9/11 context tends to dominate the domestic discourse in contemporary plays and performances of Arab Americans, the issue of Israel/Palestine is by far the most pressing international issue addressed in their works. Much like the scholars and intellectuals who created the leftist Arab American organizations in the late 1960s, these new writers and performers—especially those who identify as Palestinian Americans—have taken up the mantle of the so-called "Palestinian question" in their works. As previously demonstrated, the Arab American scholars who spearheaded the Arab American movement during the late 1960s are the literal and figurative progenitors of the contemporary Arab American playwrights studied here. In the case of Edward W. Said and Rashid Khalidi, they are the parents of two of these playwrights.

Palestinian American playwrights speak from two subject positions: Arab American and Palestinian American. Their work necessarily employs Said's concept of "double or exile perspective" as a means of understanding the Palestinian situation as it exists today.[2] These plays are works of personal and historical secondary witness trauma. The characters in the plays either foreshadow or relive the Palestinian trauma of displacement, occupation, and loss. Sometimes, however, the plays can be read through the lens of what Dominic LaCapra labels "empathic unsettlement" or "vicarious victimhood" whereby "empathy with the victim seems to become an identity."[3] By conflating the loss of Palestine with the rhetoric of absence, these playwrights sometimes create a sense of what LaCapra labels endless melancholy and impossible mourning. I believe that these plays are more of a "working through" the question of Palestine than an "acting out" of its loss. These playwrights attempt to address a Palestine they do not inhabit, but have created through their own personal investment and performative creation. Therefore, the plays occupy a complicated and conflictual space within the Palestinian American and Arab American imaginary.

First, there is a desire to retrospectively recreate Palestine as if through the historical lens of previous generations as seen in Ismail Khalidi's play *Tennis in Nablus*. Like his work *Truth Serum Blues*, *Tennis in Nablus* becomes a work of postmemory that is dominated by the narratives preceding him and was shaped by the trauma that can only be recreated through imaginative reconstruction. Second, in Betty Shamieh's play *Roar*, the characters relive the trauma of exile by attempting a reformation of their exiled lives in Detroit, Michigan. They gradually realize that they cannot escape the traumas they experienced as displaced and persecuted Palestinians in Jordan. Lameece Issaq and Jacob Kader's play *Food and Fadwa* attempts to dramatize the clash between those who decided to remain in Palestine under occupation and those who chose to immigrate to the United States. The conflict between rootedness and flight becomes an intra–Palestinian struggle that threatens to tear families apart in ways the occupation did not. In Najla Said's *Palestine* and Jennifer Jajeh's *I Heart Hamas*, contemporary Palestine is described and re-envisioned through two lenses—the writers' journeys to Palestine, and their outing as Arab/Palestinian Americans after 9/11.

There have been other playwrights and plays that have defined this genre. Kathryn Haddad and Juliana Pegues's *With Love from Ramallah* that was produced by the Arab American arts organization Mizna, premiered in 2004 at the Mixed Blood Theater in Minneapolis. In the words of Haddad and Pegues:

When we first started working on *With Love from Ramallah* in 2002 we had no lack of material, with the ongoing Al-Aqsa Intifada, the siege of Ramallah, and the Jenin massacre, all against the backdrop of an increasingly racist and hegemonic U.S. foreign and domestic policy. At the same time, the continued exclusion of Palestine from peace and justice movements pointed to the effectiveness of the media in dehumanizing Palestinians, minimizing their plight, and criminalizing their response to colonialization. This dehumanization illustrated the critical importance of highlighting the real lives of Palestinians both within Palestine and in the diaspora. We sought to portray Palestinians as political subjects but also as people who have lives and families that are at once joyful, humorous, argumentative, heated, passionate and mournful—all under the shadow of occupation.[4]

In one exchange, two Palestinian characters, Ziad and Mohammed, argue about their new found freedom in the United States. For Ziad, a shopkeeper with a fiancée in Ramallah, America is a place that will never accept Arab immigrants. His friend, Mohammed, prefers to assimilate and forget the troubles he left behind in Palestine. In one argument, they fight about the idea of remembering, and forgetting, their pasts:

> MOHAMMED: Enough! I've had enough about the past and remembering. I am tired of our past and our sad, sad story.
>
> ZIAD: Tired! Tired of our past? How can you say that?
>
> MOHAMMED: It's a terrible story, Ziad, and it will go on and on long after I'm gone.
>
> ZIAD: Yah Allah! It is our duty, Mohammed, to keep the struggle, to keep the hope, to fight on
>
> ...
>
> MOHAMMED: Duty? I'll tell you my duty. My duty is to myself. That is all!
>
> ZIAD: Yah Allah. America wannabe.
>
> MOHAMMED: This is not Ramallah, brother! This is Minneapolis. Do you see any soldiers here?[5]

By introducing characters that desperately try to survive in America while retaining their ties to Palestine, Haddad and Pegues's drama focuses on the difficulties immigrants face assimilating into American culture in Minneapolis and living under Israeli occupation in Ramallah.

Another play from this genre, Mona Mansour's *Urge for Going* that was produced at the Public Theatre LAB in New York in 2011, dramatizes the life of a young Palestinian girl growing up in a Lebanese refugee camp, living "on shaky ground, just for now, permanently impermanent."[6] The play begins with the contestatory views over the history of Palestine and the ongoing occupation and examines the notions of diasporic Palestinian identity, Arab nationalism,

Jamila (Tala Ashe) and Adham (Ramsey Faragallah) reminisce about life in London in Mona Mansour's *Urge for Going*, directed by Hal Brooks, performed at New Dramatists LAB, 2011 (© Carol Rosegg).

and Lebanese attitudes toward Palestinian refugees. By mixing Lebanese politics, Palestinian history, and popular cultural references like *Baywatch* and Joni Mitchell, Mansour offers a contemporary portrait of those who find themselves living in the precarious state of exile just miles from their homeland.

Likewise, Betty Shamieh's *The Black Eyed*, produced during the 2007-2008 New York Theatre Workshop season, is another example of a Palestinian narrative told by a chorus of historical and contemporary Palestinian women searching for their martyred families and lovers whose souls are trapped in the afterworld. Shamieh describes the play as "an extremely political and nonlinear play written in free verse with a chorus."[7] The women—including the Biblical Delilah, a Crusades-era woman named Tamam, a contemporary suicide bomber named Aiesha, and a female architect doomed to die on a plane on 9/11—muse about the past and present of Palestinian women in the post–9/11 world. Shamieh's play also deals with issues of sexuality, ethnicity, exile, and the Arab American condition that she describes as life "lived in the space between."[8] Nathalie Handal's play *Between Our Lips* is a two-person one-act about a male Palestinian American journalist named Homer and a female Palestinian photographer named Ayat. Homer comes to a holding cell where Ayat is being kept after a shooting incident that left her husband and a thirteen-year-old girl dead. The short play explores separation, lost love, and the brutality of military occupation serves as another example of how Palestinian Americans recreate the Palestinian experience under occupation through interrogating notions such as guilt, innocence, and freedom. When Ayat asks Homer what freedom is, he replies, "Freedom is when we catch life between our lips."[9] In the absence of a daily lived experience of Palestinians living under occupation, these playwrights offer words that resist that occupation from afar.

These Arab American writers are informed by their second-generation upbringing in the United States—a perspective that makes their work very different from that of their predecessors who wrote primarily from a first-generation perspective. By writing in this style, they have opted for a much more confessional mode of literary production than the more detached and factually-oriented academic writing of earlier Arab American scholars. All of these works are, in their subject matter, political; it is nearly impossible not to be political when attempting to address the Israeli-Palestinian crisis. Despite this fact, their work provides another lens by which the Israel/Palestine issue can be viewed by those who were born and raised in the United States. Despite the fact that these Arab American playwrights are decidedly pro–Palestinian in their orientation, they are also able to view the Israel/Palestine conflict with a relatively more balanced perspective than those scholars and writers who write from a purely Palestinian perspective. Some criticize this position, claiming that it is a form of self-censorship. In his essay "Arab American Theatre Caught in Censorship: A Study of Betty Shamieh's *Roar* and *The Black Eyed*," Yasser Fouad Selim writes that playwrights like Betty Shamieh who sometimes focus on the Israeli-Palestinian conflict do so with a "calculated compromise" that includes self-censorship. In Selim's view, rather than writing plays that are critical of Israeli and American Middle Eastern policies, these writers choose to censor themselves in order to remain publishable in a market that disallows critical works regarding Palestine. Instead, he believes Shamieh often portrays Arab Americans as victims and Arabs as victimizers in her plays:

> Shamieh is confused between using drama as an art of resistance to establish a postcolonial image of Arab America and her desire to cross the hyphen of Arab-Americanism and establish herself as a successful American playwright. This confusion between resistance and crossing the hyphen distorts the image of Arab America in her plays.[10]

Because of this distortion, Selim believes that Arab Americans are searching for artistic freedom and require a space where they can express their political views without repression. I am in agreement with Selim's argument about

Arab American writers who often must weigh their desire to voice their political opinions about the Middle East against their desire to have their plays produced or published. However, the post–9/11 era has proven that theatres that devote themselves to the works of Arab and Middle Eastern Americans have not only been able to produce such works, but also have audiences that are willing to attend such plays. Compared with mainstream American dramas and films, those productions are few in number and some Arab American playwrights have expressed frustration over the inability to get their works produced at larger regional theatres.

Arab American plays that address the Israel/Palestine conflict are attempts to artistically work through the history and politics of this history with the desire to both criticize, and reconcile, the situation that is taking place there. By doing so, they expand the definition of what it means to be Arab American in the post–9/11 context.

Trauma and "Postmemory"

Postmemory, diaspora, and exile are inextricably linked. In her essay "Past Lives: Postmemories in Exile," Marianne Hirsch coins the term "postmemory" and describes it as "a powerful form of memory precisely because its connection to its object or source is mediated not through recollection but through an imaginative investment and creation." Postmemory is primarily characterized experience by those who grow up with the narratives that preceded them and were shaped by traumatic events "that can be neither fully understood nor re-created."[11] Despite Hirsch's concept being mainly about what she calls Holocaust postmemory, she explains that the term is one that is applicable to a wide range of memory states that involve trauma, exile, and the re-living of traumatic events through the lives of others. For those survivors who were separated and exiled from their homelands, memory becomes more than an act of recall; it is also an act of mourning that is articulated with anger and despair. Hirsch describes postmemory as also constituted by exile from spaces of identity, diasporic experiences, and senses of belatedness and disconnection. Postmemory seeks connection as it creates what is unrecoverable. From this perspective, the lost object cannot be repaired, incorporated, or overcome.[12]

Another critical framework with which to view the works of second-generation Palestinian American playwrights is that of Dominick LaCapra's notions of trauma, absence, and loss. Specifically, LaCapra dissects the distinction between absence and loss. This distinction is crucial because, according to LaCapra, the blurring or conflation of absence and loss bears witness to the impact of the (post)traumatic condition. This conflation attests to the way one is possessed, or haunted by, the past. In the post-traumatic state where one acts out the past, the distinctions between absence and loss, the then and the now, collapse.[13] LaCapra also cautions against a situation in which "virtual experience involved in empathy gives way to vicarious victimhood, and empathy with the victim seems to become an identity."[14] This condition can lead to difficulties that include a routine methodology enacting a compulsive repetition comprised of aporia, paradox, and impasse. LaCapra argues that acting out trauma for victims and empathic unsettlement for secondary witnesses are not foreclosing attempts to work through past loss. The ability to distinguish between absence and loss is "one aspect of a complex process of working-through."[15] Absence is often converted into loss and this conversion, when narrativized, is based on misrecognition and elevates the conflation to mythic status.[16]

Each of the plays discussed here explore the trauma of displacement within the Palestinian diaspora. According to Rashid Khalidi, the traumatic events of 1947–1949, which cost Palestinians their majority in Palestine and their hopes for control of their nation, is inscribed in their history as *al-Nakba*, or "the catastrophe."[17] Khalidi argues that since *al-Nakba*, Palestinian identity is constantly reinforced in both positive and negative ways, yet is always considered suspect by non–Palestinians. Palestinian travel documents, issued by states like Egypt or Israel, list them as stateless Palestinians, which often leads to harassment and exclusion at airports and border crossings. According to Khalidi, Palestinians are among the few people in the modern era who have reached national consciousness and a defined sense of national identity, yet have not achieved national independence.[18] According to scholars Lila Abu-Lughod and Ahmad H. Sa'di, *al-Nakba* "is often reckoned as the beginning of contemporary Palestinian history, a history of catastrophic changes, violent suppression, and refusal to disappear. It is the focal point for what might be called Palestinian time."[19] Eighty percent of Palestinians became refugees following the events of 1948. Palestinian society became divided among Israel, the West and East Banks of Jordan, the Gaza Strip, in various camps within Lebanon and Syria, and as far away as Egypt and Iraq.[20] Of those who remained, 60,000 to 156,000, either became nominal citizens of Israel, or were subjected to a system of military administration by the government of Israel, the Hashemite rulers of Jordan, or the Egyptians. Following the Six-Day War in 1967, Israel annexed the West Bank, Gaza Strip, and Golan Heights, and a state of military occupation has existed since then. *Al-Nakba* has been chronicled by many Palestinian writers. Palestinian scholar Musa Budeiri writes, "The plain fact is that Palestinian society was not only socially and economically differentiated, and consequently affected in different ways by 1948 and its aftermath, but it was also geographically differentiated."[21] This geographical differentiation led to entire generations of exiled writers who were left to re-create Palestine in their imaginations.

Al-Nakba is reflected in all the plays discussed here, however not all of them refer specifically to the events of 1948. For many Palestinian scholars, it is important that *al-Nakba* not be associated solely with 1948 and the founding of the State of Israel. Instead, it must be viewed as an ongoing historical situation that will only find resolution with the recognition and reconciliation of Palestinians rights. Abu-Lughod puts it this way:

> For the Palestinian catastrophe is not just something in the past. It continues into the present in every house demolished by an Israeli bulldozer, with every firing from an Apache helicopter, with every still birth at a military checkpoint, with every village divided from its fields by the "separation" wall, and with every Palestinian who still longs to return to a home that is no more.[22]

Budeiri concurs that *al-Nakba* came later than 1948, even going so far as to cite 1967 and the Oslo Accord as events connected to *al-Nakba*.[23] Yezid Sayigh writes, "I cannot conceive of understanding 1948, nor its meaning for Palestinians today, unless it is bound internally to what went before and what came after; viewing it exclusively as the result of Zionist invasion, British conspiracy, and expropriation of Palestinian decision making by Arab states and statically fixed in time and space fails entirely to satisfy me."[24] In surveying Palestinian perspectives on *al-Nakba*, it becomes evident that the term has far greater significance than its application to the specific events of 1948.

According to Susan Slyomovics, Palestinian narratives can be explained by several Arabic terms including: flight (*hurub*), exile (*ghurbah*), resistance (*muqawamah*), steadfastness (*sumud*), and return (*awdah*). Two more terms that are appropriate are occupation (*taht al-ihtilal*) and scattering (*shatat*). I propose here that the following plays can be categorized under three of these categories that encompass these performative notions: occupation plays, resistance plays, and return plays. *Tennis in Nablus* is a resistance play that exemplifies the concepts of resistance, steadfastness, flight, and exile; *Roar* is a return play that deals with flight, exile, and return; *Food and Fadwa* is an occupation play that addresses issues of exile and steadfastness; and lastly, *Palestine* and *I Heart Hamas* are resistance plays that propose not a return to Palestine itself, but rather for a resistance against the negative impression many Americans have toward Palestinians and Arab Americans. These themes are examined in relation to these plays in order to further understand the intention of the playwrights, the messages of the plays, and the impact these plays are meant to have upon audiences. The one common factor that all of these plays share, is that all of them end with *shatat*, or scattering. In all of the plays, the families become scattered across the globe as a result of the traumas they experience as refugees and exiles. In this way, these plays are timely reflections of the Palestinian diasporic experience.

Precious Stones *and Queering the Israeli/Palestinian Conflict*

Precious Stones was the world premiere production for Silk Road Theatre Project (now Silk Road Rising). Khoury, who describes himself as "a white Arab Slovak Pole," was raised in the Antiochian Orthodox Christian tradition. His husband, and co-founder of Silk Road Rising, Malik Gillani, is an Ismaili Muslim. Their theatre, labeled by *American Theatre Magazine* as one of "a dozen young American companies you need to know" in 2004, has risen in prominence as one of the preeminent Middle Eastern-American Theatres committed, in part, to producing Arab American dramas.[25] Their first production, *Precious Stones*, set the tone for the works to come: plays that focus on playwrights of Asian and Middle Eastern backgrounds that both "enrich the fabric of American storytelling" and "advance civic engagement and public discourse."[26] The theatre was founded in 2002 as Silk Road Theatre Project as a response to the attacks of 9/11 with the aim "to educate, promote dialogue, and heal rifts through the transformative power of theatre."[27] The theatre has produced both live and video plays written by many Arab American writers including Leila Buck, Yussef El Guindi, Rana Kazkaz, Wajdi Mouawad, and Fouad Teymour. For Khoury, theatre is a means to a specific end. Khoury says, "We love the art form, but that's not where we're coming from. It's the desire to impact change."[28] Khoury (who is not of Palestinian descent) was shaped directly by his cross-cultural upbringing, his sexuality, his direct engagement with the plight of Palestinian refugees, and his personal experiences with homophobia and racism, believes in the activist potential of theatre and social media.

Khoury's play works on two very important and inter-related levels. First, it is a drama about Israel and Palestine and the Jewish and Arab diasporas. It is also one of the only Arab American dramas to dare tackle the sensitive issue of homosexuality in the Arab community. For Khoury, these are issues he cares deeply about. He worked as a refugee affairs officer in the West Bank, and he is an outspoken advocate for gay rights within and outside the Arab American community. This play, arguably at the expense of trying to do too much, tackles both issues forcefully. Andrea and Leila's relationship, though a plot contrivance, serves to create the situation in which the characters are forced to confront the issues that affect both communities.

Precious Stones is set in 1989 on Chicago's North side. It was vital to Khoury that the play take place during the first intifada, as the issues of the second intifada and the subsequent tragedies that have occurred have only obscured the original problem that is inherent to the Israeli/Palestinian conflict. For Palestinians, the first intifada was the first time that a kind of grassroots uprising took place against the Israeli occupation—one that involved stones and not guns, bombs, and suicide attacks. This intifada (or "shaking off") filled Palestinians with great pride and shed light on the brutal occupational tactics that are sometimes employed by the Israeli Defense Forces in the Palestinian Occupied Territories.

Khoury, however, prefaces his play with the note that "the play should never be presented in a tone that 'takes sides' or 'skews the arguments.' Nor should it self-consciously strive to achieve 'balance.' Audiences should be allowed to embark on their own journeys and arrive at their own conclusions. It is a play that poses questions without necessarily offering answers."[29] In this way, Khoury attempts to balance two tragic narratives: that of Holocaust survivors and their children; and that of those Palestinians who were forcibly expelled from Palestine in 1948, and their descendants who were born and raised in neighboring Arab countries. There is an uncanny parallel here, and Khoury utilizes it for his analysis and dramatization of the Israeli-Palestinian conflict. Andrea is the child of survivors of the Holocaust from Krakow; Leila is the child of parents driven from Palestine during the massacre at Deir Yassin. It is their shared, tragic history that brings the women together with a desire to form a dialogue group. Their sexual attraction for one another, although convenient for the plot of the story, adds another very difficult and painful layer to an already complicated narrative. Although Andrea's homosexuality is not as scrutinized by her community, Leila must live a closeted life and in a convenience marriage to a gay Arab man. Their marriage of convenience is one that is suitable for their situation. However, once Andrea and Leila fall in love with one another, that situation becomes untenable.

The premiere production of Khoury's play opened with the metaphor of stones. Two characters, labeled simply as "Arab" and "Jew," address the audience with short monologues about how stones have played such a vital part in the narrative of both Arabs and Jews in Palestine/Israel.[30] The "Arab" discusses how Palestinians build houses out of stones and how "our homeland, blessed with an abundance of stones, strewn generously across the landscape, blossoming ever robust with each new struggle."[31] The Arab also discusses how stones exist in Arab folklore, be it the Ka'aba in Mecca, the stone that obscured Jesus' tomb, the Dome of the Rock in Jerusalem, or the "stoning of the devil" ritual during Ramadan. The Jew speaks of the stones that built the Walls of Jericho, the stones of the Wailing Wall, the Mea Shearim, and the stone that David used in his slingshot to slay Goliath. In addition to this, Khoury also gives the Arab and Jew monologues about stoning—a punishment that ancient Arab and Jewish cultures utilized to punish adulterers and homosexuals alike. This reference is perhaps the most crucial of them all, as it deals with the issue that is central to the drama's main focus.

The initial meeting between Leila and Andrea at a coffee shop in Chicago is a dramatic equivalent of the Arab-Israeli dialogue groups that were present in the 1980s and 1990s. Andrea is clear that she wishes the group to be comprised only of women because "we need our own ideas and approaches to this conflict."[32] This feminist approach informed Khoury's approach to this work. He states, "I always thought feminism was a godsend. It was an analysis of gender, and I just ran with it. It was extraordinarily liberating. To me, the gay male identity and the feminist identity always went hand in hand."[33] Khoury, who labels himself a "queer feminist," says he was influenced at an early age by feminism and "as a teenager started identifying as a feminist."[34] This commitment to feminism is clear in the play and is expressed most clearly by the character Andrea. Leila, though also a feminist, is reticent to express her feminism outside the context of the Arab American milieu. When she is asked to do so, she recoils, sending her relationship with Andrea into turmoil.

Rachel, Andrea's ex-girlfriend, and Esther, Andrea's employer, do whatever they can to stop both the dialogue group that the women attempt to form and to put a halt to their relationship. For Rachel, the matter is one of jealousy; she expresses this jealousy by orientalizing Andrea's relationship with Leila.

> Do you have some fantasy about being in the desert and stumbling upon an oasis where you see a tent with a camel outside, and this mysterious, exotic woman stares out at you, revealing seductive, piercing brown eyes that lure you into her tent, where she feeds you figs and dates and pours fresh, cold water over your face, her hips gyrating as she begins belly dancing for you, loosening her veil then letting it fall to the floor.[35]

Rachel's reiteration of orientalist tropes both sexualizes and fetishizes Leila who, in Rachel's jealous mind, is the exotic Arab woman waiting at the oasis to be taken. Khoury's addition of this imagery highlights the modern idea of the Arab woman as the veiled, kept woman. As discussed earlier, that image transforms in the contemporary period into the female terrorist/suicide bomber. Khoury manages to reference both of these stereotypical tropes in an attempt to highlight both their ridiculous, and pervasive, nature. Rachel is also resistant to join the dialogue group. She states, "I have a lot of issues with Arabs. And not just as a Jew, okay, but as a woman, and especially a dyke. I mean, look at the way Arabs treat women. Like chattel.... And they murder gay people. I read that in Arab countries if they find out you're gay they either collapse a wall on top of you or throw you off of the highest building. Take your pick."[36] To Rachel, Arabs are uncivilized and serve to manipulate Jewish guilt. What bothers Rachel most about Leila, however, is her closeted status. Rachel is offended that Andrea is willing to be a part of a closeted relationship, especially after the battles that lesbians have fought to live openly gay lives. When Rachel asks, "Whatever happened to that nice Jewish girl you wanted to marry," Andrea replies, "She turned out to be a Palestinian Muslim."[37]

Esther, on the other hand, feels undermined by Andrea's seeming attempt to usurp her authority by beginning a dialogue group independent of the Jewish Council. For Esther, Israel is under attack and having any dialogue with "Israel's sworn enemies" is anathema. In an ironic turn, Khoury has Esther tell Andrea, "Stop being so naive, Andrea. Arabs don't believe in peace. Look at what they did to Anwar Sadat. He made peace with Israel and his own people killed him. They are dangerous people. Do you think a Jew would ever kill an Israeli Prime Minister for making peace?"[38] For Esther, Andrea's actions desecrate the memory of those who perished in the Holocaust. Esther tells Andrea, "A Jew is never to criticize Israel in front of the Goyim! We support the decisions of the government of Israel," effectively silencing any debate regarding Israeli policy toward Palestinians.[39]

The Palestinian dramatic foils to Rachel and Esther are Bassima, Leila's cousin, and Samir, Leila's husband. This paring mirrors the Rachel-Esther pair in several ways: where Rachel is Andrea's ex-lover and Samir is a gay man who pretends to be Leila's husband for the sake of propriety. Bassima, who lost her husband during the Israeli invasion of Lebanon in 1982, is a staunch anti–Israeli in the same way that Esther is staunchly anti–Palestinian. What differs with Bassima, however, is her homophobia. As the play progresses, Bassima comes to realize that Leila is not the same woman she thought she knew in the past, and this creates a rift between them that transcends the bonds of family or Arabness. Politically, Bassima cannot come to terms with dealing with Israelis believing that a Jew's only loyalty is to Israel. Bassima, like some in the Arab community, has also internalized racist ideas about Jews, telling Leila "Jews are very clever people, Leila. They control the media in this country. They run the economy. They own Congress *and* the White House."[40] For her, it is the fault of all Jews that her husband was killed in the war. She tells Leila, "I teach my children that someday they're going to avenge their father's murder. Someday they're going to avenge all that was done to us. No justice, no peace."[41] Samir, who tells Leila he works with Jews every day, is skeptical that Jews and Arabs could ever dialogue. Samir, unlike Bassima, is not prejudiced and even says that the love of his life is a Syrian Jew. He is also less threatened with his sexuality around Jews than Arabs. Both Bassima and Samir have no illusions that Arab regimes would be any kinder to Palestinians than the Israelis. For Bassima, Arabs are cowards and traitors for collaborating with the Israelis and Americans. For Samir, Leila also falls into the trap of blaming Israel for all of the Arabs' ills. He tells her, "Blame America! Blame the West! Blame the Jews! It's really tired, Leila."[42] In Samir's view, Palestinian victimhood has only restrained Palestinian rights.

Andrea and Leila's relationship is one that is also affected by issues of class. Andrea, a liberal Jewish thinker who was raised by Bundist parents, is a character who believes she is practically a socialist. Leila, who spent her childhood in poverty, has fully embraced capitalism and all of its luxuries. This class dynamic adds a third dimension to the conflict between Leila and Andrea (the first two being global and sexual politics). Leila's offers of trips to Paris and nights at the Ritz are viewed as class privilege by Andrea. In the final scene Khoury simultaneously confronts class privilege with the political issues of Israel and Palestine. The final scene between them is one where the conflicts that had surrounded them finally invade their private lives, and the scene fittingly takes place in a bedroom. Leila's denial of public affection for Andrea, her closeted lifestyle, and her embracing of her upper-class status create a rift between the women that leads to a climactic moment where the most contentious political issues emerge:

> ANDREA: If you're going to fight to liberate Palestine, you should also fight to liberate yourself.
> LEILA: I'm going to fight for gay rights in Palestine when we don't even have our own state! We're stateless and living under occupation! ... Gay rights is a luxury my people can't afford.[43]

Their final barrage of attacks unmasks their true feelings toward one another. Suddenly the facade is shattered and the two women violently attack one another.

Leila (Roxane Assaf, left) discusses living life in the closet with Samir (Nicole Pitman) in Jamil Khoury's *Precious Stones*, directed by Michael Malek Najjar, produced by Silk Road Theatre Project, 2003 (photograph by Johnny Knight, courtesy Silk Road Rising).

ANDREA: You know what I've desperately wanted to hear from you, since we first met? I've wanted to hear from your mouth that Israel has a right to exist, just as Palestine has a right to exist. It would mean so much to me to hear you say those words and mean them.

LEILA: You want me to say that Israel has a *right* to steal our land and our homes? I don't think so. And don't tell me what I should be saying. This isn't the West Bank. You're not my Israeli master here!⁴⁴

The ending is uncertain, leaving the audience asking if the two women will remain together, or if they will suffer yet another failed peace process. Khoury is among the first Arab American dramatists to introduce the issue of homosexuality within the Arab American community. Prior to *Precious Stones*, there were no plays that ventured into this contentious territory within the genre of Arab American theatre. The ending, much like the conflict itself, informs the viewer that the fundamental fact is that these two peoples are both of the same land and that there is no easy resolution to this conflict. The audience, much like those who live with the Israel/Palestine conflict itself, can only wait to see when a resolution arrives.

Tennis in Nablus: *Reimagining Palestinian History*

Khalidi's *Tennis in Nablus* is a resistance play because it imaginatively recreates the Palestinian resistance to British rule under the British Mandate of Palestine (1917–1947). Subtitled "a tragipoliticomedy in two acts," the play dramatizes aspects of the British Mandate, the growth of the Zionist movement, resistance to imperialism, and the growth of Palestinian national consciousness. Khalidi sets his play during the 1936–1939 revolt by "the indigenous Arabs of Palestine against British rule and growing Jewish immigration from 1933 onwards."⁴⁵ The nexus of British imperialism in Palestine, Ireland, and India creates the dramatic backdrop to his story. He dramatizes this triumvirate with three characters: Yusef al Qudsi, a Palestinian rebel; Michael O'Donegal, an Irish man serving in the British Army; and Rajib, a British soldier from India. The British themselves are represented by a General Falbour⁴⁶ and Lieutenant Douglas Duff, both of whom serve as comic foils, and deadly occupiers, in the play. He also includes a character Samuel Hirsch, a British-educated German Jew, who represents the voice of the European Jewish immigrant to Palestine.

Khalidi's writing is a reflection and extension of his father's academic works. According to Rashid Khalidi, the British occupation of Palestine created a complex legal and constitutional framework through which the British

O'Donegal (Michael Simpson, left), Yusef (Demosthenes Chrysan), and Rajib (Jim Sarbh) in the Alliance Theatre's 2009-10 world premiere production of Ismail Khalidi's *Tennis in Nablus*, winner of the 2010 Alliance/Kendeda National Graduate Playwriting Competition, directed by Peggy Shannon (photograph by Greg Mooney, courtesy Alliance Theatre).

created "a kind of iron cage for the Palestinians, from which they never succeeded in escaping."[47] Khalidi refers to the Balfour Declaration, a British document that promoted the idea of a national home for the Jewish people in Palestine. According to Khalidi, the declaration never cited the Palestinian people by name. Instead, despite being the majority population at that time, the Palestinians were referred to as "non–Jewish communities" or "natives" who possessed only civil and religious rights.[48] In addition, Khalidi states that historians make the false assumption that the Palestinians and the Zionists "were on equal footing vis-à-vis the British," and that the crushing of the 1936–39 revolt "marked the beginning of the end of Arab Palestine."[49] Ismail Khalidi seizes on this particular fact for the genesis of his play.

Tennis in Nablus attempts to address the issues of Palestinian identity and the Arab revolt utilizing the idea of an iron cage created by the British. At the outset of the play Yusef and his wife Ambara conduct a revolt against British forces—Yusef through tactical warfare, and Ambara through publication of articles in a periodical titled *Filasteen* (Palestine) under the alias Mohammad Ali Baybars. Their work is being undermined by several forces: the increase of Zionist influence and migration; the work of Palestinians who are profiting greatly by selling Palestinian properties to migrating European Jews; and the British, who clearly despise both peoples but obviously favor the Zionists in the struggle. Like his father before him, Khalidi clearly establishes that the Palestinians in British Mandated Palestine were fighting a losing battle as early as the 1930s.

By setting the play in the pre–1948 period, Khalidi also creates a postmemory play that examines a Palestine that existed before the establishment of the State of Israel. Khalidi's play does not attribute the loss of a Palestinian state solely on the establishment of Israel. Instead, he offers several reasons for this chain of historical events which includes Palestinians willfully leaving their land out of fear of conflict, Palestinians selling their lands for profit, and draconian British tactics that made daily existence untenable. One method he employs to dramatize the intra–Palestinian conflict is by creating conflict between Yusef and his nephew Tariq. Yusef is an older Palestinian insurgent who considers himself a rebel in the tradition of Emiliano Zapata. His nephew Tariq is a businessman working to make a profit off of the selling of Palestinian homes and lands to newly arrived immigrants from Europe. At first, it seems that Yusef is attempting to create an Arab-Jewish dichotomy regarding the migration of European Jews to Palestine. Instead, he changes the focus of the argument away from religion to the idea of origin:

> YUSEF: Well first of all you'd have to stop selling of our lands to the Europeans. That has to stop.
> TARIQ: You mean the Jews. I'd have to stop selling to Jews.
> YUSEF: No, I said Europeans. They are Europeans to me. I have no interest which way they talk to God. They are Europeans working in the interest of Europeans, and fighting side by side with the British Empire. Jews or not they are invaders and so are our enemies at this point, there's no changing that. They have arrived on our shores from elsewhere and they want the land and they'll have it before too long, mark my words.[50]

With this passage, that explains the protagonist's view of the migration to Palestine, Khalidi essentially negates the historical claims that Jews have on the land of Israel/Palestine. By simply equating the Zionist migration with European migration, he avoids the historical claim that Jews hold toward historical Israel. Near the end of the play, Khalidi does concede that the historical claim exists, yet he does not completely recognize it for the ancient Biblical claim it is:

YUSEF: I just see them as our long lost cousins coming back from years of wandering. And they've come back very much changed after all this time. And to them, we haven't changed enough and they see that as a weakness, a sign of our barbarism, so they look down upon us for it. They've come back with some of the same spite that the crusaders and the Brits carried here with them. And there are still the nomads among them, sure, the remnants of the wandering tribes, but they are the tribes of Berlin and Odessa, Vienna and Moscow. Not of this land.[51]

Despite his admission that the Jews of Europe did historically originate from the same land as the Palestinians, Khalidi's characters still attach the caveat that European Jews are "not of this land." Given this passage, it seems clear that Khalidi is drawing a sharp distinction between the Sephardic/Mizrahi Jews (Jews descended from communities in the Middle East, North Africa, and the Caucasus), and the Ashkenazi Jews of Europe. Khalidi continues this European distinction in other sections of the play where he refers to Tel Aviv as "a European city that has appeared on the coast of Palestine," to Palestinians in Jaffa staring "through the wall at Europe," and to Palestinians who work with the British and the Zionists as "monkeys ... in a nice European suit walking around the rainy streets of the imperial capital."[52] By drawing this distinction, Khalidi clarifies his political position in the play, yet he also rebuts the specific claims of Ashkenazi European Jewry to the land of Israel.

Rather than focus on the Arab-Zionist violence that consumed the discourse of the Arab Revolt, Khalidi instead turns his attention to the anti-Semitism that the British generals and soldiers brought with them to Palestine. General Falbour makes statements such as "Jews and Arabs are all alike, a beastly people, the whole lot of them not worth a single Englishman."[53] According to Falbour, Jews and Arabs are nothing more than money grubbers, murderers, and simpletons. Khalidi obviously sees the connection between moderate Palestinians and Jews as one of the more positive forces at work in this period, and he represents those moderates in the characters of Tariq and Hirsch. After Tariq is imprisoned by the British, Hirsch advocates for his release. After he does so, Tariq asks Hirsch about their future:

TARIQ: Tell me something Samuel. Can we both live here? Or is it going to be one of us?
...
HIRSCH: I want to live in Palestine, as a proud Jew. Alongside the Arabs. Safe.
TARIQ: Not you. I mean what do your leaders think? What do they want, the Begins and Ben Gurions, that crowd?
HIRSCH: Well there are always reactionaries and also sensible folks.[54]

The dichotomy between "reactionaries" and "sensible folks" is the dividing line between the radicals (Ambara, Yusef, Falbour, Duff) and the moderates (Tariq and Hirsch) in the play. While the play obviously advocates the Palestinian perspective, Khalidi does make it clear that, given the historical circumstances, there were no alternatives left to European Jews but migration to Palestine. Hirsch tells Tariq, "All of Germany is mad. There will be war and there will be nowhere to hide for us Tariq. It's become intolerable for Jews, anyone who thinks differently or looks differently. People are being shipped off in trains they say. It's going to make Palestine look like paradise, even to the non–Zionists."[55] Here Khalidi reminds readers and audience members that there were no alternatives left to them in Europe during the Holocaust. The relationship between Tariq and Hirsch is one example of how Khalidi attempts to create an Arab-Zionist connection between characters that is meant to represent the moderate perspective in the struggle.

On the Palestinian side, Khalidi attempts to equate the Palestinian struggle against the British with other historic liberation struggles. At one point Yusef says he wants to make sure the Palestinians "don't go the way of the red Indian of America, tricked and forced into cages in their own land, all in the name of progress."[56] Yusef also views his struggle as parallel with the Zapatista movement of Mexico, Gandhi's fight for liberation in India, and the Irish struggle against British control in Northern Ireland. By introducing the characters of Rajiv and O'Donegal, Khalidi further personifies and references the three groups who were most disgruntled with British rule at that time. The British officers constantly hurl epithets at the Irishman, the Indian, and the Arab and brutally lash O'Donegal when he dares confront his superiors. To further degrade their prisoners, Balfour and Duff force Yusef and Tariq to fetch their tennis balls under the scorching heat while they are both chained to one another.[57] Being subaltern subjects themselves, Rajiv and O'Donegal feel an instant connection with Yusef and Ambara; going so far as to accept Ambara's bribe to release Yusef from jail. Again, this dramatic exchange is meant to illustrate that the true enemy in the situation at that time was British Imperial rule.

The play ends with a series of symbolic images and happenings that dramatize the end of the rebellion and the dispersal of the Palestinians by the end of the British Mandate. Yusef's secret trial and summary execution can be read as the process that the British enacted to ensure that any future possibility of Palestinian self-governance was aborted before it could ever come to fruition. Yusef is hung by the neck above the tennis court to demonstrate that any resistance to British rule was tantamount to a death sentence. Tariq's departure from Palestine is symbolic of the Palestinians who left their homes after the violence made conditions unbearable. Ambara represents the Palestinians who remained under British rule and later became the Palestinians who currently live under occupation. The final symbolic gesture, Tariq's handing over of the keys to his destroyed home for his eventual return, is an image steeped in Palestinian lore. As journalist Robert Fisk writes:

> By one of the more subtle cruelties of Middle East history, the papers and keys were to prove the most symbolic and most worthless of possessions to the Palestinians. They acquired a significance that grew ever more painful as weeks and then months away from home turned into years.... For the keys—often made of thick grey iron, sometimes with decorated handles—were in a sense a promise of return, a promise that history inevitably broke. The new owners of those homes forebade any return and then changed the locks.[58]

Old keys and deeds being held by diasporic Palestinians to homes and lands they no longer inhabit was a common image among those of *al-Nakba* generation. Ambara promises Tariq she will hold the keys to his destroyed home, telling him, "they'll be right there ... talking to the sword.... Waiting for you to return."[59] Khalidi juxtaposes the image of useless keys to a destroyed home and an inert sword unable to resist occupation, with the play's final hopeful line, "the sky is clearing. The strange rain has stopped. Perhaps things will start looking up."[60] This perplexing ending, rife with both defeat and the promise of better things to come, leaves the audience with a sense of ambivalence regarding the future of Israel and Palestine.

Roar *and the Palestinian Diaspora*

Betty Shamieh's play *Roar* is a return play not because it explores a return to Palestine, but rather a return to Jordan, a country that currently contains 1.4 million Palestinians. Shamieh's play, which takes place in the immediate aftermath of the invasion of Kuwait by Iraqi forces in 1991, focuses on a family of diasporic Palestinian shopkeepers and landlords in Detroit. Ahmed and Karema Yacoub own and operate a "party store"[61] in Detroit, above which they reside. Their daughter Irene, a Palestinian American teenager, has dreams of becoming a famous American singer. When Karema's sister Hala comes to visit from Kuwait following the invasion of Iraqi forces in 1991, the family dynamic unravels. Ahmed begins longing for the relationship he and Hala once had, and for the life of the musician he once lived back in Jordan. Hala, traumatically damaged from the events of Black September and the Gulf War, cannot seem to find a place anywhere, especially in Detroit. Abe, Ahmed's brother, is a record producer who passes as Jewish and has lost all ties with his family. The play's resolution comes when Ahmed and Hala run away together to Jordan leaving Karema and Irene searching for a way forward with Abe's assistance. Shamieh's drama is focused upon the post–1967 situation of the Palestinian diaspora scattered throughout the Middle East and the United States. The central location of trauma in the play takes place during the 1970–1971 events of Black September, where Hala and Karema were attacked by Jordanian soldiers who beat them both and raped Hala.[62] Since that time Hala has been aimlessly wandering from man to man, and country to country.

The play's claim to postmemory can be found in Hala's telling line to Irene when she says, "what happened to your mother and her sister affects you in a thousand ways that you yourself will never be able to explain."[63] This directly corresponds to Hirsch's claim that the children of survivors of trauma live at a temporal and spatial remove from the decimated world of their parents and that the distance is impossible to bridge. Regardless, "the power of mourning and memory, and the depth of the rift dividing their parents' lives, impart to them something that is akin to memory."[64] Although Irene may not have

Hala (Annabella Sciorra, left) chastises Karema (Sarita Choudhury) in Betty Shamieh's *Roar*, directed by Marion McClinton at The Clurman Theater, 2004 (© Carol Rosegg).

experienced the trauma of Black September herself, her life has been forever shaped by that event.

Hala and Karema's first-hand trauma haunts them wherever they go. Karema copes with this trauma by devoting herself tirelessly to financial security. Hala, on the other hand, tries to cope with the trauma by filling her life with meaningless affairs and endless wandering. While Karema is a character who works through her trauma by attempting to realize the American dream, Hala is the one who constantly acts out through her inability to settle down and her reckless sexual exploits.

As Said wrote in his seminal essay about exile, "you are born into it, or it happens to you."[65] For the Palestinians who were exiled to countries like Jordan or Lebanon, where they are tolerated, reviled, or massacred, exile has offered no promise for a hopeful future. As Karema reminds Irene, "no one likes Jordan. It's a place you end up, not a place you go."[66] Hala puts it another way: "where your mother and I come from, you are born into one side or the other. The only choice you make is whether or not to keep breathing."[67] Arabic Studies scholar Zahia Smail Salhi writes that Arabs, no matter what the reason they have for leaving their homelands, "keep an idealized image of home as a paradise they were forced to flee, and never manage to entirely adopt their new dwellings. As such they share feelings of solitude, estrangement, loss, and longing."[68] All of Shamieh's Arab characters in *Roar* can be said to be suffering from these psychological conditions. Irene alone, the only American-born character in the play, seems to have a positive means of working through her postmemorial trauma.

Salhi writes that feelings of sorrow, tragedy, and loss are "symptomatic of the Palestinian tragedy resulting in the dislocation and exile of thousands of Palestinians ... and their continuous hope that their exile will eventually end."[69] Shamieh herself states that her writing is concerned with the particularities of Palestinian life with questions that include:

> How do you react to the erasure of your national identity and your personhood? What is reasonable? What is not reasonable? What is losing your humanity? What is retaining your rights as a human? That's the kind of thing that Palestinians talk amongst themselves and debate amongst themselves in much greater detail than we see in this country.[70]

In *Roar*, the manner in which the characters deal with this condition includes suffering through their alienation (Karema and Abe), escaping from their alienation (Hala and Ahmed), or choosing a mode of existence that removes the alienation altogether (Irene). Arguably, Palestinian American alienation is more acute than that felt by most Arab Americans because it involves the inability to return to a homeland because that homeland no longer physically exists.

The diasporic experience for the Arab American characters in the play is filled with contradictions. For instance, Karema and Ahmed wanted Irene to be brought up in the United States so she could escape the misery and suffering of Palestinians in Jordan. In doing so, Irene has embraced her Americanness and denied her Arabness completely. When Hala first tries to teach Irene Arabic music and song, Irene dismisses the gesture altogether. She tells Hala that "Arabic sounds so ugly. I never speak it in public. It sounds like spitting."[71] Later, when Hala tries to teach Irene Arabic music, Irene constantly evades her, preferring instead to sing English songs.

Another way the characters avoid their Arabness is by passing for other ethnicities. As Marvasti and McKinney explain, one manner for some subjects to pass is by trading their own ethnic identity with a less controversial one. Another strategy is to give an ambiguous account of one's ethnicity when asked to explain where one was born.[72] For instance, Karema tells Ahmed not to inform the tenants that he is the owner of the building while on repair calls. When Ahmed confronts her about this, she tells him she is afraid people would not rent the apartments if they knew Arabs owned them.[73] In another example, the character Abe passes himself off as an Egyptian Jew in order to further his career as a music producer.

> ABE: It was my first interview to be an assistant in the music industry. He asked me where I came from and I told him Egypt.
> KAREMA: First lie right there.
> ABE: But it wasn't really. I had lived in Egypt for six months before coming to the States. Egypt had just made peace with Israel. And I thought if I flat out told him I was a Palestinian, I'd never get the job. Then, he said, "there were lots of Jews in Egypt before all of the troubles" and I said "yes, there were a lot of Jews living in Egypt." So what if I somehow failed to mention that I wasn't one of them.[74]

Ironically, despite the compromises Karema has made in her own life, she considers Abe's actions reprehensible. Gradually, Abe admits that his actions were mistaken, and that "it costs me more than it ever gave me to deny who I am."[75]

In another exchange he tells Irene, "Don't mask who you are, because, if you do, nothing you achieve will be worth a damn." Being the consummate capitalist, Abe advises Irene not to change her name to something more pronounceable. Instead, he advises her, "if you make people money, trust me, they learn to pronounce your name."[76] As seen in other Arab American dramas,

Shamieh is dramatizing here that, in order to succeed in America, true identities must be sublimated. For Abe, this sublimation may have brought him wealth and prestige, but it cost him his identity. By play's end, Abe seems to be suggesting that an Arab identity can be retained but only if financially successful; otherwise, Arabs are relegated to a life of hiding their true identity. Alawi writes that self-pity is a result of the inner conflicts experienced by Palestinians who try to pass as Americans in order to secure refuge in a country "which condones violence against his people."[77] He also states that passing was easier for Palestinians in the first half of the twentieth century, before the Palestinians were equated with terrorism in the American imaginary.

Only the characters Hala and Ahmed decide that the alienation they face in America becomes too much to bear, which compels them to return to Jordan. They have their separate reasons for returning: for Ahmed, America is a place he does not belong and a place that rejects his music; for Hala, it is a place where she betrayed her sister yet again and where she will never belong. The fragmentation of the Yacoub family, first through violence and exile, and then though adultery and dislocation, is complete. Shamieh offers her own version of the *shatat*, or scattering. Karema will endure her painful exile by working to make enough money to ensure she never returns to Jordan and that her daughter can fulfill her dreams. Hala and Ahmed break their exile and return to Jordan in order to fulfill their own musical aspirations. Abe suffers his exile passing as an Egyptian Jew, devoid of family or companionship. Irene chooses her own middle path by rejecting her Arabness, embracing her American experience, and working for Abe in the hopes of becoming a famous American singer. The characters are scattered once again, exemplifying Said's view that "in a way, it's a sort of the fate of the Palestinians not to end up where they started but somewhere unexpected and far away."[78] This fate is one that befalls many characters in similar plays.

Food and Fadwa: *Life Under Occupation*

Palestinian American playwrights Lameece Issaq and Jacob Kader's play *Food and Fadwa* dramatizes life in the West Bank under occupation. The play's main character, Fadwa, lives in Bethlehem with her aging father Baba and her Aunt Samia. Her sister Dalal and fiancé Emir are preparing for their wedding and expecting the arrival of their cousin Hayat and her boyfriend Youssif, both of whom are living and working in the United States. Youssif and Fadwa once loved each other, but after leaving Palestine, Youssif and Hayat became lovers, unbeknownst to Fadwa.

Issaq explores the Palestinian situation by expressing the difficulties of living under Israeli occupation as well as the plight of those who left Palestine and established their lives in the United States. Like those in Shamieh's plays, the characters are torn between the prosperity gained in America and the loss of the culture and life they left behind in Palestine. Fadwa and her cousin Hayat represent the difference between tradition and modernity within the Palestinian and the Palestinian American diaspora. The main expression of this difference is Fadwa's passion and talent in cooking traditional Arab dishes opposed to Hayat's ability to transform those same dishes through fusion cooking. Fadwa represents the Palestinian living under occupation, trying desperately to hold on to her native culture and cuisine; Hayat represents the Arab American who attempts to fuse her Arab heritage with her American upbringing. As the play progresses the differences between the two of women become irreconcilable.

By setting the play in an olive orchard and having the protagonists' livelihoods dependent upon olive trees, Issaq centers the occupation on the symbolism of the olive tree in relation to the Israeli occupation. The father, Baba, owned an orchard of olive trees from which he made olive oil. When the Israeli Defense Forces bulldozed his orchard, Baba began a gradual descent into dementia, eventually forgetting everything and everyone around him. Issaq and Kader draw the connection between trauma and memory with the quote, "to seize an ancient olive tree is like a confiscation of memory."[79] As Hirsch reminds us, for survivors who have been separated or exiled from their ravaged worlds, memory is not only an act of recall, but also one of mourning inflected by anger, rage, and despair.[80] This connection between Palestinian livelihood and the olive tree is one that is recounted throughout Palestinian literature concerning the occupation. According to Atyaf Alwazir, the Arab-Israeli conflict is both a human and environmental disaster. The uprooting of historic olive trees is explained by the IDF as the need to build settlements, expand roads, and lay infrastructure as well as defend against snipers. Palestinians believe that the trees are being uprooted in order to destroy the Palestinian economy, to expand disputed settlements, and to force farmers from their lands.[81] Issaq plays upon this connection between the uprooting of olive trees and the uprooting of memory when Auntie Samia explains how Baba lost his memory.

> You can't imagine what it was like. Tanks and bulldozers surrounded his groves. It was harvest time—we were all there. It's a celebration—you know how we've done this for generations. We stood and watched as the army uprooted every tree. There was no reason, or warning. Just ... waste. The soldiers told us to go, but my

brother wouldn't move. He is very stubborn ... very strong. But when he came home, he just sat in this chair ... just staring. He didn't speak. When he finally did, weeks later, it was to ask where he was.... He left to try to remember.[82]

According to Alwazir, olive trees have been destroyed by soldiers, by settlers, by the inability to harvest the trees due to military curfews, and by security closures. In choosing the olive tree as a central symbol in their play, Issaq and Kader are attempting to create a connection between the uprooting of the olive tree and the uprooting of Palestinian lives living under occupation. Furthermore, since olive trees can live from 400 to 1000 years, the authors also mean to connect the age and memories of the trees with the age and memory of the older Palestinian generations, personified here by the character Baba.

Issaq and Kader also employ their own form of educational accounting in the drama, especially regarding the Israeli Occupation. Traces of occupation appear throughout the play and serve as the obstacles that impede the characters' lives. There are constant references to checkpoints, summary searches, Israeli settlers, and the separation wall that divides Israel from the occupied West Bank. In Act One, the characters find the so-called "separation fence" laughable:

> HAYAT: That wall is—I have no words. I mean, I always knew—but seeing it. It's shocking.
> YOUSSIF: It's our national landmark!
> EMIR: Yep. Our Great Wall of Palestine!
> HAYAT: It's practically in your backyard.
> DALAL: It's in everyone's backyard.
> EMIR: Yes, we own at least a kilometer.[83]

Issaq and Kader also include more specific information about the wall, such as the fact that it is 307 miles longer and 14 feet taller than the Berlin Wall. The characters joke about the names given the wall such as "separation wall," "security wall," "apartheid wall," and "a virtual gate." The characters also complain about the lack of permits and the proliferation of checkpoints throughout the West Bank. They even jokingly create a map of the West Bank with hummus, rice, chicken, napkins, and cups on the kitchen table. Despite all of the levity surrounding occupation in Act One of the play, the second act takes a much darker view of the situation.

Act Two begins with an extended Israeli Army curfew that lasts several days and forces the entire family to be incarcerated in their own home, delaying Dalal and Emir's wedding. After several days under this curfew the characters begin voicing their anger against the occupation. During their incarceration, their water and electricity are cut off, their food supply becomes dangerously low, and they are not allowed to go out to search for Baba after he escapes.

The play ends with the scattering of the family once more. In a reverse to Shamieh's play, there are those who stay to endure the occupation and those who leave to find a better life in America. Fadwa's *sumud*, or steadfastness, is rooted in her love of the land, traditions, and history. Unlike Emir, Hayat, Dalal, and Youssif, Fadwa decides to stay behind with Aunt Samia. In memory of her father and the orchard they once had, Fadwa plants olive saplings in the hopes they will one day grow to be as large as the uprooted olive trees she lost. Like *Tennis in Nablus*, the play ends on a bittersweet note: Fadwa tells the audience "Say goodbye with grace, and then, begin again."[84] The planting of the tree portends a new generation of olives and a new hope for a better future for Palestine. Issaq says, "Hope is crucial—without hope we really have nothing! And the tree represents new life—new life among destruction, death, and pain. Something can grow in place of that difficulty, and that is what keeps us going."[85]

Dalal (Maha Chehlaoui, left), Emir (Arian Moayed), Youssif (Haaz Sleiman), and Hayat (Heather Raffo) joke about the "Great Wall of Palestine" in Lameece Issaq and Jacob Kader's *Food and Fadwa,* directed by Shana Gold, performed at the New York Theatre Workshop and Noor Theatre, 2012 (photograph by Joan Marcus).

Being an occupation play, Issaq explores the lives of rooted and of diasporic Palestinians. Hirsch notes that the deep sense of displacement suffered by children of exile creates "a strange sense of plentitude rather than a feeling of absence.... The fullness of postmemory is no easier a form of connection than the absence it also generates."[86] Despite the trauma Issaq's characters endure under occupation, there is a sense of plentitude and connection found in food and tradition. The various foods that Fadwa cooks throughout the play—*baba ghanoush, hashweh, mana'eesh, tabbouli, mloukiyi*—are all expressions of love that connect and bind the family, and the culture together. Despite the fact that these foods can be changed and transformed by others like Hayat, they are the remnants of a lost culture. Regardless of the loss, there is a sense in the play that, for those who remain behind, the comforts of tradition can serve to fill the gaps left by the loss of a world decimated by war. This passing down of tradition, in the form of family recipes and embodied experience, becomes the main symbol of postmemory in the play.

Vicarious Victimhood?

These Palestinian American playwrights are all writing from a postmemorial, secondary witness position. All of these writers are American born to parents who were born outside of Palestine. Each of these writers explores the Palestinian condition of occupation, steadfastness, and resistance as if they themselves were victims. However, their vicarious victimhood is problematic since it tends to conflate the Palestinian position with the Palestinian American position. Given the fact that these writers do not live in Jordan, Lebanon, the occupied West Bank, Gaza, or Golan Heights, this calls into question whether the children of survivors of tragedies can fully comprehend the real victims' situation, or even if they have the right to take on the suffering of the Palestinian people as their own. What does constitute these as postmemorial works (according to Hirsch's definition) is that they are created through an imaginative investment. The children of exiled survivors who have lived through banishment and destruction of home, remain marginalized or exiled in the diaspora. These writers are attempting to fill in the gaps in, and absences of, their grandparents' and parents' memories of Palestine. What gives their writing credence is that they still have relatives in the West Bank and/or Gaza who are experiencing daily traumas. Sa'di and Abu-Loghod remind us that

> when the past is still entrenched in the present existential conditions of the individual, affecting the myriad aspects of her or his life, perhaps he or she cannot

secure the conditions to narrate the past. For Palestinians, still living their dispossession, still struggling or hoping for return, many under military occupation, many still immersed in matters of survival, the past is neither distant nor over.[87]

These Palestinian American playwrights, by narrating this past, may be conflating absence with loss. Viewed through the lens of resistance literature, this conflation is not one that is simply mourning loss but is rather actively working toward some kind of accounting for a present and a future. The working through is the securing of the conditions to narrate their own past and the past of their ancestors. They are struggling to come to terms with the British Mandate, the establishment of the State of Israel, the further losses of 1967 and 1973, the Gulf Wars, the 2006 Gaza War, and the repeated failed peace accords. Their works attempt to understand and reconcile a history that is still being decided in the present.

These plays, much like the Palestinian American activism that was generated from the late 1960s onward, are an attempt to speak from the Arab American positions of empathy with the Palestinians living under occupation and of Palestinian Americans working to understand their own identity. These playwrights imaginatively recreate a Palestine they know only through periodic visits, memories, and stories told by their elders. Their artistic works are a form of political activism, yet they acknowledge that they themselves are removed from the day-to-day conflicts found in the West Bank, Gaza Strip, and Palestinian refugee camps scattered throughout the Middle East. Najla Said told *New York Times*, "When I hear the word Palestine, I hear my dad's voice saying it. But I don't know what it is, because it's not a place for me.... I don't know it; I have no connection to it. Even my dad was not really connected to the actual, geographical place—for him it was an idea, a struggle for equality and human rights."[88] Similarly, Ismail Khalidi believes his work is meant to change perceptions of Palestinians.

> As a Palestinian-American playwright, I am deeply committed to challenging the myths and distortions about Palestinians that abound in American discourse. In my plays, I try to bring some light to the often obscured human dimensions of Palestinian identity. My work attempts to challenge the stereotype of the Palestinian as a violent, barbaric and inherently anti–Semitic opponent of modernity.[89]

Given the artists' stated intentions in writing these plays, it seems clear that these works are interested in restaging and reclaiming Palestinian history. These artists are committed to changing negative perceptions of Palestinians and Palestinian Americans, to reimagining their ancestral history, and to working to discover their own place within the Palestinian narrative. Unlike

Palestinian writers before them, these playwrights are able to meld both their Palestinian heritage with their American sensibilities. This melding leads to a more empathic and multifaceted voice that can simultaneously speak out for Palestinian rights while understanding and explaining the Israeli narrative. Although it is clear that these works are by no means balanced in their viewpoints, they do strive to comprehend the complications and difficulties that surround the conflict without completely attempting to claim Palestine as their own.

6

Arabs Filming Arabs: Contemporary Arab American Films

Independent filmmaker Cherien Dabis was born in 1976 and grew up in Cellina, Ohio, during the first Gulf War. Her father, a physician, lost many clients "because people didn't want to see an Arab doctor." Her family received death threats, and the Secret Service came to her high school and interrogated her seventeen-year-old sister because they erroneously received a tip that she had threatened to kill the president. It was then, at the age of fourteen, that she had what she called her political awakening. "I started really recognizing the fact that the media was perpetuating stereotypes of Arabs and Arab Americans and that we were being directly affected by people believing those stereotypes. So it kind of became my mission in life to do something to change that." Dabis felt like the bridge between American and Palestinian cultures and responsible for bringing those two worlds together. Her film, *Amreeka*, based on her aunt and cousin who immigrated to the United States and who were ultimately forced to return, became an independent and critical success. "It was always the Arabs not understanding the Americans, the Americans not understanding the Arabs, and constantly having to defend one side to the other side and explain who I was," she told an interviewer. "I never fit in here and I never quite fit in there."[1]

¤ ¤ ¤

Since the earliest films, Arabs have primarily been portrayed in two ways: in the modern period Arabs were Orientalized as exotic sheiks and sexualized belly dancers often seen riding flying carpets, luxuriating in smoke-filled harems, and riding camels on desert landscapes. In the contemporary period, that stereotypical portrayal shifted. The exotic sheik transformed into either the money hungry, lecherous oil broker or the black clad, turbaned terrorist. The harem girl also transformed; instead of being a sexualized prostitute in a harem, she became a *burqa*-clad suicide bomber. In either period, the ugly and pernicious stereotyping in mainstream films was the product of those who viewed Arabs as a foreign "Other" who had little or no relation to any "Western" values or personages. Furthermore, it was rare that Arabs actually wrote scripts or portrayed Arabs in these films. In the contemporary period, as Arabs and Arab Americans began to study film and become filmmakers, the notion of self-representation became prevalent. The screenwriters, directors, and performers discussed in this chapter decided to tell their own specific stories in deeply personal films that they believe more accurately represented their culture.

The New Wave of Arab American Filmmakers

Recently, several Arab American filmmakers have emerged whose works provide more humanistic and dimensional portrayals of Arabs and Arab Americans in film. The most notable of these are Palestinian American Cherien Dabis, writer and director of *Amreeka*; Egyptian Americans Hesham Issawi and Sayed Badreya, the co-writers and producers of *American East*; Canadian Lebanese director Ruba Nadda, the writer and director of the film *Sabah: A Love Story*; Palestinian American Jackie Reem Salloum, whose most recent documentary *Slingshot Hip Hop* has garnered critical acclaim; and Rana Kazkaz, who has written and directed several short films including *Kemo Sabe* and *Deaf Day*. These writers all have similar goals: to essentially "recast" Hollywood Arabs and Arab Americans and to represent them more truthfully than they have been represented by mainstream filmmakers.

For Issawi, the goal of *American East* was about surmounting stereotypical notions of Middle Easterners:

> Ultimately, this film is about understanding and misunderstanding, and about the difficulty of overcoming strongly-held, fixed ideas toward Middle Eastern culture. My goal was to show what happens when different cultures and mentalities collide, when dreams and realities confront each other.[2]

For Dabis, the intention for her film *Amreeka* was similar:

> I want people to walk out of the theater feeling like they know us, like they'd just celebrated the culture with us. I want them to walk out feeling a certain amount of familiarity, like 'We too are immigrants, we too have the same challenges, the same funny and strange experiences, and we've gone through so many of the same things.' And ultimately I'd like people to walk away with an idea that there are all

kinds of Middle Eastern people, that while everybody is different, we are all the same in many ways.[3]

Like other Arab American filmmakers, Dabis understands that some non-Arab filmmakers have created sympathetic portrayals of Arab Americans on film. Dabis and others like her believe that their personal stories of growing up Arab in America can, and should, be dramatized on film. For Nashef the portrayal of Arabs and Arab Americans on screen is not only an artistic choice, it is also a part of her activism. Like other Arab Americans before her, there were either negative representations of Arabs on film or none to be found at all. A motivation, therefore, for becoming a filmmaker was to tell personal stories, to represent her culture, and to bring Arab American stories to mainstream cinema. Nashef says, "Growing up I never saw people like me and my own experience in the movies.... Our experience as Arab Americans makes for great storytelling. We need to be on a screen somewhere."[4] Unlike other films, Nashef decided not to make the film political or even highlight the fact that the characters were of Arab descent. Instead, she simply uses the settings of a gas station and cell phone store that happen to be owned and operated by Arab Americans, as the setting for her film *Detroit Unleaded*.

> I think portraying Arab Americans as everyday people, as characters that non-Arabs can relate to, is a statement in itself. If I can get an audience to be thoroughly entertained and go through an emotional journey with an Arab-driven character, then they're going to have a really harder time stereotyping us or buying into all the fear factors that are out there. To me, that is my activism. I think it's important for our image to be positive in our community. That's how I believe you really reach people, because you become friends with these characters.[5]

These three films successfully present sympathetic and humanistic portrayals of Arab and Arab American lives in America. The characters in these films are actual human beings with the same hopes, dreams, and desires as would be found in any other film. This approach is guided by several factors: the frustration of growing up and watching films that dehumanized their culture, a desire to portray Arab and Arab American characters more dimensionally, and a very personal approach to telling stories that directly affected their own lives.

Jackie Salloum's Planet of the Arabs

One of the first projects by Arab American filmmaker Jackie Reem Salloum is titled *Planet of the Arabs*, based on Shaheen's book *Reel Bad Arabs*.

Salloum describes her film as "a trailer-esque montage spectacle of Hollywood's relentless vilification and dehumanization of Arabs and Muslims."[6] In it, Salloum attempts to achieve visually what Shaheen attempted textually—what she says is to "reveal truth about Arab images."[7] Salloum's work calls to mind Evelyn Alsultany's contention that, over the past four to five decades, the majority of film and television representations of Arabs and Muslims have sought to elicit celebration from the audience upon their eventual murder by the protagonist.[8] The film's title is a sardonic reference to another Hollywood classic, *Planet of the Apes*. Unlike *Planet of the Apes*, Salloum's Arabs are not in control of a future earth but rather a collection of Hollywood's portrayals of a group of violent, vicious, hateful, and angry men and women who terrorize non–Arabs. Salloum's choice of this title posits that there are the normal or "good" humans versus the abnormal or "bad" Arabs. The film begins with ominous music and a slow motion clip of hooded and armed gunmen walking down the aisle of an airplane. A mustached man stands with a gun and shouts in a heavy Arabic accent, "This is a hijacking!" Heavy metal music explodes as a montage of evil looking Arabs flash across the screen. The title "Planet of the Arabs" stamps on a white background. Then, a seemingly endless consecution of film clips goes by in rapid succession featuring stars like Chuck Norris, Michael J. Fox, Arnold Schwarzenegger, Jamie Lee Curtis, and even Daffy Duck. Suddenly, Salloum interjects a scene from Sidney Lumet's film *Network*. The character Howard Beale screams out,

> You're beginning to believe the illusions we're spinning here! You're begging to think that the tube is reality, that your own lives are unreal. You do whatever the tube tells you. You dress like the tube, you eat like the tube, you raise your children like the tube tells you. You even sex like the tube. This is mass madness you maniacs!

And here begins the underlying narrative of the film. Salloum clearly posited the sections from *Network* as the only truth among the panoply of negative images that bookend it. The final clip returns to the film *Network* where Beale screams out, "turn off you television sets! Turn them off now! Turn them off right now!" The screen fades to black.

As a response to Shaheen's book, it is helpful contrasting *Reel Bad Arabs* with *Planet of the Arabs*. Shaheen's book lists the films he indicts individually, and then critiques their most egregious scenes. In contrast, Salloum only creates a long montage of these scenes. The repetition of the scenes does little to critique them; instead, the scenes barrage the viewers, overwhelming and leaving them numb. Also, Shaheen's book lists the filmmakers, the actors, and the studios that created the films in question. Salloum's film does not give any more information to the viewer than the images themselves. Many who see the film may know the actors or films they are viewing, but have no reference to the directors, writers, or studios that created them. This de-contextualizes the film and turns the focus only on the spectacle of violence and on the actors themselves.

Perhaps the greatest difficulty with Salloum's film is her solution to the problem, or lack thereof. Shaheen's book *Guilty: Hollywood's Verdict on Arabs After 9/11* includes what he calls "Reel Solutions" to these films. His solutions include a heightened presence of Arab and Arab Americans in the film industry, the creation of what he calls "fresh films" (those that create more three-dimensional characters), and "shattering the silence" by speaking out against stereotypical films.[9] In addition, Shaheen's book analyzes, criticizes, and provides solutions to the conundrum of negative representation. By contrast Salloum's film, that ends with the *Network* character screaming "turn off you television sets! Turn them off now!" seems to advocate not for constructive dialogue, but rather for disengagement with the medium altogether. Disengagement is actually contrary to what many Arab American media critics recommend. Disengagement from the system removes the prospect of Arab American artists being able to control the means of representation themselves. However, as the following examples illustrate, simply having control over these representations does not always mean the representations will improve.

Recasting Hollywood

Arab American writer, critic, and humorist Ray Hanania grew up in a Palestinian Christian household in Chicago, Illinois. Unlike other kids, he could not passively enjoy Hollywood films the way his friends might.

> My parents hated movies that made the Arabs look bad. And nearly every Hollywood movie about the Middle East, Israel or the Arabs made the Arabs look bad. Imagine growing up as a young child, and watching movies that made people who were your father, brother or cousins appear to be brutal killers. It was like that in nearly every movie.[10]

Prior to 2009, there were no major Arab American films produced in the United States. This is startling given the fact that Arab Americans first migrated to the United States in the late–nineteenth century and have been a part of the literary landscape since the early–twentieth century. Three films, *American East*, *Amreeka*, and *Detroit Unleaded* (released in 2007, 2009, and 2012, respectively), represent the major attempts at full-length feature films written and directed by Arab Americans. The trajectories of these films were markedly different; where *Amreeka* has won multiple awards and has been screened internationally, *American East* was a direct-to-video release receiving little critical attention, despite starring and being co-produced by A-list Arab American actor Tony Shalhoub, and *Detroit Unleaded* was an official selection for the 2012 Toronto International Film Festival and has toured the film festival circuit. The reasons for these three films having such different receptions speak to the content of the films, their individual messages, and their handling of similar themes. It seems that, despite *American East* and *Amreeka* speaking to the plight of Arab Americans and their struggles in the United States in the post–9/11 context, *Amreeka* provided a more palatable message for film distributors and audiences. First, it dramatized the lives of Christian rather than Muslim Arab protagonists and it evaded many confrontational and contentious issues regarding the Israeli-Palestinian conflict. Second, it had a major backer with National Geographic Entertainment. Last, it is a more genial film and spends less time on politics and more time on the human story. *Detroit Unleaded* takes a different approach altogether. The film is an apolitical love story between an Arab American man and an Arab American woman. Politics are simply not a factor. If anything is to be garnered by critiquing these films and their contrasting receptions, it would be that, despite Arab Americans having the means to produce full-length feature films in the United States, the success of such films requires that they conform to certain standards that make them more attractive to the distributors who control the film industry.

Arab Americans on Film (or the Absence Thereof)

A great deal of attention has been given to the misrepresentation of Arabs on film by film by theorists such as Jack G. Shaheen, Evelyn Alsultany, and Tim Semmerling (to name only a few). Comparatively, very little scholarship has been devoted to the image of Arab Americans on film. This absence can be attributed mainly to the fact that there are so very few images of Arab Americans in Hollywood films at all. In their book *America on Film: Representing Race, Class, Gender, and Sexuality at the Movies*, Harry M. Benshoff and Sean Griffin write:

> Intriguingly, one of the most significant things about Arab Americans onscreen in America is their relative scarcity: Hollywood has much more regularly depicted images of *Middle Eastern Arabs* while nearly ignoring the presence of *Arab Americans* … rarely have Arabs been shown becoming part of the fabric of either Euro-

pean or American communities. There has been an attitude among many that people of Arab heritage cannot assimilate into Western society ... many today assume that Arab Americans pledge allegiance to the Muslim faith and not to the United States.[11]

Although Benshoff and Griffin attempt to make the distinction between Arab Americans and what they call "Middle Eastern Arabs," they are clear that Hollywood depictions of both are replete with negative imagery. They write that "[the] linkage of sex, violence, and (non–Christian) religion continues to mark more contemporary stereotypes of Arabs and Arab Americans."[12] Bayoumi writes, "It seems barely an exaggeration to say that Arab and Muslim Americans are constantly talked about but almost never heard from. The problem is not that they lack representations, but that they have too many. And these are all abstractions."[13] In her study of Arab Americans on film, Alsultany writes, "Although there have been abundant stereotypical representations of Arabs in the U.S. media and most notably in Hollywood cinema, portrayals of Arab Americans have been scant." In her study of the post–9/11 television landscape, she finds that there have been more representations of Arab Americans on U.S. television programs and, interestingly, these portrayals have been generally more sympathetic. However, she concludes that

> audience sympathy is evoked for the plight of the Arab American after 9/11, but the right to be racist and suspicious of Arab and Muslim Americans is affirmed, and government practices to profile racially, detain, deport, and terrorize Arabs and Muslims are accepted. Although Arab Americans are represented as victims and guilty only by their association to Arabs (non–Americans), the government's discourse about the continued Arab and Muslim threat to national security is narrated, and viewers are interpellated as citizens virtually participating in these national debates.[14]

The crises that are encountered in these television dramas are used to justify the racist views and practices of the dominant culture toward Arabs, Arab Americans, Muslims, and Muslim Americans who are portrayed as threats to the nation. They become a "racialized enemy" that the nation utilizes to legitimize its abuses of power.[15] For his part, Shaheen concludes that, "to quash the Arab stereotype we must first identify it as unacceptable and commit to its eradication by speaking out."[16] This speaking out has come mainly from scholars, but filmmakers are now utilizing their talents to speak out through filmmaking.

Arab American filmmakers, like their counterparts in theatre and performance, have committed themselves to the eradication of negative stereotyping, to writing fully dimensional characters who eschew the traditional representations of Arabs on screen, and to telling deeply personal stories that provide insight into the lives of Arabs in America. One of the difficulties these filmmakers encounter is there are few bankable Arab American actors who have the clout to get these films produced. Without Arab American actors, these artists are searching abroad for funding and this sometimes places their films outside the traditional distribution markets that would garner the attention they would require to become mainstream successes. Although these films have received critical acclaim, they remain largely unknown by most American moviegoers. There has yet to be a crossover "hit" for Arab Americans that highlights their culture in the way that *My Big, Fat Greek Wedding* did for Greek Americans or *Bend It Like Beckham* did for British Indians. Crossover has been slow to materialize partially because the subject matter of these films is much more serious and more political than other films.

Immigrant Tales

Amreeka, *American East*, and *Detroit Unleaded* are immigrant tales. *Amreeka* is about Muna and Fadi Farah, Palestinian Christians who decide to leave the West Bank for the United States after unexpectedly being granted a travel visa. Upon arriving in a small Illinois town, Muna and Fadi realize that the cookie tin, in which they secretly stashed their life savings, was accidentally disposed of by TSA officials at the airport. Luckily for them, they have Muna's sister's family, who, outwardly, are living the American dream replete with a large house, stylish clothing, and a thriving medical practice. Muna, who was trained and worked as a banker in Palestine, quickly discovers that she cannot find equal work in America and, after what little money she has left finally runs out, she decides to take a job at the local White Castle hamburger restaurant. Her son, Fadi, finds that he is discriminated against in school by a group of upperclassmen who harass him by shouting out epithets like "Osama" and "terrorist." He is unsuccessful at fitting in which leads to conflict with his classmates.

American East is the story of Mustafa (played by Badreya himself), an Egyptian immigrant who runs Habiby's Café in the "Little Arabia" district of Los Angeles. His café is in a decrepit building with plumbing and electrical problems, and Mustafa can barely make ends meet with his dwindling clientele in the post–9/11 environment. Mustafa has a daughter named Leila, who also does not fit in with her classmates at school, and a sister named Salwah, who is expected to marry a traditionally-minded Egyptian man named Sabir, which she is loathe to do. A sub-plot involves Mustafa's employee, Omar, a struggling

Hollywood actor who cannot seem to be cast in anything but terrorist roles, and Mustafa's Jewish friend, Sam (played by Shalhoub), with whom he wishes to open a restaurant.

Detroit Unleaded opens with Brahim and Miriam, an older Arab immigrant couple, going out on a date. Brahim has purchased a new car for his wife despite the fact that she does not drive. They are obviously a loving couple, but are worried about the future of their son, Sami, who wishes to move to California to study. Miriam wants her son to study somewhere closer, but Brahim urges her to allow their son to explore the world. After their discussion, he tells her he is going to work at their gas station. That night, he is killed by an armed assailant. The rest of the film takes place at the same gas station sometime later, only now it is being run by Sami and his cousin, Mike. The station is definitely in disrepair, and Sami is miserable working there, stuck working in "the cage"—a bulletproof enclosure with a cash register. One day a woman named Najla (or Naj) comes to drop off phone cards that she sells as part of her brother Fadi's cell phone business. For Sami, it is love at first sight. The relationship progresses despite the fact that Najla wants to keep it secret for fear of what others in the Arab community would say about her. Finally, after several visits, Najla is discovered in the cage with Sami by her brother Fadi. Sami finally decides to change his life, forcing his mother to throw out her mourning clothes, quitting the station, and running away. Najla leaves as well. The final scene is Sami and Najla driving away together to an unknown destination.

Amreeka, *American East*, and *Detroit Unleaded* share several common, yet slightly different, plot elements. The first major element is the protagonists who are either immigrants, exiles, or American born Arabs. Muna is a Christian Palestinian, Mustafa is a Muslim Egyptian, and Sami and Naj are Lebanese Americans. With Muna and Mustafa, both Arab immigrants, the sensitive subjects of the Israeli–Palestinian conflict, questions of assimilation and integration, and anti–Arab bias and prejudice are all addressed. For Muna and her family, discrimination impacts them on many levels. Muna's brother-in-law, a doctor named Nabeel, is losing patients who no longer wish to be seen by an Arab physician; Muna is unable to find work in the banking industry because several interviewers are afraid she'll "blow the place up," and, as mentioned earlier, her son Fadi is harassed in school by both prejudiced teachers and students alike. In a dialogue with Fadi's principal, Mr. Novatski, Muna both defends Muslims and states her own religious background.

> NOVATSKI: You know, I think you're seeing the worst of it, Mrs. Farah, I really do. Kids just don't know any better. You know, they hear about one Muslim extremist, suddenly, all Muslims are extremists.

MUNA: But they are not.
NOVATSKI: No, of course they're not.
MUNA: We are not Muslim, even.
NOVATSKI: I'm sorry, I just assumed...
MUNA: It doesn't matter. We are minority here and minority there.[17]

Muna points out that Palestinian Christians, often mistaken for Muslims, are a minority in Palestine and in America. Muna's words contradict widely held beliefs that all Palestinians are Muslims. For Mustafa in *American East*, his Muslim subject-position is stated early on in this dialogue with his son, Muhammad:

MOHAMMED: Why am I a Muslim?
MUSTAFA: What?
MOHAMMED: Why'd you have to name me Mohammed?
MUSTAFA: I named you after our own prophet and you are Muslim because I am Muslim.
MOHAMMED: Everyone at school is either Jewish or Christian.
MUSTAFA: All the same, all believe in one God.[18]

The fact that Muna is a Christian Arab and Mustafa is a Muslim Arab is central to the discrimination(s) they face. As Naber writes, "Although U.S. popular culture representations often conflate the categories 'Arab' and 'Muslim,' not all Arabs are Muslim and not all Muslims are Arabs."[19] Indeed, according to the Arab American Institute, Christian Arabs constitute the vast majority of Arab Americans.[20] Regardless of their religious background, the filmmakers are clear that protagonists and their families are viewed by their fellow Americans as foreign, dangerous, Muslim Others who must be excluded from work, school, and society despite their religious differences. In *Detroit Unleaded*, the majority of the characters are Arabs and the non–Arabs in the films, who are customers of the gas station and cell phone store, generally have good relations with them.

Another trope that *Amreeka* and *American East* employ is the benevolent Jewish benefactor. In *Amreeka*, this character is a second-generation Polish Jew named Mr. Novatski, the principle of Fadi's high school. As Fadi increasingly gets into trouble with his classmates, and as Muna finds it more difficult to acclimate to her life in America, Mr. Novatski befriends them and helps both in several ways including driving Muna to her work, discussing her problems with her, and ultimately taking responsibility for Fadi after he is arrested for attacking a classmate. In *American East*, Mustafa's Jewish friend Sam wants to start a new restaurant with Mustafa. Unlike Mr. Novatski's Polish ancestry,

Sam is a self-pronounced Israeli Jew who wears a Star of David ring on his finger, a yarmulke on his head, and drives a Mercedes with an American and Israeli flag prominently displayed on the bumper. Unlike the secular Novatski, Sam's family is Orthodox. They run the family business with Sam, but are against his going into a new venture with Mustafa. By film's end, however, Sam defies his family and helps Mustafa open his dream restaurant named *American East*. In both films, Mr. Novatski and Sam are central in making the transition and success of these Arab characters possible.

Being films about Arabs and Arab Americans, it is no wonder that discussion of U.S. involvement in Middle Eastern politics is central to these films. Muna and Fadi leave a West Bank that is infiltrated with checkpoints and violence. Unlike Muna, who struggled to leave Palestine, her sister Raghda (played by Hiam Abbass) longs to return to her homeland. Whereas *Amreeka* centers its critique on U.S. involvement in the invasion of Iraq, and makes only passing references the Israeli Occupation, *American East* confronts the Israeli-Palestinian conflict much more directly and bluntly. During one heated discussion in the café, two of Mustafa's customers, Fikry (an Iraqi Christian) and Murad (an Egyptian Muslim) have a confrontation with Sam:

Alia (Hiam Abbass, left) and Raghda (Salma Halaby) share memories in the 2009 film *Amreeka*, written and directed by Cherien Dabis (courtesy Cherien Dabis).

FIKRY: Why would anyone want to be Arab these days? To be Jewish, well ... that's cool man. You get the support of everyone.

SAM: Ah, you guys, still going on about that!

MURAD: Oppression's still going on, Sephardic Sam, why shouldn't we be going on?

SAM: The truth is ... the fact is that the Jordanians killed more Palestinians than anybody else...

MURAD: Bullshit! Bullshit! You know what, you bagel munchers, you steal their land, you destroy their homes, you shoot missiles from the skies, into streets full of innocent people...

SAM: You prefer to blow up buses and airplanes full of innocent people![21]

American East contains several of these heated dialogues that discuss the conflict in angry and confrontational terms. By contrast, *Amreeka*'s most political statement comes in the form of Muna's brother-in-law's criticism of the American war in Iraq, and the Israeli Occupation is only fleetingly discussed.

MUNA: What's happening?

NABEEL: Thirty-one Iraqis were killed in their sleep. It was an accidental bombing.

[*He laughs*] Accidental bombing. The worst calamity is one that makes you laugh. Look at this. They demolished thirteen homes in Rafah. Three Palestinians were killed. And on the American stations they're not showing any of it. It's as if it never happened.

MUNA: Enough with all this news. It's so depressing.

NABEEL: You know that we finance all this with our tax dollars.

MUNA: We have to live, Nabeel. We have to live our life.[22]

Amreeka's critique of the Israeli-Palestinian conflict is brief and muted with Muna's statement "We have to live our life." Although *Amreeka* is about Palestinians and *American East* is about Egyptians, *American East* is much more confrontational regarding the contentious and difficult issues regarding Middle East politics. Regardless, both films broach this contentious issue in ways many other American films might not.

If a major criticism could be raised against these two films, it is that, much like non–Arab films about Arabs, these stories reiterate the trope of the violent young Arab male. In *Amreeka*, after being constantly harassed and after his teenage tormentors verbally attack his mother, Fadi takes revenge by attacking the ringleader of the gang at his home, an action that subsequently gets him arrested. In *American East*, the young Arab American actor, Omar, when realizing his "big break" role has been changed to that of yet another terrorist, decides to take the film crew hostage and accidentally shoots a guard. Omar is eventually trapped and shot dead by police. Despite their trying to create more positive images of Arabs and Arab Americans in film, these films unwittingly reiterate the notion that there is something inherently violent about young Arab men. Surely this was not the intention of the filmmakers but the films read in such a way that this conclusion is unavoidable. Much like Rihani's *Wajdah*, which relies on Shakespearean tragic dramaturgy for its conflict, the three-act film structure also demands conflict that includes the film's protagonist. This invariably forces the protagonist into dramatic situations that demand conflict. This is yet another example of how, just because a film is produced by underrepresented filmmakers seeking to change misperceptions of their group, it does not necessarily follow that some of the same stereotypical tropes would not be reiterated. *Detroit Unleaded*, by not being a film that is political in nature, avoids these pitfalls. The characters definitely have interpersonal conflicts, but they do not lead to situations of physical violence.

For Issawi and Badreya, the topic of Islam in the post–9/11 context is a central theme of the film and the theme of a film-within-the-film. Mustafa's high-school aged daughter, Leila constantly defends Islam to her friends who equate the religion with terrorism. As Leila and her friend Terri sit in an old Ford Bronco smoking hashish, the topic of Islam again comes up for discussion. Terri, whose cousin is a Marine fighting in Afghanistan, asks, "How come every time I turn on the news there's some Muslim dude who's pissed off and killing everybody? Why do you hate America so much?" Leila turns to her and says, "Maybe if you'd educate yourself you would know the whole story." The scene then shifts to a colorful, graphic animation. The story begins, "Once upon a time before the oil, the sheiks and all the Saddams and Osamas, in the middle of the Arabian Desert, was this cool dude named Mohammed." In keeping with the Islamic tradition of never portraying Mohammed, the film immediately fades to a representation of the Archangel Gabriel, revealing the Koran to Mohammed. Wings flap as Koranic verses flash across the screen, and Leila's voice states, "One day an angel appeared to him with a new revelation called Islam. It means 'Submission to God.' The God of Abraham, Moses and Jesus." She then goes on to describe how, before Islam, "the bunch of yokels believed in a bunch of different gods" and how, after the angel's revelation, "they dumped the whole idol-worship thing." According to the narration, "God would free everybody from slavery. Dudes, babes, rich, poor, black, white, whatever. Everybody was equal." A map appears illustrating the spread of Islam from the Arabian Peninsula across North Africa, South Asia, and beyond.

Their conception of Islamic Civilization, where "Muslims were, like, top dog" shows Muslim thinkers painting, observing, studying, etc. When the Europeans hear of the Muslim progress, the audience is told "Europe was, like a bunch of barbarians busy barbecuing plague victims." Leila then traces the etymology of "sand nigger" to "dark dudes with sand all over their feet." The Crusades are described as "like, a downer for everybody, especially Muslims living in Jerusalem." The Crusaders in the film are shown as armored men with red glowing eyes standing before glowing red flames. The next section is about "this other really cool Kurdish Muslim dude named Saladin." According to the film, under Saladin, "there's like, this time of peace with Jews, Christians and Muslims all kicking it together." Once the Europeans returned, Leila then attempts to describe the Israeli/Palestinian conflict in this way:

> They gave the land the Palestinians were living on to the Jews and that became the new Israel. And once the Euro-honkies split, there was, like, constant fighting between the Israelis and Arabs over Jerusalem. 'Cause both the Israeli and Arab radicals wanted to have it all. If they'd just chill, they'd see Jerusalem is a spiritual place, the land of milk and honey.[23]

The arrival of the Americans is depicted with GI Joe toy soldiers who

> check out what all the fuss is about and they discover oil ... they prop up these greedy dictators who sell only to them, and they don't help the Arabs, only Israel, which pisses the Arabs off. So then you get the Israelis and Palestinians fighting over Jerusalem and blowing each other up, while the world watches and plays it all like some kind of game. And that's why the Middle East is a fricking mess. 'Cause there ain't no more cool dudes.[24]

This form of educational accounting, though visually engaging, can hardly change perceptions or the minds of those who know little about the conflicts in the Middle East. The visual history employed does little to elucidate the history of Islam, or the political consequences of foreign intervention in the Middle East. First, Terri, asks, "Why do you hate America so much?" This question is problematic because it assumes Leila is the Muslim "them" to Terri's American "us" despite the fact that they were both born and raised in the United States. Their smoking an enormous joint is both stereotypical (as if all Arabs smoke *hashish* instead of marijuana), and it makes Leila's explanation of the history of Islam suspect since she is under the influence of the drug. Instead of this educational accounting coming from a learned or sober source, it comes from an inarticulate teenager under the influence of drugs who utilizes language like "this cool dude Mohammed" and "dark dudes with sand all over their feet." The history is also incomplete, as it proclaims that, under Islamic empires, "freedom and Islam began to spread throughout Arabia, and it kept on spreading to India and all the way to China, then across North Africa to

Agent Stevens (Ray Wise, left) arrests Mustafa (Sayed Badreya) with Brad Carr in the 2007 film *American East*, directed by Hesham Issawi, produced by Zahra Pictures (courtesy Sayed Badreya).

Spain." Although Islam did spread throughout these regions, not all of those conquered may have considered it a form of freedom since obligatory allegiance was part of such a conquest. The script also glosses over historical facts such as the creation of the State of Israel and the U.S. invasion of Iraq with simplistic explanations about why these events occurred.

Issawi and Badreya also make some spurious historical claims, such as characterizing the European Early Middle Ages as a time of "a bunch of barbarians busy barbecuing plague victims" or the Muslim conquest of the Middle East, North Africa, and South Asia as a time when "everybody was equal." In addition, it grossly over-simplifies modern Palestinian and Israeli history by stating it was a "divide-and-conquer thing" and reduces the events of 1948 to "they gave the land the Palestinians were living on to the Jews and that became the new Israel." Other misleading accounts such as the United States propping up "these greedy dictators who sell only to them, and they don't help the Arabs, only Israel, which pisses the Arabs off," while having some elements of truth, still tells only a small part of the story. The conclusion, "that's why the Middle East is a fricking mess.... Cause there ain't no more cool dudes," is perhaps the most overtly ludicrous statement of all. Attempting to blame the political, social, and economic problems plaguing the Middle East on a shortage of "cool dudes" is not only senseless, but also gives audiences no concrete ideas about how the conflict can ever be resolved.

Issawi and Badreya's educational accounting cannot really be taken as a serious attempt at educating non–Arabs about the Middle East. Its brevity and colorful animation, though well-suited for short attention spans, simplifies the complex political, social, and historical situation so much that it reads like a polemic. Where the more traditional educational accounting (that found in journals and books) is arguably loquacious, at least it utilized respected sources and provided comprehensive analysis. These reductivist tactics do little to give a comprehensive or even intelligible historical account to the conflict. Therefore, while these artists are seeking to educate audiences regarding the situation in the Middle East, they only serve to provide a polemical argument that is inaccurate, thereby adding to the obfuscation and confusion that led to misinformation in the first place. Marvasti and McKinney write that "Middle Eastern Americans assume the role of educators, informing and instructing their fellow citizens about relevant topics.... Therefore, while educational accounting may be the most intelligible and productive accounting strategy for one's identity, it is also the most time-consuming and potentially misleading approach."[25] The educational accounting in *American East* unfortunately falls victim to this strategy, which is unfortunate since it could have been a vehicle for change in Arab American film.

Detroit Unleaded

Nashef's film, filled with colorful characters and much humor, includes a great deal of Arabic language with subtitles. By not writing the entire film in English, Nashef retains the reality of life in Dearborn where Arabs switch back and forth from Arabic to English (much like the *Arabeezi* mentioned earlier). She also captures the lives of many Arabs in Detroit and elsewhere, who live and work in the "cages," or bulletproof enclosures, within the gasoline stations they own. There is a cultural specificity to her film that revolves around filial duty, patriarchal strictures placed on single women, and the obligations toward family, especially regarding work. Sami's obligation to his mother, and to the memory of his father, forces him to remain working in a place that he cannot abide. Sami's mother is obligated to wear black as a sign of mourning for her late husband. Najla is expected not to date and is forced to lie about dating. Nashef successfully portrays the pressures of living in a close-knit Arab communities in the United States.

The protagonist, Sami, does not listen to Arabic music, does not speak Arabic often, and trades the Arabic food prepared by his mother for take-out food from a restaurant. He also goes by Sami even though his name is Issam. Sami represents the second generation Arab Americans who, for multiple reasons, believes they must hide their identity in order to survive. Najla, on the other hand, speaks Arabic freely. She hides her identity in a different manner—she lies about dating because otherwise she will anger her brother. Similarly, Sami's mother must wear black and refrain from visiting neighbors who invite her for coffee for the sake of respecting the dead. Although these are American characters, they are still living under the strictures of their Arab culture.

The ending, showing Sami and Naj driving away together without either being married or consulting their families, is decidedly romantic and utopian. Such an action by a couple in an Arab American community like Dearborn would be extremely controversial and scandalous. Nashef seems more interested in a happy ending than a realistic one, but that attitude is in line with her desire to write and direct films that do not "Other" Arabs, but portray them like any film would portray its protagonists. In this sense, her film breaks

Sami (EJ Assi, left) and Naj (Nada Shouhayib) secretly date in the 2010 film *Detroit Unleaded*, written and directed by Rola Nashef (courtesy Leon Toomey).

with the previous pattern of creating films that are either political or have definite political overtones that impact the themes of the films.

Relative Success

Thus far, Arab American films have been produced with small budgets, limited distributions, and critical success. None of these films have achieved mainstream success because they have not had wide national distribution in major theatre chains. As of the publication of this book, Dabis has written, directed, and starred in her second feature film, *May in the Summer*, and *Detroit Unleaded* has finally premiered in several major American cities. Dabis's second film has received some critical acclaim but, as Roya Rasteger of *The Huffington Post* wrote, the film has had detractors who are still unwilling to embrace the Arab American immigrant narrative.

> While Sundance is often criticized for making obvious film selections, some responses to *May in the Summer* beg the question of whether the industry is willing to recognize a familiar voice that tells a different story. Parochial reviews, for example, insist on gauging the film's success on the slapstick potential of "ethnic customs" and "culture clashes." One reviewer unwittingly revealed his own racist investments when he wrote that the funniest moment was an early remark by May's sister Yasmine referring to women who wear burkas as "ninjas" (a comment he wrongly attributes to May, but which Dalia promptly chastises Yasmine for being offensive). More disturbing still is the intensely gendered criticism that reared its way into much of the writing about films by female directors.... Reviewers felt entitled to comment on Dabis' appearance in crass ways, while simultaneously taking issue with the story's focus on female characters (bemoaning the grooms' absence), and then lazily judging the film according to Hollywood conventions of "chick-flicks" or "wedding romps."[26]

This review gives yet another example of how far these directors have to go before finding acceptance in the mainstream. These films are important since they mark the first feature-length Arab American films that have found relative success within the independent film market. By reappropriating the means of representation, a new generation of Arab American actors is less likely to play stereotypical, demeaning, or Orientalized roles. What is still an unfortunate truth is that many of these actors have to pay a heavy entry fee to be allowed into the Hollywood mainstream. Actors like Khalid Abdalla, Ahmed Ahmed, and Sayed Badreya all played stereotypical terrorist roles before they were allowed to play roles with depth. As with many other minority groups before them, there will be a long and difficult challenges ahead before Arab Americans are major producers of Hollywood films.

7

"A psychic civil war onstage": Arab American Solo Performance

In 1993, Iraqi American theatre artist Heather Raffo visited Iraq. The first Gulf War had ended just a few years prior, and she was eager to see her Iraqi family. She had been to Iraq before as a child, sleeping on the roof of her grandmother's house gazing at the stars. She started her journey in Amman, Jordan, taking a seventeen-hour bus ride across the desert to Baghdad. Upon arrival, she says she was warmly welcomed by the Iraqi soldier who stamped her passport. In Baghdad she met her family again, listened to their stories, and saw the horrible destruction all around her. She also visited the Amiriyya bomb shelter, where a U.S. bomb obliterated 408 men, women, and children in a place where they thought they would be safe from such horror. At the Saddam Art Center she saw galleries filled with portraits of the dictator. In the same museum, she came across one painting by a woman—the image of a nude woman, clinging to a leafless tree, the sun shining beneath a hazy sky behind her. That female artist, the curator of the center and a painter herself, was killed by a U.S. bomb. Raffo decided to write down the womens' stories she heard on her voyage back to her father's homeland. "When an Iraqi woman trusts you it is because she has come to love you," Raffo writes, "and that has been the process of finding and forming these stories."[1]

¤ ¤ ¤

In their book *O Solo Homo: The New Queer Performance* authors Holly Hughes and David Román write, "queer solo work is usually pedagogical ... to teach us about what it means to be queer and how that aspect of [their] identity intersects with various other identity factors such as race—including whiteness—ethnicity, class, gender, and region. Queer performances serve to educate queer audiences of all backgrounds even as it entertains and mobilizes

[us] politically."² I would argue that Arab American solo performance achieves the same pedagogical and identificatory functions as solo queer theatre. Both communities are marginalized within the mainstream American culture; both communities are ostracized and looked upon with suspicion; and both communities are currently asserting their identities through various mediums including performance.

This chapter specifically examines works by four female Arab American solo performers: Heather Raffo, Leila Buck, Najla Said, and Jennifer Jajeh. Their performances have had national productions, received critical acclaim, and define contemporary Arab American performance practice. I argue that these works serve much of the same pedagogical, entertainment, and political functions as queer solo performances; especially in the post–9/11 context where the Arab American community was Othered by mainstream society and many Arab Americans were either willingly or unwillingly "outed" from the non–Arab status they once embraced. In addition, these performances educate non–Arab audiences about Arabs and contribute artistically to Arab American group identity. By examining the foundations of performance practice itself, the form of solo performance, and interviews with these performers, I intend to demonstrate that these forms of solo performance serve the functions of establishing Arab American identity, educating non–Arab audiences about Arabs, and creating an empathic space within which anti–Arab prejudices and stereotypes can be challenged and overcome.

Theatre versus Performance

The American theatre establishment, a for-profit enterprise, has customarily produced works that were both commercial and non-controversial. These constraints often excluded artists of color, artists of various sexual orientations, and those who did not have the economic means by which to produce their work. This situation is self-perpetuating. Theatrical training programs teach the same canon of plays in order to train their students to work within an American theatre system that requires that actors, directors, and designers have experience with those plays. Theatres produce the same repertory of plays because audiences expect these texts to be staged for many reasons, including the fact that those are the plays most have read or seen. With more theatres facing budget shortfalls, the ability to produce previously unproduced and untried plays is continually diminished. Therefore, marginalized playwrights, often minorities, find it increasingly difficult to get their work produced.

Solo performance, therefore, became a chosen form for those marginalized voices. According to performance scholar Elin Diamond, "performance can refer to popular entertainments, speech acts, folklore, political demonstrations, conference behavior, rituals, medical and religious healing, and aspects of everyday life."[3] According to Diamond, performance is unlike theatre, where the playwright is the authority, where actors are disciplined to the task of representing fictional entities, and where spectators are "duped" into identifying with the psychological problems of characters; performance dismantles textual authority, illusionism, and the canonical actor in favor of "the polymorphous body of the performer." The performer then presents himself/herself as a "sexual, permeable, tactile body, scourging audience narrativity along with the barrier between the stage and spectator." This rise in performance over theatre in contemporary theatre shifts authority to effect and text to body, thereby allowing the spectator, not the playwright, the freedom to make and transform meanings.[4]

Where queer solo performance is concerned, Hughes and Román believe that solo performance is compelling because it is multiracial, cogendered, multisexual, and democratic. Hughes contends that solo performance is rooted in the "particularly American tradition of testifying, of witnessing history in the first person."[5] Audiences attend these performances because they trust that the performer most likely wrote the piece and that they will hear stories that actually occurred. According to Hughes, "the fact that these are 'real stories' has something to do with their critical reception," which gives the work a level of veracity not found in other forms of theatre. In addition, the autobiographical aspects of these solo performances in the queer community are a form of self-representation and identity politics that is part of what Román calls "a larger collective and ongoing process of revisionist history" and "a certain political investment in visibility."[6] The assertion of gay identity is part of this identity politics model that teaches non-queer audiences about what it means to be queer and also serves to educate queer audiences even as it entertains and mobilizes them politically. Román writes:

> The performative nature of queer lives involves a continuous negotiation between our sense of private and public selves that does not always amount to seeing these two areas as discreet. The friction between the private and the public self brings me back to the issue of the personal and the autobiographical. Not only does autobiographical work bring into representation the diversity of queer life, it also provides a space where queer people can rehearse key issues and concerns.[7]

These issues of testifying, witnessing, autobiography, and community can be applied to Arab American solo performance as well. The solo performances examined here were born of the artists' positionality as second-generation Arab Americans writing and performing about experiences they encountered while either living in or visiting the Arab countries of their ancestry. These performers examine Arab American identity, autobiography, the personal versus the political, and their feminism in their own unique ways. In my interviews with these performers I was able to glean how they created their works, the motivations behind their performances, and their ultimate intention for audience reception.

Dalia Basiouny and Marvin Carlson write that after 9/11 Arab Americans were thrust into a negative visibility through the often stereotypical portrayals of Arabs, Muslims, and Middle Easterners as the proverbial "enemy." Arab American artists responded to this by creating groups, networks, and platforms so their work would be seen by both fellow Arab Americans and the general public. They write,

> Plays were now developed to explore and express the hybrid identities of this community in these new and tension-filled circumstances, and also to present to non–Arab audiences a more accurate picture of this community and of the tensions in its various homelands than was available in the often biased and uninformed mainstream media.[8]

They also note that the majority of the artists creating this work are women, and that these works contradict the standard Western stereotypes many may have about Arab women as oppressed subjects who are unable to voice their critique of their Arabic cultures. Somaya Sami Sabry writes that Arab American solo performances foreground themselves as sites of resistance, serving as a "Sheherazadian orality" that perform "the malleability of the gaps and bridges shaping transformative cultural identities, through an interrogation of popular representations of their race and gender."[9] In their performances, these women practice their representation as active agents, creating a dynamic Arab American identity in the process. Shakir writes,

> Since the 1980s, a flood of material on Arab women has been published, much of it memoir and oral history, those first-person forms from which (although we know better) we are always hoping for unvarnished truth are always getting only a version of it. But, at least, these are versions of the women's own making. Today, as never before, if we are willing to listen, Arab women are telling us about themselves.[10]

Many Arab American female writer/performers have created these solo performances, including Elmaz Abi Nader, Laila Farah, Soha Al Jurf, Leila Buck, Kathryn Haddad, Jennifer Jajeh, Rania Khalil, Heather Raffo, Lena Rizkallah, Najla Said, and Betty Shamieh. These writer/performers create works that cover many disparate themes. Elmaz Abi Nader's *Country of Origin* is her exploration of her Lebanese immigrant roots and the difficulties she faced growing up as an Arab in America. Soha Al Jurf's *Pressing Beyond in Between* is her story of dealing with her aunt's death in Palestine. Lena Rizkallah's *Layla's Sahra* explores the rift that is created in a Lebanese family when an Arab daughter marries a non–Arab. Rania Khalil's *Flag Piece* explores the patriotic zeal most Americans felt following the 9/11 attacks. Shamieh's *Chocolate in Heat: Growing Up Arab in America* also explores the difficulties young Arab American women feel when they are expected to act a certain way with their Arab families, yet experience different and complicated emotions outside of that setting. The variety of views expressed in these works is remarkable, as they provide a pan–Arab American perspective into the lives of women who are rarely portrayed on American stages. Andrea Assaf's monodrama *Eleven Reflections on September*, a spoken word and multi-media performance piece, explores the Arab American experience through a series of poems Assaf wrote after 9/11. The performance, which explores violence and prejudice through the disintegration of language, includes video, live music, community dialogues, and panels. Assaf wrote in 2011:

> The year 2011 marks 10 years of anti–Arab, anti–Muslim prejudice and violence under the so-called War on Terror. I am Lebanese American. I'm also a New Yorker. For 10 years, I've been writing poems about this: these wars, the contradictions of identity, the many ways violence manifests in everyday life. And each year, the month of September is particularly poignant for me—full of memory, and littered with images of the fallen.[11]

Similarly, Lebanese American Laila Farah's monodrama titled *Living in the Hyphen-Nation* explores what she calls "a bicultural, biracial, bilingual ... auto-ethnographic diasporic performance."[12] In this performance, Farah seeks to problematize the racial construction of Arabs in the media and the negative exoticized and eroticized portrayal of Arab women. As both a performer and an academic, Farah creates what she describes as "a performative essay" and "living writing" which seeks to provide reflexivity, agency, political dissent, and activism.[13] Farah's goal is to inspire audiences to expand their understanding of political issues in order to change their consciousness regarding the conflicts she dramatizes. Farah embodies a range of different females in extreme circumstances: being stopped at a militia checkpoint in Beirut, being interrogated by an immigration official at an airport, watching coverage of the Iraq war on television, and being threatened in a detention center. Through her abilities as a writer, performer, and academic, Farah utilizes live performance, testimony, and lived experiences in an attempt to create social change.

Although not technically a monodrama (because it features two characters both male and female), Betty Shamieh's play *Chocolate in Heat: Growing Up Arab in America* bears mentioning here because Shamieh both wrote, and performed in, the original production and the play consists of several uninterrupted monologues. The play features two characters who speak in intermittent speeches titled "Need," "Love," "Ignorance," "Sex," and "Justice." The female, Aiesha, is an Arab American girl who is struggling to fit in with her peers and is dealing with issues of racism, sexual violence, and abuse. The male, Ahmed, is Jordanian royalty that deals with his sexuality and loneliness by writing a book about rape. Their separate stories intertwine through an unseen character, Ahmed's uncle, Lou (Lotfi). Although the play does not solely focus on Arab American issues, it does highlight the complicated sexual, personal, and political landscape Arab American females navigate from childhood to adulthood. Shamieh performed the play with fellow Arab American actor Piter Fattouche and infused the performance with music and dance. Although the play deals with serious issues, Shamieh is quick to point out that "by the way, it's also funny."[14]

Of all the modes of Arab American theatre and performance, Arab American female solo performance has created some of the most interesting stories and theatrical experiences of the entire movement. I focus on works by Heather Raffo, Leila Buck, Najla Said, and Jennifer Jajeh because they are professional actresses in addition to solo performers, and because these works have garnered attention by producers, publishers, and the media.

Female Solo Performances

Raffo's *9 Parts of Desire*, Buck's *ISite*, Said's *Palestine*, and Jajeh's *I Heart Hamas* all came about as solo performances for different reasons, adopting this form more by circumstance than by choice. For instance, Buck took a non-fiction writing class in college where she was encouraged to write a play. She began with a monologue titled "Courage Under Fire" about her life growing up in the Mid-

Andrea Assaf performs her monodrama *Eleven Reflections of September* at Pangea World Theater, 2011 (photograph by Marc Norberg, courtesy Art2Action Inc).

dle East. She realized that there was a power in telling autobiographical stories and that audiences responded differently to direct address. Said created her *Palestine* after co-founding the Arab American theatre collective *Nibras* in New York and performing their collaborative production *Sajjil*. After that production Said, Buck, and Israeli filmmaker Danae Elon decided to write individual pieces describing their personal experiences with the Israel/Palestine conflict.

Said expanded a journal entry she had written after her father, the scholar Edward W. Said passed away. She was later encouraged to develop the work further with a director and dramaturg and, in her words, "within three days I went from having a fifteen minute piece to having a fifty-four minute piece.... So I guess I didn't intend to write *any* sort of performance, let alone a solo one!"[15] In contrast, Raffo actually did set out to write a solo performance but begrudgingly, as Raffo did not really like the genre of solo performance and was not naturally inclined to write it. For her, *9 Parts of Desire* was more about telling a story in a structure that "heightens what is being said" and finding a form that matched the function of the collected consciousness and spirit of one person playing nine Iraqi women in what she calls "a psychic civil war on stage." The play required the solo performance structure only because the story she was telling required one person to inhabit nine different lives. For Raffo, *9 Parts of Desire* is more a play than a solo performance—or in her words, a combination of "storytelling, performance art, and a play." Raffo's assessment of her own work is confirmed by the fact that the play has been performed successfully both as a solo performance and with several actresses playing the various roles.

Leila Buck utilized her solo performance *ISite* in a similar manner. *ISite* is Buck's attempt to navigate all the different parts of her personality even while playing characters different from herself, such as xenophobic socialites, Orientalists, and self-obsessed college girls. Like *9 Parts of Desire*, Buck's *ISite* required the solo performance mode because it was integral to the message she was presenting. The strength of the piece is that we see each character in the performer herself and, in her words, "how the people are part of you and coming through you."[16]

Najla Said does not call *Palestine* solo performance either. She told me, "I call it my story. Really. That's it. We all have them, and the only way we can get through the political stalemate we are in is to tell our individual stories and invite people to listen. What's amazing is that they really do." All of these examples demonstrate that, just because one actress is speaking onstage, there can be no presumption that the performance was necessarily intended to be a "solo performance."[17]

Like queer identification, Arab Americans have historically found themselves either fighting for the right to "whiteness" or standing in strict opposition to such an identity. In her book *Between Arab and White: Race and Ethnicity in the Early Syrian American Diaspora*, Gualtieri writes about how early Arab immigrants to the United States fought to legally claim "whiteness" through multiple court cases in order to be a part of the "free white persons" classification. Later, especially during the post–1945 and post–1967 periods, claiming the term "Arab American" was, in Gualtieri's words, "a political act that signaled affiliation with Arabic-speaking peoples across the lines of nationality."[18] That political act extends to performers who are claiming their Arab American heritage as a primary identifier in their work.

I put this question of identification to the three performers in order to ascertain if they believe the term "Arab American" pertains to them as artists. Leila Buck accepts the moniker and believes her work is very much about being Arab American and about writing about the Arab American experience. In addition, as a performer, she enjoys writing about the topic. Buck feels strongly about identifying Arab American even in non–Arab American settings because she believes it is important to identify oneself in work, life, and art. She also notes that being known as an artist is more important than being identified as an Arab American. Heather Raffo is content with the title "Arab American," but sees it more as a label that the press requires for publicity purposes than as an identity she personally claims. Raffo believes that such titles cannot be all-encompassing, but that the term Arab American is technically correct. Najla Said believes that being both Arab and American are essential parts of her work as a writer and as the director of her play *Palestine*, but she does not necessarily identify as Arab American outside of that context. Said prefers to be known as "a human being, not for any political reason, but because I feel the very nature of an art like theatre requires the artist to remain neutral in a sense—not in the sense of having no opinions or beliefs, but rather artistically and humanly neutral so as to be able to inhabit the multiple identities which we *all* possess."[19] I found each of their answers interesting because, in their plays, they spend so much time exploring what it means to be Arab and American, and yet they do not feel it is a title they necessarily need to inhabit in their daily lives. These artists' comments defy the commonly held notion that all artists who are of Arab descent and who write about Arab American issues necessarily identify as Arab American. For some, it is an empowering identity; while for others, it is a label foisted upon them.

What is clear is that in the post–9/11 world Arab Americans were "outed" from the non–Arab closet they inhabited. All three performers believe that the Arab American label is primarily generational and that the events of 9/11 prompted a greater interest in all things Arab American and, therefore, the identity was necessary. Raffo believes that after 9/11, Arab American defined something in the artistic community that might not have existed in the theatre world before then. The audience changed, became mainstream, and began to care about what Arab Americans had to say. For Raffo, it is not a political stance to be labeled Arab American, but she believes that the "American" part of her felt "there is an injustice happening and it's my duty to speak out and let my voice be heard on behalf of those not being heard or stereotypes being perpetuated." In her play *Palestine*, Najla Said utilizes the metaphor literally by stating that she was "outed" as an Arab American after 9/11, but never felt entirely American, entirely Arab, or any combination of the two.[20]

All of this brings us to the question: Is solo performance inherently autobiographical? All three of the performers deny they are playing themselves onstage but, curiously, they also admit that the characters they portray are either amalgams or enactments of themselves. Buck feels that autobiographical performance is often biased against because it appears ego-centric and narcissistic. However, she also believes that the autobiographical elements in the performance are valuable because when standing in front of a group of people and stating what the performers actually saw and lived through the events they are describing, it decreases the audience's ability to question the veracity of the story in the way they might with a play that is purely fictional. That connection creates empathy through hearing real stories, what Buck calls "the deepest form of connection."

Raffo believes her *9 Parts of Desire* is autobiographical in the same way that a play like *Streetcar Named Desire* could be considered autobiographical. The play is not journalistic theatre where subject testimonies are recorded and performed verbatim (as, say, *The Laramie Project* or *Fires in the Mirror: Crown Heights, Brooklyn and Other Identities*), but rather it is a collage of the lives and stories of several Iraqi women. The audience sometimes imposes autobiography upon Raffo, especially when she plays the character named "The American," whom Raffo asserts is really nothing like her at all. Instead of accepting the term autobiographical, Raffo prefers to think of the piece as "deeply personal."

Said goes one step further by saying that her play *Palestine* is not at all autobiographical. This is most interesting because she performs the play as herself, in the first person, as the daughter of Edward Said. She adds, "I do think ... that in the specific case of *listening* to Palestinians and Palestinian Americans, autobiography works best. I think if I had written the same play but pretended it was fiction, people would be much more quick to find holes in the narrative. When they know it's all true, everyone is charmed and moved and shakes their head at the complexity of life." Curiously, autobiography seems to be central to these pieces but not in the personal manner that is often associated with solo performance. Instead, the writers'/performers' autobiographies are artfully concealed in the various characters they play even though they may be "playing themselves" or describing experiences they actually experienced.

The Personal and the Political

All three performers agree that their art provokes, raises questions, and implicates their audiences in one form or another. Buck believes that solo performance is meant to be entertaining but, more importantly, audiences should recognize that the performer is creating art that is meant to be used and transformed in some way to change how the audience members interact with the world. The live connection is paramount, but rather than being provocative Buck prefers it be thought of as moving:

> You have to get people at the level that is not intellectual or adversarial only but I hope it provokes empathy, feeling, dialogue, and reflection in the audience in their own role in the thing you're talking about and how it can shift in some small way and make a difference in the world. Each seed planted in someone's head will cause less fear mongering ... less willingness to bomb these places or wage war on them.[21]

For Raffo, the motivation was to speak to a Western audience about real-life Iraqis who have endured two wars, thirteen years of sanctions, and a long history of Western involvement in Iraqi affairs. Her performance is meant to say "these are who these people really are and what they really think. Most Iraqis are blown away that an Iraqi could say these things to an American audience and that any Americans care at all."[22] Because these issues are not always allowed to be confronted in the Arab world, it is incumbent upon Arab Americans to raise them in their work.

The question of whether these works could be classified as feminist is also not definite. Shakir writes, "American women of Arab heritage yearn for new narratives about themselves, their mothers, their grandmothers, and for new readings of Arab culture."[23] Rather than leveling feminist critiques, these performances seek to tell the stories of Arab women in the hopes of gaining an empathetic response from the audience. For instance, when these performers discuss issues such as anorexia, rape, prejudice against Arab women, or sexual desire, their stories are told through the vantage point of character experience rather than through the lens of political activism. For instance, Raffo believes that performances of plays like *9 Parts of Desire* are important because American audiences can no longer stereotype Iraqi women after experiencing a performance that humanizes them. Buck also believes her work may be more successful than others because the female Arab body is perceived as less threatening than the male Arab body onstage. In addition, she believes that female performers are more interested in focusing on personal stories over politicized narratives. Said says that she also does not tend to think along the lines of a feminist agenda in general.

Where feminist solo performance is committed to a political commitment and to intellectual critique as a means of analyzing the changing context of women, the performances analyzed here do not place this kind of intellectual critique at the center of the writing or performances. Instead, by inhabiting the lives of different women and sharing their experiences with the audience on a humanist level, the hope is that those who may feel prejudice or fear toward Arab women will leave the performance with changed perceptions via an empathic connection.

9 Parts of Desire: *An Iraqi American Perspective*

The most well-known Arab American monodrama is Heather Raffo's *9 Parts of Desire*. The piece premiered in 2003 at the Traverse Theatre in Edinburgh and has toured and been produced nationwide many times since. The play also won the Lucille Lortel Award and the Susan Smith Blackburn and Marian Seldes-Garson Kanin playwrighting award. As a performer Raffo was nominated for the Helen Hayes, Outer Critics Circle, and Drama League Awards.

Raffo, who initially wrote and performed the monodrama, based her play on what she calls a "life-changing trip" to Iraq in 1993. There she met many Iraqi women who inspired her to write their stories. Instead of a formal interview process, Raffo spent time living with these women who intrusted her with their personal accounts. She writes that these stories were not told to her verbatim, but were composites that were based on research and later dramatized and written in a poetic style more akin to songwriting.[24] Thus, the play does not read like a traditional drama; it is a series of monologues where the text reads like poetry.

Raffo includes nine characters: Mullaya, Layal, Amal, Huda, The Doctor,

7. *"A psychic civil war onstage"*

Heather Raffo performs in her monodrama *9 Parts of Desire* at the Manhattan Ensemble Theater, directed by Joanna Settle, 2008 (© Irene Young).

Iraqi Girl, Umm Ghada, The American, and Nanna. In the original production, Raffo changed back and forth between characters using only the traditional Muslim *abaya*. Mullaya is the woman who is hired to lead call-and-response mourning songs at Muslim funerals; Layal is an Iraqi artist; Amal is a jilted Bedouin woman; Huda is a bitter Iraqi exile living in London; The Doctor is a physician working in Basra; the Iraqi Girl is a child who lost her father to Saddam's henchmen; Umm Ghada is a mother in mourning who lost her children during the U.S. bombing of the Amiriyya bomb shelter; The American is a young American woman living in New York City watching the Iraq War on television; and Nanna is an old Iraqi woman forced to sell goods on the street. The play is structured by the five Muslim calls to prayer: dawn (*fajr*), midday (*dhuhr*), afternoon (*asr*), sunset (*maghrib*), and twilight (*isha'*).

Raffo's play, and her deeply personal performance of it, pays homage to Iraqi women who have suffered the brunt of the many difficulties faced by the Iraqi people over the past half century including the Iran-Iraq War, the two major Gulf wars, the American occupation of Iraq, and the ongoing Sunni/Shi'a/Kurdish conflicts. All of the female characters in the play have suffered from these events, and the character of Layal is killed by play's end. Layal is based on the late Iraqi artist Layla al-Attar (1940–1993), who was killed when her home was destroyed by a U.S. bomb. Other characters have also been damaged by the war. Umm Ghada, who is based on an actual woman named Fatima who lost her husband and children in the bombing, appears in the play to give audiences a virtual tour of the bomb site.

> Here, on the ceiling, you can see
> charred handprints and footprints
> from people who lay in the top bunks.
> And here a silhouette of a woman
> vaporized from heat.
> This huge room became an oven,
> and they pressed to the walls to escape from the flames.
> In the basement too
> bombs burst the pipes
> hot water came up to five feet
> and boiled the people.[25]

Huda, the Iraqi exile living in London, recounts the torture she endured in one of Saddam's prisons. The Iraqi Girl tells of how she was inadvertently responsible for her father's arrest by Saddam's henchmen. The Doctor explains how depleted uranium bullets have caused genetic defects in the pregnant women:

Look, just this month, I'll tell you, I've started counting: six babies no head, four abnormally large heads, now today another one with two heads. Such high levels of genetic damage does not occur naturally. These things you see them in textbooks.[26]

Raffo also provides an Arab American perspective through the character titled only "The American." In it, she sits transfixed by the television watching the grainy night-vision coverage of the attack on Baghdad by U.S. forces, wondering if her family living in the city has survived while she goes about her life in America working out at the gym and getting pedicures:

> I can't stop
> I wake up and fall asleep with the TV on
> holding a rosary
> watching—
> I know
> I should just
> turn it off
> but I can't
> I hate it when people say
> I don't watch it anymore
> it depresses me
> yeah
> it depresses me
> I can't
> breathe—[27]

Raffo successfully captures the dilemma many Arab Americans face watching wars on television that directly affect their relatives abroad, yet feeling helpless to intervene. That duality—having family in Arab countries that are in direct conflict with the U.S. or its allies—is one that is acutely felt by many Arab Americans during times of war. Raffo writes:

> I intended to write a piece about the Iraqi psyche, something that would inform and enlighten the images we see on T.V. However, the play is equally about the American psyche. It is a dialogue between east and west. The characters are deeply engaged in circumstances unique to them as Iraqis and yet through their passions seem to answer the concerns of the west.... I wanted the audience to see these women not as the "other" but much more like themselves than they would have initially thought.[28]

These solo performances seek to instill a radical empathy within audiences; one that demonstrates that U.S. involvement in these wars has very real and direct consequences on many Americans of Arab descent. By performing Iraqi women and dramatizing their struggles, Raffo offers a more human and humane dimension to a people who have suffered under decades of dictatorship, occupation, war, and sectarian conflict.

Palestine: *Palestinian Americans After 9/11*

Said's solo performance/monodrama titled *Palestine* comes closest to LaCapra's ideas of empathic unsettlement because, instead of creating a fictionalized re-creation of Palestine, Said provides the audience with a first-hand account of her journey to the West Bank and Gaza Strip with her father, mother, and brother. In addition, Said conflates the loss of her father, and the loss of Palestine itself, with her own corporeal absence through her struggle with anorexia. Said writes that she had to be coaxed into writing her story because of the many anxieties she had regarding her abilities as an artist and her authority to speak about the difficulties in the Middle East. However, after she began the writing process, "I realized people were willing to listen, because it was simply my story, and *precisely because* it was sort of messy and embarrassing and atypical, yet also universal in its complexity; having a mixed-up identity actually makes it easier to relate to a larger and more varied group of people."[29]

Said goes so far as to blame her anorexia on her desire to suffer for her father, and for the Palestinians themselves, writing, "the trip to Palestine added yet another dimension to my anorexia: I wanted desperately to suffer, not just for my daddy but for all of Palestine as well."[30] Her journey to this realization begins much earlier when she realizes on 9/11 that she is an Arab American. Prior to the events of 9/11, Said writes that she passed as a Jew in New York City. For instance, growing up in Brooklyn she was believed to be Jewish, and she was more likely to speak Yiddish than Arabic. She also dated more Jewish boys than gentiles, and most people would assume she was Sephardic, not Arab. This connection between Arabs and Jews, especially Palestinians and Jews, is something that is written about repeatedly in Arab American theatre and performance. It seems that these Arab American writers are attempting to create these connections in their works as a means of reconciling their political leanings with their experiences growing up in the United States.

Said's identification as an Arab American and Palestinian American is central to her monodrama. Like many Arab Americans, Said claims she had great difficulty accepting her transnational identity, opting instead for what she calls another friendly and safe version of Arab. Said notes that she spent much of her childhood avoiding acknowledging she was of Arab heritage. Said's identity crisis is compounded because she is the daughter of one of the most prominent and outspoken twentieth-century Arab American scholars. Said's performance is revealing not only of her own personal biography, but also of her father's complicated relationship with Palestine. In the BBC documentary titled *In Search of Palestine*, Edward Said says:

> My connection with Palestine was always intellectual, and cultural, and spiritual but not physical. And I've resigned myself to the loss of this place, but I still feel a moral commitment to it. It's terribly unjust and the injustice done to us has never really been acknowledged.... This is our history and it remains whether they like it or have tried to forget it or not.

Najla Said performs her monodrama *Palestine* at the Fourth Street Theatre, directed by Sturgis Warner (photograph by Sara Krulwich/*The New York Times*/Redux).

Said's choice of words, "I've resigned myself to the loss of this place," is especially telling. For Said, the loss of Palestine was equated with an absence of justice. Despite this fact, the recognition of this loss does not negate the desire to strive for a proper historical accounting of the situation. By contrast, Najla Said's connection to Palestine is rooted in her physical condition of anorexia. As stated earlier, LaCapra believes that conflating absence and loss leads to endless melancholia.[31] Hirsch states that postmemory imagines what cannot be recalled, mourns a loss that cannot be repaired, and that the lost object can never be repaired so the mourning can never be overcome.[32] Edward Said writes, "you can't go back to some earlier and perhaps more stable condition of being at home; and, alas, you can never fully arrive, be at one with your new home or situation."[33]

Exile exists in what Said calls a "median state" where exiles are neither completely whole in their new homeland nor fully disengaged from their old homeland. Becoming skilled at survival becomes imperative, and there is a danger of becoming too comfortable or secure in one's new life. These factors are at play in *Palestine*. Najla Said's exile is found within herself as she struggles as an Arab American after 9/11, and as an anorexic woman fighting for survival. Said's sense of loss is less about Palestine, the place, and more about the loss of her father to cancer.

The center of the performance is the recollection of the actual journey to the West Bank and Gaza Strip. I categorize this as an occupation play because the Israeli Occupation of the West Bank and Gaza are the primary focus of Said's memory. For her, the "promised land" is one of horrific fear, palpable tension, division, and separation. To make matters worse, the family is being followed by a British photographer who recorded their every move. His documentation of the visit makes Said feel the entire journey is farcical because of its documented, calculated, and prepared quality. "On the one hand," she writes, "it was this 'homecoming,' a 'family trip,' and on the other hand it was completely transparent and contrived."[34] Said not only experiences something for the first time, but it is being experienced in an uncanny manner that alienates her even more from her own experience.

On her trip to the West Bank and Gaza, the signs of occupation were everywhere. The settlements she saw around her look like "concrete slabs of unmovable earth" and the Israeli soldiers speak to her in Hebrew but never Arabic. They journey to Edward Said's childhood home in the Talbiya neighborhood of Jerusalem; now a place called The International Christian Embassy, which her father calls "a right-wing fundamentalist Christian and militantly pro–Zionist group, run by a South African Boer no less!"[35] As Edward Said has stated many times in his writings, his family left of their own accord for Cairo before 1948, and were able to live comfortably, unlike many Palestinian refugees who settled in camps scattered throughout the Middle East. However, Said writes that "nonetheless, their home was taken, along with all of their possessions, and they were exiled, never to be allowed back as anything but visitors."[36] Interestingly, when given the opportunity, Edward Said did not make an attempt to enter his family's old house because, if he had, it would "confirm the reality of what had happened."[37] In her interactions with Palestinian children, Najla Said notices that it is they, and not her, who are the real victims in this place:

And yet they are the ones who suffer on a daily basis in a way that I never will. They are victims of the circumstances of their birth in a way that I will never be. And they are the ones who will have to deal, not just mentally, but actually, for the rest of their lives, with the consequences of the history that they, like me, may never fully understand.[38]

In yet another postmemorial moment, Said realizes that Israeli children are much like her in that "none of us had emigrated or immigrated or fought in wars or suffered the Holocaust, but we still were the ones who had to bear the burdens of our peoples' respective histories."[39] She realizes that her father had Jewish friends, and her mother's school was in the Jewish quarter of Beirut, making her life not altogether different from the lives of Israeli children. "Each group of children has the memories of our parents' separate tragedies to defend and protect," she writes, "and none of us really get it."[40] It is here, in her realization and connection with Israeli youth, that she makes the connection between her own traumatic background and the traumatic background that haunts the Israelis she meets.

Although Said is a secondary witness to the trauma of the Palestinians, she is a primary witness to her own traumas—the recollection of living in Beirut while it was being bombed in 1983, experiencing the attack on New York City during 9/11, and enduring the Israeli attacks on Beirut in 2006. As a child, attempting to flee Beirut during a particularly terrible attack, she recounts the terrifying fear she experienced during the Lebanese Civil War. On the morning of 9/11, she has a similarly terrifying experience. If she cannot fully understand the plight of Palestinians living under occupation, she surely understood the attack on New York—her own city. Instead of allowing herself to feel the tragedy as a New Yorker, or as an American, by virtue of the fact that she was Arab, she experienced the event as an "Other." When it was announced that the perpetrators of the attack were Arab, Said writes that it was the moment that changed her life forever. Her subsequent verbal attack against someone who instantly blamed the event on Palestinians was another example of how she felt the trauma from her own double perspective—as an American and as an Arab American. From that time on, she could no longer disguise her Arabness.

September 11 was a defining moment that changed the lives of many Arab Americans living in the United States, forever removing the mask of anonymity they once possessed. After 9/11, it was no longer possible to pass for another ethnicity, or to simply claim whiteness. Instead, Arab Americans found themselves on the defensive, constantly having to prove their allegiance. The governmental apparatus that has been in place since the late 1960s was again focused upon those with Arab/Muslim heritage. This outing had yet another effect, especially among the writers and performers who self-identified as Arab American. They took it upon themselves to reclaim the mission set forth by prior Arab American activists and to speak out against the persecution they witnessed happening all around them. Said's inability to feel a combination of Arab and American is most telling here. This duality is not something easily embraced because it is an ever-shifting and unstable classification, especially during political and cultural tumult. Therefore, she reluctantly wears the mantle:

> In the last bunch of years I have been invited to speak, talk, write and create theatre as an "Arab-American." I have felt my love and happiness and connection to the Middle East grow.... I have learned to speak up about the truth of what I have seen—and NONE of that has made me less of an Upper West Side princess, none of it changes the fact that I started and finished school in America, that English is my first language, that I still live in New york. None of it.... Since 9/11 I am officially an Arab, bridging the gap between two worlds that don't understand each other.[41]

Said's personal trauma transforms her "acting out" through means of anorexia, anger, and denial into a "working through" by the means of activism, writing, and performance. LaCapra hypothesizes that working through problems requires the attempt to reinforce dimensions of the self that can both come to terms with, and counteract the forces of, the past in order to further the shaping of a livable future.[42] Said's monodrama seems to achieve this reconciliation, though she never brings closure to the issue of her anorexia. She does, however, find some meaningful way to bridge the gap between her Arab heritage and her American life through her performance.

Leila Buck and ISite

Leila Buck's play *ISite* is a one-woman drama that explores the tensions of growing up Arab American and of mixed parentage (Buck's mother is Lebanese and her father, Stephen Buck, has filial roots that date back to the Massachusetts Bay Colony in 1636). Buck is a transnational to her very core, stating "I took my first international flight in the womb. I guess that's why I've always loved takeoff. In a way, I was born in flight." Even her name becomes a point of contention; her mother wished to put her English name Kathryn first because, "that way they won't make fun of her." When asked why she did this, the character named Mom replies, "children are cruel. I want her to feel like she belongs, as an American just like you." The question of naming is a complicated one for most Arabs and is a point of contention within the Arab American community.[43] Buck writes, "I'm Katie Buck. But Leila is my ... *middle* name."[44] Over time, Leila has dropped the Kathryn altogether, and is now known only by Leila.

Part of the difficulty of identity is also found in the ability (or lack thereof) to speak Arabic. This struggle with the inability to speak Arabic is a major preoccupation with many Arab American playwrights. The Relative in the play, while speaking to Woman, says, "Why your mother didn't teach you the language of your country?!" The Woman replies, "Yes, I want to talk to you! I just—don't know how."[45] This concept of the shamefulness of not understanding or speaking Arabic becomes a major preoccupation with many second- and third-generation Arab Americans because, in Arab culture, the ability to speak Arabic is intricately tied to the concept of heritage. The loss of Arabic is equal to the loss of culture.

In the section titled "Passing," Buck asks, "So could I pass for an Arab?" Walking around the souks of Jeddah, Saudi Arabia, Woman dons an *abaya* and *ghatas* and goes into the market "fully covered for the first time." Buck realizes that

> as long as I remain silent, I belong. And I can watch this world with foreign yet familiar eyes.... I am amazed at how well I pass for an Arab.... But there is something beautiful in discovering what really makes you who you are. If everyone looks the same, you find another way to know them. So what makes me who I am?[46]

Woman can pass as an Arab, but only when fully covered and not speaking broken Arabic. It is the same with family. One's position in the world is defined by one's position in a family "because that is where your *identity*— begins."[47] Another marker of Arab identity in this play is food. According to Woman, "In the Arab world, food is love. It is also a gesture of hospitality.... To refuse food is like a personal rejection of an Arab's culture, heritage, and family. No pressure!"[48]

The transgenerational characters that haunt Buck's play are those of Teta and Jeddo (Grandmother and Grandfather, respectively). Teta and Jeddo represent Lebanon, exile, and the idea of immigration. Teta and Jeddo were immigrants as well—first to England and then to America.

> Christmas in Washington was my Jeddo's blue spruce tree. He used to decorate it every year, like a beacon welcoming us home. He planted it the year that I was born, and I've always felt like we grew up together somehow.... Now it stands two stories tall—our proof that you can put down roots wherever you're planted.[49]

In addition to this tree, Woman speaks of her grandmother's transplanting of mint, plants that were "brought from a home halfway across the world.... Like cedars transplanted, trying to put down roots in new soil."[50] The cedar, Lebanon's national symbol, is often used by Lebanese writers as a symbol of strength and a metaphor for Lebanon. Like many Arab immigrants during the late twentieth century, Teta and Jeddo moved from Lebanon because of the Lebanese Civil War, which Jeddo knew would not be a short war. Although Jeddo and Teta were proud American citizens, the play looks back sadly upon their deaths.

> Jeddo—I cry for your silence, and I'm sorry for your pain. I wish I could know how you felt here, so far away from the world that you knew. Through your death I learned the danger of clinging so strongly to one sense of yourself that without it you would cease to be. Your soul is like Lebanon. It's this beautiful, tortured place, where I could never go. And I feel your loss in the loss of you. And I feel your presence Jeddo. Your ashes feed the soil in which I grow.[51]

In addition to finding strength in her grandfather, Woman finds strength in the long line of women who preceded her. She says "I come straight up from a long line of very strong women. It started with my great-grandmother, Teta Habouba, whose family starved to death when the Ottomans besieged their village."[52] This leads Woman to a trip to the supposed site of the original Garden of Eden and to a search for the Biblical Eve in Jeddah.

> So the whole city is named for the first woman. Yet no one can say where she's buried. Now some people say they just don't want the placed mobbed by tourists, which part of me can understand. But a larger, deeper part of me knows that if *Adam's* ass were buried there, you can bet there'd be a Garden of Eden shrine and museum right on that corner.[53]

Instead, she finds a Muslim cemetery; "it matters to me where the mother of every woman who's ever walked this earth is laid to rest. And it seem sadly fitting that no one knows exactly where that is— and no one really seems to care." When she finally finds the supposed grave, she has an imaginary conversation with Eve, asking her questions ranging from what to call her to whether or not she is a feminist. "You know they tried to stop me from coming here," Woman says. "Yeah, looked at me like I was dirt. I guess some things haven't changed. But you're not alone anymore. I just thought you'd like to know."[54] Here, Woman reconnects with this early feminist by visiting Eve's grave, taking a bite of an apple, and leaving on the grave for posterity.

Buck also addresses the Palestinian issue in *ISite*. Woman's cousin, Lena, is originally Palestinian. When Lena attempts to go back to Palestine, she is

Leila Buck performs her monodrama *In the Crossing* (photograph by Hunter Canning).

placed in the line for Palestinians and not the one for Americans. There, her cousin witnesses soldiers beating an old woman.

> In Arabic class in college my American professor taught me that *Intifada* literally means shaking off. And I think sometimes about what that means to my cousins over there. Shaking off—occupation? Frustration? Degradation? The more we share the more we fight, like brother and sister who can't stand seeing themselves in each other. Everyone always says that Arabs are anti–Semitic. Well that's impossible. Arabs can't be anti–Semitic. Arabs are Semites. We come from the same land—the one we're fighting for.[55]

Another area of conflict Woman discusses is Iraq "in the final days of the Iran-Iraq war (back when America was supporting Saddam as the 'lesser of two evils....'"[56] Her father, the diplomat, was stationed there. Her father's experiences with bananas and Bahraini ambassadors, celebratory gunfire over football matches, and falling scud missiles all speak to the chaos that was wartime Baghdad.

> My mother's most vivid memory of Baghdad is of coffins on top of taxis. The Iraqi military notified a family of their son's death by sending a taxi with a coffin to their door. No letter, no notice. No yellow ribbon. Just a cold and very hard journey home.[57]

Buck's experiences growing up in the Arab world, in places as diverse as Saudi Arabia, Iraq, and Oman, inform her entire existence. For Buck, she is the sum of all of these parts—the American diplomat father and the Lebanese mother, the Palestinian cousins, all of these diverse people and experiences inform her very existence. Buck brings all of these people, places, and experiences together in her final statement of the play:

> It's touching so many shores at once that forms the shape of who I am. We all take our shape from the lands that we touch. That's what home is I guess—where you make contact with the earth. And every time I touch down in new soil I see myself for the first time.[58]

ISite focuses primarily on Buck's cross-cultural experiences of living between worlds. Like Raffo's *9 Parts of Desire*, Buck displays her writing and acting through portrayals of multiple perspectives of herself and her family at different points in their lives. Her experience of performing the play in front of audiences over many years prior to and after, 9/11 has led to many conversations with audience members. Buck's monodrama is situated at the intersection of her parents' and grandparents' transgenerational trauma, and Buck's own experiences as a bi-cultural Arab American who has, herself, experienced life in both the Arab world and in the United States during times of political upheaval. Her play offers a glimpse into the complicated allegiances, identities, and situational politics that face Arab Americans. By embodying the play herself, as a performer, Buck provides audiences with personal testimonial and theatrical storytelling. Buck believes her work "moves us across barriers toward greater understanding and empathy—and from there, toward a more just and peaceful world."[59] This idealism is at the heart of the Arab American female solo performance genre, and is shared by many of its practitioners.

Jennifer Jajeh: I Heart Hamas: And Other Things I'm Afraid to Tell You

Jennifer Jajeh, a female Palestinian American performer, has been performing her monodrama *I Heart Hamas: And Other Things I'm Afraid to Tell You* since 2008. Jajeh explains that she created the play because she was tired of explaining herself and her thoughts about the Israel/Palestine conflict. In 2000 she travelled to her parents' hometown of Ramallah where she lived for a year and a half. The 9/11 attacks occurred ten days after her return home. "I clearly had post-traumatic stress disorder from living in a war zone," she says. "'Why do these people hate us?' is what a lot of people were saying after September 11th. There's such a misunderstanding of Arabs and Muslims in general.... There was such a need of humanization of stories."[60] As an actress who was frustrated with the limited choices of roles available to her, the performance became a means for opening up the conversation about Palestine, taking the fear out of the discourse, and being more playful about the ideas within the debate. She is clear that she is not speaking for all Palestinians in her work. "I'm not representing the Palestinian perspective," she says. "I'm representing *my* Palestinian perspective."[61] By saying this, Jajeh refuses to totalize the Palestinian experience in one play. Instead, she provides audiences with a very personal reflection of her own realization as a Palestinian American who has journeyed back to her ancestral homeland and has returned very much changed.

Jajeh labels her monodrama "a tragicomic solo show." The play's provocative title, given the U.S. Department of State's designation of Hamas a terrorist organization, along with Jajeh's asking audience members to "consider the current conflict in the Middle East from the Palestinian perspective," immediately asks the audience for empathy with the Palestinian "Other." Like other Arab American writers, she too prefaces the play with a plea to not accuse the writer/performer of being anti–Semitic, reminding the audience that the word "Semite" includes Arabs. In the play Jajeh takes the audience through a journey of the frustrations she encounters being told that "there is no such thing as Palestinian" and losing acting jobs because of being Middle Eastern. Jajeh tells the audience,

> I've spent my entire life defining myself for you. Trying to make my Palestinianness easier to digest, more fun, less threatening. But you see the more I do that, the more I feel like parts, huge parts of me are being erased. Like the real me just gets watered down into a tastier, easier to swallow version.[62]

Like other Arab American performers, Jajeh reminds audiences that she is a Christian, and that there are Christian Arabs in Palestine. She also attempts to show the audience where Palestine is on a map, but there is no map she can find that actually says the word "Palestine." In the play, Jajeh's agent tells her to be cautious performing in a show that mixes business with politics since she might want to be careful who she offends.

Jajeh tells about the founding of Ramallah, Palestine. She tells the audience that her family has been living there for 450 years, and explains the history of a Christian community surrounded by Muslim neighbors. She tells a story of an interfaith marriage of a Christian girl promised to a Muslim man. When the Christian father, Sabra, changes his mind about the marriage, a terrible series of revenge killings take place, forcing Sabra to settle in the place that is now Ramallah. Jajeh traces her family's origins to that originary moment.

Like Said, Jajeh takes a transformational journey to Palestine. On her journey she falls in love, gets detained by Israeli forces at a checkpoint, and

Jennifer Jajeh explains what it means to be Palestinian in her monodrama *I Heart Hamas: And Other Things I'm Afraid to Tell You*, directed by W. Kamau Bell (photograph by Joseph Sief, courtesy Jennifer Jajeh).

spits on an Israeli soldier. When she asks, rhetorically, if spitting on soldiers was the right thing to do, she replies,

> It's hard to separate things in your mind. You have to understand what it's like there. What it feels like to be assaulted everyday. They treat us like we don't exist or we're not even human. And I've only been here, for a year. Imagine if you grew up here. It's like living in a pressure cooker. Not everyone can handle the pressure.[63]

When Jajeh arrives at a scene where children are throwing stones at Israeli soldiers, she decides to stay and film the scene. She witnessed a boy get shot, which drives her into a depression. Her boyfriend, Hakam, tells her, "Come on you have to be stronger than this if you're gonna live here." Like Said, Jajeh crosses the unimaginable line of actually empathizing with those who commit violence.

> Look, if I could snap anybody could. This idea we have of what terrorism, Hamas is. That it's some mad crazy radical person. Some religious fundamentalist driven by insane motives that we can't understand. But maybe in reality, it's just a person who's had enough and doesn't see any other options. Maybe it's just a normal human reaction against violence and oppression. After living in Ramallah for only a year and a half, I even reached a point where I could imagine blowing people up. But I had the option to leave.[64]

Jajeh ends the play by explaining that her family line, and the Christian community in Ramallah, has left Palestine. "I am the break in this 450 year chain, and as much as I try I can't seem to leave it behind. So tell me, where does that leave me?" she asks. Like other Arab American writers, Jajeh retains a deep bond with Palestine, but cannot conceive of living there. Her Palestinian identity is a part of her that she cannot forego in her work, in her relationships, or in her political views. The play's provocative title, especially in light of the recurring wars between Hamas and Israel, is one that some would automatically reject as untenable. However, Jajeh refuses to reduce the argument into absolutes—instead she embraces the complexity of the situation that faces Palestinians and Palestinian Americans. By choosing such a flagrant title, Jajeh refuses to make her play more palatable to American audiences who are looking for a less controversial viewpoint on this ongoing crisis.

What makes works by Shamieh, Said and Jajeh both compelling and complicated is the fact that they speak from a Palestinian perspective and they empathize with the Palestinian point of view regardless of the exigencies of dominant U.S. views on the conflict. Their direct confrontation with violence, poverty, and occupation coupled with their ancestral connections to Palestine, causes them to have feelings of anger and shame. These performances are their way of coping with the trauma they and their families experience. Rather than acting out with violence, they work through their postmemorial trauma by performing the experiences of their Palestinian-ness onstage, despite the risks to their careers.

With each outbreak of violence between Israel and various Palestinian factions it is clear that plays that address these issues are more timely and necessary than ever. These solo performers bring a transnational perspective to contemporary crises by creating works that dramatize their personal experiences while visiting or living in war zones that most Americans only know through news coverage. Whether it is life under dictatorship in Iraq (Raffo and Buck), surviving the Lebanese civil war (Farah), or life under occupation in Palestine (Said and Jajeh), these female performers bring powerful first-hand accounts to audiences while providing a seldom heard perspective.

Reconsidering Solo Arab American Performance

Arab American solo performance is born of the same kinds of circumstances that create solo performances in other ethnic or sexually-oriented communities. The themes of identification, testimony, witnessing, autobiography, and community run throughout all of the monodramas. Not all of the performers agree on the nature of how each of these elements manifests within their work. For some, the Arab American designation has been imposed upon them, while for others it was a conscious choice. Despite all of these performers having witnessed events they wrote about, they do not agree with the conventional wisdom that their works are purely autobiographical testimonies. Ultimately, these works are meant to combat stereotypes of Arab women, to give personal accounts of the lives of Arabs suffering through the ravages of war, occupation, and exile, and to reconfigure our preconceived notions of what it means to be living as an Arab in America today.

These solo performances also provide agency for Arab American artists who are frustrated by the lack of roles available to them as performers. These solo works are relatively inexpensive to produce, can travel easily from venue to venue, and provide these performers with a means for expressing themselves artistically while giving them the opportunity to perform for audiences nationwide. By writing these intensely personal dramas, often based on their real-life experiences living and traveling to Arab countries, they become translators for American audiences wanting to know more about the Arab world.

Conclusion

Although contemporary Arab American theatre, film, and performance has not been formally recognized as its own genre of intercultural performance by many scholars, theatre companies, or governmental arts organizations, there is no doubt that the genre exists and that it is gradually transforming the landscape of the American theatre. I have defined this genre as the works created by Arab American writers and performers as a response to the backlash against Arab Americans, with the modern period extending from 1908 to 1967, and the contemporary period extending from 1967 to the present day. This genre is defined as the plays and performances of self-identified Arab American artists who write and perform their plays in English and Arabic, utilizing modern and contemporary theatrical and filmic forms. In addition, these works are a form of resistance literature interested in issues of assimilation, acculturation, and political themes. Furthermore, these works focus on issues that are controversial for many within the Arab community in the United States.

In this book I suggest that contemporary writers and performers are attempting to recast and restage Arab Americans in theatre, film, stand-up comedy, and solo performance by utilizing educational, confrontational, passing, and humorous accounting methods. They are the contemporary artistic counterparts to the academic work that preceded them following the previous backlash against Arab Americans following the 1967 Six-Day War. Arab American is defined here as an ethno-racial construction based upon Omi and Winant's class and nation based theory of cultural nationalism whereby a group underscores their identity based on the centrality of cultural domination and racial oppression, and the importance of cultures of resistance that unifies and promotes the collective identity of the oppressed.

The writers and performers who comprise the contemporary Arab American theatre, film, and performance genre are mainly first and second generation Arab Americans who were born during the 1960s and 1970s, and who self-identify as Arab Americans. These artists made the conscious decision to speak from, and create works focused on, their Arab American identity. After the attacks on 9/11, whatever claims to whiteness that Americans of Arab Descent once held were removed, and these artists were outed as Arab Americans. Instead of denying or escaping their Arabness, these writers, filmmakers, and performers embraced this identity and made the conscious decision to create their performances from this subject position. In doing so, they confronted issues such as governmental persecution, racial profiling, renditions, black sites, and torture. In addition, these works confront other issues that concern Arab Americans such as the Israel/Palestine conflict, negative stereotyping of Arabs in popular entertainment, and intra–Arab conflicts within the United States.

Three recent Arab American dramas, Denmo Ibrahim's *Ecstasy: A Water Fable*, Yussef El Guindi's *Pilgrims Musa and Sheri in the New World*, and Stephen Karam's *Sons of the Prophet*, offer a glimpse at the future of an Arab American art form that is not constrained by the preoccupations of racial profiling, governmental persecution, and abjection that have been a hallmark of previous dramas and comedies. Instead, these plays integrate the history, mythology, and culture of Arab Americans within an American context, thereby freeing the form from its need to constantly engage in protest and resistance.

Ecstasy: A Water Fable

Denmo Ibrahim's imagistic play, *Ecstasy: A Water Fable*, is based on the ancient Sufi myth known as "When the Waters Were Changed." Ibrahim's retelling of this myth is not particularly faithful to the original tale, relying instead on three simultaneous times, plots, and character journeys. The first, that of Picture Lady, is one that takes place in a mythic/dream world; the second, that of Pipeman, takes place in the ancient world, and the third scenario, that of Mona and Jack, takes place in the modern world. The main theme of the play is reconnection with origin—something shared by all three characters throughout the drama, and a central tenet of Sufism. Picture Lady is described as old, lost in a world of pictures, struggling to re-member her life. The Pipeman is a Sufi who was expelled from his community when he refused to drink the waters that changed. Mona, the contemporary Arab American character in the play, is separated from family, history, and her ancestry, causing her to be an insomniac who cannot seem to reconnect with her own life. Ibrahim writes, "the piece weaves through these three parallel, seemingly disparate worlds into what becomes a very intimate portrayal of an estranged mother and daughter."[1] The play, a non-linear, imagistic, ensemble-based work, is meant for a physical and musical storytelling ensemble. Unlike other works that preceded it, *Ecstasy* is not political and deals with its Arab themes metaphorically rather than realistically.

Of all the dramas presented here, this play is the most "Middle Eastern" in the sense that it does not necessarily root itself specifically within Arab culture. Rather, the play speaks to a broader Middle Eastern audience that could include any ethnic group from the Middle East, though it does contain themes specific to Muslim culture such as the *wail* (or "freestyle vocal *calling* ... and particularly elements of the Imam's Call to Prayer") and the *wudu* (or "the cleansing done by Muslims before prayer"). Though the play is not specifically

The Pipeman's community (Ryan Burke, Sunil Homes, Jerilyn Armstrong, and Lilly Lion) comfort the Pipeman (Alex Mentzel, center) in Denmo Ibrahim's *Ecstasy: A Water Fable,* directed by Michael Malek Najjar, produced by the University of Oregon (photograph by Ariel Ogden).

a Muslim tale, if any specific religion could be discerned, it would be those rituals specific to Sufi Islam.

Water is, of course, the primary element in the play.[2] Throughout the play are notes about stage properties that pertain to water: jars of water, glasses of water, water spouts, buckets of water, and bowls of water. The scenes have water titles as well. The Picture Lady states at the opening of the play that "where I come from, story comes from mouth. / What will occur has already occurred. It is written in the water."[3] Story is the other vital component to the drama. By recounting stories of relatives, loved ones, and lost friends, the Picture Lady states that she has kept tradition, preserved history, and remembered her life.[4]

Ecstacy: A Water Fable, though based on a fifth century Sufi tale, is a story of faith, family, and reconnecting with the place we all come from, but have lost. One character, known only as Birthsong, is the personification of that lost song that once resided in all humans, but has been forgotten. Mona's searching ends once she reconnects with her mother, but only after a journey into her past and her re-connection with herself. Likewise, the Pipeman, who has been outcast by his community and thought mad, finally relents and drinks the water that makes him whole again.

The play's non-linear format, reliance on ensemble storytelling, and references to Sufi Islam conjoin to make the play both compelling and disorienting. By eschewing fixed characters, linear structure, and an expected ending, *Ecstasy: A Water Fable* provides an unexpected departure from the Arab American dramas that preceded it. Free from the constraints of making political statements or polemical arguments, Ibrahim creates a visually compelling and deeply thought-provoking experience.

Pilgrims Musa and Sheri in the New World

Playwright Yussef El Guindi's 2011 comedy *Pilgrims Musa and Sheri in the New World*, premiered in 2011 at Seattle's ACT, directed by Anita Montgomery, and starring Shanga Parker and Carol Roscoe. The play is a departure from El Guindi's more political works, dealing instead with the life of an Muslim Egyptian American cab driver named Musa, his betrothed Egyptian Muslim fiancée Gamila, his friend Tayyib, and a smart-alecky street-wise American waitress named Sheri. In this case, the political is personal as Musa, who is expected to uphold the norms of being a good Muslim male, has broken with his family's traditions and fallen for a non–Muslim woman. When Gamila,

Musa's betrothed comes to visit, a crisis ensues forcing Musa to choose between them.

The play does not deal with issues of political persecution or discrimination, but rather with the internal struggles Muslim immigrants face being torn between their obligations to their faith, family, and religion and their desire for independence and free will. When Gamila confronts Musa about the need to conform to societal norms, he exclaims,

> I don't want roots! I want things I know nothing about. I want a life where I don't know where it goes. With us, the story it would be—it would be very clear—and customs and tradition and family; and this is who we are and where we started and this is where we are going. All the way to when they bury me. I don't want the rest of my life to be what I know.[5]

El Guindi offers a vision of Muslim American life that does not include allegiance to family, mosque, or community. Musa represents a character who is willing to break the ties with all of these institutions in order to live the life

Musa (Shanga Parker) and Sheri (Carol Roscoe) reconcile in *Pilgrims Musa and Sheri in the New World*, directed by Anita Montgomery, performed at A Contemporary Theatre (ACT), Seattle, 2011 (photograph by Chris Bennion).

he envisions for himself. El Guindi's comedy continues his tradition of dramatizing characters who are complicated, unpredictable, and flawed. The ending, with all of the characters making their individual pilgrimages, provides a vision of escape, release, and thanks for an unknown future.

Sons of the Prophet

Stephen Karam's serio-comedy *Sons of the Prophet*, that premiered in 2011 at the Laura Pels Theatre to critical acclaim, was a finalist for the 2012 Pulitzer Prize for Drama, and winner of the Drama Critics Circle, Outer Critics Circle, and the Lucille Lortel and Hull-Warriner Awards for Best Play. Karam's previous play, *Speech & Debate*, premiered at the Roundabout Theater Company and was called a "runaway hit" by *New York Times*. Karam also co-wrote a chamber opera with composer Nico Muhly titled *Dark Sisters* that was co-produced by Gotham Chamber Opera, MTG, and Opera Company of Philadelphia in 2012. Karam grew up in Scranton, Pennsylvania, and graduated from Brown University. He also taught at Brown University, New York University, the University of Scranton, Fieldston School in New York, and The New School.

The play centers on the character Joseph, an Olympic trials running hopeful who is suffering from injuries (both physical and psychological). Joseph's father, who died of a heart attack after an accident where he was forced to swerve off the road to avoid a deer decoy that was placed there by a college athlete named Vin as a practical joke, is a ghostly presence in the play. Joseph's older, and inappropriate, Uncle Bill and his younger brother Charles, are desperate to understand why Vin, a college football star, would dare play such a prank. Joseph's employer Gloria, a publisher who wishes to exploit the family's ties to famed Lebanese author Kahlil Gibran, is also coming unhinged after her best-selling Holocaust memoir is disgraced for being inauthentic. The hilarious climax throws all of the characters into a harsh relief that changes them forever.

The filial ties to Gibran and their Maronite Christian heritage serve as a backdrop for the characters, yet the play remains a universal American story. In an interview about the play, Karam describes his relationship with Gibran as "love/hate." Karam admires Gibran's success and ability to become such a renowned artist despite his impoverished beginnings, but he feels his poetry is "often too Hallmark Hall of Fame" for him. However, it was Gibran's optimism that attracted him to the subject.

Gibran's writing offers a big, cosmic, warm, hopeful picture of God and the reason for human suffering; I'm more interested in how to write about specific people with specific problems and still get a big, cosmic payoff. Gibran is interested in helping people cope with the despair that can creep into everyday life. So we're similar in that regard—and we're both fairly optimistic.[6]

Karam centers Gibran and Lebanon in the American experience both metaphorically and literally. The play's setting of Lebanon, Kansas (cited as the geodetic center of the United States), figures heavily into the drama. The spectre of the Maronite Saint Rafka, whose icon appears on the wall of the Douaihy house, is a reminder of their ties to their ancient religion and homeland. Despite Joseph and Charles being third generation removed from Lebanon, the spectre of the country and its suffering (at one point Charles tells Gloria, "Lebanon looks like a man's face, in pain, screaming") is a larger metaphor for the suffering of the Douaihy family.

Karam denies that *Sons of the Prophet* is his "family play," noting that, if it were, it would need supernumeraries given the size of his father's family.[7] The play attempts to dramatize a Lebanese American family struggling to fit

Joseph (Santino Fontana) tries to restrain his uncle Bill (Yusef Bulos) in Stephen Karam's *Sons of the Prophet*, directed by Peter DuBois, performed at the Roundabout Theater Company, 2011 (photograph by Sara Krulwich/*The New York Times*/Redux).

into the complicated cultural mosaic that is America. Karam explains his family's own dilemma with assimilation:

> for my grandfather (who was born in Zgharta, Lebanon, and arrived in the U.S. around 26 years of age), assimilation was the priority. He died speaking only broken English when my dad was a teenager. My dad's the ninth of ten siblings, and the Arabic proficiency in the family has a funny sliding scale.... So I grew up in Pennsylvania with a father who was assimilated, which allowed me to focus on the joys of being the first gay member of a devout Maronite Catholic family.[8]

The characters, all of whom carry tremendous pain inside, survive despite themselves. As one character tells Joseph, "you also can't stand in your pain too long. It's like quicksand, you'll sink, never get past it."[9] Karam's ability to connect disparate issues of heritage, sexuality, tradition, and forgiveness has made this play one of the most interesting Arab American dramas of the past decade.

Looking Forward

Perhaps the greatest force in opposition to this Arab American performing arts movement can be found within the Arab community itself. In her speech to the ADC titled "Arab Americans in the Performing Arts," Shamieh told the audience that Arab American artists need more support from their community in order to promote issues that are important to Arab Americans:

> I was told all my life in different ways by Palestinians and non–Palestinians that I would never make it as a Palestinian working in American theater, that it would be impossible for me to have an impact or a voice. Whatever small success I have achieved has been in spite of the constant messages of defeatism that are rife within the Arab-American community.[10]

Because Arab Americans traditionally gravitate toward fields such as business or the sciences, they rarely find the pursuit of careers in the arts or humanities worthy. There are currently no governmental programs, scholarships, or funding organizations that specifically promote Arab American performing artists. Because of the negative representations of Arabs and Arab Americans in American popular entertainment, little desire exists for parents to direct their children into this field. Furthermore, Arab Americans often create plays, films, and performances that speak directly to their condition even if the subject matter does not always reflect the majority opinion of the community itself. Playwright Yussef El Guindi wrote,

> Because there are so few depictions of Arab-American life in our theatre, people have wanted me to just give a very, very affirmative view of who we are. Some have asked me, why are you, for instance, depicting homophobia? There are so many other issues to deal with. But in order to humanize a people, you need to show them warts and all. Our humanity lives in our cracks and wounds. How can you affirm something, without talking about everything?[11]

Contemporary Arab American playwrights, filmmakers, and performers are continually reimagining and reshaping what it means to be Arab American. Their work, which is not widely produced or published, strives to speak for a community that often does not support its artists. The challenge ahead lies in the need for Arab American artists to continually engage with Arab Americans, to encourage them to attend their films and performances, and to bridge the gap that currently exists between the arts and the community.

The rise of theatre companies that are devoted to the works of Middle Eastern American plays such as Silk Road Rising, Golden Thread Productions, and Noor Theatre can be credited with producing the vast number of plays and performances of Arab Americans that have been staged during the last decade. In addition, organizations such as the RAWI Screenwriters' Lab/The Royal Film Commission-Jordan are creating valuable opportunities for Arab and Arab American filmmakers to create films. These theatres and organizations are vital for the longevity and health of this genre.[12]

Getting produced as an Arab American playwright remains a challenge. In a panel hosted by Chicago Public Radio in April of 2008 titled "Political Acts: the Emerging Arab American Theatre Movement," playwrights Yussef El Guindi, Heather Raffo, and Betty Shamieh discussed the difficulties of getting their work staged in American theatres. Shamieh's view is that most not-for-profit theatres only produce a play by a playwright of color once a year, leaving Arab American playwrights in competition with other minority playwrights. El Guindi states that "it's a struggle, it's a constant struggle to expand the cultural conversation to say, look at these stories, there are so many different groups with different stories and you need to start letting these stories become part of the cultural conversation."[13] Despite these difficulties, there has been a gradual increase in the production and publication of these plays. In addition to the aforementioned anthologies, several prominent magazines have printed Arab American writers' plays and several respected regional theatres have produced their works. Recently, *American Theatre Magazine* published two Arab American dramas: *Pilgrims Musa and Sheri in the New World* by Yussef El Guindi, and *Sons of the Prophet* by Stephen Karam. Arab American plays have been produced by several regional theatres that do not have a Middle Eastern

American drama mandate including ACT Theatre (Seattle); Alliance Theatre (Atlanta); Center REPertory Company (Walnut Creek, CA); Portland Center Stage (PCS); Manhattan Ensemble Theater; New York Theatre Workshop; The Wilma Theatre (Philadelphia). Cherien Dabis's films, *Amreeka* and *May in the Summer*, have found tremendous support through the Sundance Film Festival and Sundance Institute.

As this genre develops and matures and as the cultural climate transforms, Arab American writers' plays and films will continue to become a part of the tapestry that makes up American theatre and film. New works are constantly being written and produced. Leila Buck's *In the Crossing* was performed and read at Silk Road Rising in April of 2009; Sharif Abu-Hamdeh's *Habibi* was staged by Campo Santo (San Francisco) in October of 2010; Michael Malek Najjar directed a staged reading of his play *Talib* at Silk Road Rising in August 2010; Denmo Ibrahim staged her monodrama *Baba* at the Minnesota Fringe Festival in August 2011; Heather Raffo has collaborated with composer Tobin Stokes on *Fallujah: The First Opera about The Iraq War*, that was workshopped at City Opera Vancouver in 2011; Ismail Khalidi's play *Sabra Falling* received a staged reading at Noor Theatre in 2012; Mona Mansour's *Urge for Going* was produced by Golden Thread Productions in 2013, and Mansour received the 2014 Middle East America Distinguished Playwright Award; and Yussef El Guindi's *Threesome* is to be staged at Portland Center Stage in 2015.

In his essay "Toward an Arab American Theatre Movement" Jamil Khoury writes,

> I want an Arab American theatre movement that creates great theatre. I want an Arab American theatre movement that develops and catapults Arab American artists. I want an Arab American theatre movement that challenges racism and Islamophobia and racial profiling. I want an Arab American theatre movement that depicts us as who we are: your neighbors and colleagues and friends and loved ones. I want an Arab American theatre movement that is proud to be Arab American.[14]

This generation of playwrights, filmmakers, and performers have taken it upon themselves to address a range of issues that concern Arab Americans in particular, and American society in general. This creativity is born of a need change the world they have experience at home and abroad. James Zogby puts it this way:

> the measure of America's success as a multiethnic democracy lies in its continued ability to fully integrate the talents and skills of various people and accept the dignity of their heritage. Doing that will point us toward a more unified, smarter, and stronger America—a country true to its promise of inclusion.[15]

These writers can inform both Arab and American audiences about the experiences of living in both worlds, bridging the gap between them. This cross-cultural dialogue can also constructively address the problems facing our world today by utilizing a performative context to do so. With this generation of playwrights, filmmakers, and performers it seems, Arab Americans will no longer play the "tiny, marginal, and unimportant role" Edward W. Said believed they had been assigned to playing for over a century in American culture.

Appendix: Abridged Chronology of Arab American Drama, Film and Performance, 1896–2015

1896 *Andromak* by Syrian Youth Society. Performed April 18.
1908 *Riwayah* by Joseph A. Nasr. Published in *Al-Mohajer*.
1909 *Wajdah* by Ameen F. Rihani. Published in 2001.
1916 *The Chameleons* by Gibran Khalil Gibran. Published in *Al-Sa'ih*, April 20. Translated into English by Nefertiti Takla, 2012.
1919 *The Syrian Conference* by Sadeq Kabbash. Published in *Al-Sa'ih*, January 16.
1931 *Antar Ben Shaddad*, produced by the Syrian Dramatic Club at the Public Hall's Little Theatre, Cleveland, Ohio.
1933 *A Village Tyrant* by Yusuf Ghassub. Published in *Al-Machriq* 31 (1–4).
1965 *An Oasis in Manhattan* by S.K. Hershewe, directed by Mesrop Kesdekian. Performed in 1965 at the Stage Society Theatre, Los Angeles. Restaged at the Venture Theatre, Burbank, in 1990 starring Vic Tayback, directed by T.J. Castronovo.
1977 *Wedding and a Slice of Life* by Ala Fa'ik. Produced at the University of Missouri.
1984 *Shaleelah wa Dhay'a Ras-ha (A Tangled Yarn)* by Husam Zoro, directed by Salah Kalatoo, produced by Baghdad Theater Company, Detroit, Michigan.
1989 *The Festival: A Musical Play in Two Acts* by Hammam Shafie, adapted by Amira Assaly with music composed by Faheem Sadi. Produced by the Arab American Children's Theater, Los Angeles.
1996 *Mahjar* by Ahmed Ahmed and Fadwa El Guindi. Premiered at the Ruby Theatre at The Complex, Los Angeles, California.
2000 *Living in the Hyphen-Nation* written and performed by Laila Farah, performed at multiple venues including New York University, Lebanese American University, and DePaul University.

2002 *Sajjil (Record)*, conceived, written, performed, and directed by members of Nibras. Performed at the International Fringe Festival, New York.

2003 *9 Parts of Desire* by Heather Raffo, directed by Joanna Settle. Premiered at the Traverse Theatre, Edinburgh.

Precious Stones by Jamil Khoury, directed by Michael Malek Najjar. Staged by Silk Road Theatre Project at the Chicago Cultural Center.

2004 *Roar* by Betty Shamieh, directed by Marion McClinton. Presented at the New Group at the Clurman Theatre, New York.

With Love from Ramallah by Kathryn Haddad and Juliana Pegues, directed by Dipankar Mukherjee. Performed at the Mixed Blood Theater, Minneapolis, Minneapolis.

Browntown by Sam Younis. Staged at the Krane Theatre. Directed by Abigail Marateck.

Live! With Pascale and Chantal by Leila Gazale and Jana Zenadeen. Staged at the New York Fringe Festival. Directed by Maha Chehlaoui.

2005 *Chocolate in Heat: Growing Up Arab in America* by Betty Shamieh, directed by Sam Gold. Produced at The Tank Theatre, New York.

Between Our Lips by Nathalie Handal. Produced at the Blue Heron Theatre, New York.

2006 *Back of the Throat* by Yussef El Guindi. Staged at Theater Schmeater. Directed by Mark Jared Zufelt.

Ten Acrobats in an Amazing Leap of Faith by Yussef El Guindi. Staged at Silk Road Theatre Project. Directed by Stuart Garden.

In the Crossing by Leila Buck, directed and developed by Shana Gold. Performed at multiple venues.

2007 *Territories* by Betty Shamieh, directed by Jessica Heidt. Produced by Magic Theatre, San Francisco, California.

American East, screenplay by Hesham Issawi and Sayed Badreya, directed by Hesham Issawi.

Kemo Sabe, a film written and directed by Rana Kazkaz.

The Black Eyed by Betty Shamieh, directed by Sam Gold. Produced at the New York Theatre Workshop, New York.

2008 *Jihad Jones and the Kalishnikov Babes* by Yussef El Guindi, directed by Mark Routhier. Produced by Golden Thread Productions, San Francisco, California.

Our Enemies: Lively Scenes of Love and Combat by Yussef El Guindi, directed by Patrizia Acerra. Produced by Silk Road Rising, Chicago, Illinois.

2009 *Shoufou Al Wawa Wayn (Where Does It Hurt)* by Najee Mondalek. Produced at the Ford Community & Performing Arts Center, Dearborn, Michigan.

Palestine by Najla Said, directed by Sturgis Warner. Produced at the Fourth Street Theatre, New York.

Amreeka, written and directed by Cherien Dabis. Premiered at the Sundance Film Festival.

Ecstasy: A Waterfable by Denmo Ibrahim, directed by Evren Odcikin and produced by Golden Thread Productions, July–August. The play was restaged at the University of Oregon in 2014, directed by Michael Malek Najjar.

2010 *Language Rooms* by Yussef El Guindi, directed by Blanka Zizka. Performed at the Wilma Theatre, Philadelphia, Pennsylvania.

Tennis in Nablus by Ismail Khalidi, directed by Peggy Shannon. Produced by the Alliance Theatre, Atlanta, Georgia.

2011 *Sons of the Prophet* by Stephen Karam, directed by Peter DuBois. Produced by the Roundabout Theatre Company, New York.

Pilgrims Musa and Sheri in the New World by Yussef El Guindi, directed by Anita Montgomery. Produced by ACT Theatre, Seattle.

Eleven Reflections on September, written, directed, and performed by Andrea Assaf. Premiered at Pangea World Theatre, Minneapolis, Minnesota.

2012 *The Country Within* by Faiza Shereen, directed by C. Julian White. Produced at the Irvine Barclay Theatre, California.

I Heart Hamas: And Other Things I'm Afraid to Tell You by Jennifer Jajeh, directed by W. Kamau Bell. Premiered at Metro Madina Theatre, Beirut, Lebanon.

Detroit Unleaded, written and directed by Rola Nashef. Premiered at Toronto International Film Festival.

Food and Fadwa by Lameece Issaq and Jacob Kader, directed by Shana Gold. Produced by the New York Theatre Workshop and Noor Theatre, New York.

Urge for Going by Mona Mansour, directed by Hal Brooks. Produced by the Public Theatre, New York.

2013 *Sabra Falling* by Ismail Khalidi. A staged reading co-presented by Mizna and Pangea World Theater.

Fit for a Queen by Betty Shamieh. Directed by Lisa Peterson. Presented by Noor Theatre, New York.

May in the Summer, written and directed by Cherien Dabis. Premiered at Sundance Film Festival.

2014 *Baba* by Denmo Ibrahim, directed by Sara Razavi. Performed by Denmo Ibrahim. Produced by Alter Theatre, San Rafael, California.

Anna Asli Suriyah: I Come from Syria by Sarah Badiyah Sakaan, directed by Jessica Brater. Produced by Polybe + Seats, Brooklyn, New York.

2015 *Threesome* by Yussef El Guindi. Produced by Portland Center Stage, Portland, Oregon.

Chapter Notes

Preface

1. Werner Sollors, *Beyond Ethnicity: Consent and Descent in American Culture* (New York: Oxford University Press, 1986).
2. Harold Clurman, *The Collected Works of Harold Clurman: Six Decades of Commentary on Theatre, Dance, Music, Film, Arts and Letters* (New York: Applause, 1994).
3. It should be noted here that Gibran's name is actually Gibran Khalil Gibran. The name was shortened, and changed, by publishers.
4. In her fascinating essay, "Prophet Motive: The Kahlil Gibran Phenomenon," Joan Acocella writes that Gibran's *The Prophet* has sold more than nine million copies in the American edition alone. She also writes that Alfred A. Knopf, Gibran's publisher, believed that those who were purchasing the book must belong to a "cult."
5. One such anthology is Nishan Parlakian's *Contemporary Armenian American Drama: An Anthology of Ancestral Voices* (New York: Columbia University Press, 2004).
6. See "Afterword: Toward an Arab American Theatre Movement" in *Four Arab American Dramas: Works by Leila Buck, Yussef El Guindi, Jamil Khoury, and Lameece Issaq & Jacob Kader*, edited by Michael Malek Najjar (Jefferson, NC: McFarland, 2014), 187–92.
7. See Barbara Harlow, *Resistance Literature* (New York: Methuen, 1987), 1–30.
8. Homi K. Bhabha, *The Location of Culture* (New York: Routledge, 2004), 3.
9. Bhabha, *Location of Culture*, 2.
10. Jack G. Shaheen, *Guilty: Hollywood's Verdict on Arabs After 9/11* (Northampton, MA: Olive Branch, 2008), 68.
11. "Introduction," in *Post-Gibran: Anthology of New Arab American Writing*, ed. Munir Akash and Khaled Mattawa (Syracuse: Syracuse University Press, 1999), xi.
12. Holly Arida, *Etching Our Own Image: Voices from Within the Arab American Art Movement*, ed. Anan Ameri and Holly Arida (Newcastle: Cambridge Scholars, 2007), 1.
13. Peggy Phelan, *Unmarked* (New York: Routledge, 1993), 26.
14. Ala Fa'ik, "Issues of Identity: In Theater of Immigrant Community," in *The Development of Arab-American Identity*, ed. Ernest McCarus (Ann Arbor: University of Michigan Press, 1994), 107–18.
15. Dina Amin, "What's in a Hyphen?" in *Salaam, Peace: An Anthology of Middle Eastern-American Drama* (New York: Theatre Communications Group, 2009), 380.
16. Dalia Basiouny and Marvin Carlson, "Current Trends in Arab-American Performance," in *Performance, Exile and "America"* ed. Silvija Jestrovic and Yana Meerzon (New York: Palgrave Macmillan, 2009), 208–19.
17. Basiouny and Carlson, "Current Trends," 208–19.
18. Anneka Esch-Van Kan, "Amazing Acrobatics of Language: The Theatre of Yussef El Guindi," *American Studies Journal* no. 52 (2008), http://www.asjournal.org/archive/52/157.html.
19. Fa'ik, "Issues of Identity," 107–18.
20. Erith Jaffe-Berg, "Deterritorializing Voices: Staging the Middle East in American Theatre," in *Performance, Exile and "America"* ed. Silvija Jestrovic and Yana Meerzon (New York: Palgrave Macmillan, 2009), 179–207.
21. Somaya Sami Sabry, *Arab-American Women's Writing and Performance: Oriental-*

ism, Race and the Idea of The Arabian Nights (London: I.B. Tauris, 2011).

22. Jack G. Shaheen, *Guilty: Hollywood's Verdict on Arabs After 9/11*.

23. Judith Butler, *Precarious Life: The Powers of Mourning and Violence* (London: Verso, 2004).

24. Marianne Hirsch, "Past Lives: Postmemories in Exile," *Poetics Today* 17 (1996): 659–86.

25. Dominick LaCapra, "Trauma, Absence, Loss," *Critical Inquiry* 25 (1999): 696–727.

26. Nadine Naber, *Arab America: Gender, Cultural Politics, and Activism* (New York: New York University Press, 2012), 65.

27. Amira Jarmakani, *Imagining Arab Womanhood: The Cultural Mythology of Veils, Harems, and Belly Dancers in the U.S.* (New York: Palgrave Macmillan, 2008), 6.

Introduction

1. David W. Dunlap, "Little Syria (Now Tiny Syria) Finds New Advocates," *New York Times*, January 1, 2012, http://cityroom.blogs.nytimes.com/2012/01/01/little-syria-now-tiny-syria-finds-new-advocates.

2. According to Jack G. Shaheen, this term, which is often conflated with the term Islamophobia, connotes "irrational fears and/or prejudices toward Arabs, Muslims, and Islam that stir symptoms of loathing." See *Guilty: Hollywood's Verdict on Arabs After 9/11*, Kindle Edition, loc. 407.

3. Jean Gibran and Kahlil Gibran, *Kahlil Gibran: His Life and World* (New York: Avenel, 1981), 36–37.

4. Nijmeh Hajjar, *The Politics and Poetics of Ameen Rihani: The Humanist Ideology of an Arab-American Intellectual and Activist* (London: Tauris Academic Studies, 2010), 5.

5. Nada Najjar, "The Space In-Between: The Ambivalence of Early Arab-American Writers" (Ph.D. diss., University of Toledo, 1999), ii.

6. Sarah Gualtieri, *Between Arab and White: Race and Ethnicity in the Early Syrian American Diaspora* (Berkeley: University of California Press, 2009), 22.

7. Ibid., 26.

8. Kahlil Gibran, *A Treasury of Kahlil Gibran*, ed. Martin L. Wolf, trans. Anthony R. Ferris (New York: Open Road Media, 2011).

9. Ameen Rihani, "Palestine and the Proposed Arab Federation," *Annals of the American Academy of Political and Social Science* 164 (November 1932): 67.

10. Naimy, quoted in C. Nijland, *Mīkhāʾīl Nuʿaymah: Promoter of the Arabic Literary Revival, Nederlands Historisch-Archaeologisch Instituut te Istanbul* (1975), 76.

11. Yossi Shain, "Arab-Americans at a Crossroads," *Journal of Palestine Studies* 25 (Spring 1996), 46.

12. Arab American can be written either with or without a hyphen. For the purposes of this study I will utilize the non-hyphenated usage of the word since this study is not based on the concept of hybridity, I will instead utilize the word "Arab" as an adjective for the word "American." I will focus on the intervening space between these two identities, and therefore not utilize the hyphen.

13. Gary C. David, "The Creation of 'Arab American': Political Activism and Ethnic (Dis)Unity 1," *Critical Sociology* 33 (2007): 833–62.

14. Michael Omi and Howard Winant, *Racial Formation in the United States: From the 1960s to the 1990s*, 2d ed. (New York: Routledge, 1994), 30.

15. "On Arabs and Arabness" by Nasser Rabbat, *The Thistle* 10(15) states, "As identities go, Arabness is one of the most complex, varicolored, and historically and politically contested designations. Millions of people believe in it, swear by it, and yearn for it, yet no one can conclusively define it. It is supposed to denote a nation, yet there is no inclusive political entity that currently engenders it. Nor has there been any in the past, except for disappointingly short periods and in exceedingly limited geographical extents."

16. For an excellent examination of this period of Arab American history, see Gualtieri, *Between Arab and White*, chapter two.

17. Gibran wrote two of his plays in English—*Lazarus and His Beloved* and *The Blind*. Ameen Fares Rihani also wrote his play *Wajdah* in English. Mikhail Naimy, however, wrote his play *Fathers and Sons* in Arabic.

18. For more information on contemporary Arab Theatre, I recommend Eyad Houssami, Dalia Khamissy, and Elias Khoury's *Doomed by Hope: Essays on Arab Theatre* (London: Pluto, 2012) and Don Rubin's *The World Encyclopedia of Contemporary Theatre,* Vol. 4: *The Arab World* (London: Routledge, 1994–2000).

19. Islamophobia is defined as "close-minded prejudice against or hatred of Islam and Muslims." See *Same Hate, New Target: Islamopho-*

bia and Its Impact in the United States, January 2009–December 2010 (Washington: Council on American-Islamic Relations, 2009–2010).

20. Steven George Salaita, *Arab American Literary Fictions, Cultures, and Politics* (New York: Palgrave Macmillan, 2007), 1.

21. Gregory Orfalea and Sharif Elmusa, eds., *Grape Leaves: A Century of Arab American Poetry* (Salt Lake City: University of Utah Press, 1988), xxi–xxii.

22. Hayan Charara, *Inclined to Speak: An Anthology of Contemporary Arab American Poetry* (Fayetteville: University of Arkansas Press, 2008), xiii–xiv.

23. Nabil Alawi, "Arab American Poets: the Politics of Exclusion and Assimilation," in *Narratives of Resistance: Literature and Ethnicity in the United States and the Caribbean*, ed. Ana M. Manzanas and Jesus Benito (Castilla-La Mancha: University of Castilla La Mancha, 2000), 53.

24. Darcy Zabel, *Arabs in the Americas: Interdisciplinary Essays on the Arab Diaspora* (New York: Peter Lang, 2006), 2.

25. Nadine Naber, "The Rules of Forced Engagement," *Cultural Dynamics* 18 (2006): 240.

26. Hatem Bazian, "Virtual Internment: Arab, Muslims, Asians and the War on Terrorism," *The Journal of Islamic Law and Culture* 9 (Spring/Summer 2004): 5-6.

27. Carol Fadda-Conrey, *Contemporary Arab-American Literature: Transnational Reconfigurations of Citizenship and Belonging* (New York: New York University Press, 2014): 5.

28. Judith Butler, *Precarious Life*, 33–34.

Chapter 1

1. Edward W. Said, *Out of Place: A Memoir* (New York: Knopf, 1999), 140–41.

2. See Michael Suleiman, ed., *Arabs in America: Building a New Future* (Philadelphia: Temple University Press, 1999); Orfalea, 2006.

3. Omi and Winant, 1994, 15–16.

4. Assimilation, which occurs when a group considers their cultural/ethnic maintenance less important than acceptance by the host society, became the new form of ethnic identity in the United States. Assimilationists abandon their ethnic identity, preferring to adopt the values, beliefs, and lifestyles of the host society. "Assimilation takes on a variety of forms, each of which represents a higher level of individual and institutional transformation, and each is determined by factors that are internal to the group or to the host society" (Hayani, "Arabs in Canada," in *Arabs in America: Building a New Future*, ed. Michael Suleiman, 290).

5. Gualtieri, *Between Arab and White*, 54.

6. Ibid., 67.

7. Omi and Winant, *Racial Formation*, 15.

8. Alixa Naff, *Becoming American: The Early Arab Immigrant Experience* (Carbondale: Southern Illinois University Press, 1985), 123.

9. Ibrahim Hayani, "Arabs in Canada: Assimilation or Integration?" in *Arabs in America: Building a New Future*, 290.

10. Suleiman, *Arabs in Amerca*, 5.

11. Gualtieri, *Between Arab and White*, 169.

12. Ibid., 169.

13. Orfalea, *Arab Americans*, 189.

14. It is important to note that both non–Arabs and Americans of Arab descent have been guilty of this negative stereotyping in their own ways. Although the plays, films, and television productions were mainly created by non–Arabs, many Americans of Arab descent acted in these productions, and some even became famous for doing so.

15. Omi and Winant, *Racial Formation*, 99.

16. Bhabha, *Location of Culture*, 2.

17. Ibid., 3.

18. Suleiman, *Arabs in America*, 1.

19. Abdeen Jabara, "The AAUG: Aspirations and Failures," *Arab Studies Quarterly* 17 (2007): 15–9.

20. Naseer Aruri, "AAUG: A Memoir," *Arab Studies Quarterly* 3/4 (2007): 35.

21. Hayani, "Arabs in Canada," 290.

22. Nabeel Abraham, "Arab-American Marginality: Mythos and Praxis," *Arab Studies Quarterly* 11 (1989): 25.

23. Hayani, "Arabs in Canada," 288.

24. For a comprehensive understanding of this topic see Sarah M.A. Gualtieri's *Between Arab and White: Race and Ethnicity in the Early Syrian American Diaspora* (Berkeley: University of California Press, 2009).

25. Nabeel Abraham and Andrew Shryock, eds., *Arab Detroit: From Margin to Mainstream* (Detroit: Wayne State University Press, 2000), 29.

26. Abraham and Shryock, *Arab Detroit*, 29.

27. Ibid., 17–8.

28. Omi and Winant, *Racial Formation*, 4.

29. Ibid., 10.

30. Ibid., 40.
31. Ibid., 44.
32. Ibid., 42.
33. Charara, *Inclined*, xix.
34. Falguni Sheth, *Toward a Political Philosophy of Race* (Albany: State University of New York, 2009), 24.
35. Sheth, *Toward a Political Philosophy*, 24.
36. Ibid., 111.
37. Ibid., 90.
38. Aboul-Ela, Hosam, "Edward Said's *Out of Place:* Criticism, Polemic, and Arab American Identity," *MELUS* 31 (2006): 21.
39. Evelyn Shakir, *Bint Arab: Arab and Arab American Women in the United States* (Westport, CT: Praeger, 1997), 10.
40. *Arabs in America*. 13.
41. Samir Kassir, *Being Arab* (New York: Verso, 2006), 2.
42. Ibid., 2.
43. Ibid., 4.
44. Halim Barakat, *Days of Dust* (Wilmette, IL: Medina University Press International, 1974), 163.
45. Jamil Jreisat, "Organizing Arab-American Professionals: AAUG and Me," *Arab Studies Quarterly* 29 (2007): 140.
46. Edward Said, *In Search of Palestine* (BBC documentary, 1998).
47. Alia Malek, *A Country Called Amreeka: Arab Roots, American Stories* (New York: Free, 2009), 49.
48. Barakat, *Days of Dust*, xxviii.
49. Robert Ruby, "A Six-Day War: Its Aftermath in American Public Opinion," *Pew Forum on Religion and Pubic Life*, http://www.pewforum.org/2007/05/30/a-six-day-war-its-aftermath-in-american-public-opinion/.
50. Baha Abu-Laban, "Reflections on the Rise and Decline of an Arab-American Organization," *Arab Studies Quarterly* 29 (2007): 48.
51. Rashid Bashshur, "Unfulfilled Expectations: The Genesis and Demise of the AAUG," *Arab Studies Quarterly* 29 (2007): 7.
52. Elaine Hagopian, "Reversing Injustice: On Utopian Activism," *Arab Studies Quarterly* 29 (2007): 57.
53. Michael Suleiman, "'I Come to Bury Caesar, Not to Praise Him': An Assessment of the AAUG as an Example of an Activist Arab-American Organization," *Arab Studies Quarterly* 29 (2007): 76.
54. It is interesting to note here that prior to 1967, the title "Orientalist" did not have a negative connotation.
55. Bashshur, "Unfulfilled Expectations," 9.
56. Ibid., 10.
57. It is interesting to note here that the members of the AAUG did not consider Palestinians only to be Arabs. It seems from this statement that their vision of a Palestinian country would not exclude citizens based on their religion.
58. Gualtieri, *Between Arab and White*, 171–3.
59. Orfalea, *Arab Americans*, 215–6.
60. Fouad Moughrabi, "Remembering the AAUG," *Arab Studies Quarterly* 29 (1997): 98–99.
61. Gualtieri, *Between Arab and White*, 174.
62. Abbas Alnasrawi, "Reflections on the Rise and Decline of AAUG," *Arab Studies Quarterly* 29 (1997): 116.
63. Hani A. Faris, "The AAUG Experience: An Assessment," *Arab Studies Quarterly* 29 (1997): 119.
64. Suleiman, "'I Come to Bury Caesar,'" 78.
65. Nakleh, "AAUG: A Personal Introspection," *Arab Studies Quarterly* 29 (1997): 109.
66. Ibid., 109.
67. Terry, "Introduction," *Arab Studies Quarterly* 29 (1997): 3–4.
68. David Greenberg. *Nixon's Shadow: The History of an Image* (W. W. Norton, 2003): 100–101; Orfalea, *Arab Americans*, 216; "3 Acquitted In Nixon Plot," *Pittsburgh Post-Gazette*, 18 July 1969, 22.
69. "U.S. Checks Arabs to Block Terror: Residents and Travelers Are Being Screened to Protect Israelis in the Country," *New York Times*, 5 October 1972: 97.
70. Naber, "The Rules of Forced Engagement: Race, Gender, and the Culture of Fear," 34.
71. Malek, *A Country Called Amreeka*, 50.
72. Naber, "The Rules of Forced Engagement: Race, Gender, and the Culture of Fear," 34.
73. The 2013 film *American Hustle*, directed by David O. Russell, dramatizes some of the events of the ABSCAM operation.
74. Malek, *A Country Called Amreeka*, 99–100. Malek focuses on an important point—namely the charge of anti–Americanism in relation to Arabs and Arab Americans. The ABSCAM scandal was one that attempted to create the false connection between Arabism and anti–Americanism. Decades later, this anti–Americanism would become linked with Islam.
75. http://www.democracynow.org.

Notes. Chapter 1

76. Malek, *A Country Called Amreeka*, 187.
77. Ibid., 241.
78. Orfalea and Orfalea, *Arab Americans*, 312.
79. Sevandal, "Special Registration: Discrimination in the Name of National Security," *The Journal of Gender, Race, & Justice* 735 (2004–2005): 736.
80. Gana, "Introduction: Race, Islam, and the Task of Muslim and Arab American Writing," *PLMA* 123 (2005): 1576.
81. http://www.adc.org.
82. http://www.adc.org.
83. Malek, *A Country Called Amreeka*, 101.
84. Gualtieri, *Between Arab and White*, 179.
85. http://www.aaiusa.org.
86. Edward Said, Covering Islam: How the Media and the Experts Determine How We See the Rest of the World (New York: Random House, 1997), x.
87. Said, *Covering Islam*, x.
88. Ibid., xv.
89. Ibid., xvi.
90. Ibid., xviii.
91. Ibid., xviii.
92. Ibid., xxvi.
93. Jack Shaheen, *Reel Bad Arabs: How Hollywood Vilifies a People* (New York: Olive Branch, 2001), 7.
94. Ibid., 11.
95. Ray Hanania, *I'm Glad I Look Like a Terrorist: Growing Up Arab in America* (Tinley Park, IL: Urban Strategies Group, 1996), 47.
96. Ibid., 49.
97. Gualtieri, *Between Arab and White*, 9.
98. Gana, "Introduction," 1577.
99. Bazian, "Virtual Internment," 5–6.
100. Ibid., 6.
101. Ibid., 8.
102. Vitello, "Muslims Say F.B.I. Tactics Sow Anger and Fear," *New York Times*, December 12, 2009, A1 (New York edition).
103. Jerry Markon, "Tension Grows Between Calif. Muslims, FBI After Informant Infiltrates Mosque," *The Washington Post*, Decmeber 5, 2010, http://www.washingtonpost.com/wp-dyn/content/article/2010/12/04/AR2010120403710.html.
104. Said as quoted in Orfalea, *Arab Americans*, 174–75.
105. Suleiman, "I Come to Bury Caesar," 90–91.
106. Fa'ik, *Issues of Identity*, 108–109.
107. "Political Acts: The Emerging Arab-American Theatre Movement." Hosted by Jason Loewith. WBEZ 91.5 *Chicago Amplified*, 21 April 2008. http://www.wbez.org/episode-segments/political-acts-emerging-arab-american-theatre-movement.
108. Harlow, *Resistance Literature*, xvi.
109. Ibid., xviii.
110. Ibid., 22.
111. Salaita, *Arab American Literary Fictions*, 4.
112. Nouri Gana, "Everyday Arabness: The Poetics of Arab Canadian Literature and Film," *CR: The New Centennial Review*, Vol. 9, No. 2 (Fall 2009): 27.
113. Charara, *Inclined to Speak*, xxx.
114. Karen Shimakawa, *National Abjection: The Asian American Body on Stage* (Durham, NC: Duke University Press, 2002), 2.
115. Shimakawa, *Abjection*, 2.
116. Ibid., 3.
117. Ibid., 4.
118. Yvonne Haddad and Jane Smith, *Muslim Communities in North America* (Albany: State University of New York Press, 1994), xxvi.
119. Moustafa Bayoumi, *How Does It Feel to Be a Problem? Being Young and Arab in America* (New York: Penguin, 2008), 3.
120. Bayoumi, *How Does It Feel*, 6.
121. Shakir, *Bint Arab*, 1.
122. Ibid., 3.
123. Jarmakani, *Imagining Arab Womanhood*, 3–4.
124. It should be noted that, for some, assimilation may not be a choice. The tremendous pressures that are placed on some immigrants force them to take accent reduction classes, change their appearance, and adopt lifestyles they may, or may not, have otherwise adopted in order to find acceptance in society.
125. Bhabha, *Location of Culture*, 8.
126. Both German Chancellor Angela Merkel and British Prime Minister David Cameron have claimed that multiculturalism has failed in their countries, specifically citing Islam as the cause. (see Jaime Doward, "David Cameron's Attack on Multiculturalism Divides the Coalition," in *The Guardian*, 5 February 2011, http://www.theguardian.com/politics/2011/feb/05/david-cameron-attack-multiculturalism-coalition; Matthew Weaver, "Angela Merkel: German Multiculturalism has 'Utterly Failed,'" in *The Guardian*, 17 October 2010), http://www.theguardian.com/world/2010/oct/17/angela-merkel-german-multiculturalism-failed).

127. Sandra Mattar, "A Quest for Identity: Racism and Acculturation among Immigrant Families," in *The Psychology of Prejudice and Discrimination*, ed. Jean L. Chin (Westport, CT: Praeger), 138.
128. Mattar, "A Quest for Identity," 144.
129. Ibid., 147.
130. Ibid., 158.
131. Najla Said, *Palestine*. Unpublished playscript, 24.
132. Toufic El Rassi, *Arab in America* (Gardena, CA: SCB Distributors, 2007), 6.
133. Hanania, *I'm Glad I Look Like a Terrorist*, 6.
134. Ibid., 7.
135. In Arabic, *kaffir* means *apostate*.
136. Hanania, *I'm Glad I Look Like a Terrorist*, 8.
137. Elin Diamond, *Performance and Cultural Politics* (New York: Routledge, 1996), 1.
138. Diamond, *Performance*, 1.
139. Ibid., 1.
140. Ibid., 2.
141. Ibid., 2.
142. These strategies were originally created by Joe R. Feagin and Karyn D. McKinney in *The Many Costs of Racism* (2005) and applied specifically to discrimination of African Americans.
143. Amir Marvasti and Karyn McKinney, *Middle Eastern Lives in America* (Lanham, MD: Rowman & Littlefield, 2004), 91.
144. Ibid., 90.
145. Ibid., 90.
146. Ibid., 99.
147. Ibid., 99–100.

Chapter 2

1. Michael W. Suleiman, *The Arab-American Experience in the United States and Canada: A Classified, Annotated Bibliography* (Ann Arbor, MI: Pierian Press, 2006), 488.
2. Nada Najjar, "The Space In-Between: The Ambivalence of Early Arab-American Writers" (Ph.D. diss., The University of Toledo, 1999), 8.
3. Ibid., 5.
4. Nijmeh Hajjar, *The Politics and Poetics of Ameen Rihani: The Humanist Ideology of an Arab-American Intellectual and Activist* (London: Tauris Academic Studies, 2010), 23.
5. These sketches can be seen in the Ameen Rihani family museum in Freike, Lebanon.
6. According to Dr. Ameen A. Rihani, this is the same play, *The Tragedy of Shammar*, first written in Arabic and later rewritten in English by the author.
7. Hajjar, *The Politics and Poetics of Ameen Rihani*, 28.
8. This information was given to me by Dr. Ameen Albert Rihani via email on November 19, 2013.
9. Ibid.
10. http://www.ameenrihani.org
11. Hajjar, *The Politics and Poetics of Ameen Rihani*, 32.
12. Ameen F. Rihani, *The Rihani Essays: Ar-RIHANIYYAAT*, trans. Rula Zuheir Baalbaki (Washington, DC: Platform International, 2010), 89.
13. Rihani, *The Rihani Essays*, 252.
14. Ibid., 444–45.
15. Wail S. Hassan, "The Rise of Arab-American Literature: Orientalism and Cultural Translation in the Work of Ameen Rihani," *American Literary History* 20 (2008): 259. http://muse.jhu.edu/journals/alh/summary/v020/20.1hassan.html.
16. Hassan, "The Rise of Arab-American Literature," 259.
17. Edward Said, *Orientalism* (New York: Pantheon, 1978), 222.
18. Practicable or practical means that it should be constructed so that actors can utilize the set piece.
19. Ameen F. Rihani, *Wajdah* (Washington, DC: Platform International, 2001), 17.
20. For more information on Orientalist imagery see *Interrogating Orientalism: Contextual Approaches and Pedagogical Practices*, eds. Diane Long Hoeveler and Jeffrey Cass (Columbus: Ohio State University Press, 2006).
21. Rihani, *Wajdah*, 47.
22. Jarmakani, *Imagining*, 4–5.
23. Naimy, *Gibran*, 337.
24. Ibid., 338.
25. Suheil B. Bushrui, and Joe Jenkins, *Kahlil Gibran, Man and Poet: A New Biography* (Boston: Oneworld, 1998), 38.
26. Ibid., 158.
27. Robin Waterfield, *Prophet: The Life and Times of Kahlil Gibran* (New York: St. Martin's, 1998), 265.
28. Waterfield, 340.
29. Kahlil Gibran and Jean Gibran, introduction to *Dramas of Life* (Philadelphia: Westminster, 1981), 26.
30. Gibran and Gibran, *Dramas of Life*, 36.
31. Ibid., 37.

32. Kahlil Gibran, *The Chameleons,* trans. Nefertiti Takla. Unpublished playscript, 2011, 1.
33. Ibid., 7.
34. Ibid., 3.
35. Ibid., 1.
36. Kahlil Gibran, "I Believe in You," in *Mirrors of the Soul* (New York: Open Road Media, 2011), ebook.
37. Gibran and Takla, 2.
38. Ibid., 7.
39. Ibid., 8.
40. Ibid., 2.
41. Ibid., 2–4.
42. Ibid., 4.
43. Ibid., 5.
44. Ibid.
45. Ibid., 9.
46. Ibid., 10.
47. Kahlil Gibran, *A Treasury of Kahlil Gibran,* ed. Martin L. Wolf (New York: Citadel, 1951), ebook.
48. Kahlil Gibran and Mary Haskell, Beloved Prophet: The Love Letters of Kahlil Gibran and Mary Haskell and Her Private Journal. (New York: Knopf, 1972), 306.
49. Hussein Dabbagh, *Mikhail Naimy: Some Aspects of His Thought as Revealed in His Writings* (Durham, England: University of Durham, Centre for Middle Eastern and Islamic Studies, 1983), 7.
50. According to University of Washington Assistant to the Registrar Christine Fish, Naimy's bachelor of laws degree was converted to a J.D. degree in 1969.
51. Mikhail Naimy, *Parents and Children,* trans. by Nefertiti Takla. Unpublished playscript. 2.
52. Ibid., 2.
53. Ibid., 3.
54. Ibid.
55. Ibid., 4.
56. Ibid.
57. Ibid., 1.
58. Ibid.
59. Ibid., 2.
60. Elsaid Badawi, "Arab Theatre and Language: The Continuing Debate," in *The World Encyclopedia of Contemporary Theatre, Vol. 4: The Arab World* (London: Routledge, 1994), 19.
61. Alyn Desmond Hine, "Russian Literature in the Works of Mikhail Naimy" (Ph.D. diss., University of London, 2011), 133.
62. For an excellent comparison between Turgenev's novel and Naimy's play within a Russian literary context, see Aida Imangulieva, *Gibran, Rihani & Naimy: East-West Interactions in Early Twentieth-Century Arab Literature* (Oxford: Inner Farne, 2009).
63. Ibid., 159.
64. Naimy and Takla, 7.
65. Dawud replies, "Perhaps that which you don't know is known by the force that leads us from the darkness of the womb to the darkness of the tomb and shows us that flash of lightning in between that makes us love life." Forty years later Beckett would write in his play *Waiting for Godot:* "They give birth astride a grave, the light gleams an instant, then it's night once more."
66. Naimy and Takla, 13.
67. Ibid., 14.
68. Ibid., 29.
69. Ibid.
70. Ibid., 49.
71. Ibid., 67.
72. M. M. Badawi, ed., *Modern Arabic Literature* (New York: Cambridge University Press, 1992), 356.

Chapter 3

1. John Limon, *Stand-Up Comedy in Theory, or, Abjection in America* (Durham, NC: Duke University Press, 2000), 4.
2. Limon, *Stand-up,* 5.
3. Ibid., 6.
4. Ibid., 7.
5. "Newcomers: Only a Few Are Funny," *LIFE Magazine,* January 10, 1944, 77. http://books.google.com/books?id=2FYEAAAAMBAJ&printsec=frontcover&dq=life+magazine&hl=en&sa=X&ei=ydQeUqaAK6XJiQL6tIHwCA&ved=0CD4Q6wEwAQ#v=onepage&q=life%20magazine&f=true.
6. "Danny Thomas," in *United Cerebral Palsy Associations, Inc. Souvenir Program,* August 25, 1950. Thomas's biography in this program claims, "His people are pure Labanites from Biblical times" and that Thomas was "called the greatest story-teller in the world."
7. Danny Thomas, "Why I Vowed to Help Sick Kids," in *Family Weekly,* February 20, 1972, 14, http://news.google.com/newspapers?nid=1696&dat=19720220&id=ZdMdAAAAIBAJ&sjid=JUcEAAAAIBAJ&pg=5704,2904818.
8. Danny Thomas, "Trouble: It's Wonderful." *The American Magazine,* November 1955, 104.

9. Danny Thomas, *An Ode to a Wailing Syrian*, film, *All Star Revue*, NBC, October 13, 1951.

10. The only copies of this film are located at the Library of Congress (Washington, DC), UCLA Film & Television Archive (Los Angeles, CA), and the Paley Center for Media (Beverly Hills, CA).

11. Ibid.
12. Ibid.
13. Ibid.
14. Ibid.
15. Ibid.
16. Ibid.

17. *LIFE Magazine*, January 10, 1944, 77.

18. Johnny Sippel, "Nightclub Reviews," *Billboard*, January 19, 1946, 32, http://books.google.com/books?id=dBgEAAAAMBAJ&pg=PT31&dq=thomas+%22ode+to+a+wailing+syrian%22&hl=en&sa=X&ei=QuQeUpuAB4H9igLon4HQBw&ved=0CC0Q6AEwAA#v=onepage&q=thomas%20%22ode%20to%20a%20wailing%20syrian%22&f=false.

19. Johnny Sippel, "Nightclub Reviews," *Billboard*, November 25, 1950, http://books.google.com/books?id=8B0EAAAAMBAJ&pg=PA45&dq=thomas+%22ode+to+a+wailing+syrian%22&hl=en&sa=X&ei=QuQeUpuAB4H9igLon4HQBw&ved=0CDkQ6AEwAw#v=onepage&q=thomas%20%22ode%20to%20a%20wailing%20syrian%22&f=false.

20. Thomas, "Trouble," 104.

21. Danny Thomas and Bill Davidson, *Make Room for Danny* (New York: Putnam, 1991), 184.

22. Marla Brooks, *The American Family on Television: A Chronology of 121 Shows, 1948–2004*. (Jefferson, NC: McFarland, 2005), 22.

23. Thomas, "Trouble," 104.

24. For more on this history, see Michael Provence, *The Great Syrian Revolt and the Rise of Arab Nationalism* (Austin: University of Texas Press, 2005).

25. During the current Syrian civil war (2011–), another street singer named Ibrahim Qashoush, who wrote a song about the Syrian uprising and who had taken part in riots against the Assad regime, was murdered and his vocal cords were ripped from his throat. See "Syria Undercover." *Frontline*, November 8, 2011, http://www.pbs.org/wgbh/pages/frontline.

26. Sylvie Drake, "Stage Notes: Actors Studio, Playwrights Split," *Los Angeles Times*, April 24, 1974, http://www.proquest.com.

27. Program notes, *An Oasis in Manhattan*, 1990. Burbank: Venture Theatre.

28. "'Oasis in Manhattan' Premieres Wednesday," *Los Angeles Times*, October 31, 1965, http://proquest.com/?.

29. Cecil Smith, "'Oasis' Refreshing at Stage Society," *Los Angeles Times*, November 5, 1965, http://www.proquest.com/?.

30. Margaret Harford, "Radio Veteran Finds 'Oasis,'" *Los Angeles Times*, December 30, 1965, http://proquest.com/?.

31. Pat McDonnell Twair, "Comedy Dispels Arab-Jewish Bigotry," *Washington Report on Middle East Affairs*, March 1990, http://wrmea.org/.

32. Myrna Oliver, Myrna, "Vic Tayback; Actor Best Known as Mel in 'Alice' TV Series," *Los Angeles Times*, May 26, 1990, http://www.articles.latimes.com/.

33. T. H. McCulloh, "Bridging a Cultural, Generation Gap in 'Oasis,'" *Los Angeles Times*, February 16, 1990.

34. Bruce Feld, "An Oasis in Manhattan," *Drama-Logue*, February 15–21, 1990.

35. McDonnel Twair, "Comedy."

36. Vic Tayback, "St. Louie & Moh," A Vic Tayback/BRB Entertainment Production. Unpublished teleplay, 1986.

37. Ibid.

38. Vic Tayback, Papers. Christopher Tayback Personal Archives.

39. Harry C. Ford, "Why I Wrote a Syrian Play," *Syrian World* 2 (July 1927): 33–34.

40. Ford, 33–34.

41. McDonnel Twair, "Comedy."

42. Gualtieri, *Between Arab and White*, 143.

43. S. K. Hershewe, *An Oasis in Manhattan*. Unpublished playscript.

44. Janice Arkatov, "New Role Takes Vic Tayback Back to Origins," *Los Angeles Times*, January 7, 1990, http://www.articles.latimes.com/.

45. Naff, *Becoming American*, 329.

46. Ajyal Theater Group, http://www.ajyal.us/aboutus.html.

47. Najee Mondalek, *Smile You're in America*. Author's translation.

48. Mondalek, *Smile*.

49. Francis Fukuyama, *America at the Crossroads: Democracy, Power, and the Neoconservative Legacy* (New Haven, CT: Yale University Press, 2007).

50. "The Ninth Annual New York Arab-American Comedy Festival Is Returning to New York from October 18–20, 2012," New York Arab-American Comedy Festival, www.arabcomedy.com/pages/2012.

51. Fukuyama, *America at the Crossroads*.
52. Ibid.
53. Ibid. Note: There have been other stand-up comedy groups that predated 9/11, including the *Infidels of Comedy, or the Christian Arab Comedy Tour*, featuring Nasry Malak, Maria Shehata, and Ray Hanania, who focused their attention on Christian Arab comedy (http://www.infidelsofcomedy.com).
54. *America at a Crossroads: STAND UP: Muslim American Comics Come of Age*, DVD, directed by Glenn Baker, (Washington, DC: PBS Home Video, 2007).
55. Ibid.
56. Ibid.
57. Ibid.
58. Ibid.
59. Ibid.
60. *The Arab American Comedy Tour*, DVD (Seattle, WA: Arab Film Distribution, 2006).
61. *Axis of Evil*.
62. Fukuyama, *America at the Crossroads*.
63. *The Axis of Evil Comedy Tour*.
64. *The Arab American Comedy Tour*.
65. Ibid.
66. Ibid.
67. Ibid.
68. Jarmakani, *Imagining Arab Womanhood*, 8.
69. Ahmed Al Omran, "Not Just for Laughs," http://www.alomran.me. March 22, 2011. www.alomran.me/comedy.
70. *Just Like Us* (Santa Monica, CA: Lionsgate, 2010).
71. Ibid.
72. Ibid.

Chapter 4

1. Jane Mayer, "The Black Sites: A Rare Look Inside the C.I.A.'s Secret Interrogation Program," *The New Yorker*, August 13, 2007, http://www.newyorker.com/reporting/2007/08/13/070813fa_fact_mayer.
2. Amardeep Singh "'Are Not the Enemy': Hate Crimes Against Arabs, Muslims, and Those Perceived to be Arab or Muslim After September 11," *Human Rights Watch* 14 (2002).
3. Singh, "Are Not the Enemy," 15.
4. Ibid., 34.
5. In their December 17, 2009, *New York Times* article, "Muslims Say F.B.I. Tactics Sow Anger and Fear," Paul Vitello and Kirk Semple write: "Since the terror attacks of 2001, the F.B.I. and Muslim and Arab-American leaders across the country have worked to build a relationship of trust, sharing information both to fight terrorism and to protect the interests of mosques and communities. But those relations have reached a low point in recent months, many Muslim leaders say. Several high-profile cases in which informers have infiltrated mosques and helped promote plots, they say, have sown a corrosive fear among their people that F.B.I. informers are everywhere, listening."
6. Said, "The Arab Portrayed," 5.
7. Ibid., 4.
8. Ibid., 1.
9. Harry Benshoff and Sean Griffin, *America on Film: Representing Race, Class, Gender, and Sexuality at the Movies* (Malden: MA: Blackwell, 2004), 70–73.
10. Benshoff and Griffin, *America on Film*, 74.
11. Tim Semmerling, *"Evil' Arabs in American Popular Film: Orientalist Fear* (Austin: University of Texas Press, 2006), 2.
12. Ibid., 25–26.
13. Kofi Annan, "Confronting Islamophobia: Education for Tolerance and Understanding," United National Press Release, December 7, 2004.
14. Butler, *Precarious*, 20.
15. Ibid., 22.
16. Ibid., 28.
17. Ibid., 33–34.
18. Ibid., 32.
19. Ibid., 39.
20. Ibid., 63.
21. Ibid., 76–77.
22. Ibid., 77.
23. Naber, "The Rules of Enforced," 236.
24. Ibid.
25. Arab American scholar Hatem Bazian proposes a similar concept that he calls "virtual internment," which he defines as "a quasi-visible but repressive, intimidating, and confining structure employed by the U.S. administration and its allies on a global scale against individuals, communities, and organizations deemed unsupportive, and possibly hostile, in their worldview toward American and 'global' interests" (Bazian, "Virtual Internment: Arabs, Muslims, Asians and the War on Terrorism").
26. Naber, "The Rules of Forced," 240.
27. Ibid., 255.
28. Khalidi, *Truth Serum Blues*. Unpublished playscript, 3.
29. Ibid., 4.
30. Ibid., 7.

31. Ibid., 15.
32. Ibid., 23.
33. Ibid., 24–25.
34. Ibid., 29.
35. Ibid., 33.
36. Ibid., 36–37.
37. Ibid., 48–50.
38. Fractured Atlas, http://www.fracturedatlas.org.
39. Voice of America, http://www.voanews.com.
40. Najla Said, *Looking for Palestine: Growing Up Confused in an Arab-American Family* (New York: Riverhead, 2013), 218.
41. Michael Malek Najjar, "Writing from the Hyphen: Arab American Playwrights Struggle with Identity in the Post–9/11 World," *Gale eNewsletters Arts & Humanities Community News*, September 2004, accessed September 7, 2013, http://www.silkroadrising.org/news/writing-from-the-hyphen-arab-american-playwrights-struggle-with-identity-in-the-post-911-world.
42. Antonio Sacre, "nytheatre.com review," 15 August 2002. http://www.nytheatre.com/Review/antonio-sacre-2002-8-15-sajjil-record.
43. Ibid.
44. Ibid.
45. Ibid.
46. Voice of America, website, http://www.voanews.com.
47. Ibid.
48. Liesl Schillinger, "Theater; The New 'Arab' Playwrights." *New York Times* 4 April 2004. http://www.nytimes.com/2004/04/04/theater/theater-the-new-arab-playwrights.html.
49. Ibid., par 14.
50. Said, *Looking for Palestine*, 226.
51. James Asher, e-mail message to author, July 8, 2009.
52. Nibras, *Sajjil*, 4–5.
53. Ibid., 5.
54. Ibid., 6.
55. Ibid., 44.
56. Ibid., 12.
57. Ibid., 16.
58. Ibid., 32.
59. Ibid., 33.
60. Joshua Tanzer, "Camel Lot? Maybe Not" (OffOffOff Theater, 2002), accessed April 21, 2014, http://www.offoffoff.com/theater/2002/sajjil.php, par 8.
61. Nibras, *Sajjil*, 26–7.
62. Ibid., 31.
63. Ibid., 43.
64. Ibid., 36.
65. Ibid., 36–37.
66. Ibid., 41.
67. Ibid., 42.
68. Ibid., 44.
69. Ibid., 15.
70. Lawrence Joseph, "Sand Nigger" poets.org, accessed May 3, 2014, www.poets.org/poetsorg/poem/sand-nigger.
71. Steven Salaita, *Modern Arab American Fiction: A Reader's Guide* (Syracuse, NY: Syracuse University Press, 2011), 19.
72. Salaita, *Modern Arab American Fiction*, 22.
73. Ibid., 37.
74. Said, *Looking for Palestine*, 228.
75. Najjar, "Writing from the Hyphen."
76. Email interview with Maha Chehlaoui, March 27, 2014.
77. Here I am specifically utilizing the concepts of Michel Foucault and his text *Discipline and Punish: The Birth of the Prison* (New York: Vintage, 1995).
78. Interestingly, these plays are linked through the character of Khaled who, in *Language Rooms*, has been interrogated by Ahmed and Nasser. This point was verified by the playwright in a personal correspondence.
79. Yussef El Guindi, *Language Rooms*, in *Here's to a Theatre of Defiance: Manifesto Series Vol. 3*, edited by Naomi Iizuka (Seattle: Rain City Projects, 2007), 44.
80. Yussef El Guindi, *Back of the Throat* (New York: Dramatists Play Service, January 29, 2007), 49.
81. Yussef El Guindi, *Back of the Throat*, *Theatreforum* (Summer/Fall 2006): 26.
82. Walter Bilderback, "Interview with Playwright Yussef El Guindi," 9 February 2010, http://www.wilmatheater.org/blog/interview-playwright-yussef-el-guindi#bottom.
83. Naber, "The Rules of Forced Engagement," 236.
84. El Guindi, *Back of the Throat*, 30.
85. Nadine Naber, "'Look, Mohammed the Terrorist Is Coming!' Cultural Racism, Nation-Based Racism, and the Intersectionality of Oppressions After 9/11," in *Race and Arab Americans Before and After 9/11: From Invisible Citizens to Visible Subjects,* ed. Amaney Jamal and Nadine Naber (Syracuse, New York: Syracuse University Press, 2008), 288.
86. Gana, "Introduction," 1576.
87. El Guindi, *Back of the Throat*, 40.
88. Ibid., 42.

89. Ibid., 48.
90. Ibid., 8–9.
91. Ibid., 44.
92. Ibid., 18.
93. Bayoumi, *How Does It Feel*, 2.
94. Ibid., 3.
95. El Guindi, *Back of the Throat*, 34.
96. El Guindi, *Language Rooms*, 29.
97. Adams quoted in Sollors 1986.
98. Sollors, *Beyond* 6.
99. El Guindi, *Back of the Throat*, 35.
100. Ibid., 45.
101. Benshoff and Griffin, *America on Film*, 72.
102. El Guindi, *Language Rooms*, 69.
103. Butler, *Precarious*, 33–34.
104. Ibid., 81.
105. El Guindi, *Back of the Throat*, 49.
106. Fadda-Conrey, Carol, *Contemporary Arab-American Literature*, 170.
107. Arab American Institute (2014). *American Attitudes Toward Arabs and Muslims, July 29, 2014.* Poll retrieved July 29, 2014, from www.aaiusa.org.

Chapter 5

1. Shamieh, Betty, "Lives I Could Not Have Led," *American Theatre Magazine* (New York: Theatre Communications Group, 2003), 32, 71.
2. Edward Said, "Intellectual Exile: Expatriates and Marginals," *Grand Street* 47 (1993): 122.
3. LaCapra, "Trauma, Absence, Loss," 699.
4. Kathryn Haddad and Juliana Pegues, "From the Playwrights," in *With Love from Ramallah*, program notes, 2004.
5. Kathryn Haddad, "With Love from Ramallah," *Mizna* 7, no. 1 (2005): 33.
6. Mona Mansour, *Urge for Going*. Unpublished playscript, 12.
7. Betty Shamieh, "Introduction" in *The Black Eyed and Architecture* (New York: Broadway Play, 2008), 9.
8. Shamieh, *Black Eyed*, 70.
9. Nathalie Handal, *Between Our Lips* in *Salaam, Peace: An Anthology of Middle Eastern-American Drama*, ed. Holly Hill and Dina Amin (New York: Theatre Communications Group, 2009), 105.
10. Yasser Fouad Selim, "Arab American Theatre Caught in Censorship: A Study of Betty Shamieh's *Roar* and *The Black Eyed*," *International Journal of Humanities and Social Science* Vol. 4, No. 3 (February 2014): 87.
11. Hirsch, "Past Lives: Postmemories," 662.
12. Ibid.," 664.
13. LaCapra, "Trauma," 698.
14. Ibid., 699.
15. Ibid.
16. Ibid., 701.
17. Rashid Khalidi, *Palestinian Identity: The Construction of Modern National Consciousness* (New York: Columbia University Press, 1997), 178.
18. Ibid., 11.
19. Ahmad Sa'di and Lila Abu-Lughod, *Nakba: Palestine, 1948, and the Claims of Memory* (New York: Columbia University Press, 2007), 5.
20. Rashid Khalidi, *The Iron Cage: The Story of the Palestinian Struggle for Statehood* (Boston: Beacon, 2006), 137.
21. Budeiri, "Reflections" 31.
22. Abu-Lughod, "Return to Half-Ruins" 103.
23. Mamdouh Nofal et al., "Reflections on Al-Nakba," *Journal of Palestine Studies* 28 (1998): 32.
24. Nofal et al., "Reflections," 20.
25. Reid, Kerry, "Silk Road Theatre Project, Chicago," *American Theatre Magazine*, December 2004. Web. 25 September 2014.
26. "About." *Silk Road Rising*. Web. 26 September 2014.
27. Ibid.
28. "Jamil Khoury, the Theater Activist." Chicagoreader.com. 22 December 2011. Web. 26 September 2014.
29. Khoury 2014, 46.
30. It is important to note that Khoury writes, "Please note that all Christian and Muslim references have been assigned to the 'Arab,' as Arabs are both Christians and Muslims."
31. Khoury 2003, 1.
32. Khoury 2014, 48.
33. Sura Faraj, "Crossing Boundaries, Creating Intersections: Jamil Khoury Does Both with 'Precious Stones.'" *Queer Life News*, February 2005. http://www.silkroadrising.org/news/crossing-boundaries-creating-intersections-jamil-khoury-does-both-with-precious-stones.
34. Ibid., 15.
35. Khoury, 2014, 49.
36. Ibid., 54.
37. Ibid., 81.
38. Ibid., 56.
39. Ibid., 59.

40. Ibid., 57.
41. Ibid.
42. Ibid., 52.
43. Ibid., 85.
44. Ibid., 86.
45. Ismail Khalidi, *Tennis in Nablus: A Tragipoliticomedy in Two Acts*. Unpublished playscript, 2.
46. An obvious reference to British General Arthur James Balfour (1848–1930). Balfour was prime minister of Great Britain from 1902 to 1905 and foreign secretary from 1916 to 1919. Balfour wrote the Balfour Declaration in 1917 which supported "the establishment in Palestine of a national home for the Jewish people" (*Encyclopaedia Brittanica Online*).
47. Khalidi, *Iron Cage*, 31.
48. Ibid., 32–3.
49. Ibid., 64.
50. Khalidi, *Tennis in Nablus*, 23.
51. Ibid., 71.
52. Ibid., 71, 75, 43.
53. In their book *One Palestine, Complete: Jews and Arabs Under the British Mandate*, Tom Segev and Haim Watzman write, "There were those who identified with the Arabs. There were those who found both repugnant. 'I dislike them all equally,' wrote General Sir Walter Norris 'Squib' Congreve. 'Arabs and Jews and Christians, in Syria and Palestine, they are all alike, a beastly people. The whole lot of them is not worth a single Englishman!" (9)
54. Khalidi, *Tennis in Nablus*, 80.
55. Ibid., 81.
56. Ibid., 45.
57. Šegev and Watzman write, "People played soccer in Palestine even before the Mandate, but the British brought tennis; it was part of their colonial culture and mentality.... Colonial Secretary Lord Milner came to visit Palestine. He drank tea with the governor of Hebron and his guests and afterward they went to play tennis. Two Arab criminals were brought specifically from the prison to run around the court and collect the balls; their legs were in irons throughout the game" (*One Palestine*, 8).
58. Robert Fisk, *Pity the Nation: Lebanon at War* (New York: Oxford University Press, 1990), 19.
59. Khalidi, *Tennis in Nablus*, 104.
60. Ibid.
61. A party store is described by Shamieh as "a liquor store that also sells some food items and there is one on practically every corner of downtown Detroit" (*Roar* 1).
62. Mamdouh Nofal, et al., "Reflections on Al-Nakba." *Journal of Palestine Studies*, volume 28, no. 1 (1998): 34. Nofal et al. write, "June 1967 was the historical divider between 'before' and 'after,' but in retrospect the events of 1970 drove home in personal terms the meaning of identity and the dimensions of defeat"
63. Betty Shamieh, *Roar* (New York: Broaday Play, 2005), 47.
64. Hirsch, "Past Lives: Postmemories," 662.
65. "Reflections on Al-Nakba," 184.
66. Shamieh, *Roar*, 50.
67. Ibid., 11.
68. Zahia Salhi and Ian Netton, *The Arab Diaspora: Voices of an Anguished Scream* (London: Routledge, 2006), 3.
69. Ibid., 2.
70. *Political Acts*.
71. Shamieh, *Roar*, 30.
72. Marvasti and McKinney, *Middle Eastern Lives*, 97.
73. Shamieh, *Roar*, 34.
74. Ibid., 65.
75. Ibid., 64.
76. Ibid., 68.
77. Alawi, "Arab American Poets," 45.
78. Said, *In Search of Palestine*.
79. Lameece Issaq and Jacob Kader, Food and Fadwa in *Four Arab American Plays: Works by Leila Buck, Jamil Khoury, Yussef El Guindi, Lameece Issaq and Jacob Kader*, ed. by Michael Malek Najjar (Jefferson, NC: McFarland, 2014), 182.
80. Hirsch, "Past Lives: Postmemories," 661.
81. Atyaf Alwazir, "Uprooting Olive Trees in Palestine," http://www1.american.edu/ted/ice/olive-tree.htm.
82. Issaq and Kader, *Fadwa*, 182–83.
83. Ibid., 154.
84. Ibid., 185.
85. Ibid., 140.
86. Hirsch, "Past Lives: Postmemories," 664.
87. Sa'di and Abu-Lughod, *Nakba*, 10.
88. Felicia Lee, "Identity Found: On West Side Via West Bank," *New York Times*, February 8, 2010, C1.
89. Ismail Khalidi "Debunking the Palestinian Stereotype," *Atlanta Journal-Constitution*, February 9, 2010.

Chapter 6

1. (www.bombsite.com/issues/109/articles/3328) *Viewpoint with James Zogby*, Interview, 10/1/09.

2. Issawi, American East Press Kit, 6.
3. Dabis, Amreeka Press Kit, 9.
4. Scott Macaulay, "25 New Faces of Independent Film," *Filmmaker Magazine*, 2011, accessed September 9, 2013, http://filmmakermagazine.com/series/25-new-faces-of-2011/.
5. Cosima Amelang, "Rola Nashef, Detroit Unleaded," *ScreenDaily*, September 11, 2012, accessed September 9, 2013, http://www.screendaily.com/reports/one-on-one/rola-nashef-detroit-unleaded/5046450.article.
6. http://www.jsalloum.org.
7. Shaheen, *Guilty*, 85.
8. Evelyn Alsultany, "The Primetime Plight of Arab-Muslim-Americans Post–9/11: Configurations of Race and Nation in TV Dramas," in *From Invisible Citizens to Visible Subjects: Arab American Identitites Before and After September 11th*, ed. Amaney Jamal and Evelyn Alsultany (New York: Syracuse University Press, 2008), 204.
9. Shaheen, *Guilty*, 54–84.
10. Hanania, *I'm Glad I Look Like a Terrorist*, 50.
11. Benshoff and Griffin, *American on Film*, 71–72.
12. Ibid., 72.
13. Bayoumi, *How Does It Feel*, 5.
14. Alsultany, *Prime Time* 225.
15. Ibid., 228.
16. Shaheen, *Guilty*, 68.
17. Cherien Dabis, *Amreeka* (Virgin Films and Entertainment, 2010), 1:00–1:01.
18. Sayed Badreya and Hesham Issawi, *American East* (MGM Films, 2008), 1:25–2:00.
19. Nadine Naber, *Arab America: Gender, Cultural Politics, and Activism* (New York: New York Univesity Press, 2012), 5.
20. http://www.aaiusa.org.
21. Badreya and Issaw, *American East*.
22. Dabis, *Amreeka*.
23. Badreya and Issaw, *American East*.
24. Ibid.
25. Marvasti and McKinney, *Middle Eastern Lives*, 93, 96.
26. Roya Rastegar, "May in the Summer: Sundance 2013 Review," in *The Huffington Post*, 31 January 2013, http://www.huffingtonpost.com/roya-rastegar/may-in-the-summer-sundance_b_2577019.html

Chapter 7

1. Heather Raffo, "Author's Note" in *Heather Raffo's 9 Parts of Desire* (New York: Dramatists Play Service, 2006), 5.

2. Holly Hughes and David Roman, *O Solo Homo: The New Queer Performance* (New York: Grove, 1998), 5.
3. Diamond, *Performance*, 2.
4. Ibid., 3.
5. Hughes and Roman, *O Solo Homo*, 2.
6. Ibid., 4.
7. Ibid., 7.
8. Basiouny and Carlson, "Current Trends," 209.
9. Sabry, "Arab-American Women's Writing," 129.
10. Shakir, *Bint Arab*, 9.
11. Andrea Assaf, "Eleven Reflections on September," accessed September 20, 2013, http://www.usaprojects.org.
12. Laila Farah, "Dancing on the Hyphen: Performing Diasporic Subjectivity," *Modern Drama*, 48:2 (Summer 2005): 317.
13. Ibid., 318.
14. Betty Shamieh, "Chocolate in Heat." www.bettyshamieh.com.
15. Heather Raffo, e-mail interview with author, May 6, 2010.
16. Leila Buck, e-mail interview with author, May 13, 2010.
17. Najla Said, e-mail interview with author, May 24, 2010.
18. Gualtieri, *Between Arab and White*, 167.
19. Said, e-mail interview.
20. Said, *Looking for Palestine*, 24–5.
21. Buck, e-mail interview.
22. Raffo, e-mail interview.
23. Shakir, *Bint Arab*, 3.
24. Heather Raffo, *Heather Raffo's 9 Parts of Desire* (Evanston, IL: Northwestern University Press, 2006) ix–x.
25. Ibid., 29–30.
26. Ibid., 21.
27. Ibid., 47.
28. Heather Raffo, "From Heather Raffo," accessed July 26, 2014, http://www.heatherraffo.com/projects/nine-parts-of-desire/.
29. Said, *Looking for Palestine*, 254.
30. Ibid., 173.
31. LaCapra, "Trauma," 715.
32. Hirsch, "Past Lives: Postmemories," 664.
33. Said, "Intellectual Exile," 117.
34. Najla Said, *Looking for Palestine*: Growing Up Confused in an Arab-American Family (New York: Riverhead, 2013), 161.
35. Ibid., 163.
36. Ibid., 164.
37. In the BBC film titled *In Search of Palestine*, the moment where Edward W. Said ap-

proaches the old home and remarks about his journey back to Palestine is documented.

38. Said, *Palestine*. Unpublished playscript, 11.
39. Said, *Looking for Palestine*, 166.
40. Ibid., 167.
41. Said, *Palestine*, 25, 29.
42. LaCapra, *Trauma*, 181.
43. In his article "Arab Despise Thyself," Nouri Gana writes, "So, by calling your child Ray or Isabelle, do you think, given the intensive profiling systems and the unquenchably crooked interest in people's ethnicities, do you think you're building a better future for your child or that you're somewhat protecting him or her from the radar of ethnic profiling? … What if your sensitive and anti-imperialist child grows up one day and accuses you of treachery, of giving her a name that does not coincide with her cultural allegiances or affiliations? What if? How would you feel as a parent? … Do you think we should let history determine our fates or determine the direction of history through our familial, local and grassroots struggles even with little and small-scale actions, as small as the decision upon the name of your next child?"
44. Buck, *ISite*, 24.
45. Ibid., 26.
46. Ibid., 26–27.
47. Ibid., 9. Emphasis in original.
48. Ibid., 30.
49. Ibid., 36.
50. Ibid.
51. Ibid., 37.
52. Ibid., 38.
53. Ibid.
54. Ibid., 40.
55. Ibid., 41.
56. Ibid.
57. Ibid., 41–42.
58. Ibid., 44.
59. Ibid., 23.
60. Weenta Girmay, "Jennifer Jajeh and *I Heart Hamas*." Pghcitypaper.com, October 20, 2010, accessed September 13, 2013, http://www.pghcitypaper.
61. Ibid.
62. Jennifer Jajeh, *I Heart Hamas: And Other Things I'm Afraid to Tell You* (solo performance, 2009), 5.
63. Ibid., 25.
64. Ibid., 30.

Conclusion

1. Ibrahim, *Ecstasy: A Water Fable*. Unpublished playscript, 4.
2. The company that performed the world premiere of the production was even called The Water Project Ensemble.
3. Ibrahim, *Ecstasy*, 6.
4. Ibid., 7.
5. Yussef El Guindi, *Pilgrims Musa and Sheri in the New World*, in *American Theatre Magazine*, September 2012, 78.
6. Jon R. Baitz "Modes of Compassion: An Interview with the Playwright," *American Theatre Magazine,* February 2012, 65.
7. Rob Weinert-Kendt, "Darkly Comic Voice Adds a Libretto to His Résumé," *New York Times*, October 6, 2011, accessed September 9, 2013, http://theater.nytimes.com/2011/10/09/theater/stephen-karams-sons-of-the-prophet-and-dark-sisters.html.
8. Baitz, "Modes of Compassion," 64–5.
9. Stephen Karam, *Sons of the Prophet*, *American Theatre Magazine*, February 2010, 83.
10. M. Scott Bortot, "Playwright Betty Shamieh Outlines Keys to Success for Arab-American Artists," *IIP Digital*, June 11, 2010, http://iipdigital.usembassy.gov/st/english/article/2010/06/20100610164948smtotrob0.6660272.html#axzz30hNy9UFZ.
11. Misha Berson, "Yussef El Guindi: Are We Being Followed?" *American Theatre Magazine* 23 (2006): 53.
12. There have been several attempts at creating Arab American Theater ensembles. These include the Arab American Children's Theater (Los Angeles), Nibras (New York City), and Ajyal Theatrical Group (Dearborn). Of these, only Ajyal Theatrical Group is still producing works, primarily in Arabic.
13. "Political Acts."
14. See "Afterword: Toward an Arab American Theatre Movement" in *Four Arab American Dramas: Works by Leila Buck, Yussef El Guindi, Jamil Khoury, and Lameece Issaq & Jacob Kader*, edited by Michael Malek Najjar (Jefferson, NC: McFarland, 2014), 191.
15. James Zogby "Arab Americans: Bridging the Divide" in *Arab Voices: What They Are Saying to Us and Why It Matters* (New York: Palgrave Macmillan, 2010), 186.

Works Referenced

Abdulhadi, Rabab, Evelyn Alsultany, and Nadine Naber. *Arab & Arab American Feminisms: Gender, Violence, & Belonging.* Syracuse, NY: Syracuse University Press, 2011.
Abraham, Nabeel. "Arab-American Marginality: Mythos and Praxis." *Arab Studies Quarterly* 11 (1989): 17–43.
_____, and Andrew Shryock. *Arab Detroit: From Margin to Mainstream.* Detroit: Wayne State University Press, 2000.
Abu-Laban, Baha. "Reflections on the Rise and Decline of an Arab-American Organization." *Arab Studies Quarterly* 29 (3 & 4): 47–56.
Ajyal Theater Group. http://www.ajyal.us/aboutus.html.
'Akash, Munir, and Kahled Mattawa. *Post-Gibran Anthology of New Arab American Writing.* Syracuse, NY: Kitab, Syracuse University Press, 1999.
Akatov, Janice. "New Role Takes Vic Tayback Back to Origins." *Los Angeles Times*, 1990.
Al Omran, Ahmed. "Not Just for Laughs." www.Alomran.me. March 22, 2011. http://alomran.me/comedy.
Alawi, Nabil. "Arab American Poets: The Politics of Exclusion and Assimilation." In *Narratives of Resistance: Literature and Ethnicity in the United States and the Caribbean*, ed. by Ana Manzanas and Jesus Benito. Castilla-La Mancha: University of Castilla La Mancha, 2000.
Alsultany, Evelyn. "The Primetime Plight of Arab-Muslim-Americans Post–9/11: Configurations of Race and Nation in TV Dramas," in *From Invisible Citizens to Visible Subjects: Arab American Identitites Before and After September 11th*, ed. by Amaney Jamal and Evelyn Alsultany. New York: Syracuse University Press, 2008.
_____. *Arabs and Muslims in the Media: Race and Representation After 9/11.* New York: New York University Press, 2012.
Alwazir, Atyaf. "Uprooting Olive Trees in Palestine." *ICE,* November 2002. http://www1.american.edu/ted/ice/olive-tree.htm#r5.
Amin, Dina A. "What's In a Hyphen?" In *Salaam, Peace: An Anthology of Middle Eastern-American Drama*, ed. by Holly Hill and Dina A. Amin. New York: Theatre Communications Group, 2009.
Annan, Kofi. *Confronting Islamophobia: Education for Tolerance and Understanding.* United Nations Press Release, December 7, 2004.
Arktov, Janice. "New Role Takes Vic Tayback Back to Origins." *Los Angeles Times*, January 7, 1990. http://www.articles.latimes.com/.
Aruri, Nasser H. "AAUG: A Memoir." *Arab Studies Quarterly* 3 & 4 (2007): 33–46.
Asher, J. B., Leila Buck, Omar Khoury, Omar Metwally, Najla Said, Afaf Shawwa, and Maha Chehlaoui. *Sajjil.* Unpublished playscript, last modified 2002, Microsoft Word file.
Assaf, Andrea. "Eleven Reflections on September." http://www.usaprojects.org.
Badaw, M. M. *Modern Arabic Literature.* New York: Cambridge University Press, 1992.
Badawi, Elsaid. "Arab Theatre and Language: The Continuing Debate." In *The World Encyclopedia of Contemporary Theatre, Vol. 4: The Arab World.* London: Routledge, 1994.

Badreya, Sayed, and Hesham Issawi. *American East.* MGM Films, 2008. 110 minutes.
Baitz, Jon R. "Modes of Compassion: An Interview with the Playwright." *American Theatre Magazine,* February 2012.
Barakat, Halim I. *Days of Dust.* Wilmette, IL: Medina University Press International, 1974.
Bashshur, Rashid. "Unfulfilled Expectations: The Genesis and Demise of the AAUG." *Arab Studies Quarterly* 29 (2007): 7–13.
Basiouny, Dalia, and Marvin Carlson. "Current Trends in Arab-American Performance." In *Performance, Exile and "America"* ed. by Silvija Jestrovic and Yana Meerzon, 208–19. New York: Palgrave Macmillan, 2009.
Bayoumi, Moustafa. *How Does It Feel to Be a Problem: Being Young and Arab in America.* New York: Penguin, 2008.
Bazian, Hatem."Virtual Internment: Arab, Muslims, Asians and the War on Terrorism." *The Journal of Islamic Law and Culture* 9 (2004): 1–26.
Benshoff, Harry M., and Sean Griffin. *America on Film: Representing Race, Class, Gender, and Sexuality at the Movies.* Malden, MA: Blackwell, 2004.
Berson, Misha. "Yussef El Guindi: Are We Being Followed?" *American Theatre Magazine* 23 (2006): 53.
Bhabha, Hami K. *The Location of Culture.* London: New York, Routledge, 2004.
Bilderback, Walter. "Interview with Playwright Yussef El Guindi." February 9, 2010. http://www.wilmatheater.org/blog/interview-playwright-yussef-el-guindi
Bortot, M. Scott, "Playwright Betty Shamieh Outlines Keys to Success for Arab-American Artists." *IIP Digital.* June 11, 2010. http://iipdigital.usembassy.gov/st/english/article/2010/06/20100610164948smtotrob0.6660272.html#axzz30hNy9UFZ.
Brooks, Marla. *The American Family on Television: A Chronology of 121 Shows, 1948–2004.* Jefferson, NC: McFarland, 2005.
Buck, Leila. *ISite* in *Four Arab American Plays: Works by Leila Buck, Jamil Khoury, Yussef El Guindi, and Lameece Issaq & Jacob Kader,* edited by Michael Malek Najjar, 22–44. Jefferson, NC: McFarland, 2014.
Butler, Judith. *Precarious Life: The Powers of Mourning and Violence.* New York: Verso, 2004.
Carlson, Marvin A. *Performance: A Critical Introduction.* New York: Routledge, 2004..
Charara, Hayan. *Inclined to Speak: An Anthology of Contemporary Arab American Poetry.* Fayetteville: University of Arkansas Press, 2008.
Council on American-Islamic Relations. *Same Hate, New Target: Islamophobia and Its Impact in the United States, January 2009–December 2010.* Washington, DC: Council on American-Islamic Relations, 2009–2010.
Clurman, Harold, Glenn Young, and Marjorie Loggia. *The Collected Works of Harold Clurman: Six Decades of Commentary on Theatre, Dance, Music, Film, Arts and Letters.* New York: Applause, 1994.
Dabbagh, Hussein. *Mikhail Naimy: Some Aspects of His Thought as Revealed in His Writings.* Durham, England: University of Durham, Centre for Middle Eastern and Islamic Studies, 1983.
Dabis, Cherien. *Amreeka.* Virgil Films and Entertainment, 2010, 96 minutes.
David, Gary C. "The Creation of 'Arab American': Political Activism and Ethnic (Dis)Unity 1." *Critical Sociology* 33 (2007): 833–62.
Diamond, Elin. *Performance and Cultural Politics.* New York: Routledge, 1996.
Doward, Jaime, "David Cameron's Attack on Multiculturalism Divides the Coalition," *The Guardian,* February 5, 2011, http://www.theguardian.com/politics/2011/feb/05/david-cameron-attack-multiculturalism-coalition.
Drake, Sylvie. (1974). "Stage Notes: Actors Studio, Playwrights Split." *Los Angeles Times,* April 24, 1974, http://www.proquest.com.
Dunlap, David W. "Little Syria (Now Tiny Syria) Finds New Advocates." *New York Times,* January 1, 2012. http://cityroom.blogs.nytimes.com/2012/01/01/little-syria-now-tiny-syria-finds-new-advocates.
El Guindi, Yussef. "Back of the Throat." *Theatre Forum* 29 (2006): 25–50.
_____. *Back of the Throat.* New York: Dramatists Play Service, 2007.
_____. *Language Rooms* in *Here's to a Theatre of Defiance: Manifesto Series Vol. 3,* ed. by Naomi Iizuka, 1–45. Seattle, WA: Rain City Projects, 2007.

_____. *Pilgrims Musa and Sheri in the New World. American Theatre Magazine*, September 2012.

_____. *Our Enemies: Lively Scenes of Love and Combat* in *Four Arab American Plays: Works by Leila Buck, Jamil Khoury, Yussef El Guindi, and Lameece Issaq & Jacob Kader*, ed. by Michael Malek Najjar, 87–138. Jefferson, NC: McFarland, 2014.

El Rassi, Toufic. *Arab in America*. San Francisco: Last Gasp, 2012.

Esch-Van Kan, Anneka. "Amazing Acrobatics of Language: The Theatre of Yussef El Guindi." *American Studies Journal* 52 (2008), http://www.asjournal.org?archive/52/157.html.

Fadda-Conrey, Carol. *Contemporary Arab-American Literature: Transnational Reconfigurations of Citizenship and Belonging*. New York: New York University Press, 2014.

Fa'ik, Ala. *Issues of Identity: In Theater of Immigrant Community: The Development of Arab-American Identity*. Ann Arbor: University of Michigan Press, 1994.

Farah, Laila. "Dancing on the Hyphen: Performing Diasporic Subjectivity." *Modern Drama*, 48:2 (Summer 2005): 317.

Faraj, Sura. "Crossing Boundaries, Creating Intersections: Jamil Khoury Does Both with 'Precious Stones.'" *Queer Life News*, February 2005, http://www.silkroadrising.org/news/crossing-boundaries-creating-intersections-jamil-khoury-does-both-with-precious-stones.

Feagin, Joe R., and Karen D. McKinney. *The Many Costs of Racism*. Lanham, MD: Rowman & Littlefield, 2003.

Feld, Bruce. "An Oasis in Manhattan." *Drama-Logue*, February 15–21, 1990.

Fisk, Robert. *Pity the Nation: Lebanon at War*. New York: Oxford University Press, 1990.

Ford, Harry C. "Why I Wrote a Syrian Play." *Syrian World* (1927): 33–34.

Foucault, Michel, and Alan Sheridan. *Discipline and Punish: The Birth of the Prison*. New York: Vintage, 1995.

Fukuyama, Francis. *America at a Crossroads: Democracy, Power, and the Neoconservative Legacy*. New Haven, CT: Yale University Press, 2007.

Gana, Nouri. "Arab Despise Thyself." *Counterpunch*, February 17, 2010, http://www.counterpunch.org/2010/02/17/arab-despise-thyself/

_____. "Introduction: Race, Islam, and the Task of Muslim and Arab American Writing." *PMLA* 123 (2008): 5.

Gibran, Jean, and Kahlil Gibran. *Kahlil Gibran: His Life and World*. New York: Avenel, 1981.

Gibran, Kahlil. *A Treasury of Kahlil Gibran*. New York: Citadel, 1951.

_____. *The Treasured Writings of Kahlil Gibran*. New York: Open Road, 2011.

_____, and Jean Gibran. *Dramas of Life*. Philadelphia: Westminster, 1981.

_____, and Mary Haskell. *Beloved Prophet; The Love Letters of Kahlil Gibran and Mary Haskell and Her Private Journal*. New York: Knopf, 1972.

Girmay, Weenta. "Jennifer Jajeh and I Heart Hamas." Pghcitypaper.com, October 20, 2010, http://www.pghcitypaper.

Greenberg, David. *Nixon's Shadow: The History of an Image*. New York: W. W. Norton, 2004.

Gualtieri, Sarah M. A. *Between Arab and White: Race and Ethnicity in the Early Syrian American Diaspora*. Berkeley: University of California Press, 2009.

Haddad, Kathryn. "With Love From Ramallah." *Mizna* 7, no. 1 (2005): 22–33.

_____, and Juliana Pegues. "From the Playwrights." In *With Love from Ramallah*, program notes, June 2004.

Haddad, Yvonne Y. *Not Quite American?: The Shaping of Arab and Muslim Identity in The United States*. Waco, TX: Baylor University Press, 2004.

_____, and Jane I. Smith. *Muslim Communities in North America*. Albany: State University of New York Press, 1994.

Hagopian, Elaine C. "Reversing Injustice: On Utopian Activism." *Arab Studies Quarterly* 29 (2007): 57–73.

Hajjar, Nijmeh. *The Politics and Poetics of Ameen Rihani: The Humanist Ideology of an Arab-American Intellectual and Activist*. New York: Tauris Academic Studies, 2010.

Hanania, Ray. *I'm Glad I Look Like a Terrorist: Growing Up Arab in America*. Tinley Park, IL: Urban Strategies Group, 1996.

Handal, Nathalie. *Between Our Lips* in *Salaam.Peace: An Anthology of Middle Eastern-American Drama*, ed. by Holly Hill and Dina Amin (New York: Theatre Communications Group, 2009), 93–108.

Harford, Margaret. "Radio Veteran Finds 'Oasis.'" *Los Angeles Times*, December 30, 1965. http://proquest.com/?.
Harlow, Barbara. *Resistance Literature*. New York: Methuen, 1987.
Hassan, Waïl S. *Immigrant Narratives: Orientalism and Cultural Translation in Arab American and Arab British Literature*. New York: Oxford University Press, 2011.
_____. "The Rise of Arab-American Literature: Orientalism and Cultural Translation in the Work of Ameen Rihani." *American Literary History* 20 (2008): 259, http://muse.jhu.edu/journals/alh/summary/v020/20.1hassan.html.
Hayani, Ibrahim. "Arabs in Canada: Assimilation or Integration?" In *Arabs in America: Building a New Future*, ed. by Michael W. Suleiman, 284–303. Philadelphia: Temple University Press, 1999.
Hershewe, S. K. *An Oasis in Manhattan*. Unpublished playscript, 1965.
Hill, Holly, and Dina A. Amin. *Salaam, Peace: An Anthology of Middle Eastern-American Drama*. New York: Theatre Communications Group, 2009.
Hine, Alyn Desmond. "Russian Literature in the Works of Mikhail Naimy." Ph.D. diss., University of London, 2011.
Hirsch, Marianne. "Past Lives: Postmemories in Exile." *Poetics Today* 17 (1996): 659–86.
Hoeveler, Diane L., and Jeffery Cass. *Interrogating Orientalism: Contextual Approaches and Pedagogical Practices*. Columbus: Ohio State University Press, 2006.
Houssami, Eyad, Dalia Khamissy, and Elias Khoury *Doomed by Hope: Essays on Arab Theatre*. New York: Pluto, 2012.
Hughes, Holly, and David Román. *O Solo Homo: The New Queer Performance*. New York: Grove, 1998.
Ibrahim, Denmo. *Ecstasy: A Water Fable*. Unpublished playscript, 2009.
Imangulieva, Aida. *Gibran, Rihani & Naimy: East-West Interactions in Early Twentieth-Century Arab Literature*. Oxford: Inner Farne, 2009.
Ireland, Susan, and Patrice J. Proulx. *Textualizing the Immigrant Experience in Contemporary Quebec*. Westport, CT: Praeger, 2004.
Issaq, Lameece, and Jacob Kader. *Food and Fadwa*. In *Four Arab American Plays: Works by Leila Buck, Jamil Khoury, Yussef El Guindi, and Lameece Issaq & Jacob Kader*, ed. by Michael Malek Najjar, 139–186. Jefferson, NC: McFarland, 2014.
Jabara, Abdeen. "The AAUG: Aspirations and Failures." *Arab Studies Quarterly* 29 (2007): 15–19.
Jaffe-Berg, Erith. "Deterritorializing Voices: Staging the Middle East in American Theatre." In *Performance, Exile and "America"* ed. by Silvija Jestrovic and Yana Meerzon, 179–207. New York: Palgrave Macmillan, 2009.
Jajeh, Jennifer. *I Heart Hamas: And Other Things I'm Afraid to Tell You*. Solo performance, 2009.
Jarmakani, Amira. *Imagining Arab Womanhood: The Cultural Mythology of Veils, Harems, and Belly Dancers in the U.S.* New York: Palgrave Macmillan, 2008.
Jreisat, Jamil. "Organizing Arab-American Professionals: AAUG and Me." *Arab Studies Quarterly* 29 (2007): 139–54.
Karam, Stephen, *Sons of the Prophet*. New York: Dramatist's Play Service, 2012.
Kassir, Samir. *Being Arab*. New York: Verso, 2006.
Khalidi, Ismail. "Debunking the Palestinian Stereotype." *Atlanta Journal-Constitution*, February 9, 2010.
_____. *Tennis in Nablus: A Tragipoliticomedy in Two Acts*. Unpublished playscript, 2011.
_____, and Bassam Jarbawi. *Truth Serum Blues*. Unpublished playscript, 2005.
Khalidi, Rashid. *The Iron Cage: The Story of the Palestinian Struggle for Statehood*. Boston: Beacon Press, 2006.
_____. *Palestinian Identity: The Construction of Modern National Consciousness*. New York: Columbia University Press, 1997.
Khoury, Jamil. *Precious Stones* in *Four Arab American Plays: Works by Leila Buck, Jamil Khoury, Yussef El Guindi, and Lameece Issaq & Jacob Kader*, ed. by Michael Malek Najjar, 47–86. Jefferson, NC: McFarland, 2014.
LaCapra, Dominick. "Trauma, Absence, Loss." *Critical Inquiry* 25 (1999): 696–727.
Lan, Stephen. "Amreeka: A Film by Cherien Dabis." Press Kit, www.stephenlan.com/images/press_kits/Pkit-AMREEKA.pdf.

Lee, Felicia R. "Identity Found: On West Side via West Bank." *New York Times*, February 8, 2010, C1.
LIFE Magazine, January 10, 1944, 77.
Limon, John. *Stand-Up Comedy in Theory, or, Abjection in America*. Durham, NC: Duke University Press, 2000.
Macaulay, Scott. "25 New Faces of Independent Film." *Filmmaker Magazine*, 2011, http://filmmakermagazine.com/series/25-new-faces-of-2011/.
Macron, Mary Haddad. *Arab-Americans and Their Communities of Cleveland*. Cleveland: Cleveland State University, 1979.
Malek, Alia. *A Country Called Amreeka: Arab Roots, American Stories*. New York: Free, 2009.
Mansour, Mona. *Urge for Going*. Unpublished playscript, 2011.
Marvasti, Amir B., and Karyn D. McKinney. *Middle Eastern Lives in America*. Lanham, MD: Rowman & Littlefield, 2004.
Mattar, Sandra. "A Quest for Identity: Racism and Acculturation Among Immigrant Families." In *The Psychology of Prejudice and Discrimination*, ed. by Jean L. Chin, 137–59. Westport, CT: Praeger, 2004.
Mayer, Jane. "The Black Sites: A Rare Look Inside the C.I.A.'s Secret Interrogation Program." *The New Yorker*, August 13, 2007, http://www.newyorker.com/reporting/2007/08/13/070813fa_fact_mayer.
McCulloh, T. H. "Bridging a Cultural, Generation Gap in 'Oasis.'" *Los Angeles Times*, February 16, 1990. http://articles.latimes.com/1990-02-16/entertainment/ca-590_1_dead-end.
McDonnell Twair, Pat. "Comedy Dispels Arab-Jewish Bigotry." *Washington Report on Middle East Affairs*. Washington, DC, 1990.
Mondalek, Najee. "Smile You're in America." Ajyal Theatrical Group.
Moughrabi, Fouad. "Remembering the AAUG." *Arab Studies Quarterly* 29 (1997): 97–103.
Naber, Nadine C. *Arab America: Gender, Cultural Politics, and Activism*. New York: New York University Press, 2012.
———. "Look, Mohammed the Terrorist Is Coming!: Cultural Racism, Nation-Based Racism, and the Intersectionality of Oppressions after 9/11." In *Race and Arab Americans Before and After 9/11: From Invisible Citizens to Visible Subjects*, ed. by Amaney Jamal and Nadine Naber, 276–304. New York: Syracuse University Press, 2008.
———. "The Rules of Forced Engagement: Race, Gender, and the Culture of Fear Among Arab Immigrants in San Francisco Post–9/11." *Cultural Dynamics* 18 (2006): 235–67.
Naff, Alixa. *Becoming American: The Early Arab Immigrant Experience*. Carbondale: Southern Illinois University Press, 1985.
Naimy, Mikhail. *Parents and Children*. Translated by Nefertiti Takla. Unpublished playscript, 2014.
Najjar, Michael M., ed. *Four Arab American Plays: Works by Leila Buck, Jamil Khoury, Yussef El Guindi, and Lameece Issaq & Jacob Kader*. Jefferson, NC: McFarland, 2014.
———. "Writing from the Hyphen: Arab-American Playwrights Struggle with Identity in the Post–9/11 World." *Gale eNewsletters Arts & Humanities Community News*, September 2004, http://www.silkroadrising.org/news/writing-from-the-hyphen-arab-american-playwrights-struggle-with-identity-in-the-post-911-world.
Najjar, Nada. "The Space In-Between: The Ambivalence of Early Arab-American Writers." Ph.D. diss., University of Toledo, 1999.
Nakleh, Khalil. "AAUG: A Personal Introspection." *Arab Studies Quarterly* 29 (2007): 105–10.
"Newcomers: Only a Few Are Funny," *LIFE Magazine*, January 10, 1944, 77. http://books.google.com/books?id=2FYEAAAAMBAJ&printsec=frontcover&dq=life+magazine&hl=en&sa=X&ei=ydQeUqaAK6XJiQL6tIHwCA&ved=0CD4Q6wEwAQ#v=onepage&q=life%20magazine&f=true.
Nijland, C. *Mikhā'īl Nu'aymah: Promoter of the Arabic Literary Revival*. Istanbul: Nederlands Historisch-Archaeologisch Instituut, 1975.
Nofal, Mamdouh, Fawaz Turki, Haidar Abdel Shafi, Inea Bushnaq, and Yezid Sayigh, (1998). "Reflections on Al-Nakba." *Journal of Palestine Studies* 28 (1): 5–35.
"'Oasis in Manhattan' Premieres Wednesday," *Los Angeles Times*, October 31, 1965. http://proquest.com/?.
Oliver, Myrna. "Vic Tayback: Actor Best Known as Mel in 'Alice' TV Series." *Los Angeles Times*, May 26, 1990. http://www.articles.latimes.com/.

Omi, Michael, and Howard Winant. *Racial Formation in the United States: From the 1960s to the 1990s*. New York: Routledge, 1994.
Orfalea, George. *The Arab Americans: A History*. Northampton, MA: Olive Branch, 2006.
_____, and Sharif Elmusa. *Grape Leaves: A Century of Arab-American Poetry*. New York: Interlink, 2000.
Parlakian, Nishan. *Contemporary Armenian American Drama: An Anthology of Ancestral Voices*. New York: Columbia University Press, 2004.
Phelan, Peggy. *Unmarked: The Politics of Performance*. New York: Routledge, 1993.
"Political Acts: The Emerging Arab-American Theatre Movement." Hosted by Jason Loewith. WBEZ 91.5 *Chicago Amplified*, April 21, 2008, http://www.wbez.org/episode-segments/political-acts-emerging-arab-american-theatre-movement.
Provence, Michael. *The Great Syrian Revolt and the Rise of Arab Nationalism*. Austin: University of Texas Press, 1993.
Rabbat, Nasser, "On Arabs and Arabness." *Thistle* 10.15, http://web.mit.edu/thistle/www/v10/10.15/arabness.html.
Raffo, Heather. E-mail interview with author, 2010.
_____. *Heather Raffo's 9 Parts of Desire: A Play*. Evanston, IL: Northwestern University Press, 2006.
_____. "Introduction." In *Salaam, Peace: An Anthology of Middle Eastern-American Drama*, edited by Holly Hill and Dina A. Amin. New York: Theatre Communications Group, 2009.
Rastegar, Roya, "May in the Summer: Sundance 2013 Review." *The Huffington Post*, January 31, 2013, http://www.huffingtonpost.com/roya-rastegar/may-in-the-summer-sundance_b_2577019.html
Rihani, Ameen F. "Palestine and the Proposed Arab Federation." *Annals of the American Academy of Political and Social Science* 164 (1932): 67.
_____. *The Rihani Essays: Ar-RIHANIYYAAT*. Washington, DC: Platform International, 2010.
_____. *Wajdah*. Washington, DC: Platform International, 2001.
Ruby, Robert. "A Six-Day War: Its Aftermath in American Public Opinion." *Pew Forum on Religion and Public Life*, http://www.pewforum.org/2007/05/30/a-six-day-war-its-aftermath-in-american-public-opinion/.
Sa'adi, Ahmad H., and Lila Abu-Lughod, eds. *Nakba: Palestine, 1948, and the Claims of Memory*. New York: Columbia University Press, 2007.
Sabry, Somaya S. *Arab-American Women's Writing and Performance: Orientalism, Race and the Idea of The Arabian Nights*. New York: I. B. Tauris, 2011.
Sacre, Antonio, nytheatre.com review. August 15, 2002, http://www.nytheatre.com/Review/antonio-sacre-2002-8-15-sajjil-record.
Said, Edward W. "The Arab Portrayed." *The Arab World* 14 (1970): 1–9.
_____. "Intellectual Exile: Expatriates and Marginals." *Grand Street* 47 (1993): 112–24.
_____. *Orientalism*. New York: Pantheon, 1978.
_____. *Orientalism*, 25th ed. New York: Vintage, 2003.
_____. *Out of Place: A Memoir*. New York: Knopf, 1999.
Said, Najla. E-mail interview with author, May 24, 2010.
_____. *Looking for Palestine: Growing Up Confused in an Arab-American Family*. New York: Riverhead, 2013.
Salaita, Steven. *Anti-Arab Racism in the USA: Where It Comes From and What It Means for Politics Today*. Ann Arbor, MI: Pluto, 2006.
_____. *Arab American Literary Fictions, Cultures, and Politics*. New York: Palgrave Macmillan, 2007.
_____. *Modern Arab American Fiction: A Reader's Guide*. Syracuse, NY: Syracuse University Press, 2011.
Salhi, Zahia S., and Ian R. Netton. *The Arab Diaspora: Voices of an Anguished Scream*. London: Routledge, 2006.
Salloum, Jaqueline, and Jack Shaheen. *Planet of the Arabs*. September 4, 2006, nine-minute online video. http://www.informationclearinghouse.info/article14836.htm.
Schillinger, Liesl. "Theater: The New 'Arab' Playwrights." *New York Times*, April 4, 2004. http://www.nytimes.com/2004/04/04/theater/theater-the-new-arab-playwrights.html.

Segev, Tom, and Haim Watzman. *One Palestine, Complete: Jews and Arabs Under the Mandate.* New York: Metropolitan Books, 2000.
Selim, Yasser Fouad. "Arab American Theatre Caught in Censorship: A Study of Betty Shamieh's *Roar* and *The Black Eyed*." *International Journal of Humanities and Social Science* Vol. 4, No. 3: February 2014: 81–88.
Semmerling, Tim J. *"Evil" Arabs in American Popular Film: Orientalist Fear.* Austin: University of Texas Press, 2006.
Sevandal, Mary M. "Special Registration: Discrimination in the Name of National Security." *The Journal of Gender, Race & Justice* 8 (2005): 735–63.
Shaheen, Jack G. *Guilty: Hollywood's Verdict on Arabs After 9/11.* Northampton, MA: Olive Branch, 2008.
_____. *Reel Bad Arabs: How Hollywood Vilifies a People.* New York: Olive Branch, 2001.
Shain, Yossi, and Merkaz Tami Shtainmets le-mehkere shalom (Israel). *Arab-Americans in the 1990s: What Next for the Diaspora?* Tel Aviv, Israel: Tel Aviv University, Tami Steinmetz Center for Peace Research, 1996.
Shakir, Evelyn. *Bint Arab: Arab and Arab American Women in the United States.* Westport, CT: Praeger, 1997.
Shamieh, Betty. *The Black Eyed & Architecture.* New York: Broadway Play, 2008.
_____. "Chocolate in Heat: Growing Up Arab in America In Shattering the Stereotypes: Muslim Women Speak Out," ed. by Fawzia Afzal-Khan. Northampton, MA: Olive Branch, 2005.
_____. "Lives I Could Not Have Led." *American Theatre Magazine* 20 (2003): 71.
_____. *Roar.* New York: Broadway Play, 2005.
Sheth, Falgani A. *Toward a Political Philosophy of Race.* Albany: State University of New York Press, 2009.
Shimakawa, Karen. *National Abjection: The Asian American Body on Stage.* Durham, NC: Duke University Press, 2002.
Shohat, Ella, and Evelyn Alsultany. *Between the Middle East and the America: The Cultural Politics of Diaspora.* Ann Arbor: University of Michigan Press, 2013.
Singh, Amardeep. "'We Are Not the Enemy.' Hate Crimes Against Arabs, Muslims, and Those Perceived to Be Arab or Muslim After September 11." *Human Rights Watch* 14 (2002).
Sippel, Johnny. "Nightclub Reviews." *Billboard*, January 19, 1946. http://books.google.com/books?id=dBgEAAAAMBAJ&pg=PT31&dq=thomas+%22ode+to+a+wailing+syrian%22&hl=en&sa=X&ei=QuQeUpuAB4H9igLon4HQBw&ved=0CC0Q6AEwAA#v=onepage&q=thomas%20%22ode%20to%20a%20wailing%20syrian%22&f=false.
_____. "Nightclub Reviews." *Billboard*, November 25, 1950. http://books.google.com/books?id=8B0EAAAAMBAJ&pg=PA45&dq=thomas+%22ode+to+a+wailing+syrian%22&hl=en&sa=X&ei=QuQeUpuAB4H9igLon4HQBw&ved=0CDkQ6AEwAw#v=onepage&q=thomas%20%22ode%20to%20a%20wailing%20syrian%22&f=false.
Slyomovics, Susan. *The Object of Memory: Arab and Jew Narrate the Palestinian Village.* Philadelphia: University of Philadelphia Press, 1988.
_____. "'To Put One's Finger in the Bleeding Wound': Palestinian Theatre Under Israeli Censorship." *TDR* 35 (1991): 18–38.
Smith, Cecil. "'Oasis' Refreshing at Stage Society." *Los Angeles Times*, November 5, 1965. http://www.proquest.com/?.
Sollors, Werner, *Beyond Ethnicity: Consent and Descent in American Culture.* New York: Oxford University Press, 1986.
Suleiman, Michael W. *The Arab-American Experience in the United States and Canada: A Classified, Annotated Bibliography.* Ann Arbor, MI: Pierian, 2006.
_____. *Arabs in America: Building a New Future.* Philadelphia: Temple University Press, 1999.
_____. "'I Come to Bury Caesar, Not to Praise Him': An Assessment of the AAUG as an Example of an Activist Arab-American Organization." *Arab Studies Quarterly* 29 (2007): 75–95.
"Syria Undercover." *Frontline*, November 8, 2011. http://www.pbs.org/wgbh/pages/frontline.
Tanzer, Joshua. "Camel Lot? Maybe Not." OffOffOff Theater, http://www.offoffoff.com/theater/2002/sajjil.php, par 8.
Tayback, Vic. *St. Louie & Moh.* A Vic Tayback/BRB Entertainment Production. Unpublished teleplay, 1986.

Thomas, Danny. *An Ode to a Wailing Syrian*. A film, All Star Revue, NBC, October 13, 1951.
_____. "Trouble: It's Wonderful." *The American Magazine* (November 1955): 17–19, 102–104.
_____. "Why I Vowed to Help Sick Kids." *Family Weekly*, February 20, 1972, 14, http://news.google.com/newspapers?nid=1696&dat=19720220&id=ZdMdAAAAIBAJ&sjid=JUcEAAAAIBAJ&pg=5704,2904818.
_____, and Bill Davidson. *Make Room for Danny*. New York: Putnam, 1991.
Vitello, Paul, and Kirk Semple. "Muslims Say F.B.I. Tactics Sow Anger and Fear." *New York Times* (New York Edition), December 12, 2009, A1.
Waterfield, Robin. *Prophet: The Life and Times of Kahlil Gibran*. New York: St. Martin's, 1998.
WBEZ. "Political Acts: The Emerging Arab-American Theatre Movement." *Chicago Amplified*, April 21, 2008, http://www.wbez.org/episode-segments/political-acts-emerging-arab-american-theatre-movement.
Weinert-Kendt, Rob. "Darkly Comic Voice Adds a Libretto to His Resume." *New York Times*, October 6, 2011, http://theater.nytimes.com/2011/10/09/theater/stephen-karams-sons-of-the-prophet-and-dark-sisters.html.
Zabel, Darcy. *Arabs in the Americas: Interdisciplinary Essays on the Arab Diaspora*. New York: Peter Lang, 2006.
Zogby, James. *Arab Voices: What They Are Saying to Us, and Why It Matters*. New York: Palgrave Macmillan, 2010.

Index

Page numbers in **_bold italics_** indicate pages with illustrations.

Abbass, Hiam **_196_**
'Abd al-Hamid, Sultan 18
Abdalla, Khalid 203
Abdul-Aziz, King 74
Abdul-Rashid, Mujahid **_153_**
Abie's Irish Rose (Nichols) 108
abjection concept 61–62, 64–66, 99
Aboul-Ela, Hosam: "Edward Said's Out of Place: Criticism, Polemic, and Arab American Identity" 42
Abourezk, James 49, 51
Abraham, Nabeel 39–40
Abu-Hamdeh, Sharif: *Habibi* 240
Abu-Laban, Baha 44
Abu-Lughod, Ibrahim 43–44, 46
Abu-Lughod, Lila 162, 163, 183–184
acculturation, viewpoints on 24, 39, 63–64; *see also* immigration patterns
Acocella, Joan: "Prophet Motive: The Kahlil Gibran Phenomenon" 247n4
action-oriented resistance strategies 67–68
actors, status of 90
Actors Studio, Playwrights Unit 106
Adams, John Quincy 151
African Americans, and racism 150
Afzal-Khan, Fawzia: *Shattering the Stereotypes: Muslim Women Speak Out* 3
Ahmed, Ahmed 98, 116, 118–119, **_118_**, 120–121, 203; *Just Like Us* 117, 121–124
AJYAL (Generations) Theatrical Group 23, 112–116, 124
Akhtar, Ayad: *Disgraced* 155
Ala Fa'ik 9
al-Attar, Layla 216
Alawi, Nabil 27, 179
Alexander, Ronald 105
al-Husayn, 'Ali Ibn (King) 74
Al Jurf, Soha: *Pressing Beyond in Between* 207–208

All Star Revue (television show) 100–101, 103
The Allah Made Me Funny Tour 116
Alliance Theatre, Atlanta 240
al-Naqqash, Marun 91–92
Alnasrawi, Abbas 47
Al Omran, Ahmed 121–122
Alsultany, Evelyn 189, 191, 192
American-Arab Anti-Discrimination Committee (ADC) 21, 49, 51–52, 127, 238
American Arab University Graduates (AAUG) 21, 45–48
American Civil Liberties Union (ACLU) 56
American East (Issawi and Badreya) 190–191, 193–201, **_200_**
American Theatre Magazine 239
Amin, Dina 9
Amreeka (Dabis) 186, 187–188, 190–191, 193, 194–197, **_196_**, 240
Anna Ascends (Ford) 109–110, 111
Annan, Kofi 128
anorexia, treatment of *see Palestine* (N. Said)
anti–Arab racism, as the New Anti-Semitism 54
Anti-Terrorism and Effective Death Penalty Act (1996) 50
Arab American civil rights movement 6–7, 9, 33, 35–36, 51–52
Arab American Comedy Tour 116, 117, 118
Arab American drama, as genre 8–9, 15–29; conclusion 231–241; contemporary drama 17, 20–21; criteria for 22–26; modern drama 16–20, 37; and origins of Arab American identity 20, 21–22; political impulse in 26–29; *see also* specific playwrights
Arab American Institute (AAI) 21, 51, 52, 154–155, 195
"Arab American Theatre Caught in Censorship: A Study of Betty Shamieh's *Roar* and *The Black Eyed*" (Selim) 160–161

269

Index

Arab American, use of term 8, 13, 26, 33, 211; *see also* identity formation, among contemporary Arab Americans
"Arab Americans in the Performing Arts" (Shamieh's ADC speech) 238
Arab Canadians 60
"Arab Despise Thyself" (Gana) 260n43
Arab in America (El Rassi) 64–65
"The Arab Portrayed" (E. Said) 7, 47, 127
Arab Studies Quarterly (ASQ) 46–47
ArabDrama listserv 125, 135
Arabeezi (bicultural language) 113–115
Arabic and Broud (Mondalek) 115
Arabic language 26, 223; *fusha* vs. *aamiyah* (high vs. low) 23, 91–92, 96; usage of in arts 18, 23, 24, 37, 74, 76–79, 82, 91, 96, 100–103, 113–114
Arabism vs. Phoenicianism 19
Arab-Israeli War (1967) 44–45, 162–163; postwar context 7, 20, 21, 31–32, 42, 43–44, 127; and Tayback's tv show proposal 106–108, 112
Arabness, use of term 22, 248n15
Arabophobia 8, 15, 25, 154, 248n2
Arabs in the Americas: Interdisciplinary Essays on the Arab Diaspora (Zabel) 27
Arabs, in U.S.: Christian Arabs 195, 227; governmental surveillance and persecution of 29, 41–42, 48–49, 56, 126–127, 186, 255n5
Arida, Holly 6
Arida, Nasib 71, 88, 89
Armstrong, Jerilyn *233*
Ar-Rihaniyyaat (Rihani) 74–75
Aruri, Naseer H. 38
Ashe, Tala *159*
Asher, James 135, 137, 140, *153*
Asian Americans 61
Assaf, Andrea: *Eleven Reflections on September* 208, *209*
Assaf, Roxane *169*
Assi, EJ *202*
assimilation, viewpoints on 28, 34–35, 38–40, 63, 111; *see also* immigration patterns
Aswad, Adnan 45
Aswat: Voices of Palestine (New York Theatre Workshop) 143
attitudinal coping mechanisms 67
Awake and Singing: 7 Classic Plays from the American Jewish Repertoire (Schiff) 4
Axis of Evil Comedy Tour 116, 117, 118, 122
Ayoub, Raschid 89

Baba (Ibrahim) 240
Back of the Throat (El Guindi) 28, 125, 143–154, *149*, 256n78
Badawi, Elsaid 92
Badawi, Muhammad 95–96
Badreya, Sayed 203; *American East* 187, 190–191, 193–201, *200*
Bahout, Wadi 89
Balfour Declaration (1967) 20, 46, 171, 258n46

The Banshee (Gibran) 82
Barakat, Halim: *Days of Dust* 43
Barrymore, Lionel 82
Bashshur, Rashid 44, 45–46
Basiouny, Dalia 9, 207
Bayoumi, Moustafa 62, 150, 192
Bazian, Hatem 27–28, 55–56, 255n25
Becoming American: the Early Arab Immigrant Experience (Naff) 111
The Beginning of the Revolution (Gibran) 82
Bell, W. Kamau 228
Bend It Like Beckham (film) 193
Benshoff, Harry M. 127–128, 151; *America on Film: Representing Race, Class, Gender, and Sexuality at the Movies* 191–192
Between Arab and White: Race and Ethnicity in the Early Syrian American Diaspora (Gualtieri) 211
Between Night and Morn (Gibran) 82
Between Our Lips (Handel) 159–160
Beyond Ethnicity (Sollors) 151
Bhabha, Homi K. 36, 59, 63; *The Location of Culture* 5
Bint Arab: Arab and Arab American Women in the United States (Shakir) 42, 62
biological race (BR) (Sheth) 41
The Black Eyed (Shamieh) 159
black sites *see* war on terror
The Blind (Gibran) 82, 83
The Book of Khalid (Rihani) 3, 15, 73, 77–78
British imperialism 170–171, 174
Brooks, Hal 159
Brooks, Marla 103–104
Bruce, Lenny 99
Buck, Leila 135–136, 143–144, 164, 205, 207, 211–213; "Courage Under Fire" 209–210; *In the Crossing* *225*, 240; *ISite* 209–210, 222–226
Budeiri, Musa 163
Bulos, Yusef *237*
Burke, Ryan *233*
Bush Administration (G.W.B.) 50, 56, 131, 144, 146, 152–153
Bushrui, Suheil 82, 87
But Still, Like Air, I'll Rise: New Asian American Plays (Houston) 4
Butler, Judith 11, 28, 115, 129–130, 152–153; *Precarious Life: the Powers of Mourning and Violence* 128–129; *see also* post-9/11 Arab American drama

Campo Santo, San Francisco 240
Carden, Stuart 149
Carlson, Marvin 9, 207
Carr, Brad *200*
Castronovo, T. J. 107
Catzeflis, William 89
Caucasians 34
censorship, in the Middle East 122
Center REPertory Company, Walnut Creek, California 240

Chahlaoui, Maha *182*
Chamberlain, Richard 107
The Chameleons (Gibran) 18, 81–87
A Chant of Mystics and Other Poems (Rihani) 74
Charara, Hayan 26–27, 41, 60
Chehab, Fouad 73
Chehlaoui, Maha 135, 143
Chekhov, Anton 88, 96; *Uncle Vanya* 92
Chicago Public Radio: "Political Acts: the Emerging Arab American Theatre Movement" 239
Chocolate in Heat: Growing Up Arab in America (Shamieh) 207–208, 209
Choudhury, Sarita *176*
Christian Arabs 33, 195, 227
Christian mystics *see* Gibran, Kahlil; Naimy, Mikhail
City Opera Vancouver 240
civil rights *see* Arab American civil rights movement; civil rights movement (1960s)
civil rights movement (1960s) 9, 33, 38
class and nation based theory 40
Clinton Administration 50
Clurman, Harold 3
The Clurman Theater 176
The Colored Faces (Gibran) 82; *see also The Chameleons* (Gibran)
comedy and stand-up performance 98–124, 255*n*53; *AJYAL* (Generations) Theatrical Group 112–116; current stand-up comedians, listing of 116; *An Oasis in Manhattan* (Hershewe) 105–112; "Ode to a Wailing Syrian/Lebanese" (Thomas) 98, 99–105; post-9/11 stand-up comedy 99, 116–123
Company of Angels 107
confrontational accounting resistance strategies 67–68
Congressional Scorecard (AAI) 52
consent relations (Sollors) 151
contemporary Arab American drama (1967–present) 17, 20–21; *see also* specific playwrights
Contemporary Armenian American Drama: An Anthology of Ancestral Voices (Parlakian) 4
A Contemporary Theatre (ACT), Seattle 234, 235, 240
A Country Called Amreeka (Malek) 44
Country of Origin (Nader) 207–208
"Courage Under Fire" (Buck) 209–210
Covering Islam: How the Media and the Experts Determine How We See the Rest of the World (E. Said) 52–54
The Crescent Moon: A Fantasy in One Scene (Rihani) 73
cultural hybridity 59–61
cultural nationalism (Omi and Winant) 22, 40–41, 231
cultural pluralism 34
cultures of resistance 22

Dabis, Cherien: *Amreeka* 186, 187–188, 190–191, 193, 194–197, *196*, 240; *May in the Summer* 203, 240
The Danny Thomas Show see Make Room for Danny (television show)
Dark Sisters opera (Karam and Muhly) 236
David, Gary C. 22
Days of Dust (Barakat) 43
"Dead Are My People" (Gibran) 19
Deaf Day (Kazkaz) 187
derealization (Butler) 11, 28, 129, 152; *see also* post-9/11 Arab American drama
descent relations (Sollors) 151
Detroit Unleaded (Nashef) 188, 190–191, 193, 194–195, 198, 201–203, *202*
Diamond, Elin 206; *Performance and Cultural Politics* 66, 67
discrimination, and resistance strategies (Marvasti and McKinney) 67–68
disengagement 190
Disgraced (Akhtar) 155
drag acts 113, 115, 130–131
drama *see* Arab American drama, as genre; specific plays and playwrights
Drama Critics Circle 236
Drama League Award 214
dual citizenship 28, 58
DuBois, Peter 237
Du Bois, W.E.B.: *The Souls of Black Folks* 150

Ecstasy: A Water Fable (Ibrahim) 232–234, *233*
educational accounting resistance strategies 67–68, 122, 181, 199–201
"Edward Said's Out of Place: Criticism, Polemic, and Arab American Identity" (Aboul-Ela) 42
Election Report (AAI) 52
Eleven Reflections on September (Assaf) 208, *209*
El Guindi, Yussef 23, 59, 68, 164, 238–239; *Back of the Throat* 28, 125–126, 143–154, *149*, 256*n*78; *Language Rooms* 125–126, 143–154, *153*, 256*n*78; *Pilgrims Musa and Sheri in the New World* 232, 234–236, *235*, 239; *Threesome* 240
Elmusa, Sharif 26, 87
Elon, Danae 210
El Rassi, Toufic: *Arab in America* 64–65
empathic unsettlement (LaCapra) 157, 162, 218, 219
English language, immigration patterns and 35
enhanced interrogation techniques 126, 144
entertainment industry: anti-Arab bias in 42–43, 54; Arab/Muslim derealization in 127–128; globalization of 124; stereotypes in 6, 7, 98, 105, 118–119, 120–121, 127–128, 186–187, 190, 191–192
The Envious One (*al-Hasud*) (al-Naqqash) 92
Esch-Van Kan, Anneka 9
ethnic integrationism 38–39

ethnic isolationism 38–39
ethnicity paradigm (Omi and Winant) 33–36
ethnicity theory 40
"Everyday Arabness" (Gana) 60
Executive Decision (film) 118–119

Fadda-Conrey, Carol 28, 154
Faithful Time (Rihani) 73
Fallujah: The First Opera about The Iraq War (Raffo and Stokes) 240
Faragallah, Ramsey *159*
Farah, Laila: *Living in the Hyphen-Nation* 207–208
Faris, Hani A. 47
Farsad, Negin 124
Fathers and Sons (Naimy) 18, 88; see also *Parents and Children* (Naimy)
Federal Bureau of Investigation (FBI) 48–49, 52, 56, 127, 255n5
feminism, treatment of see *Precious Stones* (Khoury); solo performance
films, contemporary Arab American 186–203; absence of Arab Americans in Hollywood films 191–193; *Detroit Unleaded* (Nashef) 201–203; immigrant tales 193–201; new wave of filmmakers 187–188; *Planet of the Arabs* (Salloum) 188–190; recasting Hollywood 190–191; relative success of 203; see also specific films
films, three-act screenplay structure 24
Fisk, Robert 175
Flag Piece (Khalil) 207–208
Fontana, Santino *237*
Food and Fadwa (Issaq and Kader) 157, 179–183, *182*
Ford, Harry Chapman: *Anna Ascends* 109–110, 111; "Why I Wrote a Syrian Play" 109
Four Plays: Works by Leila Buck, Jamil Khoury, Yussef El Guindi, and Lameece Issaq & Jacob Kader (M. Najjar) 1–2
Fourth Street Theatre 219
"From Brooklyn Bridge" (Rihani) 74–75
Fulvio, Richard 106
al-Funun (The Arts) 72, 88

Gallup polls 44
Gana, Nouri 28–29, 146; "Arab Despise Thyself" 260n43; "Everyday Arabness" 60; "Writing While Muslim, Writing While Arab" 55
Gibran, Jean 83
Gibran, Kahlil 7, 15, 17–20, *72*, *83*, 88, 89, 96–97; background of 18–19, 29, 71–75; *The Banshee* 82; *The Beginning of the Revolution* 82; *Between Night and Morn* 82; *The Blind* 82, 83; *The Chameleons* 18, 81–87; *The Colored Faces* 81, 82; "Dead Are My People" 19; "Gibran's Message to Young Americans of Syrian Origin" 84; *The Hunchback or the Man Unseen* 82; *The Invisible Man* 82; *Jesus, Son of Man* 18; Karam on 236–237; *The King and the Shepherd* 82; *The Last Unction* 82; *Lazarus and His Beloved* 82–83; "My Countrymen" 86–87; poet-prophet ideal 32–33; *The Prophet* 3, 18, 85, 247n4; relations with Rihani 74
Gibran, Kahlil (cousin) 18
Gibran Museum, Lebanon *83*
"Gibran's Message to Young Americans of Syrian Origin" (Gibran) 84
Gillani, Malik 164
Gold, Shana 182
Golden Thread Productions 153, 239, 240
Gotham Chamber Opera 236
governmental arts grants 57
"The Great City" (Rihani) 75
Greater Syria 18, 82, 104; see also Lebanon (formerly Syria)
Griffin, Sean 127–128, 151; *America on Film: Representing Race, Class, Gender, and Sexuality at the Movies* 191–192
Gualtieri, Sarah M.A. 19, 28–29, 36, 55, 109–110; *Between Arab and White: Race and Ethnicity in the Early Syrian American Diaspora* 211
Guantanamo Bay detentions, treatment of see *Truth Serum Blues* (I. Khalidi)
Guilty: Hollywood's Verdict on Arabs After 9/11 (Shaheen) 190

Habibi (Abu-Hamdeh) 240
Haddad, Abd al-Massih 71, *72*, 83
Haddad, Kathryn 207; *With Love from Ramallah* 157–158
Haddad, Yazbeck 61–62
Hagopian, Elaine C. 44–45
Hajjar, Nijmeh 18, 74
hakawati (storytelling) 81
Halaby, Salma *196*
Hamide, Khader 50
Hanania, Ray 65, 190; *I'm Glad I Look Like a Terrorist: Growing Up Arab in America* 54
Handal, Nathalie : *Between Our Lips* 159–160
Harlow, Barbara 4–5; *Resistance Literature* 58
Harout, Magda 106
Haskell, Mary 87
Hassan, Waïl S. 78
hate crimes 127
Hayani, Ibrahim 39
Helen Hayes Award 214
Hershewe, S.K. *110*; *An Oasis in Manhattan* 7–8, 16–17, 105–112; *A Toy for Carmen* 106
Hickey, Tom *149*
Hirsch, Marianne 180, 183, 219; "Past Lives: Postmemories in Exile" 161
Homeland Security Act (2002) 50
Homes, Sunil *233*
homosexuality, treatment of 25, 204–205, 206; see also *Precious Stones* (Khoury)
House of Representatives: Hearing on

Ethnically Motivated Violence against Arab-Americans (1986) 52
Houston, Velina Hasu: *But Still, Like Air, I'll Rise: New Asian American Plays* 4
al-Huda (*Guidance*) 72
Hughes, Holly 206; *O Solo Homo: The New Queer Performance* 204–205
Hull-Warriner Awards for Best Play 236
Human Rights Watch: "We Are Not the Enemy" 126–127
humorous accounting resistance strategies 67–68, 99; *see also* comedy and stand-up performance
The Hunchback or the Man Unseen (Gibran) 82

I Heart Hamas: And Other Things I'm Afraid to Tell You (Jajeh) 157, 163, 209, 226–229, **228**
Ibn Sa'ud, King 74
Ibrahim, Denmo: *Baba* 240; *Ecstasy: A Water Fable* 1, 232–234, **233**
identity formation, among contemporary Arab Americans 31–69; and AAI 51, 52; AAUG and intellectual movement 45–48; abjection concept 61–62, 64–66; and ADC 51–52; and Arabic language 26; constrained scholarship and coerced imaginations 54–56, 59; cultural production 36–38, 56–57; culture of resistance 38–40; diversity within 25–26, 136; forty years of institutionalized racism 48–51; and hybridity 59–61; identity and difference 67–68; and immigration patterns 32–36; media war 44–45; and negative stereotyping 52–54; origins of 20, 21–22; post-1967 context 33, 43–44; post-9/11 context 6, 221–222; and race theory 22–23, 34, 40–43; recasting and restaging 66–67; resistance literature 56–60; searching for identity 62–64
identity negotiation 24
Illegal Immigration Reform and Immigrant Responsibility Act (IIRIRA) 50
I'm Glad I Look Like a Terrorist: Growing Up Arab in America (Hanania) 54
Imangulieva, Aida 96
Immigration Act (1965) 35
Immigration and Naturalization Acts (1906/1952) 34, 35
immigration patterns 32–36; contemporary wave (1967–present) 33, 35–36; early immigrants (1880–1945) 33, 34–35; Omi and Winant's ethnicity paradigm 33–36; post–World War II (1945–1965) 33, 34–35
in-between spaces (Bhabba) 36
In Search of Palestine (BBC) 219
In the Crossing (Buck) **225**, 240
Institute in Nazareth, Palestine 88
interminably spectral (Butler) 28, 129–130, 152–153; *see also* post-9/11 Arab American drama
internal colonialism 27
International Fringe Festival, New York 135

internment of the psyche (Naber) 27–28, 130–131, 146; *see also* post-9/11 Arab American drama
interstitial space: Arab American writers within 89, 159; identity formation and expression within 36–37; recasting and restaging within 36–37; the space in-between (N. Najjar) 19, 58; in-between spaces (Bhabba) 36
The Invisible Man (Gibran) 82
Iraq 48, 204, 213, 214, 216
ISite (Buck) 209–210, 222–226
Islam 25, 36, 41, 52–53; *see also* Muslims, in U.S.
Islamophobia 8, 25, 128, 134, 154, 248*n*19
Israel 42, 43–44, 48, 49, 51, 162–163, 173, 229; *see also* Arab-Israeli War (1967)
Issaq, Lameece: *Food and Fadwa* 157, 163, 179–183, **182**
Issawi, Hesham: *American East* 187, 190–191, 193–201, **200**

Jabara, Abdeen 45
Jacobs, Amos *see* Thomas, Danny
Jaffe-Berg, Erith 9
Jajeh, Jennifer 205, 207; *I Heart Hamas: And Other Things I'm Afraid to Tell You* 157, 163, 209, 226–229, **228**
Jarmakani, Amira 62, 80, 121
Jenkins, Joe 87
Jesus, Son of Man (Gibran) 18
Jewish Defense League (JDL) 52
Job (Naimy) 88
Jordan 175, 177
Joseph, Lawrence 142
Jreisat, Jamil 43
Just Like Us (Ahmed) 117, 121–124

Kader, Jacob: *Food and Fadwa* 157, 163, 179–183, **182**
Karam, Nihat Biyar 73
Karam, Stephen: *Dark Sisters* 236; *Sons of the Prophet* 232, 236–238, **237**, 239; *Speech & Debate* 236
Kassir, Samir 43
Kaufmann, Moisés 136
Kazkaz, Rana 164; *Deaf Day* 187; *Kemo Sabe* 187
Kemo Sabe (Kazkaz) 187
Kesdekain, Nesrop 106
Khalidi, Ismail 59, 68, 184; *Sabra Falling* 240; *Tennis in Nablus* 157, 163, 170–175; *Truth Serum Blues* 28, 131–135, 157
Khalidi, Rashid 131, 156, 162, 170–171
Khalil, Rania: *Flag Piece* 207–208
Khoury, Jamil 4; *Mosque Alert* 155; *Precious Stones* 1, 164–170, **169**; "Toward an Arab American Theatre Movement" 240
The King and the Shepherd (Gibran) 82
Kovacs, Bryan **108**

LaCapra, Dominic 157, 161–162, 218, 219, 222
Language Rooms (El Guindi) 125–126, 143–154, *153*, 256n78
The Laramie Project (Kaufmann) 136
The Last Leaf (Naimy) 88
The Last Unction (Gibran) 82
"Laughing Without Teeth Tour" (Zayid) 124
Laura Pels Theatre 236
Layla's Sahra (Rizkallah) 207–208
Lazarus and His Beloved (Gibran) 82–83
Lebanese Civil War 221
Lebanese Maronite Church 87
Lebanon (formerly Syria) 35, 48, 51, 75, 177, 224
Limon, John: *Stand-up Comedy in Theory, or, Abjection in America* 99
Lion, Lilly *233*
Little Syria, New York City 15–16
Living in the Hyphen-Nation (Farah) 207–208
The Location of Culture (Bhabha) 5
Lucille Lortel Awards 214, 236
Lumet, Sidney 189

Mahfouz, Naguib 138
Make Room for Danny (television show) 103, 104
Malek, Alia 49, 51–52; *A Country Called Amreeka* 44
Manhattan Ensemble Theater 215, 240
Mansour, Mona: *Urge for Going* 158–159, *159*, 240
Maronite Christians 15–16, 18–19, 37
Marvasti, Amir 99, 120, 178, 201; *Middle Eastern Lives in America* 67–68
Mattar, Sandra: "A Quest for Identity: Racism and Acculturation Among Immigrant Families" 63–64
mattawa (religious police) 122
Mattawa, Khaled 5–6
May in the Summer (Dabis) 203, 240
Mayer, Jane 126
Mazzacurati, Renato Marino 73
McCarran-Walter Act (1952) 49–50
McClinton, Marion 176
McCulloh, T.H. 107
McKinney, Karyn D. 99, 120, 178, 201; *Middle Eastern Lives in America* 67–68
media, anti–Arab bias in 31, 42–45, 47, 52–53, 127–128
median state (E. Said) 219–220
Mentzel, Alex *233*
Middle East America Distinguished Playwright Award 240
Middle Eastern American drama 8
Middle Eastern Lives in America (Marvasti and McKinney) 67–68
Minnesota Fringe Festival 240
Mir'at al-Gharb (*Mirror to the West*) 71–72
The Miser (Moliere) 91–92
Mixed Blood Theater, Minneapolis 157

Mizna 157
Moayed, Arian *182*
modern Arab American drama (1908–1967) 16–20, 37; *see also* specific playwrights
Molière 96; *The Miser* 91–92
Mondalek, Najee 23, 112–116, *113*; *Arabic and Broud* 115; *Smile You're in Dearborn* 113–115
Montgomery, Anita 234
A Month in the Country (Turgenev) 92
Morrow, Vic 107
Mosque Alert (Khoury) 155
Mouawad, Wajdi 164
Moughrabi, Fouad 46–47
MTG 236
Muhly, Nico 236
multicultural theatre 24
multiculturalism 63
Muslims, in U.S.: anti–Muslim bias 53; dehumanization of (Butler) 129–130; derealization in film and media 125–128; governmental surveillance and persecution of 29, 41–42, 48–49, 56, 126–127, 186, 255n5; hate crimes against 127; neo–Muslim movement 39; ongoing anti–Muslim prejudice 154–155; viewed as community of suspicion (Bayoumi) 61–62
The Muslims Are Coming! (Obeidallah and Farsad) 124
"Muslims Say F.B.I. Tactics Sow Anger and Fear" (*New York Times*) 56
My Big, Fat Greek Wedding (film) 193
"My Countrymen" (Gibran) 86–87

Naber, Nadine 27, 48–49, 146; "The Rules of Forced Engagement" 130–131; *see also* post–9/11 Arab American drama
Nadda, Ruba: *Sadah: A Love Story* 187
Nader, Elmaz Abi: *Country of Origin* 207–208
Naff, Alixa: *Becoming American: the Early Arab Immigrant Experience* 111
Naimy, Mikhail 7, 15, 17–20, *72*, *89*; background of 18–19, 29, 70, 71–72, 88–89; *Fathers and Sons* 18, 88; on Gibran 82; *Job* 88; *The Last Leaf* 88; *Parents and Children* 88–97, 111; poet-prophet ideal 32–33; relations with Rihani 74; *Seventy* 20, 92; Shakespeare's influence on 91, 96; on theatrical art 90; use of Arabic language 23
Naimy, Nadeem 88
Najjar, Fawzi 45
Najjar, Michael Malek: as director 1, 3, 96, 169, 233; *Four Plays: Works by Leila Buck, Jamil Khoury, Yussef El Guindi, and Lameece Issaq & Jacob Kader* 1–2; *Talib* 1, 240
Najjar, Nada 19, 71–72; *The Space In-Between: The Ambivalence of Early Arab-American Writers* 58
al-Nakba (the catastrophe) 162–163
Nakleh, Khalil 47–48
naming of children 222–223, 260n43

Nashef, Rola: *Detroit Unleaded* 188, 190–191, 193, 194–195, 198, 201–203, **202**
National Geographic Entertainment 191
National Objection: The Asian American Body Onstage (Shimakawa) 61
National Playwrights Company 106
National Security Entry-Exit Registration System (NSEERS) 50–51
nativism 34–35
"Needed, a Nixon Declaration for Five Million Jewish, Christian, and Moslem Palestinians" (AAUG) 46
Network (film) 189, 190
"New Anti-Semitism" (Shaheen) 54
New Dramatists LAB 159
New York Arab American Comedy Festival 116, 124
New York Theatre Workshop 143, 159, 182, 240
newspapers 71–72
Nibras Theatre Collective: *Sajjil* 125, 135–143, **137**, 210
Nichols, Anne: *Abie's Irish Rose* 108
Nimoy, Leonard 107
9 Parts of Desire (Raffo) 1, 209–210, 212, 214–218, **215**, 226
Nixon Administration 46, 48
Noor Theatre 182, 239, 240

O Solo Homo: The New Queer Performance (Hughes and Román) 204–205
OAPEC oil embargo (1973) 49
An Oasis in Manhattan (Hershewe) 7–8, 16–17, 105–112
Obama Administration 56
Obeidallah, Dean 98, 116–118, 121; *The Muslims Are Coming!* 124
"Ode to a Wailing Syrian/Lebanese" (Thomas) 98, 99–105
Odeh, Alex 52
Omi, Michael 33–34, 231; cultural nationalism 22, 40–41, 231; ethnicity paradigm 33–36; *Racial Formation in the United States from the 1960s to the 1990s* 36; rearticulation 36, 37
"On Arabs and Arabness" (Rabbat) 248n15
Opera Company of Philadelphia 236
Operation ABSCAM (1978) 49
Operation Boulder (1972) 48–49
Operation TIPS 50, 126, 146
Orfalea, Gregory 26, 57, 87
Orientalism (E. Said) 6–7, 47, 52, 78, 127, 134
"Orientalism and the October War: The Shattered Myths" (E. Said) 47
Orozco, José 83
Oslo Accord 163
Othering: derealization (Butler) 11, 28, 129, 152; internment of the psyche (Naber) 27–28, 130–131, 146; political othering (PO) (Sheth) 41; and skin color 39; *see also* stereotypes

Our Lady of Lebanon Maronite Catholic Cathedral 16
Out of Place (E. Said) 32
Outer Critics Circle Award 214, 236

Palestine 20, 31–32, 35, 42, 43–44, 46, 162–163, 218, 220, 227–228; *see also* Arab-Israeli War (1967)
Palestine (N. Said) 64, 157, 163, 209–210, 212–213, 218–222, **219**
"Palestine and the Proposed Arab Federation" (Rihani) 20
Palestinian American playwrights 156–185; Arabic terms in narratives 163; *Food and Fadwa* (Issaq and Kader) 157, 163, 179–183, **182**; *Precious Stones* (Khoury) 164–170, **169**; *Roar* (Shamieh) 157, 160–161, 163, 175–179, **176**; *Tennis in Nablus* (I. Khalidi) 157, 163, 170–175; trauma and postmemory 161–164; and vicarious victimhood 183–185
Palestinian Americans 44
Pangea World Theater 209
Paouli, Petro 73, 104
Parents and Children (Naimy) 88–97, 111
Parker, Shanga 234, **235**
Parlakian, Nishan: *Contemporary Armenian American Drama: An Anthology of Ancestral Voices* 4
passing/avoiding accounting resistance strategies 67–68
"Past Lives: Postmemories in Exile" (Hirsch) 161
The Path of Vision (Rihani) 74
Pegues, Juliana: *With Love from Ramallah* 157–158
The Pen League 8, 15, 70, 71, **72**, 74, 82, 88, 89
Performance and Cultural Politics (Diamond) 66, 67
Phelan, Peggy 6
Phoenicianism 18–19, 37
Pilgrims Musa and Sheri in the New World (El Guindi) 232, 234–236, **235**, 239
Pitman, Nicole **169**
Planet of the Arabs (Salloum) 188–190
pluralist anarchy (Bhabha) 63
poet-prophet ideal 18–19, 32–33, 37
"Political Acts: the Emerging Arab American Theatre Movement" (Chicago Public Radio) 239
political othering (PO) (Sheth) 41
Popular Front for the Liberation of Palestine (PFLP) 49–50
Portland Center Stage (PCS) 240
postmemory (Hirsch) 161, 183, 219
post-9/11 Arab American drama 125–155; Arab/Muslim derealization, history of 126–127; Arab/Muslim derealization, in film and media 127–128; derealization in *Back of the Throat* and *Language Rooms* 143–154, **153**, 256n78; derealization, spectrality and intern-

ment of the psyche 128–131; Nibras and *Sajji* 125, 135–143; ongoing anti-Muslim prejudice 154–155; *Truth Serum Blues* 131–135
post-9/11 context: and AAI 52; anti-Muslim bias 53; Arab American identity 6, 221–222; impact on cultural production 55, 65–67; need for multiple categories of Arab American works 3–4; pervasive suspicion of Arab Americans 62; political self-identification 23; resistance literature 58–59, 60; surveillance and persecution of Arab Americans 56, 64; U.S. governmental persecution of Arab Americans 21–22
Precarious Life: The Powers of Mourning and Violence (Butler) 128–129
Precious Stones (Khoury) 1, 164–170, **169**
Pressing Beyond in Between (Al Jurf) 207–208, 198
The Prisoners, or Abdul Hameed in Asitana (Rihani) 73
The Prophet (Gibran) 3, 18, 85, 247n4
"Prophet Motive: The Kahlil Gibran Phenomenon" (Acocella) 247n4
Pryor, Richard 99
Public Theatre LAB, New York 158
Pulitzer Prize for Drama 236

queer solo performance 204–205, 206
"A Quest for Identity: Racism and Acculturation Among Immigrant Families" (Mattar) 63–64

Rabbat, Nasser: "On Arabs and Arabness" 248n15
al-Rabitah al Qalamiyah *see* The Pen League
race theory, and Arab American identity 22–23, 34, 40–43
Racial Formation in the United States from the 1960s to the 1990s (Omi and Winant) 36
racism 48–51, 54, 63–64, 130, 142, 150, 192
Raffo, Heather 23, 59, **182**, 204, 205, 207, 211–214, 239; *Fallujah: The First Opera about The Iraq War* 240; *9 Parts of Desire* 1, 209–210, 212, 214–218, **215**, 226
Rahme, Rudy 83
Rasteger, Roya 203
RAWI Screenwriters' Lab/The Royal Film Commission- Jordan 239
rearticulation (Omi and Winant) 36, 37
recasting, use of term 36–37
Reed, Alan 106
Reel Bad Arabs (Shaheen) 188, 189–190
The Register of Repent (Rihani) 73
resistance literature 4–5, 21, 56–60, 163–164; *see also* specific works
Resistance Literature (Harlow) 58
resistance strategies (Marvasti and McKinney) 67–68
restaging, use of term 5, 36–37
Rihani, Ameen Albert 74
Rihani, Ameen Fares 17–20, **73**, 88, 89, 96–97; *Ar-Rihaniyyaat* 74–75; background of 18–19, 29, 71–72; *The Book of Khalid* 3, 15, 73, 77–78; *A Chant of Mystics and Other Poems* 74; *The Crescent Moon: A Fantasy in One Scene* 73; *Faithful Time* 73; "From Brooklyn Bridge" 74–75; "The Great City" 75; "Palestine and the Proposed Arab Federation" 20; *The Path of Vision* 74; poet-prophet ideal 32–33; *The Prisoners, or Abdul Hameed in Asitana* 73; *The Register of Repent* 73; relations with Gibran 74; relations with Naimy 74; "The Spirit of the Language" 76; *The Tragedy of Shammar* 73; *The Tragedy of the Rasheed Family* 73; *The Travellers: a Vision of the Eternal Dual* 73; *The Trilateral Treaty in the Animal Kingdom* 73; *Wajdah* 7, 16–17, 73–81, **77**, 198
Rizkallah, Lena Riz: *Layla's Sahra* 207–208
The Road to Lebanon (Thomas) 105
Roar (Shamieh) 157, 160–161, 163, 175–179, **176**
Román, David 206; *O Solo Homo: The New Queer Performance* 204–205
Roscoe, Carol 234, **235**
Roundabout Theater Company 236, 237
Ruby, Robert 44
"The Rules of Forced Engagement" (Naber) 130

Sabra Falling (I. Khalidi) 240
Sabry, Somaya Sami 9, 207
Sacre, Antonio 136
Sadah: A Love Story (Nadda) 187
Sadat, Anwar 48, 167
Sa'di, Ahmad H. 162, 183–184
Said, Edward W. 20, **32**, 44, 57, 81, 138–140, 141, 156–157, 177, 179, 219–220, 241; "The Arab Portrayed" 47, 127; background of 31–32; *Covering Islam: How the Media and the Experts Determine How We See the Rest of the World* 52–54; as founder of *Arab Studies Quarterly* 46–47; *Orientalism* 6–7, 47, 52, 78, 127, 134; "Orientalism and the October War: The Shattered Myths" 47; *Out of Place* 32
Said, Najla 125, 135, 136–137, 143, 184, 205, 207, 211, 214, 229; *Palestine* 64, 157, 163, 209–210, 212–213, 218–222, **219**
Saint Joseph's Roman Catholic Maronite Church 15–16, **16**
St. Jude Children's Research Hospital 99, 100
St. Louie & Moh (television show proposal) 107–108, 112
Saint-Saens, Camille 101
Sajjil (Nibras Theatre Collective) 125, 135–143, **137**, 210
Salaam, Peace: An Anthology of Middle Eastern-American Drama (Theatre Communications Group) 3
Salaita, Steven 8, 25–26, 59–60, 142
Salhi, Zahia Smail 177

Salloum, Jackie Reem: *Planet of the Arabs* 188–190; *Slingshot Hip Hop* 187
sand nigger, use of term 142, 199
Al-Sayeh (The Traveler) 72, 83, 87
Sayigh, Yezid 163
Schiff, Ellen: *Awake and Singing: 7 Classic Plays from the American Jewish Repertoire* 4
scholarships 52
The School of the Americas *see* Western Hemisphere Institute for Security Cooperation (WHINSEC)
Sciorra, Anabella *176*
Selim, Fouad: "Arab American Theatre Caught in Censorship: A Study of Betty Shamieh's *Roar* and *The Black Eyed*" 160–161
Semmerling, Tim J. 128, 191
Settle, Joanna 215
Seventy (Naimy) 20, 92
Shaheen, Jack G. 5, 7, 9, 191, 192, 248n2; *Guilty: Hollywood's Verdict on Arabs After 9/11* 190; on New Anti-Semitism 54; *Reel Bad Arabs* 188, 189–190
Shain, Yossi 20
Shakespeare 73, 76, 78–81, 91, 96
Shakir, Evelyn 207, 213; *Bint Arab: Arab and Arab American Women in the United States* 42, 62
Shalhoub, Michel *see* Sharif, Omar
Shalhoub, Tony 191
Shamieh, Betty 23, 57, 59, 156, 207, 229, 239; "Arab Americans in the Performing Arts" (ADC speech) 238; *The Black Eyed* 159; *Chocolate in Heat: Growing Up Arab in America* 207–208, 209; *Roar* 157, 160–161, 163, 175–179, *176*
Sharif, Omar 31
Shattering the Stereotypes: Muslim Women Speak Out (Afzal-Khan) 3
Shehadeh, Michel 50
Sheherazadian orality (Sabry) 207
Sheth, Falguni A. 41
Shimakawa, Karen: *National Objection: The Asian American Body Onstage* 61
Shouhayib, Nada *202*
Shryock, Andrew 39–40
Silk Road Rising 4, 149, 164, 239, 240
Silk Road Theatre Project 164, 169
Sinitski, Sean *149*
Sleiman, Haaz *182*
Slingshot Hip Hop (Salloum) 187
Slyomovics, Susan 163
Smile You're in Dearborn (Mondalek) 113–115
Smith, Idleman 61–62
social movements 36
Sollors, Werner 2; *Beyond Ethnicity* 151
solo performance 204–230; female performances 209–213; *ISite* (Buck) 222–226; *9 Parts of Desire* (Raffo) 214–218; *Palestine* (N. Said) 218–222; personal and political aspects 213–214; theater versus performance 205–209; *see also* specific performers and performances
Sons of the Prophet (Karam) 232, 236–238, *237*, 239
The Souls of Black Folks (Du Bois) 150
the space in-between (N. Najjar) 19, 58
The Space In-Between: The Ambivalence of Early Arab-American Writers (N. Najjar) 58
Special Registration program 50, 126, 146
Speech & Debate (Karam) 236
"The Spirit of the Language" (Rihani) 76
Stage Society Theater 106
stand-up *see* comedy and stand-up performance
Stand-up Comedy in Theory, or, Abjection in America (Limon) 99
stereotypes: in academia 51–52; advocacy groups against 51–52; of Arab women 62–63, 79–80; in entertainment industry 6, 7, 98, 105, 118–119, 120–121, 127–128, 186–187, 190, 191–192; formations of negative 52–54; post–Arab-Israeli War (1967) context 7, 31–32, 127; post-9/11 context 6; in U.S. media 31; *see also* Othering
Stokes, Tobin: *Fallujah: The First Opera about The Iraq War* 240
Strasberg, Lee 106
Streetcar Named Desire (play) 212
Suleiman, Michael W. 38, 42, 45, 47, 57, 81
Sullivan, Ed 104
Sundance Film Festival 240
Sundance Institute 240
Susan Smith Blackburn and Marian Seldes-Garson Kanin playwright award 214
Syrian civil war (2011–) 254n25
The Syrian World 72
Syrian-Mount Lebanon Relief Committee 19, 82
Syrian Youth Society: *Andromak* 71

Tabbak, Victor *see* Tayback, Vic
Takla, Nefertiti 81
Talib (M. Najjar) 1, 240
Tanzer, Joshua 139–140
Tayback, Vic 106–108, *108*, 111, 112
Tchaikovsky 100, 101
Tennis in Nablus (I. Khalidi) 157, 163, 170–175
"Tension Grows Between California Muslims, FBI After Informant Infiltrates Mosque" (*Washington Post*) 56
Teymour, Fouad 164
theater versus performance 205–209
Thomas, Danny *105*; *Make Room for Danny* (television show) 103, 104; "Ode to a Wailing Syrian/Lebanese" 98, 99–105; *The Road to Lebanon* 105
Thoreau, Henry David 70
Threesome (El Guindi) 240
Tolstoy, Leo 94–95
Toronto International Film Festival 191

"Toward an Arab American Theatre Movement" (Khoury) 240
A Toy for Carmen (Hershewe) 106
The Tragedy of Shammar (Rihani) 73
The Tragedy of the Rasheed Family (Rihani) 73
transliteration and nomenclature 13
transnational perspective (Fadda-Conrey) 28
The Travellers: A Vision of the Eternal Dual (Rihani) 73
Traverse Theatre, Edinburgh 214
The Trilateral Treaty in the Animal Kingdom (Rihani) 73
Truth Serum Blues (I. Khalidi) 28, 131–135, 157
Turgenev, Ivan: *A Month in the Country* 92

Uncle Vanya (Chekhov) 92
United States: domestic policy 41–42; foreign policy 24–25, 26, 39, 41–43, 46–49; immigration policy 21, 34–36; surveillance and persecution of Arabs/Muslims in 29, 41–42, 48–49, 126–127, 186, 255n5; *see also* specific legislation and agencies; war on terror
University of Oregon 233
Urge for Going (Mansour) 158–159, *159*, 240
USA PATRIOT Act 50, 126
U.S.-VISIT technology 51

Valentino, Rudolph 109
Venture Theatre 106–107
vicarious victimhood 58; *see also* empathic unsettlement (LaCapra)
Viewpoint (AAI television show) 52
virtual internment (Bazian) 27–28, 55–56, 57, 255n25

Wajdah (Rihani) 7, 16–17, 73–81, 198
wally, Omar Met 136
war on terror 50; black sites 125, 126, 129, 133, 146, 152; dehumanization of Arabs/Muslims in (Butler) 129–130; derealization in 28; enhanced interrogation techniques 126, 144; guilt by association (Bazian) 55; and U.S. hegemony 152–154
Warner, Sturgis 219
The Watch List 116
A Water Fable (Ibrahim) 1
Waterfield, Robin 82
"We Are Not the Enemy" (Human Rights Watch) 126–127
Western Hemisphere Institute for Security Co-operation (WHINSEC) 126
"Western" Realism 24
"When the Waters Were Changed" (Sufi myth) 232
whiteness 23, 34, 58, 125, 211, 221, 232
"Why I Wrote a Syrian Play" (Ford) 109
The Wilma Theatre, Philadelphia 240
Winant, Howard 231; cultural nationalism 22, 40–41, 231; ethnicity paradigm 33–36; *Racial Formation in the United States from the 1960s to the 1990s* 36; rearticulation 36, 37
Wise, Ray **200**
With Love from Ramallah (Haddad and Pegues) 157–158
women: comics in Saudi Arabia 122; feminism 62; in Gibran's writings 84, 86; in Naimy's writings 95; in Rihani's writings 79–81; solo performances of 209–213; stereotypes of Arab 62–63, 79–80; *see also* specific authors and playwrights
World Congress of Orientalists (1967) 45
World Trade Center 15, 16
"Writing While Muslim, Writing While Arab" (Gana) 55

You Can't Take It with You (Kaufman and Hart) 108

Zabel, Darcy 27
Zayid, Maysoon 116, 117, 119–120, 121; "Laughing Without Teeth Tour" 124
Zogby, James 52, 240

www.ingramcontent.com/pod-product-compliance
Ingram Content Group UK Ltd.
Pitfield, Milton Keynes, MK11 3LW, UK
UKHW041929140426
5217IPUK00014B/383